The Eyes of Discovery

VERRAZANO · 1524
NARVAEZ and
CABEZA DE VACA · 1528-36
CARTIER · 1534-35
DE SOTO · 1539-42
ALARCÓN · 1540
CORONADO · 1540-42
CABRILLO · 1542
DRAKE · 1579
CHAMPLAIN · 1603-04
SMITH · 1606-14
LA SALLE beginning 1666
WEISER · 1729-33
VÉRENDRYE and SONS · 1742
(Approximate Route)
PORTOLÁ · 1769-70
LEWIS and CLARK · 1804-05

HUDSON
1609

LOUISVILLE
CUMBERLAND
GAP

WISCONSIN R.
FOX RIVER
ST. LOUIS
ARKANSAS R.
RED RIVER
GALVESTON IS.

PLATTE R.
ARKANSAS R.

BISMARCK
PIERRE

YELLOWSTONE R.
YELLOWSTONE
PARK

GRAND
CANYON

DRAKE'S
BAY

FARALLONES IS.

The Eyes of Discovery

THE PAGEANT OF NORTH AMERICA
AS SEEN BY THE FIRST EXPLORERS

John Bakeless

DOVER PUBLICATIONS, INC.
NEW YORK

By the author:
ECONOMIC CAUSES OF MODERN WAR
ORIGIN OF THE NEXT WAR
MAGAZINE MAKING
CHRISTOPHER MARLOWE, THE MAN IN HIS TIME
DANIEL BOONE, MASTER OF THE WILDERNESS
THE TRAGICALL HISTORY OF CHRISTOPHER MARLOWE
LEWIS AND CLARK, PARTNERS IN DISCOVERY
FIGHTING FRONTIERSMAN: LIFE OF DANIEL BOONE
BACKGROUND TO GLORY: LIFE OF GEORGE ROGERS CLARK
TRAITORS, TURNCOATS AND HEROES
ADVENTURES OF LEWIS AND CLARK
   with Katherine Bakeless:
THEY SAW AMERICA FIRST, published in England as
  EXPLORERS OF THE NEW WORLD

Standard Book Number: 486-20761-7
Library of Congress Catalog Card Number: 61-19591

Manufactured in the United States of America
Dover Publications, Inc.
180 Varick Street
New York, N. Y. 10014

PREFACE

The Eyes of Discovery is an effort to describe North America as the first white men in each area saw it: landscapes, forests, plains, animals, plants, streams, and Indians, as they existed before the inevitable change that began almost from the instant of the first white settlement. It is neither a story of adventure nor a book about Indians nor a history of exploration and colonization. Where the life of an explorer is touched upon at all, it is merely to explain who the man was and how he came to make his discoveries when he did. Because of this approach, many a great name of the ever-moving frontier does not appear at all.

Such an attempt as this faces one inevitable difficulty. The first explorer in each part of the United States often took but a brief glimpse and then departed before putting on record any detailed account of what he saw. Luckily, the country was so new and strange that many of the discoverers were sufficiently impressed with what they saw to give fairly detailed descriptions, but in many other cases one can only fill in a description of what the first arrival must have seen, from accounts given by much later and more leisurely travelers, who, facing less difficulty, hardship, or danger, had more time to look about them. Often it is possible to find good descriptions of primitive conditions in the books of visitors to America long after settlement had begun, for such things as waterfalls, prairie fires, buffalo, moose, lakes, rivers, and Indian ways changed very slowly.

A further difficulty has been the queer bits of information that such an undertaking as this involves. The ordinary methods of historical investigation apply, to be sure; but one is constantly running into puzzling problems in botany, zoology, ecology, dendrology, climatology, anthropology, and half a dozen other sciences. Fortunately, I have been able to correct and expand my own meagre acquaintance with innumerable specialties by the generous help of a great number of careful and minute students, whose aid is acknowledged in a separate section. It is pleasant to recall that in four years' work, I have never once asked for a specialist's aid without finding prompt, willing, and competent response.

I owe special gratitude to Mr. George Stevens, who had the original idea for the book and suggested my writing it; to Mr. Donald Culross Peattie, who has cheerfully submitted to a series of botanical and ecological inquiries for the last four years; and to Mr. Bernard DeVoto, who has lent of his wide knowledge of the West. Perhaps I owe most of all to the late D. S. Hartline, for many years head of the Department of Biology in the State Teachers College at Bloomsburg, Pennsylvania, who through many years was always willing to let an awkward, interested boy hang about the laboratory or "tag along" on field trips in woods and mountains and beside the streams, with an instant and friendly answer to any question about the queer and beautiful things that are in them.

JOHN BAKELESS

Great Hill,
Seymour, Connecticut

ACKNOWLEDGMENTS

WHILE SPACE, AS usual, makes it impossible to acknowledge all the friendly aid I have received in the course of this study, certain debts are too great to be ignored. Any book of this sort owes a great deal to librarians. Through the courtesy of Mr. James T. Babb, Librarian of Yale University, I have had the constant use of the Yale Library and the constant assistance of the library staff. Mr. Nelson W. Mc-Combs, Librarian of the Washington Square College Library, New York University, has assisted in running down rare European and American sources. At the New York Public Library, Mr. Gerald D. McDonald, Mr. F. Igor D. Avellino, Mr. Sylvester Vigilante, Miss Shirley Barker, Mr. Henry Kapenstein, and the pages of the American History Room have given every possible help.

In various bibliographical problems, I have had the help of Miss Rose Demorest, of the Carnegie Library, Pittsburgh; Mrs. Anne Mc-Donnell, assistant librarian of the State Historical Society of Montana; Mr. Charles van Ravenswaay, director, and Miss Barbara Kell, librarian, of the Missouri Historical Society; Miss Louise Bercaw, of the Department of Agriculture Library; Miss Helen M. McFarland, of the Kansas State Historical Society; Miss Alice J. Pickup, of the Buffalo Historical Society; Mr. Milton E. Lord, Librarian, and Mr. Richard G. Hensley, of the Boston Public Library; Miss Alice C. Moore, of the Public Library, Sunbury, Pa.; Miss Lillian M. Evans, of the Juniata College Library; Miss Irene Janes, Free Public Library, Paterson, N. J.; Mr. Guy C. Miller, of the Palo Alto Public Library; Mr. Joseph A. Belloli, of the Stanford University Library; and Miss Caroline E. Jakeman, of the Harvard College Library.

Acknowledgments

At Yale, Mr. David H. Clift, Associate Librarian; Messrs. Paul Winkler and Archibald Hanna, of the Coe Collection; Miss Dorothy Bridgwater, Miss Emma Stephenson, and Miss Betty Kinard, of the Reference Department, have done everything in their power to make the resources of their great institution available. Mr. J. S. Holliday, of the Coe Collection, generously placed at my disposal his copy of a frontier manuscript.

In finding maps and pictures I have had the help of the staff of the Public Archives of Canada; Mr. Arthur J. O. Anderson, of the School of American Research; Mr. Perry T. Rathbone, Director of the City Art Museum, St. Louis; Mr. Erle Kauffman, editor of *American Forests*; Mr. R. P. Wentworth, of the Quetico-Superior International Peace Memorial Forest; the U. S. Forest Service, especially Mr. Leland J. Prater; the National Park Service, especially Mr. Hillory A. Tolson, Assistant Director; Mr. Horace A. Dough, Custodian of the Kill Devil Monument National Memorial; Mr. H. C. Bryant, Superintendent of the Grand Canyon National Park; and Mr. David de L. Condon, Chief Park Naturalist of the Yellowstone; the North Carolina Department of Conservation, especially Mr. A. W. Postel; and Mr. G. S. Hume, Chief of the Geological Survey of Canada.

On scientific questions I have had the aid of Mr. George W. Goodwin and Mr. John C. Armstrong, of the American Museum of Natural History; the late Dr. Brayton Eddy, of the New York Zoological Society; Dr. Kimber Kuster, of the State Teachers College, Bloomsburg, Pa.; Mr. Van Lawrence, Mr. Carl W. Moen, and Mr. John B. Moyle, of the Minnesota Department of Conservation; Mr. Lyle M. Thorpe, of the Connecticut Board of Fisheries and Game; Mr. Leo Luttringer and Mr. Robert E. Latimer, of the Pennsylvania Game Commission; Dr. J. J. Hambleton, of the Beltsville agricultural experiment station; Mr. Clyde Spry, Assistant Secretary of Agriculture, of Iowa.

On various questions relating to the American Indian I have had the assistance of Dr. Gregory Mason, of New York University; Mr. H. Geiger Omwake, of Lewes, Delaware; Miss Grace Lee Nute, Mr. G. Hubert Smith, and Miss Lucile Kane, of the Minnesota Historical

Acknowledgments

Society; Mr. Charles S. Deppen, of Dalmatia, Pa.; and Mr. E. C. Oberholtzer, of the Quetico-Superior Council.

Strictly local information confirming much earlier observation by the pioneers has been supplied by Mr. Lyon N. Richardson, of Western Reserve University; Mr. Gordon W. Thayer, of the Cleveland Public Library; Mr. Robert A. Baylor, of Danville, Pa.; Mr. Morris Bishop, of Cornell University; Mr. Carl Carmer, Mr. R. E. Caudle, of the Missouri Pacific Lines; and Mr. Earl B. Strower, of the Buffalo Niagara Electric Corporation.

Special bibliographical information has been supplied by Mr. S. E. Morison, of Harvard University; Mr. C. W. Tebeau, of the University of Miami; Dr. John Goggin, of the University of Florida; Messrs. John O. Beaty, Herbert Gambrell, and Samuel Wood Geiser, of Southern Methodist University; Mr. H. E. Bolton, of the University of California; Mr. John Witthoft, State Anthropologist of Pennsylvania; Mr. Merle H. Deardorff, of Warren, Pa.; Dr. Ernst Antevs, of the Southwest Archeological Expedition; Dr. E. N. Transeau, of Ohio State University; Mr. Earle R. Forrest, of Washington, Pa.; Mr. John Bartlet Brebner, of Columbia University; and Col. H. W. Shoemaker, of Harrisburg, Pa.

Contents

Contents

List of Illustrations

List of Illustrations

List of Illustrations

The Eyes of Discovery

I

The White Discoverers

It was midnight of October 11–12 and the whole course of world history was going to change forever in just two hours more. Nobody quite realized that. But every man in the fleet, from the Admiral to the smallest page boy, was tensely alert. There was a reward of ten thousand maravedis up for the man who first sighted land; and everyone knew by this time that the long voyage was nearly over. Sometime, soon, something was going to come up over that western horizon, where for so long eager eyes had seen nothing but waves and more waves, endlessly tossing.

As midnight approached, their three little ships were scudding ahead through a clear, moon-and-starlit night, with a following gale of wind. The moon, past full, was riding high, behind them. Providentially, it chanced to be in the one best position to reveal whatever lay ahead in the mysterious, unknown sea to westward, which no white man's eye had ever seen and to which all eyes were straining now.

Nerves were tense in all three crews. For more than a month they had been at sea—sailing always to the west—until the chance that anyone of them would ever return at all seemed well-nigh impossible. Never anything on the horizon but the eternal ocean, more of it than they—or any human being, then—had ever dreamed could possibly exist. Once, on September 25 Martín Alonso Pinzón, one of the captains, thought he saw land. He was wrong. We know now that the three ships were, at that deluding moment, almost exactly in mid-Atlantic, with no land near for more than a thousand miles. Then, once more, on October 9, *Niña* had been so sure of a landfall that she joyfully broke out her flag and fired a signal gun. Wrong again! A crestfallen captain ruefully hauled down his flag.

It was the birds that really set them on the right course. October is the great migration month in that North America toward which the three ships were unknowingly headed, a forested land that had in it then more birds than it would ever have again. The fleet had chanced upon the season when feathered millions fly south, some of them plunging across the Gulf of Mexico for South America, while others come down the coast by way of Bermuda to the West Indies.

It was a huge flock of the latter group of migrants that caught the anxious eye of Christopher Columbus. They were winging WSW. Where birds are flying, there must be land. Columbus altered course to follow them. Two nights later the crews could hear more birds calling overhead in the darkness and occasionally could see them, briefly silhouetted against the brilliant tropical moon.

In spite of such encouraging signs there was mutiny on *Santa Maria* next day; but it was quelled and the fleet sailed ahead. Then *Niña* fished out of the water a branch bearing small blossoms. *Pinta* collected from the sea a cane, a stick, a piece of board, a plant that obviously had grown on land, and finally "another little stick fashioned, as it appeared, with iron." (Captain Pinzón did not know what an Indian carpenter could do with a stone chisel.) Only the flagship, *Santa Maria,* seems to have found nothing of the sort.

After these bits of flotsam turned up, the grumbling stopped. There was no doubt now they were approaching land, and inhabited land at that. At ten o'clock on the night of the eleventh, just before the moon rose, Columbus, eagerly pacing his quarter-deck, saw his famous "light." It is easy enough to laugh at him now, for with modern charts we know well enough that he was at that moment still thirty-five miles from any possible landfall. Columbus himself was none too sure. What he saw, or thought he saw, was "so uncertain a thing that he did not wish to declare that it was land." Straining his eyes, one Pedro Gutiérrez also thought he saw that dubious flicker, but a certain Rodrigo Sánchez, when appealed to, "saw nothing because he was not in a position where he could see anything." It would have been easy enough to move to a better place, but Rodrigo, anticipating modern historians, was obviously skeptical about that light. Then Columbus thought he saw it again, "like a little wax candle rising and falling."

Presently a seaman, Pedro Yzquierdo, saw it too, and let out a yell: "Lumbre! Tierra!"

"It's already seen by my master," Columbus's page told him coldly.

Many an ingenious effort has been made by many a modern writer to explain this light that never was on sea or land. The schoolbooks say, with calm assurance, that it was a torch carried by an Indian. If so, that hypothetical redskin carried a marvelous torch indeed—a torch throwing a beam vastly more powerful than the modern lighthouse which now stands upon that very coast. Other hopeful souls say it must have been Indians spearing fish by torchlight—as if any Indian ever paddled thirty-five miles out to sea in a dugout canoe in a gale of wind in the middle of the night, when there were plenty of fish right at home. It has even been suggested that this was a supernatural light, sent to guide the explorers; but in that case Providence was a little behindhand, for in the whole course of his voyage Columbus had never needed guidance less than he needed it at this particular moment. There was no question now about his reaching land. After his long discouraging years, the time had come at last when he could not possibly miss it.

The fleet had altered course—straight to the west again—at sunset on the eleventh. Both changes of course had been fortunate ones, though Columbus probably never guessed how very fortunate they were. If he had failed to follow those migratory birds, passing overhead at just the right time, he would have sailed into the Gulf Stream, of whose existence no one then had the least suspicion. In that case, he would have been carried up the coast. He would have landed on the mainland of North America—if he had landed at all; but the chances are that he would have been wrecked on the unknown Florida coast, where many a mariner left his bones in the years that followed.

If he had failed to alter course to the west again on October 11, he would have brought up somewhere south of San Salvador, with an unfriendly island shore just under his lee, in a very dangerous situation. Luck and the migrating birds brought him to the southern end of San

Salvador, so that he could come up its west coast in the lee of the island to a good safe anchorage, easily and quickly.

Captain Martín Alonso Pinzón, on *Pinta,* led the fleet that night, and it was Rodrigo de Triana, lookout on *Pinta's* forecastle, who first saw something that looked like the gleam of a white, sandy cliff standing out in the moonlight, westward, far ahead. He looked again. Now there were two white cliffs and a low dark shadow that had to be land, which seemed to connect them.

"Tierra! Tierra!" bawled Rodrigo and, with that exultant shout, disappears from history forever.

Captain Martín Alonso Pinzón, having been conspicuously wrong about the mistaken landfall two weeks earlier, had learned caution. This time he waited to make sure, but even hasty verification left no room for doubt.

The ship's biggest piece of artillery, a "lombard," had been standing, loaded and primed, ready to fire a signal the moment there was news. Now its fat black muzzle nosed out through a porthole, just above the rolling Caribbean waves.

"Bang!" went the lombard.

North America had been discovered.

It had been discovered a good many times before—by Indians coming in the other direction, from Asia across Bering Strait; by Norsemen; probably by Breton or Basque fishermen, who, having found good fishing grounds preferred to keep them secret. But this was the first time anybody did anything about it.

It is interesting to think of the vast continent as it lay for a few hours before dawn in the darkness of that moonlit October night and of its unconcerned red inhabitants, still ignorant of that momentous instant. In Mexico, only a few hundred miles west of San Salvador, where Columbus landed, the Aztec civilization was at its height of grace, cruelty, and power, though already showing faint signs of corruption at its heart. The Lord Montezuma, or his predecessor, slept quietly, not guessing that a Cortez would follow a Columbus.

In the southwestern United States, where dawn was at that moment not yet ready to break, the peaceful Indians of the Pueblos would wake to the life they had been living for at least a thousand years, worshipping the rain-gods with ceremonial dances, harvesting their crops, managing their irrigation, fearing nothing. Were not their painted deserts a protection? Undisturbed in their majesty, giant redwoods that had been growing when Rome was still an empire, looked through the fogs toward the Pacific waves breaking on the California coast. Northward, on the Columbia, Chinook and Klamath had relaxed from the ardors of the salmon fishing. From the Rockies to the forests of Pennsylvania black, gigantic buffalo herds were beginning to stir in the morning and think of grass and forage. Wolf, cougar, lynx, weasel, wildcat, fox were nearly ready to den up for their daytime rest. Between the Mississippi and the Pacific, the giant grizzlies prowled, lords of plain and mountain, certain of their power, contemptuous of the frail, red creatures who, with bows and arrows, occasionally disturbed them briefly. And over it all, through the autumn night, swept the miraculous millions of the migrant birds.

Just west of the Mississippi, in their leather tepees, dwelt the Sioux, a rather weak tribe who had as yet never dreamed of the horses, the mounted buffalo-hunting, the cavalry war that would make them the rich and powerful terrors of the plains. Through Canada, about the Great Lakes, into New England and down the coast, ranged various Algonkian tribes, hunters, trappers, canoemen. In upper New York State the great Iroquois statesmen, Dekanáwida and Hayowentha had only recently established the League of the Iroquois, the Five Nations, who were just beginning to develop their power, when on that fateful October morning *Pinta* fired the signal gun that marked the coming of the master race and the red man's loss of a continent that he had held since the last glacier.

There were not really very many of these red men. Some parts of the huge continent were wholly empty. Even where powerful tribes controlled the forests or the plains, the land seemed empty to invaders who came from settled Europe.

To all appearance, the life of the whole great continent, that fateful October morning in 1492 was wholly unchanged. Save on one insignificant island, there was no stir that day and no excitement. Yet the arrival of these three small ships, bobbing in the warm blue waves off San Salvador, meant that all this life of plains, mountains, lakes, and forests was now an insubstantial pageant soon to fade.

Earlier strangers—Orientals, perhaps, as well as Europeans—had come, had vanished, and had made no special difference. A Chinese legend of the sixth century says that one Hoei-Sin sailed four thousand miles east from Japan and there found a continent called Fusang. America? No one knows. There is not much doubt that occasional junks did now and then get blown clear across the Pacific but, if so, they left no traces.

The Norsemen were of little more importance. They came, they settled, fought the "Skraellings"—who may have been either Eskimos or Indians—and left again. Of North America they tell us nothing save that it was inhabited; that there grew in its forests such timber as they had never seen; that the winter days were longer than in Greenland. Like all travelers they were impressed by the grapevines which sprawled and scrambled over most of the continent, and so named the new country "Vineland the Good." No Indian legend mentions the Norsemen. They built, perhaps—it is very dubious—the round tower at Newport. Perhaps again—and this is still more dubious— they penetrated into Ontario about the year 1000 and into the Red River country in Minnesota in 1362. A "Viking Find"—a sword, an axe, an iron handle of a shield—is supposed to have been unearthed from a grave on Lake Nipigon, near Port Arthur, Ontario, in 1930. Authorities say the weapons are genuine enough and date from about A.D. 1000; but it has been suspected they were brought, as curiosities, in modern times by some modern Norwegian settler. The Kensington Stone, found in Minnesota in 1898, describes in runic characters the massacre of Scandinavian explorers by Minnesota Indians in 1362 and the plight of the survivors. If it is genuine, a party of Norwegians and Swedes traversed half of North America 130 years before Columbus. And it is true that a certain Paul Knudsen was sent by the Norwegian king on an exploring expedition from which he seems never to have returned, just about that time.

But for present purposes, none of this is of any great importance. Genuine or spurious, these archeological curiosities tell nothing of what the country was like before Columbus. That is a story which must still be patched together from the casual observations of weary men, often in danger of their lives, mostly untrained in observation, almost always so exhausted by the mere effort to stay alive that they had small leisure or energy for the scanty notes and journals that they left behind.

II

The Red Discoverers

NORTH AMERICA HAD been there a long, long time, in many shapes and forms and with varying extents and elevations. Great seas had flowed in what is now the Mississippi Valley, and elsewhere. Then the land had risen under geological force and the seas had drained away, leaving traces in subterranean salt seas, and beds of salt beneath the earth, and in briny springs that bubble up to the surface still.

Never, until the fourth and last glacier was in retreat, did mankind see America. For countless millennia, the Great Ice had been sliding, grinding, scraping its way relentlessly southward. It had scoured Canada down to its primeval rock—formed long before in the fires of the early earth. The huge, hard, heavy frozen mass scooped out as it went innumerable hollows in the ancient granite, which one day would become endless chains of wooded northern lakes, their exquisitely clear water floating and reflecting the white birchbark canoes of the Algonkian tribes.

Down across the Canadian border and into the future United States swept the ice until, at its greatest extent, it covered all of New England and New York, the northern halves of New Jersey and Pennsylvania, most of Ohio, Indiana, and Illinois, reaching south along what would one day be the west bank of the Mississippi into Kansas and Missouri, its edge then swinging northward until it met the chill and icy Pacific not very far south of the Canadian boundary. Ice covered Europe as far south as Kiev, Cracow, Prague, and London. In Asia there was less ice—or perhaps we only think so because we know so little about it.

Still, there was enough to cover northern Siberia, reach over into America to bury Alaska, and make a solid crystal bridge across Bering Strait, providing passage for any primitive men or animals of Asia adventurous enough to seek the uninhabited American shore.

Whether any took advantage of that opportunity, we do not know. Mankind—black, yellow, red, or white—could not find life upon that enormous, frigid, glittering mass very inviting. The modern Eskimo have shown that human life can sustain itself there if it has to. But in Europe and Asia mankind clung upon its edges. In North America, or so the best evidence indicates, the human race had not yet even arrived, when the glaciers covered the land. The southern United States was always clear of ice, but nothing even remotely human lived there.

Accumulated through many centuries, the Great Ice went on melting through other centuries. Slowly the glaciers drew back, creeping an ever-shorter distance south each winter, withdrawing a little farther into the North each spring, as the sunlight grew slowly warmer with each passing century. Huge streams formed by the melting ice went roaring down the valleys where smaller rivers run today. In most American valleys you can find the water-rounded stones of the old river beds, high up the slopes where, now, even the spring floods never reach. As the ice drew sullenly back into the Arctic, the plants and animals that it had once forced southward began to wander north again, into a continent no modern man would recognize.

The melting snow and ice made not only rivers but lakes, larger than any that we know. Up the rushing rivers, into the still icy lakes came fish that had survived farther south. They did not all come at the same time. The immense lake trout of interior Canada and the northern states, for example, were early comers, pushing their way up great glacial rivers so deep that they drowned out what now are waterfalls. Swimming over them easily, the lake trout reached their present waters. But when the first ancestors of that angler's prize, the brook trout, began exploring for new homes, the glacial rivers had shrunk. The brook trout could not get over the big falls, and so are now found naturally, only in brooks below falls like St. Anthony's and

Niagara. Artificial stocking alone has, in recent years, brought them into the upper streams.

Musk-ox and reindeer came, paused a little while, geologically speaking, in the United States, then followed the Great Ice into the North forever. Various horses came—strange creatures with several toes—mammoths and mastodon, camels, giant bison, enormous bears, the forefathers of the American fauna the first explorers were to find. Many returning animals remain, but these have disappeared. Some, like the mammoth, must have vanished just before the white man came. Indeed, it is by no means impossible that, while Columbus was skirting the American coast, the last of the mammoths were dying in Kentucky.

A few of the lesser glacial animals survive to this day in a few favored spots in the United States, which still approximate conditions of the Ice Age. The great Kadiak bear is one. Even more interesting is the little White Mountain butterfly *(Oeneis semidea)*, which, when the Great Ice was withdrawing, fluttered up into the colder air on Mount Washington in New Hampshire and one other peak—in Colorado. There, to this day, their descendants remain, the two colonies separated by thousands of miles, prisoners on the peaks which, to the little grey butterflies, are life-saving islands of cold amid the deadly warm air of the modern valleys. Nowhere else in North America does this strange winged relic of the Ice Age appear, until you reach Labrador, where it can still find the cold it grew to love in the days of the great glacier.

By about 40,000 to 20,000 B.C.—dates which are at best mere guesses—North America must have reached nearly the condition in which Columbus found it. Slowly, new soil had formed again where the glaciers had planed down to the bare barren rock, or where they had left only deposits of glacial sand. The soil made plant life possible. The plants, within a few generations, began to make more soil. More plants grew, and animals followed the plants. Forests of conifers and deciduous trees began to cover New England and the central states, with the woods buffalo, not quite the same animal as the great bison of the prairies, living here and there among them. In Illinois and Kentucky, patches of open meadow and canebrakes began to appear. From the

Panel from a map made in 1711. "A view of the Industry of the Beavers in Canada in making dams to stop the course of a rivulet to form a great lake, about which they build their habitations." Also an early drawing of Niagara Falls.

A view of the Falls of St. Anthony, showing the site of the city of Minneapolis. The earliest known American magazine engraving of the Mississippi River, from the *New York Magazine*, May, 1796.

Mississippi to the Rockies stretched the great plains, kept clear of trees by prairie fires and by enormous herds of buffalo, sometimes miles across, moving north each summer and south each winter, following the grass, grazing as they moved, their "chips" and in the end their bones slowly, through centuries, fertilizing what would one day, centuries later, be rich, western farming land.

The Rockies must have looked always very much as they look today, their peaks glittering in the sun so that the first white men called them "the Shining Mountains," perhaps translating an earlier Indian name. Untouched through all the centuries, the changeless summits remain as they were when the first wandering copper-colored immigrants looked up at them with wonder. The Appalachians, in the East, are older mountains, worn down through millennia before mankind, red or white, ever saw them.

Beyond the Rockies, in Oregon and Washington and part at least of California, the land was covered with gigantic fir, ten feet through at the base, towering two hundred feet, the ground beneath them a hopeless tangle through which even a red hunter could hardly penetrate, passable only here and there by game trails. Often swamps lay between the thickest growths of timber. A little farther south, in California, where the fogs sweep in from the Pacific, stood the giant redwoods, thirty feet at the base, reaching three hundred feet and more into the air—not the isolated groves at which tourists gape today, but solid forests of the giant trees, moss-grown, with ferns and moss beneath them, silent, stretching from the rocky cliffs along the coast back to the foothills of the towering Rockies.

No human eye had ever seen these romantic, unspoiled, lovely landscapes, for as yet the human race had never entered North America. Sea lions barked along the California coast. Sea otter swam and dived in the Columbia and among Pacific kelp beds. The salmon came rushing up the Columbia to the spawning grounds each spring, with nothing to fear save a few hungry animals along the bank, watching for wounded or straggling fish. There were no Indians, and it would be many thousand years before the white man would arrive, bringing trouble with him. Only elk, deer, bear, the mountain lion, and other animals looked out from time to time over the Pacific, boiling away toward Asia, without so much as a canoe, still less a sail, least of all a steamer's smoke, to mar its surface.

Six thousand miles away, across that blue and heaving surface, something was happening in Asia. As the Asiatic glaciers drew back, other plants began to follow the retreating ice, and, as always, animals followed the plants. That had happened in America. But in Asia there was a difference; and that difference was Man. Mongoloid hunters began to follow the animals—north, north, always north, until after generations they came at last to Bering Strait where, from the shores of Asia, they could look across to Alaska. Behind them, doubtless, other tribes were pressing. Ahead was ever the lure of game.

Somehow, on rafts or in canoes, perhaps upon the ice, they crossed. Then slowly, as the news spread and more hunters came, they began moving south. It is very likely they kept on crossing and moving southward for many centuries—little bands of various tribes, without much knowledge of their fellow immigrants and no interest at all in each other. The bands that led the southward movement probably neither dreamed nor cared that other Mongoloid bands were following far behind.

Slowly the red invaders of this empty land crept south and then east. Some passed the Isthmus of Panama and peopled South America. Of these some remained in savagery, others—Toltec, Maya, Aztec, Inca—created great civilizations.

In the United States and Canada nothing that can quite be described as an Indian civilization ever grew up, though the Iroquois built up in New York an empire as unscrupulously powerful as the most modern white man's and—like the Five Civilized Tribes in the Southeast and the various tribes called Pueblos in the Southwest—established a secure and settled mode of life which might, in a few centuries more, have developed all the white man's arts. Elsewhere—in the severe climates of Canada and Alaska, in the sunny comfort of California, on the Great Plains, and in the barren foothills of the Rockies—the red men remained wandering hunters.

These were the people whom Columbus called Indians because he thought he had sailed to India. They have been called so ever since, mainly because no one has ever thought of a better name. Mostly they had only tribal names for themselves. There was no real need for a racial name. For thousands of years it never occurred to any Indian that there could be a race that was not "red." Some of them had words like the Algonkian "anishinábek," "the original people," for their kind. Many of the tribal names meant about the same thing— "the real people," a bit of not-too-innocent vanity from which the human race has never recovered.

Though the idea that the Indians' ancestors came from Asia across Bering Strait is now generally accepted, it is not, of course, the only theory. Some of the early guesses, though far less sensible, were at least amusing. The first white travelers soon discovered that the North American Indians had many customs shared by primitive peoples the world over. For example, most tribes separated menstruating girls, providing a special lodging for them. Women underwent a ritual cleansing after childbirth. (Some branches of the Christian church still retain a ritual of the same sort, though they rarely practice it, nowadays.) The white men were familiar with similar observances in the Old Testament. A few amateur philologists were sure they heard traces of Hebrew in the half-understood, badly translated sounds the red men uttered—a more recent amateur is quite sure he hears Old Norse!

The conclusion was obvious: here were the lost Ten Tribes of Israel at last! They seemed to have wandered a long distance from Palestine, but that merely explained why they had never turned up anywhere else. It was well along in the nineteenth century before the sciences of anthropology and philology developed far enough to end that absurd and unfounded notion, once for all.

Cotton Mather had a still more enlivening theory: He believed that the devil had personally conducted the Indians to America to keep them "out of the sound of the silver trumpets of the gospel" and thus prevent their salvation.

Other speculations were nearly as wild as Mather's. Even the early American scientist Bartram thought the Indians might be descendants of forgotten Norse colonists or of Egyptian, Phoenician, or Carthaginian sailors, blown across the Atlantic. He was not by any means sure that the story that the American aborigines originated from a band of

Welshmen led across the Atlantic by a mythical Prince Madoc was "meer fiction." Bartram also entertained the Asiatic theory, since there might be land "most of the way from *America* to *Japan,* at least islands."

No one had any doubt that the Indians were completely human—the Indian girls soon proved that; and if they were human, then, to the theological mind, there was no real problem about their origin. Said Roger Williams: "From Adam and Noah that they spring, it is granted on all hands."

Some other early ideas were more reasonable and may hold a little truth. Though there is no longer any real doubt that Indians did arrive in North America by way of Bering Strait and Alaska, it is also possible that other Asiatics were simply blown across the Pacific and stayed in North America because they had no way to go home. There have been enough similar incidents in historical times to show what could—and perhaps did—happen.

There is even a theory (which recent [1947] experiments with a raft manned by white men, but wholly driven by wind and current, make plausible) that some of this involuntary migration went the other way. If that is true, the Pacific Islands were at least partly populated by Indians, carried by winds or currents westward from the coast of Peru. If part of the aboriginal population of North America—even a small part—really did arrive across the Pacific from southern Asia, that might help explain some of the curious resemblances that some students think they have noted between ancient stone ruins in Mexico and Asia.

When the first red immigrants crossed Bering Strait, they brought with them skillfully chipped stone arrowheads, and probably axes, spearheads, awls, and scrapers. There seem to be no genuine "paleoliths" in North America. The crude chipped stone instruments, once supposed to be paleolithic, are now thought to be "rejects"—that is, half-finished stones that some pre-historic craftsmen commenced working on and then discarded as unsatisfactory, when only half complete. Stone tools excavated on the campus of the University of Alaska, probably the most ancient manufactures ever found in North America, are clearly neolithic. Indeed, they are very much like neolithic tools found in the Gobi Desert—perhaps because the ancestors of their Mongoloid makers started both west and east from a common center.

Once the red adventurers had reached the empty continent, especially after they had gone far enough south to reach a temperate climate, they must have had a rather easy time. There were no hostile inhabitants to oppose their coming. Food must have been less of a problem for them than it ever was for the later Indians. Game, which included even more species than the white man found, was plentiful and—since it had never been hunted—without any fear of man.

The mysterious Indians who left their exquisitely wrought arrow points at Folsom, Colorado, successfully hunted the great pre-historic bison—even larger than the half-ton buffalo bull the white man exterminated. We know that, because the early hunters accommodatingly left their easily recognized stone "Folsom points" in the animals' bones, and because surviving skeletons lack the tail vertebrae—plain evidence that ancient hunters skinned the carcasses.

However long the mammoth lasted in America—the writer's own guess is that it was still here as late as 1500 or even 1600—there is no doubt that it was here in the millennia before Christ, when the red man came. The huge beast was hard to kill with stone spears and axes but—stampeded over a cliff or stuck in a bog—it could occasionally be made to provide meat. Killing a mammoth meant tons of it.

The later Indians who gravely assured Thomas Jefferson that the hairy mammoth still existed in the wild interior of North America may have been simply wrong, or may have been mistranslated, or may —as Indians do—have simply been trying to tell the white brother what they thought he would like to hear. It is quite as likely, however, that they were remembering tribal traditions not more than a century or two old. The great bones in Kentucky lay on or near the surface of the ground, showing that the huge creatures had not long been dead. Hunters of Daniel Boone's day found the enormous vertebrae very comfortable camp seats, admirably rounded to accommodate a hunter's weary rump.

When these larger animals failed, there were always deer and fish and a great variety of wild game birds, including the passenger pigeons whose flocks (literally) darkened the sky and which could be netted or snared with ease.

With their tools and weapons—not quite all of stone, since they also used wood, bone, claws, horn, shells, and the sharp tail of the horseshoe crab—the red newcomers began to spread over the continent, drawn by the search for new hunting grounds, pushed on by other Asiatics more or less akin, coming in behind them. There were migrations in two directions—one straight south along the mountains, the other eastward. Toward the end of the red man's supremacy there was even a return migration westward into the Great Plains. Languages, traces of culture, legends show which group traveled southward. We know some of them today as Pueblos, Apaches, Navajos, Utes, Aztecs. The savage Utes, well to the north, speak a language that is undoubtedly related to that of the civilized Aztecs. Probably this means that, as the original stock passed south, the Utes halted in an environment less favorable to development than their Aztec kin found in Mexico. The Apaches of the American Southwest and the distant Athapascans of Canada also speak cognate languages. The Apaches settled almost due south of their Canadian kindred, though separated from them by thousands of miles.

The ancestors of the Iroquoian Indians (the Iroquois themselves, the Hurons, Cherokees, Eries, the "Neutral Nation," and many others) moved directly across the northern tier of the United States. Somewhere along the Canadian border and north of it, through Canadian lakes and forests came most of the ancestors of the great Algonkian group, (Ojibway, or Chippewa, and Cree). Other Indians of the same group, notably the Shawnee and Delaware, seem to have moved eastward through plains and forests, just south of an entirely separate Iroquois migration. The New England tribes for whom, between 1661 and 1663, John Eliot published his Indian Bible were another part of the Algonkian group.

Algonkian languages have always remained pretty much alike. If you speak reasonably good twentieth century Ojibway you can read Eliot's Pequot translation of the Scriptures; or you can guess correctly the meaning of the few recorded Shawnee taunts that the Indians flung across the stockade at Daniel Boone and his men during the

siege of Boonesborough in 1778. French and Italian are no closer together than the Algonkian languages. "Anim," says the Cree, for
"dog." "Animush," says the Ojibway. "Nipa" is modern Ojibway for
"sleep." It was a good Shawnee word—with the same meaning—in
the eighteenth century, and it is still in use on the Shawnee reservations today.

When we find "Siouan" languages being spoken in Pennsylvania
and Carolina about the time the white man came, by tribes long
established in the East, we can guess at the course of their ancestral
migration. The ancient Siouan group must have parted company at
the Mississippi. The Mandans—also Siouan—probably dropped off
somewhere along the Missouri. The Sioux proper, as we know them,
swung up the Mississippi, then back into the West. Another branch
moved on into the southeastern United States to form the tribes of
Tutelo, Sapony, and others.

Sometimes there are tribal traditions, set down by white men who
took an interest in such matters one or two hundred years ago, when
the stories still were fresh in the minds of the Indians themselves and
uncontaminated by white influence. These more or less confirm what
linguists and anthropologists more or less know must have happened.

When in the eighteenth century the Moravian missionary, Heckewelder, came among them, the older Delawares still remembered
their ancient traditions. They had reached the Mississippi, aged warriors told their Moravian friend, only to find the land on the east
bank already occupied by other Indians. As native diplomacy required,
they asked for permission to pass through the tribal territory of the
strange Indians. It was duly granted; but, when the other Indians saw
how numerous the Delawares were, they took fright and refused to
let them pass. Just then the Delawares discovered that the Iroquois
had also reached the Mississippi, immediately above them, and were
also endeavoring to cross. Together they attacked the inhabitants of
the east bank—migrants from the West still earlier than themselves—
and defeated them.

This may have happened around the year 1300 or even earlier.
Though the tradition does not say so, linguistic and anthropological
studies show that during the next few centuries, the ancestors of the

Iroquois must have made a series of moves. They had crossed the Mississippi somewhere south of St. Louis after a period of settlement in Missouri and Arkansas. The east bank Indians with whom they fought were perhaps the proto-Muskogean ancestors of the Creeks, Chickasaws, Choctaws, and Seminoles.

After crossing the Mississippi, the Delaware and Iroquois together must have forced their way northeast through Kentucky. Thence most of the Iroquoian tribes moved still farther in the same direction to the banks of the St. Lawrence. Somewhere along the way, the related Hurons, Eries, and the "Neutral Nation" must have broken off from the Iroquoian group for when, with the first Jesuit missionaries, written history begins, they are independent and even hostile tribes.

From the banks of the St. Lawrence, the hostile Adirondacks, an Algonkian tribe already in possession, forced them back into New York State. The Iroquois had left behind them, on the way, remnants of the Iroquoian stock, notably the Cherokee, who settled in Tennessee and South Carolina and stayed there till the white man moved them out.

Part of this story the Delaware tradition confirms. It says simply that the Iroquois moved to the St. Lawrence, while the Delaware settled south of them in Pennsylvania, New Jersey, and Maryland. Then, when the Iroquois began to move into New York State, they clashed with their old Delaware friends and allies.

The Iroquois migration is one of the rare cases where an event in "pre-history" can be roughly dated within a few centuries. It is known that the League of the Iroquois was formed in New York some time in the 1500's. This was the story they told the white men, arriving only about a hundred years later, when the oldest Indians remembered fairly well a tradition which at that time was not very ancient. They must have spent at least the fifteenth century along the St. Lawrence— in fact Cartier found some of them there as late as 1535, though they had vanished by the time Champlain arrived.

Allow one more century for the long, slow journey on foot from the Mississippi to the St. Lawrence. Remember this was not a definite, swift movement with a specific purpose by a hardy band of warriors moving to a definite goal. The ancestral Iroquois did not know where they were going. They were looking for any land where there was good hunting and where they could grow corn. Remember that they had women, children, and baggage to encumber every movement. Remember that they were delayed by the necessity of hunting, halting to make winter shelter, preserving food, building canoes, and cutting firewood—all with stone implements. Probably there were a good many halts of a year or more to grow a crop or two and lay in a fresh reserve of food. Remember also that, year by year as they moved, they were in constant danger of attack from tribes already in possession of the land, who resented them as interlopers and were certainly handy with bow, arrow, war club, and stone axe. Probably the early Iroquoians had to take time out for a good many small wars, before they made their way through the Middle West and the middle Atlantic states. On such a basis, one might say that, while Chaucer was writing the *Canterbury Tales,* the Iroquois and the Delaware were moving into the eastern United States.

How long all this required, what struggles, hardships, and adventures, what wars, what deaths, what tortures, how many tribes had vanished utterly, long, long before the white man, no one knows. The things we do know, as well as the things we guess at, are a combination of archeological excavation, the relationship of Indian languages, anthropological studies showing physical measurements of modern Indians and physical resemblances, and tribal legends, critically compared and checked against each other.

III

The Red Man's Dixie

THE LAND THAT was one day to be Dixie already possessed, in pre-Columbian days, a good many of the characteristics for which it is still famous. It was agricultural, richly productive, fertile, and very beautiful. It was also hospitable. It became famous for good Indian food and good Indian cooking. Elsewhere in North America, dining with the Indians was likely to be a nauseating experience, endurable only by a very strong or a very empty stomach. But the southern Indians, says James Adair, who lived long among them, could "diversify their courses, as much as the English," and all their food was "grateful for a wholesome stomach."

Their cornmeal flour, made of selected white kernels, and their special flour of mixed ground corn, beans, and potatoes made really good bread, particularly as it was refined by sifting through sieves made of cane. Baked either in thin cakes moistened with bear's oil, or as large loaves, placed on the hot earth where a campfire had been and then covered with an earthen pot and hot coals, the results were excellent. "This method of baking is as clean and efficacious as possibly could be done in any oven," wrote Adair, who often watched the squaws at work. "When they take it off, they wash the loaf with warm water, and it soon becomes firm, and very white. It is likewise very wholesome, and well-tasted to any except the vitiated palate of an Epicure."

In this prehistoric southern cooking, potatoes and other roots were boiled and roasted. Pumpkins were barbecued over the fire. Persimmons were dried, mashed with parched corn, and baked into cakes, which were stewed with fat venison or bear's oil, of which a single animal might yield fifteen gallons (while the giant grizzlies of the West yielded much more). Later, oranges were abundant, growing in groves of thousands, sometimes covering several acres. The fruit was roasted and, since it was much sourer than the improved varieties of modern commerce, was sometimes opened and filled with honey. The black mulberry was also dried into cakes and stewed with bread, parched cornmeal, and oil. The reputation of southern cookery had begun long before the southern white man had arrived and before plantations were even dreamed of.

This pre-Columbian South even had its store of southern belles. Though anthropologists like to represent the Indians' love life as "rather simply physical" and are in the main probably right about it, romance was not wholly unknown. The Cherokee girls had an especial reputation for beauty, which some of the other tribes shared. When the woman chief of Cofitachequi (not far from Augusta, Georgia,) was borne on the shoulders of her subjects to De Soto's camp, in 1540, "in a litter covered with delicate white linen," the susceptible Spaniards thought her "a young girl of fine bearing," admiring the poise and self-possession with which she addressed their commander "quite gracefully and at her ease."

Historians have habitually made fun of the story of Pocahontas' romantic rescue of Captain John Smith, but there are so many similar stories from other sources that Smith's tale is probably true. The Spaniard, Juan Ortiz, left behind in Florida by the Narváez expedition in 1528 and captured by the Indians was saved from burning by the chief's daughter, just as Smith was saved by Pocahontas from having his brains beaten out. When the chief later changed his mind and decided to use Ortiz as a human sacrifice, the enamoured girl helped him to flee and even guided him until he was well started on the path to a safer village.

Otherwise, it was a Dixie very different from anything that Robert E. Lee ever dreamed of. The whole of what is today the South was forested, from the Atlantic coast to the Mississippi River and the Gulf of Mexico. Virginia was the meeting place of northern and southern forests, the species of both growing here intermingled, as they do today, though nowadays their numbers are dismally reduced. From Virginia southward, typically southern trees like the magnolia, the persimmon, the southern longleaf pine began to appear. In the Carolinas the palmetto flourished, and thence southward the forests stretched away to the Gulf and Florida, where they became definitely sub-tropical.

Kentucky and the Shenandoah Valley were, for a time, neutral hunting grounds, entered only by hunters and war parties, the latter coming down the Warriors' Path, through Kentucky from Lake Erie. Kentucky itself was thickly forested and filled with game. In the Shenandoah, as in much of Piedmont Virginia and the Middle West, the Indians had for years kept the level ground burned free of trees, to make it easier to see the game. The meadowland was, therefore, covered mainly with canebrakes and waving grass, through which wandered buffalo, elk, and deer—pursued by wolves and panthers, while foxes preyed upon the smaller animals.

The river valleys everywhere, beginning with the Ohio, the Shenandoah, the Kentucky rivers, and on southward, were covered with a luxuriant growth of cane, the "brakes" often extending for miles in every direction. No one, for the last hundred years, has seen anything like the tremendous growth of these primitive canebrakes. Brakes still exist, but they are poor and pitifully reduced descendants of the luxuriant growth whose tasseled tops once waved over mile upon mile of fertile plains. The fertility of the land on which they grew destroyed them quickly. They disappeared early because the first white settlers were quick to realize that a flourishing canebrake was a sign of first-class farm land, with the added advantage that the stalks, which could be slashed away like corn, were much easier to clear than thick-set forest trees.

In the luxuriant South, in pre-Columbian days, a single brake, two or three miles wide, might extend for a hundred miles, filling rich river valleys and crowding out all other plant life. The jointed stalks were enormously strong and tall, sometimes reaching thirty—or perhaps occasionally, forty—feet. The leaves were long and green, like corn. The tops were tasseled. The stalks of cane themselves were so

Canebrake in Alabama, which formerly covered vast areas
in the Southeast and lower Mississippi region. From
Economic Botany of Alabama by Roland M. Harper, 1913.
Courtesy of the author.

Florida swamp. From *Picturesque America*, 1872.

strong and so rigid that, with their ends sharpened, the Indians could use them to spear fish.

Broken, they were razor-sharp. A "cane stab," the wound made by stepping on a stub left erect in the ground, was one of the most dreaded of injuries. So sharp was the outer glasslike cortex that Indians lacking flint sometimes improvised knives from its sharp edges. Faggots of dried cane made convenient torches, which lighted wild midnight dances.

Canebrakes were perfect hiding places for fugitives, since if they turned and doubled in their tracks, it was impossible to find them. In a really large brake a man on horseback could hide himself without dismounting. Innumerable records tell the stories of white pioneers who escaped the Indians only by diving in time into a handy canebrake.

But even cane could not crowd out the trees. Both banks of the Mississippi were forested all the way to the sea, except where the Indians had cleared away occasional fields for corn and beans. Cottonwood, poplar, cane, tangles of brier and grapevines edged both the eastern and the western banks, in the southern part of the great valley. Five or six miles back from the river, where water was not quite so plentiful as in the sodden bottom lands, open prairie began, with mulberry and persimmon trees—and with vines still climbing everywhere.

Farther west, along prairie streams, cottonwoods and willows were very nearly the only trees. In the southern reaches of the Mississippi and its tributaries, they reached such dimensions that the Indians could find trunks big enough to make dugout canoes forty and fifty feet long, with a beam of three feet. Here also grapes hung thickly from the trees. The hungry or thirsty traveler could pick them from vines on trees that overhung the river, without even leaving his canoe.

Throughout most of the pre-Columbian South, the Indians enjoyed abundance, though in Western Texas food was often scarce. Elsewhere the menace of winter famine, from which the northern tribes were never free, was unknown. Bear fat and walnut oil were stored in calabashes. Great fields of corn spread in all directions. The land produced two crops a year, in spite of occasional raids by buffalo and deer. Most of the game animals of the North, except moose and elk,

were present in the South, though naturally the fur-bearers grew more
and more infrequent.

Waterfowl, after nesting in the northern United States and Canada,
came south for the winter in the incredible numbers then common in
North America; but though they could be killed easily, the southern
Indians did not have to use them very much for food. Bartram describes them as "approaching like Clouds in the air." When disturbed,
they took wing "like a Vast dark thunder Storm," by day, while if
disturbed by night "the Thunder of their Wings, with their united
squaling Tongues exhibits a scene of confusion & bableing as if the
desolution of Nature was at hand."

Deer were as common here as they were everywhere. Pigeons were
even more plentiful than wild ducks and wild geese. Sassafras and
wild cinnamon flavored the bear fat that the Indians kept from winter
to winter in earthen jars. Maple sugar, which the northern tribes used
for the same purpose, seems to have been unknown here.

The southern Indians all raised about the same crops as their
northern brothers—corn, potatoes, tobacco, beans, peas, melons,
squashes, sunflowers, and pumpkins, called "pompions" by some of
the early white travelers. As in the North, the fields were cleared by
girdling the trees with stone hatchets or by burning them down.

Into this luxuriant land by way of its most luxuriant part, the
Florida Peninsula, came the Spaniards, not greatly interested in the
fertile acres they traversed, but with dreams of more golden empires to
despoil, such as they had looted in Peru and Mexico. Long before
the Virginia colonists or the Pilgrim Fathers landed, they had covered
the South and Southwest from coast to coast, reaching at least as far
north as the Blue Ridge, Tennessee, and Kansas.

Spanish exploration naturally began in Florida, close to the Caribbean islands, with which the Spaniards were already familiar. It moved
west and northwest, because the Spaniards, looking for gold in a land
where there was practically none, kept moving hopefully on and on—
encouraged by the dubious tales of Indians, who were chiefly interested
in getting these intruders out of their own territory and into somebody
else's. Spanish adventures in the Old South led to nothing very permanent except in Florida. The conquistadors were mere get-rich-quick

adventurers, not farmers and home-builders. In consequence, despite Spanish interest, the English had settled the country as far south as Georgia before the Spaniards could make good their claims.

Quite probably, adventurous Spaniards had mapped the Florida Peninsula by 1502 or earlier; but, if so, they left no positive record. The first explorer of whom we can be sure today was Juan Ponce de León, who visited Florida in 1513, seeking the fountain of eternal youth, which formed part of Indian mythology. The quest itself so absorbed him that he left little or no account of what he saw in the strange new land. Francisco Fernández de Córdoba, in 1517, had not really meant to land in Florida at all. Driven off by the fierce warriors of Yucatan, however, he let his pilot, who had been in Florida with Ponce de León, take him thither. He left little more description than Ponce de León or the numerous Spanish slave-raiders who sailed the Atlantic coast between 1521 and 1525, no one knows how far northward.

The first really serious Spanish attempt to found a colony in the southeastern United States was led in 1526 by Vásquez de Ayllón, who after looking for gold and jewels near Cape Fear, spent a disastrous winter on a river which may have been the Pedee, in South Carolina. About a hundred and fifty men got home alive, leaving Ayllón dead in the wilderness.

Then, in 1528, came Captain Pánfilo de Narváez, an adventurer who really looked the part. One-eyed (he had lost the other eye fighting against Cortez), with a bass voice so deep that it seemed to come from a cavern rather than a human larynx, he was "tall and strong-limbed, his face long, with a red beard and an agreeable presence." With him came four hundred hopeful colonists, all but five of them doomed to various unpleasant forms of death, along with their commander. Rich but reputed stingy, intelligent but careless, Narváez had to a hideous degree the cold brutality of the Spanish conquistadors. He is the man who on one occasion sat his horse, quietly watching his men butcher two thousand friendly and defenseless Indians, for no particular reason except that at the moment they felt like it.

He landed on the west side of Tampa Bay in April, 1528. Sailing up the Gulf coast of Florida, the Spaniards from their ships could see

primitive Florida as a later traveler described it: An "amazing extent
of uncultivated land, covered with forests, and intermixed with vast
lakes and marshes of stagnated fresh water." The forests included
many "large pine-trees" which were, of course, southern longleaf pines,
though it was a long time before botanists like Bartram began to distinguish the species. "The country," wrote William Roberts much later
"abounds with all kinds of timber, particularly pines, cedar, palms,
laurel, cypress, and chesnut trees; but, above all, sassefras is found in
the greatest plenty; excellent limes and plums also grow here in great
abundance. There were also many vines, wild cotton, hemp, and flax."

Luxuriant, semi-tropical beauty and agricultural possibilities, however, did not interest Narváez and his conquistadors. Gold and
jewels were what they were after. The Indian village near which they
landed—its site is still marked by enormous mounds of shells—was
empty, the inhabitants having prudently fled when they saw strangers.
One of the soldiers, rummaging among Indian fishing nets, soon
found a gold object, described as a "rattle," or "tinklet." This, and a
few other gold articles, easily convinced Narváez that he was approaching another great empire, like the Aztecs' or the Incas', with immense
wealth.

A patrol, pushing north into Old Tampa Bay, caught a few
Timucuas—a tribe extinct since the eighteenth century. These Indians
led them to another village at the head of the bay. Here the Spaniards
found "many cases, such as are used to contain the merchandise of
Castile," wool, linen, and canvas cloth, iron, and other obviously
European objects. These, the Indians explained by signs, had been
taken from a ship, wrecked in Tampa Bay. In spite of much guesswork, no one has ever determined whose ship this was.

When the Spaniards inquired by signs where the golden objects came
from, the Timucuas exclaimed "Apalachen" and pointed north. The
Apalachee tribe—the final -*n* seems to have been merely a grammatical
ending—lived in northwestern Florida, around Pensacola, Tallahassee,
and St. Marks. Long since extinct, they are remembered now only
because their name is preserved by the Appalachian Mountains and a
few other geographic names. The Apalachee got some of their gold
by barter with the Indians of northern Georgia, where some nuggets

were, in primitive times, washed out of the river sands. But there was also gold in Florida. The town of Apalachee was probably on Lake Miccosukee, just south of the Georgia-Florida border. Narváez rashly struck off overland to find it, leaving only vague orders for his ships to proceed to a harbor rumored to lie farther up the coast and there wait for him. In case he did not appear, the ships were to search one year before giving up the attempt to find him. As the port he had in mind lay to the south instead of to the north, it is hardly surprising that the expedition and its ships never saw each other again.

In early May Narváez moved north, keeping close to the sea and thus avoiding the worst of the Florida swamps. At first he met with very little difficulty. The country was level and sandy, broken here and there by clumps of tall pines. The Spaniards would have had no trouble at all had it not been for the swamps, creeks, and rivers that lay across their path. These were full of fallen trees and tangled reeds. Strange to say, neither the Narváez nor the De Soto expedition had any trouble, either with the poisonous snakes or with the alligators which must have swarmed there and which, though rarely aggressive, are always willing to fight it out if cornered or annoyed.

Some thirty years later, the French explorers along the Florida, Georgia, and South Carolina coasts and on the Mississippi observed the alligators at once. It is true that Father Marquette failed to see any in the Mississippi, but he did not go below the mouth of the Arkansas River, which was about the northern limit of their range. They were, says one account, "much bigger than the crocodiles of the Nile," which is probably an exaggeration, like the stories of eighteen- and twenty-footers, which persisted into the nineteenth century. Elsewhere, the French say, they were only twelve to thirteen feet long— quite big enough for comfort—though even today a really big bull alligator may reach sixteen feet. The Indians killed them by thrusting a sharp pole into the open mouth and down the gullet, after which they turned the struggling beast upside down and beat it with clubs, meantime shooting arrows into the soft belly. The meat, one French explorer reports, was "tender, white as veal, and had almost the same taste." They had a musky odor which led one Indian, taken as a guest to the French Court, to complain that all the men smelled like alligators. He had recognized the perfumer's musk then affected by the courtiers!

Though the alligators do not seem actually to have attacked travelers along the rivers very often, they certainly terrified them with great regularity, rushing toward canoes ferociously and then diving their huge scaly lengths under the keel. The canoeist never knew when one of the huge brutes might rise beneath his craft, throwing him into the water where he was at the mercy of their huge jaws. Most canoeists got out of their way with speed and alacrity.

Fishermen were in special danger because the scent of their catch attracted the reptiles. William Bartram's party, in 1773, having just caught enough fish for supper, were attacked by three of "monstrous size," which "rush't out of the weeds, & stop't before us who seemed inclin'd to dispute the pass, however we pusht on towards them. One rush't through the water at us heaved his enormous body streight up out of the water near breast high, close by the side of our canoe, & open'd a dreadfull pair of jaws, & a bellowing throat; The other rose up behind us in like maner, pierceing the water with his strongplated Tail 5 or 6 feet high flourishing it in the air. lashing the River into a foam, & roaring like furious waters breaking out of the earth then plunging & rushing through the waters around us."

The canoeists scrambled for shore, amid a "terrible roaring." Bartram was chased to within three yards of his tent, where he snatched up a fusee loaded with buckshot. One alligator, seeing him return, started after him again, received the whole charge at point-blank range, and died then and there. The noise of the shot at first frightened the others off, but more alligators "in prodigious numbers" assembled as soon as the party began cleaning their fish for supper, "some rising their huge bodies out of the water, & roaring like terrible thunder & lashing the waters with mighty bodies, they drew near to us & one rise up & with a sweep of his Tail had like to robbed us of our fish." Probably the alligators were merely after the fish, but it was disconcerting all the same.

Next day, the travelers could hear the alligators roaring around them for miles, as was usual in the spring mating season. "Their noise is louder then the bellowing of the most furious Bull, or a Lyon, more like the latter, the water rattling in their throats, which they force out in froth & foam, & makes the earth to tremble, & our little Island shook as by an earth quake; When they roar their Body is swoln like an empty Hogshead on the water their head and Neck raisd out of the water, his Tail raised 5 or 6 feet in the air waving too & fro, & lashing the surface of the water in a terrible maner as they utter their terrable Voice their body sinks gradually in the water then swelling again rises up thus alternately as they continue their bellowing. The deep swamps & banks of the river's & Forest reechoing the dreadfull roar, the noise is communicated from one to another fills the whole country with a noise like dreadfull thunders." It was these descriptions of Bartram's that Coleridge later worked into "The Ancient Mariner."

Being in alligator country in the spring both the Narváez and the De Soto expeditions certainly heard them roar and must have seen a good many. But they were intent on treasure, not saurians. They can perhaps be forgiven for not observing an obscurer species, the American crocodile (not an alligator at all). This odd beast remained concealed in the swamps of southeast Florida, known only to Indians, until its discovery in the nineteenth century.

When the column reached the vicinity of the Witlacoochee River, Álvar Núñez Cabeza de Vaca—a junior officer of noble Spanish blood, destined to become the most famous member of the expedition—was sent to the coast to look for the ships. He and his men had to wade part of the time, "treading on oysters, which cut our feet badly," and at length found the river's mouth. But there was no sign of the ships they sought.

Thus far the Spaniards had seen few Indians, but in mid-June they were startled by the sound of music. Presently Indians appeared, "playing of flutes of reed," and escorting a local chief. The flute music to greet visitors was a widespread custom among southern Indians. A chief greeting the French, some years later, brought with him twenty of these pipers "making the wildest kind of noise, without any harmony or rhythm, each blowing with all his might as if to see who could blow the loudest. Their instruments were thick reeds, like organ pipes or whistles, with only two openings. They blew into the top hole, while the sound came out the other end."

The chief volunteered to go with them to Apalachee, but it took an entire day to make a canoe and ferry the expedition across the wide and swift Suwannee River—which Stephen Foster was later to choose, quite at random, and make immortal with a song. One man and one horse were drowned. The Spaniards, who seem to have done little hunting, were so hungry for fresh meat that "the horse afforded supper to many that night."

North of the Suwannee, the country became "very difficult to travel and wonderful to look upon." They had the luck to pass to the west of the big and, in those days, nearly impenetrable swamps of Fayette County, but along the coast, according to Cabeza de Vaca, were "vast forests, the trees being astonishingly high. So many were fallen on the ground as to obstruct our way in such a manner that we could not advance without much going about and a considerable increase of toil. Many of the standing trees were riven from top to bottom by bolts of lightning which fall in that country of frequent storms and tempests." Such tangles of fallen timber became wearisomely familiar to later explorers of eastern and southern forests; but they were probably worse than anywhere else in Florida, which received the full force of hurricanes sweeping in from the Gulf.

Here, again, the Spaniards had the luck to escape three more dangerous reptiles. Of these, the worst were the big diamondback rattlesnake and the small but deadly coral snake. The diamondback rattler, though its venom is not so strong as that of some other serpents, is the most deadly of American poisonous reptiles because of its size. Specimens more than eight feet long and weighing about fifteen pounds have been recorded by sober herpetologists. The amount of poison such a creature can inject, sometimes to a depth of a full inch, is very great.

The coral snake, brilliant in scarlet, blue-black, and yellow, is small. One early observer gives a maximum length of five feet, though none so large are seen today. But it produces a special venom of its own which, drop for drop, is far more lethal than a rattler's—more lethal, even, than a cobra's. Worse still, it has the unique and nasty habit of first striking, then holding on and chewing, so as to work the poison from its short fangs deeply into the victim's flesh. Water moccasins, being mostly in streams, were no great danger to troops on the march.

In Florida, the diamondbacks live in pine swamps and hummock lands, through both of which the expedition passed. The coral snakes live under the débris of the forest floor. The Spaniards must have tramped over them again and again, but there is no suggestion in the narratives that any one was bitten. In fact, there is no mention of poisonous snakes at all except once, long afterward, when Cabeza de Vaca was deep in the heart of Texas. Out on the arid plains along the coast, nobody could overlook the big rattlers that, quite at leisure, dragged their slow length along the sandy, open ground.

It was easy for the Spaniards to take possession of the town of Apalachee; for Narváez had the luck to arrive when all the men were absent, and when the warriors came hurrying home, surprised and disorganized, they were easily driven off. The village contained stores of green and dried corn, which the invaders seized without scruple. The town consisted of some forty thatched huts "surrounded by very dense woods, large groves, and many bodies of fresh water." The forest was mostly walnut, laurel, liquidambar, cedar, oak, pine, and palmettos, with edible "hearts." Here, too, the Florida woods were full of large fallen trees, "rendering travel difficult and dangerous."

Not all the land was forested. There were many cornfields and "fine pastures for herds." Geese, ducks, herons swarmed on the lakes, and the woods were full of partridges, though strange to say, there is no mention of wild turkeys. There were three species of deer, rabbits, hares, bears, "lions," i.e., cougars, and a remarkable "animal with a pocket on its belly, in which it carries its young until they know how to seek food, and if it should happen that they should be out feeding and any one come near, the mother will not run until she has gathered them in together." It was the first white man's record of the opossum, which was to astonish white travelers for two centuries to come.

After less than a month, Narváez had had enough. The country beyond Apalachee, he learned, was thinly peopled. Westward, a few friendly Indians told him, lay only "great lakes, dense forests, immense deserts and solitudes." There was no trace, in all this wilderness, of rich cities, like those of the Aztecs and the Incas, which he had come to seek. He decided to move south to the native coastal town of Aute, somewhere near modern St. Marks.

The first day's march toward Aute was not opposed. The Indians waited till the Spaniards were struggling through a lake, tangled with snags and fallen trees, and floundering in water up to their breasts. Then the arrows came down in showers, the almost invisible warriors shooting from behind trees along the shore. The Timucuas were big, powerful men—one skeleton unearthed in modern times is said to have been seven feet tall!—and their bows, "as thick as the arm, of eleven or twelve palms in length" drove arrows two hundred paces (which is almost "battle sight" for the U.S. Army's Springfield rifle) "with so great precision that they miss nothing," which is more than you can say for the average G.I. The striking power and penetration of these arrows was very great. The Spaniards soon found that "the good armor that they wore did not avail." Headed with snake-teeth, bone, or flint, the reed arrows would penetrate steel. Some dead Spaniards were found, "their corpses traversed from side to side with arrows; and for all some had on good armor, it did not give adequate protection." One man died from an arrow clear through the neck. Worst of all were arrows with only the sharpened reed itself for point. Hitting a shirt of chain mail, this would splinter, inflicting multiple wounds through the interstices of the mail.

Charging cavalry could scatter the native archers but the Indians made most of their attacks in thick woods where horsemen could not move. Somehow, Narváez got most of his men through to the coast, alive.

At St. Marks Bay, he halted. There was no sign of his fleet. He must have known by this time there never would be. The expedition was plainly a failure. The problem now was to get away. He decided to improvise boats and try to sail along the shore of the Gulf to the Spanish colonies in Mexico.

On the beautiful, coastal lands stretching green from Apalachee Bay to the Mississippi—five hundred miles of unspoiled, perpetual verdure, past which they sailed—they made no comment, being wholly concerned with the problem of survival. From a less perturbed later traveler—with more time to observe, since he wasn't fleeing for his life—we learn that western Florida was "wonderfully delightful & fertile, abounding with various herbs, shrubs, evergreens, and meadows." Captain Thomas Robinson in 1754 placidly observed St. Marks Bay, which Narváez and his men had been lucky to reach alive. "Looking which way I pleased, I was equally attracted with a view of the most ravishing prospects. The shore level, rising gradually into eminencies, cloathed with the finest verdure, and spontaneous productions, interspersed promiscuously, as mulberry, cedar, cocoa, vanilla, moho [a shrub which provided hemp], and cabbage-trees [palmettos], &c. the last towering their round tops above the rest, as if conscious of their sovereign dignity." The grapes were like Muscadines. Inland, around St. Marks, were many fine mulberry trees, bearing better fruit than the mulberry trees of Italy.

Eighty miles farther along the coast, between the Cape and the Mosquito River, "the scene entirely changed from the most delightful prospect and fertile soil to the most barren mountains."

Narváez took no time for landscapes. Realizing that there was no longer hope that his fleet would ever appear, he prepared to build the best substitutes he could. All spare metal was assembled—stirrups, spurs, crossbows—and made into nails, rude saws, and axes, the blacksmith using a clumsy bellows improvised from wood pipes and deerskin. No one knows how these desperate fellows made pipes out of logs. Certainly they had no augurs long enough; but they may have split the logs in quarters, chopped out the centers and then bound the four parts together.

Slowly they cut enough timber for five boats, calking the seams with palmetto fibre. They seized several hundred bushels of corn from the Indians, gathered shellfish at the risk of their lives, with Indians sniping at them whenever they could. They ate their horses, carefully working cylinders of hide off the legs first, and saving them to make water bottles for the journey.

Why, with some of the finest fishing in North America right in front of them, the Spaniards had trouble getting food, is something hard to understand; but in spite of his long experience as an officer, the science of logistics was never Narváez's strong point. He was just the kind of blundering commander who forgets essential supplies.

Still, the hungry troops might have used the nets they found in the Indian villages, if they had thought of it in time; but Cabeza de Vaca says specifically that they got very few fish.

Eventually, the expedition crawled from St. Marks out to sea in their crazy, unseaworthy craft, crowded with men, the gunwales so nearly awash that the wretched occupants had to add "waist-boards" from captured Indian canoes, after which the sides still rose only "two palms above the water." Propelled by oars and by sails made of their shirts, they managed to creep along the coast for a month, "finding occasionally Indian fishermen, a poor and miserable lot." There was no trace of the land of gold they had come to find, no hopeful sign they were nearing the new Spanish colonies in Mexico.

After five days without water—so Cabeza de Vaca says, though the thing seems incredible—they met a fleet of canoes filled with friendly Indians, perhaps in Pensacola Bay. A chief wearing a robe of civet-marten, still fragrant with the animal's musk, greeted them. Parching with thirst, the white men saw that "before their dwellings were many clay pitchers with Water, and a large quantity of cooked fish, which the chief of these territories offered to the Governor." Narváez, in return presented some dried corn and "many trinkets."

But in spite of this initial friendliness, the Indians attacked them suddenly about midnight. The Spaniards stood off two more attacks before dawn, then huddled miserably by the shore, keeping off the cold by burning the canoes of their late hosts, "without daring to go to sea, because of the rough weather upon it."

When the weather improved, Narváez and his Spaniards crawled on along the coast, fighting Indians once more, and passing a "broad river," which may have been the Mississippi. Having the best boat-crew, Narváez finally deserted the others, callously calling across the waves "that each should do what he thought best to save his own life; that he so intended to act; and saying this, he departed with his boat." One finds it hard to regret that he was shortly afterward blown out into the Gulf of Mexico, almost alone in an improvised boat, and never seen again.

Cabeza de Vaca, who lived to write the terrible story, struggled on in his craft, in company with another boat until he lost it in a storm.

On November 6, 1528, according to his own reckoning, a huge wave tossed his craft on the beach somewhere near Galveston, Texas, perhaps on San Luis Island, southwest of Galveston Island. Friendly Indians brought them food; and after several days' rest they tried to launch their boat, which turned bottom up, killing three.

With much trepidation they let the Indians take them to their village. Some Spaniards feared this meant they would be sacrificed to the gods, after the Aztec fashion—the heart torn from the living victim —but there was nothing else they could do. The Indians, however, proved hospitable and friendly. Presently Cabeza de Vaca saw one of them with "an article of traffic I knew was not one we had bestowed." Whence had it come? An Indian pointed back the way they had come. "It had been given by men like ourselves who were behind." He started two Spaniards and two Indians off to see who else had survived; but his messengers had hardly left the village when they met the other boat's crew, coming to look for them.

Selecting the four healthiest men, the Spaniards set them on the way west to Mexico on foot and themselves settled down to live with the Indians till help reached them. The Spaniards had sailed past the rich country east of the Mississippi, where they might have survived ashore, and had been cast away on the Texan plains, far south of the buffalo country. It was, in those days, a desolate land, where even the Indians found it hard to survive.

The valiant four perished in their desperate effort to reach Mexico, and the Spaniards they had left behind waited in vain for any sight of rescue. One by one they died in that cruel country. Bad weather came. Food ran short for red and white alike. Some of the Spaniards horrified the Indians by resorting to cannibalism. Soon only fifteen of the original eighty white survivors remained.

Gradually—the records do not explain why—Indian kindness ceased. The Spaniards became mere slaves, horribly treated. Eventually Cabeza de Vaca escaped to the Indians of "Charruco"—a place otherwise unknown, but probably somewhere in Texas; set himself up as a trader; located three other scattered survivors of the expedition, including the Moroccan-born Negro slave, Estebánico; wandered with the tribes in search of prickly pears, an important source of food and drink; suffered agony from mosquitoes—"there is no torment in this world that can equal it."

The four were the first Europeans to see buffalo—"hunch-backed cows," which Cabeza de Vaca described thus: "They have small horns like the cows of Morocco; the hair is very long and wooly like a rug. Some are tawny, others black. To my judgment the flesh is finer and fatter than those from here"—that is, from Spain.

It is strange that Cabeza de Vaca and his companions had not already seen buffalo in Florida, where they roamed in considerable numbers as late as the eighteenth century. In fact, there were so many of them that one Spanish garrison was in 1718 expected to subsist mainly on what buffalo meat it could kill. Nevertheless, there is no mention of them in the narrative until Cabeza de Vaca is far to the west, and it is possible that buffalo did not actually arrive in Florida until some time between 1550 and 1700. By 1693, they were found in Pensacola, where French hunters found them again in 1708, and there were plenty of them near Biloxi in 1699.

Some time in September of 1533, the three surviving Spaniards resolved "not to live this life, so savage and so divorced from the service of God and all good reason." Taking the Negro, Estebánico, they fled west across the plains. They fell in with friendly Indians. When some of these complained of headaches, one of the Spaniards "made over them the sign of the Cross, and commended them to God." The redskins were instantly cured—or thought they were. In gratitude, they brought presents of prickly pears and venison. The news of these medical marvels spread. Other patients poured in. The cures always worked. Once Cabeza de Vaca raised an Indian from the dead—anyhow, he seemed dead, "his eyes rolled up, and the pulse gone, he having all the appearances of death."

From one unidentifiable tribe to another they passed, living on prickly pears in season, fish when they could get them, sometimes scraping bits of flesh from hides ready to be tanned. When a white man got a piece of meat he ate it instantly, without waiting to roast it, lest some passing savage take it from him. Armed and traveling farther north, they might have fared sumptuously on buffalo beef; but they did not know that; and few buffalo came south to the Texan coast, to which they clung as their only guide. Somewhere along that coast they knew, were the Spanish colonies.

Meantime, in the northern part of that Mexico which was their only hope, a certain Nuño de Guzmán, an enemy of Cortez, the viceroy, had made himself supreme. He was a violent and bloody man, greedy for loot and Indian slaves. In April of 1536 a troop of his cavalry was on the Petatlán, or Sinaloa, River in the province of Sinaloa. A mounted patrol of four men, scouting along the river, beheld in amazement a white man and a Negro, bearded, coming toward them out of that North where no white man had ever been. There was an escort of Indians with them.

The troopers, says Cabeza de Vaca, "stood staring at me a length of time, so confounded that they neither hailed me nor drew near to make an inquiry." When the strange, ragged creature with the beard asked in good Castilian to be taken to their commanding officer, they took him back to camp. Captain Diego de Alcaraz sent three troopers and some Indians, guided by the Negro, Estebánico, to bring in the other two, who were some twenty-five miles behind. Safe under military escort, they pushed on to Mexico City, to be received by an astonished viceroy.

IV

De Soto Tours the New World

CABEZA DE VACA got safely back to Spain—very lucky to be alive at all —just as Hernando de Soto was equipping a new expedition for Florida. De Soto, "an inflexible man, and dry of word," was an experienced conquistador. Like most of his kind, he was a good deal of a brute, as well. "Much given to the sport of hunting Indians," he had an even more unpleasant habit of throwing natives of whom he did not approve to his pack of savage, powerful dogs to be torn to pieces. He burned one Indian alive in the presence of some fellow tribesmen, because the brave and loyal redskin refused to betray the hiding place of his chief. De Soto had hoped to frighten the others into betrayal. When they, too, stood firm, he burned them all. He also went in for slashing off hands and noses as minor punishments for red men; and he had no hesitation at all about sentencing his white followers to hanging or beheading, when he thought it would improve discipline.

De Soto was, however, no worse than other Spaniards, who in those days thought nothing of casual contests in beheading Indians, just to test the relative keenness of their blades and their own mastery of the sword. De Soto was something more than a mere greedy brute. He was all that, of course, but he was also a bold and skillful leader who, in the strange and savage new land of North America, where his predecessors had ignominiously failed, marched a force smaller than a modern battalion over 350,000 square miles of mostly hostile territory, with a total loss of about fifty per cent in four years of constant fighting—for combat infantry almost a unique record. From Florida to North Carolina and Tennessee, through Alabama and Mississippi and north nearly to Memphis, Tennessee, west into Arkansas and Oklahoma, then into Texas, and finally back to Arkansas and then in improvised ships down the Mississippi to Mexico, his daring little expedition marched and counter-marched—making the last part of the journey without their commander, who died along the Mississippi.

Where other expeditions perished of starvation, De Soto thought out his logistical problem—he took thirteen hogs along and bred them on the march, so that by the following spring he had three hundred, a number which rose to five hundred by fall. At his death his swine had so multiplied that the leader's share alone was seven hundred. With quartermaster supplies like that, grunting along behind the column, you simply couldn't starve. The spectacle of armored Spanish cavalry, lance in hand, with sturdy Spanish infantry (in those days the best there was), followed by a baggage-train of chained Indian slaves, carefully herding their squealing swine through the alligator-infested swamps of Florida, driving them through forests, carrying them in canoes across the Mississippi, over the plains, and south and west and then east again until the final feast of pork along the Mississippi, is unique in the annals of exploration anywhere. It must have been astonishing to see and equally astonishing to hear! Even the Indians took to raising swine and on the return journey were, however reluctantly, able to supply pork to the invading Europeans. It is said that the vicious and dangerous wild hogs that still lurk in the Okefenokee Swamp—locally known as "piney woods rooters"—are descended from swine which escaped from De Soto's droves in Georgia, and have, in the intervening centuries, grown huge and savage on the lush vegetation there.

Perhaps the pigs, which are adroit and deadly snake-killers, help explain the expedition's immunity from snakebite. Like Narváez, De Soto seems to have lost no men at all from venomous reptiles with which the country swarmed.

De Soto, who had served in Nicaragua and had been with Pizarro in Peru, had come home to Spain so rich that even royalty condescended to borrow from him. He now hoped to grow still richer in

North America. Cortez had found immense wealth in Mexico. Pizarro had found immense wealth in Peru. De Soto thought it only reasonable to expect another native empire, abounding in gold and jewels, to the north. "It was his object to find another treasure like that of Atabalipa, lord of Peru."

The queer thing is that De Soto still entertained these ardent hopes after the bedraggled Cabeza de Vaca had returned to Spain with his tale of suffering and privation. Perhaps it was because that worthy man certainly did not tell the whole truth. He was, he suggested, "sworn not to divulge certain things." He would not join De Soto, when invited to return to North America—no, not he!

De Soto went, but he went far better equipped than Narváez. With six hundred troops, 213 horses, a pack of fighting hounds—to which he casually tossed offending Indians—and his herd of swine, he landed in Florida May 28, 1539, either at Tampa Bay or at Charlotte Harbor, farther south. No one has ever understood why he chose the very country where the Narváez expedition had found nothing but disaster.

Shortly after they had landed, De Soto's men, in pursuit of Indians, were astounded to hear one of them shout in Spanish to the nearest horseman: "Do not slay me, cavalier; I am a Christian!" They had had the luck to find the last survivor of the Narváez expedition, Juan Ortiz, nobleman of Seville.

It was a great piece of luck. Ortiz—who had lived so long among the Indians that he had almost forgotten Spanish—soon recovered his native language, and became an almost perfect interpreter. Even he, however, was no use as a guide; for, like the Indians themselves, he knew nothing of the country fifty or sixty miles from his own village.

When De Soto found that neither Ortiz nor the Indians could tell him anything about cities filled with gold, he sent out a reconnoitering party; but all it found was more country "low, very wet, pondy, and thickly covered with trees"—probably the Polk County lakes, east of Tampa. Food was short, for De Soto was saving his pigs. The men ate water cresses, corn, and cabbage palm, instead. There were not enough pigs, as yet to have supplied the army, even if De Soto had been willing to slaughter them. A relief party found one group of Spaniards disconsolate in a swamp, "eating herbs and roots roasted and others boiled without salt, and what was worse, without knowing what they were." That must mean they feared the herbs were poisonous but were so hungry they ate them anyhow. There was some compensation in the "very delicious wild chestnuts," which the Spaniards found "rich and of very good flavour." There was nothing unusual about this, for most Europeans were pleasantly surprised by the American chestnut, which an English visitor long afterward described as "very sweet, as if mixt with sugar."

More or less following the trail of Narváez, they pushed on to Apalachee. Sometimes the Indians received them with the flute-playing that had greeted Narváez. More often they fought. Captured Indians were put in irons and used as slaves to carry the baggage. Once, unconsciously anticipating Mr. Whittaker Chambers, De Soto hid documents in a pumpkin, leaving a sign above his cache, so that the Spaniards following him could find it. Besides pumpkins, the Indians were raising corn, beans, cucumbers, and plums. (Old plum orchards still often mark a forgotten Indian village.)

In October, they found the place, near St. Marks, where Narváez had built his boats. Remnants of the mangers were still there and skulls of the horses that had eaten from them.

Wintering in this general vicinity, De Soto started for Georgia in March, 1540, reaching the Blue Ridge somewhere near the headwaters of the Broad River, and pushing on, in the general direction of Augusta, toward the South Carolina border.

Marching through Georgia, the Spaniards found the country "abundant, picturesque, and luxuriant, well watered, and having good river margins." Most of the route, from the moment they landed in Florida and far on into Georgia and the Carolinas, was covered with longleaf pine. They had already begun to admire the pines in Florida—"well proportioned and as tall as the tallest in Spain." Some of the country, especially Florida and southern Georgia, was "low, having many ponds." Elsewhere there were "high and dense forests, into which the Indians that were hostile betook themselves, where they could not be found; nor could horses enter there." This was unlike most northern forests where, from Virginia north, horses could move easily in spite of the heavy growth of trees. Northern Georgia and South Carolina country was "delightful and fertile, having good interval lands upon the streams; the forest was open, with abundance of walnut [probably hickory or pecan] and mulberry trees." The mulberries, De Soto's secretary noted, were "quite like those of Spain, just as tall and larger, but the leaf is softer and better for silk, and the mulberries are better eating and larger than those of Spain, and they were frequently of great advantage to the Spaniards for food." Sometimes the column passed large empty spaces, overgrown with grass, where towns had once stood—abandoned now, the Indians explained, because of pestilence two years before.

Though the Indians here "never lacked meat, killing deer, wild turkeys, rabbits, and other game," De Soto's six hundred men were often glad to eat dogs, since their commander was still saving his pigs for emergencies. Sometimes, powerful local chiefs supplied the expedition on a grand scale. One chief sent a single carrying party of four hundred Indians. "Tamemes," or baggage carriers, alone could negotiate the narrow, winding forest trails. There was no beast of burden in North America, except the dog, which plains tribes sometimes used as a pack animal and sometimes to draw the travois—two sticks tied to the animal's shoulders, with their ends dragging on the ground. Wheels had never been invented in the western hemisphere. Dogs, though better than nothing on the plains, were not much use in the eastern forests.

Another chief sent two thousand Indians, loaded with "rabbits, partridges, cornbread and many dogs, but only two wild turkeys." This was odd—a Cherokee chief in North Carolina made a gift of seven hundred turkeys.

These birds flourished in the prehistoric South and were remarkably good eating. American pioneers used slices of the white meat of the breast instead of the bread they could not get in the wilderness. Wild turkeys then were about as large as the biggest modern domesticated fowl. A really big gobbler might stand three feet high and weigh twenty to forty pounds. There are even tales of fifty-pound birds in the North. From March to April, they made the early morning ring with their gobbling from the magnolia trees in which they roosted.

It is hard to see why the Spaniards fail to mention the dawn-gobbling of the turkeys. Certainly they heard it regularly, and it was a sound that ought to have impressed any traveler. The calls started at the first hint of dawn and continued till the sun was over the horizon.

"The high forests ring with the noise, like the crowing of the domestic cock, of these social centinels," wrote Bartram, "the watchword being caught and repeated from one to another for hundreds of miles around; insomuch that the whole country is for an hour or more in a universal shout. A little after sun-rise, their crowing gradually ceases, they quit their high lodging places, and alight on the earth, where expanding their silver bordered train, they strut and dance round about the coy female, while the deep forests seem to tremble with their shrill noise."

When he left Florida and passed into Georgia, De Soto entered the territory of the Creek Confederacy, a group of tribes which had achieved something very like civilization and a life of great security and comfort, though not the boundless wealth De Soto sought. They were governed by powerful chiefs, some of whom were women. They had a well-developed agriculture, lived in comfortable thatched cabins, and dressed in white garments described as "linen." Probably they really were, for though these tribes made good cloth out of mulberry bark, they seem also to have used the fibres of wild hemp and wild flax.

They lived in neat cabins with gable roofs, built partly of planks split from tree trunks with wooden wedges—something the northern tribes never learned to do—and partly of bark and saplings. The houses were plastered, inside and out, with a tough mortar mixed with grass. In order to confuse raiding enemies, they adopted the extraordinary device of making loopholes for defensive fire in the walls of each house, and then plastering them over outside. An approaching foe would have no idea that the houses were defensible. Inside, each loophole was carefully indicated by a circle. At the critical moment, the owners punched through the holes and opened fire. Being made largely of cypress planking, fastened to southern pine, locust, or sassafras logs driven into the ground, these houses were almost indestructible. All the enemy could do was try to set them on fire, and that was difficult since the wood was covered with plaster.

The houses were whitewashed with ground oyster shells—later to be used by white settlers as a lime substitute—or else with white chalk or white clay. A prosperous warrior's household would have a corncrib—the design of which the whites later imitated—and as soon as they began to raise poultry, a poultry pen. The pigs and horses, which they also took over from the white man, ran mostly wild. The virtues of Indian bacon were celebrated, since the hogs lived largely on forest nuts and acorns.

There was a curious custom of maintaining a "hot house," where, even in the South, a continuous fire was kept burning with "heat so great that cloaths are not to be borne the coldest day in winter."

Interiors of the dwellings were furnished with couches raised from the ground on forked sticks, "to give the swarming fleas some trouble in their attack, as they are not able to reach them at one spring." These were covered with cane, then with mattresses filled with splinters of cane, and finally with buffalo, panther, bear, elk, and deer skins, dressed with the hair on and "as soft as velvet." Male babies were reared on panther skins, little girls on the skins of fawns or buffalo calves, to ensure their growing up with suitable virtues. The floor was covered with carpets woven from wild hemp, painted in bright designs. The Indians also wove hempen garters, sashes, pouches, and belts. Yarn from spun buffalo wool was used as a base for beadwork. The Choctaws made blankets of turkey feathers twisted into hemp thread.

The summer "visiting dress" of the southern warriors was a shirt of dressed deerskin. Winter hunting clothes were made of otter or beaver, which would be priceless on Fifth Avenue but which were ordinary enough to the savages, sometimes of the less valuable skin of panthers, bucks, or bear. By exquisitely skillful tanning, these, too, were "always softened like velvet-cloth." Winter clothing was worn with the hair inside.

Women wore a broad band of skin or of several skins, sewn together with bone or horn needles and thread of sinews or of spun hemp. They were not averse to revealing, as far as the knees, what

Adair appreciatively describes as "exquisitely fine proportioned limbs." In cold weather they wore the soft tanned skin of very young buffalo.

Hunters wore high deerskin leggings reaching up to long hunting coats, which protected them among twigs, underbrush, and brambles. All men wore the breech-clout, for the Indians had no use at all for the "pinching custom" of wearing trousers. Everyone went barefoot when possible, ignoring possible and plentiful snakes; but in cold weather moccasins of bear or elk skin protected the feet.

Headdresses were important. Many of these Indians flattened their heads—something which, curiously enough, the western tribe of "Flat-heads" never did—and they jeered at the white men with their normal skulls as "long heads." Like the medals and decorations of more civilized warriors, and presented with quite as much ceremony, were the war bonnets of swans' feathers—called "crowns" by early white men—awarded to successful warriors in the southern cause. These were quite unlike the flowing bonnets of eagle feathers worn by the western Sioux, Crows, Blackfeet, and others, which have caught the public fancy and which are now nearly a trade mark for Indian impersonators, but they served the same purpose.

The southern tribes had an advanced agriculture, cultivating "many fine fields," in which they raised the usual Indian crops, including two kinds of corn—yellow for ordinary eating, white for flour. Near each Indian dwelling was a small field, fenced with saplings fastened to stakes in the ground. More distant fields, too big to fence, were not planted until the wild fruit began to ripen, drawing the birds away from the new seed. The planting date for these big communal fields was set by an old warrior, bearing the usual ceremonial title of "old beloved man," who gave warning to his village the day before the planting was to begin. Everyone, including the most distinguished chiefs and warriors, turned out to help with the planting. Everyone worked from one field to another till the seed was all in, their labors cheered by story-tellers, singers, and musicians performing on deer-skin drums.

The planting was not very skillful, the cornstalks being only two inches apart (one foot is an absolute minimum in modern agriculture); and the squaws, like many modern gardeners, were often rather careless about weeding and cultivating; but the richness of their soil made up for everything.

The fields were constantly guarded. Old women watched from high scaffoldings by day to frighten marauding birds away. Being at a distance from the village, they were not infrequently surprised and slaughtered by hostile Iroquois bands from New York, who found old women, helpless and alone, a safe and convenient source of scalps.

The Creeks also raised "dogs of a small size that do not bark," by which the puzzled Spaniards apparently meant domesticated opossums. They were, says Ranjel, "good eating." If they really were opossums, he has ample subsequent gastronomic opinion to support his judgment.

Game was especially common and palatable in the southern states, where winter privations did not exhaust the animals and where food was always to be had. There were plenty of deer, bear, squirrels, rabbits, waterfowl, and turkeys; and the streams were full of fish, though with so much game about many of the southern Indians fished for sport rather than for food.

Mere sport gave them all they wanted to eat. They shot fish in the water with arrows; speared them with stalks of cane, which were stout enough to bring up fish two feet long; caught them in long stone weirs ending in fish-trap baskets woven of cane or grapevines, into which the fish were driven; or poisoned the water with roots, walnut bark, or ground horse-chestnuts, gathering in the fish as they rose gasping to the surface.

Some Indians caught the big southern catfish by diving into the water with any red object for bait and, as the fish tried to swallow it, grasping the creature and dragging it to the surface and ashore. They could not do this, of course, with the huge Mississippi catfish, which weighed one or two hundred pounds. The Chickasaws and some other tribes formed lines of men, who swam under water holding hand nets in front of them until lack of breath or the weight of their catch forced them to bring their nets and their noses to the surface. The trouble with this method was that it brought in about as large a stock of watersnakes as of fish.

There was a special technique in using the cane fish-spear, because the cane was not strong enough to haul a fish out at the first thrust.

Once transfixed, a big one was allowed to run, exactly as if he had been harpooned or taken on a light line. When the reed spear came bobbing to the surface again, the fisherman gave a new thrust. When the fish was worn out, it could be hauled in.

Even without their well-tended crops, the southern Indians could have lived on the natural produce of their forests. A good many excellent foods grew wild. So rich was the country that James Adair, who knew it well in later years, wrote: "If an Indian were driven out into the extensive woods, with only a knife and tomohawk, or a small hatchet, it is not to be doubted but he would fatten, even where a wolf would starve."

Passing through the country in the spring, the Spaniards saw the pre-historic South at its very best. "They found there along the trails countless roses growing wild like those of Spain; and although they have not so many leaves since they are in the woods they are none the less fragrant and finer and sweeter." They admired the great forests of southern longleaf pine, "walnuts" (which may have been hickory nuts), oak, live oak, cedar, liquidambar, the fertile fields, the rich dress of the natives.

The newcomers were particularly impressed, as were all later Europeans, by the wild strawberries, "very savoury, palatable, and fragrant," rather better than those in Europe, "a finer delicate fruit." The plants grew in a thickness inconceivable today. One traveler notes that strawberries of large size "covered the ground as with a red cloth." Wild potatoes and the "nuts," i.e., roots, of wild flag added to the varied diet, which could at need be supplemented by green salad herbs or potherbs, of which the American woodlands and meadows, even today, produce an abundance—poke, lamb's-quarters, milk weed, purslane, nettle, wild spinach, wild onion—which for the most part goes to waste.

Though the southern Indians usually detested salad greens as heartily as the average American male of the twentieth century, they did, in springtime, eat green herbs. When game ran short while De Soto was still jealously conserving his pork for emergencies, the Spanish soldiers made out very well on "bledo," or "blite"—that is, wild spinach or similar green herbs—though they do not seem to have been enthusiastic about it. They were lucky in not eating the wrong thing. Kentucky pioneer women in the eighteenth century, collecting spring greens in a new country, made it a rule to watch the cattle. From the plants which the cows ate, they chose the more appetizing to feed their families.

Though there is not much poisonous vegetation in North America—despite the fears of timid townsmen—it was on the whole a wise precaution. Strange plants could sometimes be dangerous. Coronado lost one or two men who died from eating the wrong herbs—or so he thought. In New England in the seventeenth century, John Josselyn wrote: "Always observe this rule in taking or refusing unknown fruit: if you find them eaten of the fowl or beast, you may boldly venture to eat of them, otherwise do not touch them." Certainly one or two species of amanita mushrooms, the "Indian turnip," or Jack-in-the-pulpit root (unless prepared by the Indian method), skunk cabbage, unripe persimmons, peyotl, or loco-weed, and even acorns unless treated for removal of their tannin, were not very good for the health. There are even some trustworthy records of deaths from eating amanitas, and various other mushrooms can make a man rather ill. It is perhaps fortunate that the early travelers were not gourmets and so not interested in mushrooms, though the Lewis and Clark expedition once had very little except morels to eat.

"Hickory milk," or "powhicora"—a drink popular among the Indians from Virginia south—pleased the critical Spanish palates, as it did those of later travelers. Using a round stone upon another stone, hollowed out for the purpose, the squaws pounded up acorns, hickory nuts, walnuts, and probably pecans, which they dropped, shell and all, into the water. The fragments of shell sank, after which the thick, white, oily "milk" was skimmed off and eaten with cornbread, hot from the fire. It tasted something "like cream or rich new milk." As a "thin drink," it was sometimes mixed with cornmeal or flavored, to taste, with the ashes of burnt straw. Ashes of various kinds were a flavoring much enjoyed by eastern and southern Indians, the Iroquois being especially fond of wood ashes, or even lye, with certain foods.

Gideon Lincecum, a naturalist of early days, gives an idea what the nut harvest was like along the Tombigbee River, near the Alabama-Mississippi line: "The autumnal leaves and nuts were clattering down everywhere. Shellbarks, hickory-nuts, and chestnuts strewed the ground, and grapes, muscadines, persimmons and various wild autumnal fruits were plentiful. It was delightful to observe the women and children wallowing in the dry leaves in the evening, and gathering such quantities of nuts as to require assistance to get them into camp."

Although few modern Europeans can be persuaded to like cornpone, De Soto's Spanish soldiery, hungry after long marches, fell to with a will on "an abundance of corn cakes," given them by the Indians together with "no end of oil from walnuts and acorns, which they know how to extract very well, which was very good and contributed much to their diet. Yet some say that the oil from nuts produces flatulence. However, it is very delicious." Many of the "walnuts" were probably pecans—at least the "little walnut of the country, which is much better than that here in Spain," as described by one chronicler, sounds more like a pecan than like anything else.

Thus far, De Soto had not really been doing badly. He had not, to be sure, found any golden empires to plunder. Clearly this land, however fertile, was neither another Mexico nor another Peru; and since De Soto saw himself as a new Cortez or Pizarro, it was time to move on. There had been no sign of anything like treasure, except freshwater pearls, extracted from river mussels, but there were quantities of these. The woman chief of Cofitachequi—who ruled the Indians on the South Carolina and Georgia sides of the Savannah River, around Augusta—gave De Soto a whole necklace of them.

Robbing a tomb, the Spaniards found corpses, "the breasts, belly, necks and arms and legs full of pearls." In all, they collected about two hundred pounds—all of which would eventually prove quite worthless by European standards. Even De Soto's men soon realized that a good many had been ruined by "being bored with heat, which causes them to lose their hue." But as the country produced so many pearls and as Indians were using them for ornaments all over the South, they felt sure they could secure others that had not been spoiled. A little later Jean Ribault's French expedition of 1562–1563, found similar pearls among the South Carolina Indians, likewise damaged by heat, not because these Indians used heat to bore them but because they cooked the mussels before taking out the pearls.

There was much excitement when the grave-robbers found in a tomb "something green like an emerald of good quality," but the crest-fallen thieves soon realized it was nothing but glass and European glass at that. Near the "emerald" lay other glass beads, rosaries, iron axes—remnants of Ayllón's disastrous expedition thirteen years before. Later, they even found an iron dirk.

Still, whatever its shortcomings as a source of treasure, this was "a good country, and one fit in which to raise supplies." Some of the Spaniards wanted to stay. "It seemed an error to leave that country," but De Soto "would not be content with good lands nor pearls."

The free life of the Indians appealed to some of the Negro slaves, who slipped away into the forest to spend the rest of their lives in this glorious land of freedom. It was rumored, too, that the woman chief of Cofitachequi, when she escaped from De Soto, took with her a black paramour. Even a few Spaniards, here and there along the way, found Indian life and ardent Indian ladies so attractive that they deserted and, when located, could not be persuaded to return. One sent back his signature, to prove he was alive and well. But return he would not. Twenty-some years later, one of the men in the expedition of the French Huguenot, Ribault, joined the Indians in South Carolina, rather than risk the sea journey back to France. Life in the wilds with an Indian girl—or several Indian girls—was more attractive than the prospect of more years of marching through forests, swamps, rivers, brambles, and canebrakes that never seemed to end and never led to gold. A later expedition in 1560 learned that a Negro slave and a deserter from De Soto's expedition had been living here and there among the Indians for ten or twelve years.

But these men were a minority. Before most of the Spaniards the prospect of cities filled with gold still glimmered. The Indians had for some time been telling De Soto about "a province called Cuça, a plentiful country having very large towns." This was probably the Creek town of Kusa, later well known to the white men, situated in the middle of Alabama, one of the sacred cities of refuge for "those who kill undesignedly."

Thither De Soto made up his mind to go, swinging first through South Carolina, North Carolina, and Tennessee, before turning south into Alabama and Mississippi. He thus passed from Creek tribal territory into that of the Cherokee, the Cheraw, and the Chickasaw, then back into Creek territory. The Cherokee were of Iroquoian, the Cheraw probably of Siouan stock, while the Chickasaws were closely related to the Creeks. Though of different origin, all these tribes were on about the same relatively high level, almost approaching civilization. The Spaniards seem to have noticed little difference between them.

Cutting across western South Carolina, to enter western North Carolina, they passed through "a high range," with "rough and lofty ridges," plainly the Great Smokies, or southern end of the Blue Ridge, and came after about a fortnight's travel to a place they describe as Xualla probably in Swain County, North Carolina. Thence they moved to Guaxulle, which may have been near Cartersville, Georgia, where the Indians presented them with three hundred "dogs"—perhaps opossums again—as food. A neighboring town sent twenty men, loaded with mulberries. Each village as De Soto passed supplied carrying parties for his baggage—the main idea apparently being to give these queer but dangerous white creatures anything they wanted, and get rid of them. Later a chief gave them a guide who had private instructions to take them some place—any place—where they would starve to death. Occasionally, the Spaniards also demanded women, whom the villages usually supplied, sometimes twenty, thirty, or more at a time.

One chief gave De Soto his daughter, "a fine young girl." Not to be outdone, another gave one of his wives, "blooming, and very worthy," plus his sister and a third squaw. Another chief presented the Spanish leader with his two sisters, one of whom is described as utterly charming, though the other was not too attractive. De Soto still had Indian women with him when he died.

Soldiers being soldiers, some of the men probably picked up willing Indian girls of their own, who traveled with the expedition. Occasionally the troops could simply buy a few squaws in exchange for mirrors and knives. A survivor of the expedition, somewhat confused between biology and doctrinal theology, later explained that "the

women they desired both as servants and for their foul uses and lewd-
ness, and that they had them baptized more on account of carnal inter-
course with them than to teach them the faith."

The column must have presented a remarkable appearance, as it
wound in single file along the narrow wilderness trails: caballeros
with swords, lances, and armor, rather dingy and a bit rusty by this
time; infantry cursing the weight of their packs and armor; arquebusiers, crossbowmen; squealing, rebellious hogs; Indian prisoners in
chains; other Indian tamenes, or bearers; and the copper-colored
ladies, who must have been fairly attractive (as Creek girls often
were), or they wouldn't have been asked to go along.

By this time, careful breeding en route had increased the herd of
swine to several hundred. Anyone who has ever tried to persuade
an unwilling pig to go in any given direction will appreciate the
labors of De Soto's swineherds. They coaxed hundreds of hogs through
forests filled with edible nuts, succulent roots, and other porcine tidbits,
over wilderness trails, with chances of escape into the bushes on every
hand, with wild animals hungry for a little pork each night, for a
distance of several thousand miles, from Florida to Texas, to Oklahoma, and half way back! There has been nothing like it since the
Odyssey; and even in the *Odyssey,* the pigs stayed at home.

Reaching Coca, June 16, 1540, De Soto was met outside the town
by the chief, "borne in a litter on the shoulders of his principal men,
seated on a cushion, and covered with a mantle of marten-skins, of
the size and shape of a woman's shawl: on his head he wore a diadem
of plumes, and he was surrounded by many attendants playing upon
flutes and singing" the usual ceremonial of formal welcome.

De Soto gazed about him. This was no wilderness. Central Alabama
was covered with the Indians' fields of corn and beans, stretching from
one village to the next, as did the orchards and cornfields in Indiana,
which astonished Anthony Wayne in 1794. The "barbacoas," or store-
houses—from which the white man later took the design of modern
corncribs—were elevated on posts to keep them out of reach of rats
and vermin.

"The country, thickly settled in numerous and large towns, with
fields between extending from one to another, was pleasant, and had

a rich soil with fair river margins. In the woods were many plums, as well those of Spain as of the country; and wild grapes on vines growing up into the trees, near the streams; likewise a kind that grew on low vines elsewhere, the berry being large and sweet, but, for want of hoeing and dressing, had large stones." Some of the "plums of the country" were undoubtedly persimmons, not yet touched by frost. Luckily for themselves, the Spaniards found these golden but deceptive fruits at a season when there was no temptation to try them. Otherwise they would have found (as did incautiously experimental colonists in Virginia) that the astringency of the unfrosted fruit draws "a man's mouth awry with much torment." Since the fruit was not yet ripe, they had no opportunity to sample the persimmon bread of the southern Indians, of which later white travelers and traders became very fond.

They found also "many plums like the early ones of Seville, very good," and "wild apples" but rather "small in size." Some of the plums were probably the Chickasaw plum *(Prunus chicàsa)*, which was much cultivated by the Indians. Bartram, in the eighteenth century, often found it growing wild, but only near abandoned Indian villages —precisely as one finds old roses and forgotten orchards near old New England farms that have gone back to brush.

For nearly a month, the expedition rested in this pleasant region. De Soto made a good many of these long halts—perhaps to feed the pigs as much as for any other purpose. The old records do not tell how these much-traveled swine were kept alive or how the little pigs kept up with their mothers on the march; but clearly they had to be turned into the rich southern woods from time to time to forage for themselves. Farrowing sows had to be given some attention, and their litters certainly had to grow a while before they could keep up with the expedition. This was not impossible, since in settled country where corn could be gotten, the column moved only twelve or fifteen miles ("five or six leagues") a day, though through uninhabited forests it moved hard and fast in forced marches.

Near Mauvilla, somewhere in Greene County, Alabama, De Soto and an advance party were received with the usual songs and flute-playing. But a quarrel with the chief of Tastaluça, whom De Soto was dragging with him, led to violence and then to a pitched battle in which the Spaniards were driven out of the town "at more than a walk." The line of chained Indian slaves rushed into the village, where their kinsmen armed them. Two Spaniards were disarmed and red warriors laid about mightily with the captured swords and halberds. Luckily, De Soto's main force of cavalry and infantry arrived in the nick of time. About 2,500 Indians and eighteen or twenty Spaniards were killed before the town was burned and the Creeks driven out. When it was over, 250 Spaniards had been wounded, most of them several times, "bearing upon our bodies seven hundred and sixty injuries from their hands." Rodrigo Ranjel got back to headquarters bristling with arrows like a porcupine. More than twenty were pulled out of his loose, quilted armor. Medical stores, the pearls and a good deal of the baggage had been destroyed. The Spaniards had to dress their wounds "with the fat of the dead Indians," as there was no medicine left.

At this critical moment, word reached De Soto secretly from the Gulf coast. His ships were only six days' march away. But they came at the wrong time. More than a year of exploration had produced no treasure except his stack of pearls—and they had just been lost in the fire. Worse, he had lost just over a hundred men from wounds and sickness and had absolutely nothing to show for it.

Rather than have the news of such failure get back to Cuba, the conquistador prepared to turn north, deeper into the heart of the dark continent, "because the pearls he wished to send to Cuba for show, that their fame might raise the desire of coming to Florida, had been lost, and he feared that, hearing of him without seeing either gold or silver, or other thing of value from that land, it would come to have such reputation that no one would be found to go there when men should be wanted: so he determined to send no news of himself until he should have discovered a rich country."

Amusing themselves by burning over the country around Mauvilla, the Spaniards rested there about a month and then pushed on into Mississippi, meeting a good deal of not very formidable Indian hostility. About a fortnight's march through almost unbroken forest took them to Chicaca, a village of some twenty lodges, near the modern town of Redland, in Pontotoc County, Mississippi. This was fertile country, mostly under cultivation. The corn crop was in and De Soto soon had supplies for the winter. The local chief good-naturedly presented the Spaniards with 150 rabbits, Indian shawls, and leather clothing, of which—after their losses of clothing at Mauvilla—the Spaniards must have been in need. De Soto introduced the Chickasaws to pork, of which they became so fond that there was an epidemic of pig-stealing from "some houses where the hogs slept." Characteristically, De Soto ended it by having two thieves shot with arrows and a third sent home with both hands cut off.

The expedition had now come into the country of the Chickasaws, closely related to the Creeks and Choctaws, living along the Mississippi River in Mississippi and Tennessee. At first everything seemed peaceful and the Spaniards rested here for about two months; but when, about March 8, 1541, De Soto found the Chickasaws reluctant to provide the two hundred bearers for whom he asked, he prepared for trouble. It came early next morning, an attack from four different directions. The town was soon in a blaze. The Spaniards, waking in confusion, could not find their arms or their horses. One caballero tumbled ingloriously from his mount with his first lance thrust, not having had time to saddle properly. As the men ran from the burning village, arrows from the darkness cut them down. In the end the Indians were frightened off by horses which had gotten loose and were charging about in the darkness without riders.

When the shaken Spaniards took stock in daylight, they found many of the troops literally naked, their clothing having been burned. Arms and saddles had been lost. The heat had destroyed the temper of swords and lances. Some horses had burned to death. Only one hundred pigs were left of the drove with which they had entered Mauvilla some months earlier. Stark naked, the white men huddled about large fires. They must have made perfect targets for prowling Indian archers; but the warriors were gone. After daylight, they improvised "mats of dried grass sewed together, one to be placed below, and the other above." No troops in military history can ever have looked so much like hula dancers! Even their disconsolate comrades laughed.

No disaster, however, stopped De Soto. He set up a forge and put a blacksmith to work retempering the arms. When a new attack came, he was ready for it and beat the Indians off. By the end of April he was on his way through the forested and almost uninhabited northwest corner of Mississippi, pausing only to destroy a palisaded Indian fort somewhere near New Albany, Mississippi.

Northwest Mississippi and southeastern Tennessee proved to be "a wilderness, having many pondy places, with thick forests." They could ford most of the little lakes they had to cross, though once or twice the expedition had to swim for it. The change in the country was a sign that they were approaching the Mississippi, whose oxbows, bayous, and sluggish tributaries made most of the trouble. They struck the great river first at a village called Quizquiz, not far south of the Tennessee border.

Exhausted and hungry, the leader decided to "try to have peace," in which he was much assisted by a local legend. These Indians "had knowledge from their ancestors that they were to be subdued by a white race."

Looking over the river either at Council Bend or at Walnut Bend in Tunica County, Mississippi, well south of Memphis, De Soto decided to build boats and cross.

The muddy river was about a mile and a half ("near half a league") across, so wide that a man standing on the opposite shore "could not be told, whether he were a man or something else. The stream was swift, and very deep; the water, always flowing turbidly, brought along from above many trees and much timber, driven onward by its force." According to Ranjel: "Many of these conquerors said this river was larger than the Danube"—they were right about that. In time of flood, some parts of the lower Mississippi were fifty miles across.

Presently the chief from the opposite bank appeared, with two hundred canoes. It was an astonishing spectacle—the fleet moving across the muddy water, each canoe filled with warriors painted with ochre, their shields ornamented with feathers, their beads gleaming in the sun, their heads crested with "great bunches of white and other plumes of many colours." "These were fine-looking men, very large and well-formed; and what with the awnings, the plumes, and the shields, the pennons, and the number of people in the fleet, it appeared like a famous armada of galleys." Wicker shields protected the men at the paddles, while from stem to stern stood warriors with their arrows ready. The canoes were heavy, stable, river dugouts, not the light and "tippy" bark canoes of the northern Indians. In the flagship of this formidable fighting fleet sat the chief, under an awning in the stern, issuing orders to subordinate commanders under awnings of their own. Though this was plainly a demonstration in force, the Indians were friendly and brought with them three "barges," loaded with fish and bread made of persimmon pulp.

Suspecting a trick, the Spaniards opened with their crossbows, whereupon the fleet drew off in good order, the men at the paddles keeping their posts even when those next them were hit. Strange to say, there was no further trouble with this powerful tribe.

Resting there for thirty days, De Soto built four boats, put an advance guard over to protect his landing and crossed with his whole force, pigs included. Safely over, he had the boats knocked to pieces, thriftily saving the iron spikes. Once in Arkansas, he had trouble with more swamps, bayous, bends, and oxbows—"having to go round the bays that swell out of the river." All one day "until sunset, he marched through water, in places coming to the knees; in others, as high as the waist." No Indians seemed to live in these bays—"the worst tract for swamp and water that they had found."

One of the worst of their difficulties must have been the canebrakes, which in Arkansas and many other parts of the lower Mississippi were unusually thick and luxuriant. U.S. Dragoons, advancing into Arkansas in the early nineteenth century, found the cane "an apparently impenetrable breastwork of dense green." The stalks, according to one of the cavalrymen, "were so large and close together that our horses could not move forward without breaking through by main force." The commander of another military exploring detachment thought his mounted troops, struggling through a canebrake, looked like "a company of rats traversing a sturdy field of grass."

After struggling through this sort of thing, De Soto's column emerged joyfully in northeastern Arkansas. This was good country, "higher, drier, and more level than any other along the river that had been seen until then. In the fields were many walnut trees, bearing tender-shelled nuts in the shape of acorns [pecans?], many being found stored in the houses. The tree did not differ in any thing from that of Spain, nor from the one seen before except the leaf was smaller. There were many mulberry-trees, and trees of plums (persimmons), having fruit of vermilion hue, like one of Spain, while others were gray, differing, but far better. All the trees, the year round, were as green as if they stood in orchards, and the woods were open." Most of neighboring Arkansas country for two days' march was cultivated. Villages were large and numerous, "two or three of them to be seen from one." These Indians had plenty of woven "shawls," deer, bear, "lion" and catskins, also "shields of raw cowhide"—in other words, buffalo hide.

There was no end of fish, because all that country is flooded by the great river when it overflows its banks. One chief kept a kind of artificial fish pond. The huge Mississippi catfish surprised the Spaniards as it surprised all later explorers of the Mississippi. To Europeans, who had never seen anything like it, it was an odd animal—"the third part of which was head, with gills from end to end, and along the sides were great spines, like very sharp awls. Those of this sort that lived in the lake were as big as pike; in the river were some that weighed from one hundred to one hundred and fifty pounds."

De Soto's men also observed the spadefish (*Polyodon spatula,* Linn.), now very rare in the Mississippi but then so common that many travelers mention it. *Polyodon spatula* was one of those ichthyological oddities you can't forget—"the snout a cubit [18 inches] in length, the upper lip being shaped like a shovel."

While resting here, De Soto sent a reconnoissance party north. It came back with the news that there were few inhabitants but many buffalo. "The cattle were in such plenty, no maize could be protected from them, and the inhabitants lived upon the meat."

This was the first real report of the teeming herds of the buffalo plains. Cabeza de Vaca had learned a little about the buffalo. De Soto himself certainly saw buffalo hide skins, which, one of his officers reports, made good bedcovers, "as they were very soft and the wool like

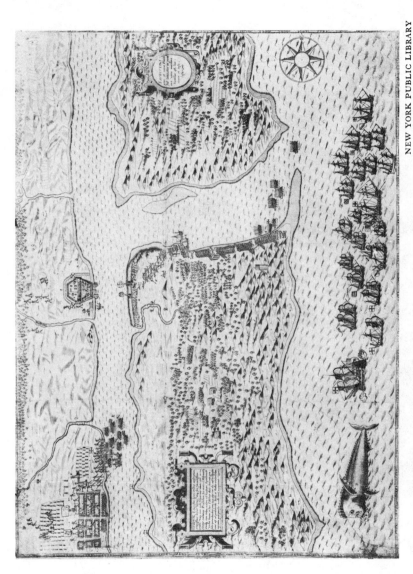

St. Augustine, Florida, 1586. The earliest known view of a city in the United States.

A magnolia swamp on the lower Mississippi. From *Picturesque America*, 1872.

that of sheep," but in all their journeys most of the Spaniards did not see more than a few live buffalo.

Though De Soto had no idea how easily he could have subsisted his command on the great herds of the prairies, had he gone a little farther north, he still had his much-traveled pigs as a meat reserve. What he now wanted was corn; and he turned south and west to get it.

He pushed farther on into Arkansas, a country at first "level and fertile, having rich river margins, on which the Indians made extensive fields," and then half way to Little Rock through "an immense pathless thicket of desert for seven days, where they slept continually in ponds and shallow puddles"—L'Anguille River, Big Creek, Bayou de Vue, and Cache River.

These bayous and tangles in the lower Mississippi country were often very picturesque, though that fact made little appeal to the floundering Spaniards. A much later writer says: "That part of the bayou into which the canal flows is a hundred feet wide at the most. Its muddy banks are hidden by high tufts of reed and rush, behind which rises a beautiful forest of sumacs, cotton woods, and walnut trees of various species, covered with black creepers and long twigs [moss?], which hang from the higher branches. White creepers with fragrant flowers, ivy, and convolvulus surrounded the trunks of old trees and rejuvenated them with their green shoots; and on younger trees *herbe-à-la-puce* [perhaps trumpet vine] opened its red bell-flowers. The bayou water, thick and reddish, was very quiet and reflected the rays of a beautiful sun. Many alligators were asleep on the surface and looked like stumps of trees rather than living creatures."

However bad the traveling, country like that provided easy food. There were so many fish that the travelers simply clubbed them; and when the chained Indian slaves shuffled through the mud, "the fish, becoming stupefied, would swim to the surface, when as many were taken as were desired." The north central part of the state had a very rich soil, yielding so much corn that the Indians had to throw away stored grain to make room for new. The inevitable beans and pumpkins were "larger and better than those of Spain." Corn, wrote one hidalgo, was "the best fodder that grows."

As the winter of 1541 drew on, even De Soto was ready to give up. Somewhere near Fort Smith, Arkansas, he passed across the border into Oklahoma, and thence turned eastward, seeking a way to the sea, where he proposed to build ships. For the worst three winter months he camped in Arkansas, the men feasting on corn, beans, walnuts, and dried persimmons—also rabbits, which the Indians taught the white men to snare. Spring found him near Arkansas Post, on the Arkansas River, near the Mississippi. He moved south to the vicinity of Arkansas City, where he found it impossible to march overland to the Gulf of Mexico "on account of the great bogs that came out of the river, the canebrakes and thick scrubs there were along the margin." This part of the Mississippi's banks seemed entirely uninhabited.

On May 21, 1542, despondent and sick with a "putrid fever," De Soto died. His successor, Luis de Moscoso, tried to persuade skeptical and not overfriendly Indians that the dead leader had ascended into the skies for a visit but would return. When the Indians found loose soil around the grave, he exhumed the body and sank it in the river. De Soto's property—which included seven hundred swine—was auctioned off and everyone feasted upon pork.

Moscoso pushed southwest into Texas, somewhere near Texarkana, through "great heats," scrub and forest, but, finding nothing of value, journeyed back across Arkansas. Near Arkansas City, where "for the building of ships better timber was found than had been seen elsewhere in all Florida," he began to build vessels, calked with native hemp and ravelings from Indian shawls, armored with reed mats to stop arrows, and equipped with anchors made by melting down old iron stirrups, and cables made of mulberry bark. In June, 1543, a convenient flood floated these crazy craft into the river and so down to the Mississippi, the Gulf, and safety in Mexico. Three hundred and eleven men had survived four years of De Soto's exploration.

De Soto never guessed that he had passed close to the country where there really was a little gold. The French under Jean Ribault and René de Laudonnière, who sailed along the coast of Florida, Georgia, and the lower part of South Carolina, not very far from De Soto's earlier line of march, found that "many of the men wore round flat plates of gold, silver, or brass, which hung upon their legs, tinkling like little bells." The "brass" was probably Lake Superior copper, passed from hand to hand and tribe to tribe in the long processes of native trade; but the gold was genuine and probably also the silver. Most of it, the Indians said, came from the Apalatcy (Appalachian) Mountains. The Indians dug ditches in sandy river beds. Into these the heavy nuggets or gold dust, washed down by the streams, sank, and it was then easy to gather up the sand in hollow reeds, "shaking them about, whereby the grains of gold and silver appear." This gave a clue to veins of ore in the mountains from which the streams flowed. A good deal more gold was brought down the St. Johns River to the west coast in canoes. An artist with one French expedition even made a drawing of Indian placer mining. If De Soto had gone a little farther east, he would have found gold, though not the immense quantities for which he thirsted.

For all its gallantry and skillful leadership, De Soto's venture had simply been the most spectacular of Spanish failures. It brought death to the leader, death to half his followers. It found no empires, seized no gold. But it was the most complete exploration of North America yet undertaken, save for the march of Coronado, which it just failed to meet.

V

Coronado's Country

THE RETURN OF Cabeza de Vaca aroused as much interest in Mexico as it did in Spain. Even before the survivors of the Narváez expedition came staggering out of the wilderness, Nuño de Guzmán, viceroy of Mexico, had been interested in the stories of a half-breed named Tejo, a trader's son. Tejo had told the greedy and credulous Guzmán "that when he was a little boy his father had gone into the back country with fine feathers to trade for ornaments, and that when he came back he brought a large amount of gold and silver, of which there is a good deal in that country."

Guzmán organized an expedition and started off, but never got out of Mexico. Learning that his bitter enemy, Cortez, was returning to Mexico "with great favors and estates"—having straightened out the little matter of strangling his wife—Guzmán hurried back to protect his interests, and in the meantime Tejo most inconveniently died. Eventually Guzmán went to jail for official abuses, and his exploring days were thus quite definitely ended.

There the matter rested, when Cabeza de Vaca arrived with new tales of the Seven Cities of Cíbola. It was true he had not seen them, but he had heard all about them from various tribes through whose territory he had passed. They were "large and powerful villages, four and five stories high"—the pueblos of Arizona and New Mexico. The viceroy, Don Antonio de Mendoza, passed the word to one of his provincial governors, Francisco Vásquez de Coronado.

By way of preliminary reconnoissance, the obvious thing was to send back into the country either Cabeza de Vaca or one of his companions. But Cabeza de Vaca himself had long since had enough; and there is no reason to suppose that either of his Spanish companions had any greater wish to traverse again the country where they had already suffered so much. But there was always the Negro, Estebánico. Estebánico was a slave. He could be sent wherever his master wished. Mendoza bought him and sent him off with Fray Marcos de Niza, reconnoitering for the expedition which Coronado was to lead.

From Estebánico's point of view, it was an admirable arrangement, especially as he preceded Fray Marcos by several days' journey. In Mexico he had been a mere chattel. But in the wilderness he was an important and independent person—well known to the Indians, among whom he had traveled with Cabeza de Vaca, a powerful medicine man, known to have effected remarkable cures. Probably he was especially admired because of his color, for when Lewis and Clark took the latter's Negro slave, York, on their expedition, the black man was a far greater sensation among the Indians than the white men. There is every reason to believe that Estebánico was an equal *succès fou*.

The journey had other more intimate triumphs for him. The love life of a Negro slave, distinctly inhibited in sixteenth century Mexico, was not in the least inhibited out on the lonely desert. From the very start, the bearded Negro met with disapproval from the friar, "because he took along the women that were given to him." Almost as regrettable was the further fact that he "collected turquoises, and accumulated everything," instead of handing his acquisitions over to his betters. It was annoying, improper, irregular; but, once they were beyond the Mexican settlements, there was no way to control Estebánico, who by this time did not feel in the least like anybody's slave.

Now, for the first time, Estebánico was entirely uninhibited. Indian maids were willing mates, free from race prejudice, and not by any means prudish. Even on occasions when they proved skittish, Estebánico had his own ways of handling the situation. When he found red wenches insufficiently complaisant, the Pueblos complained later, "he assaulted their women," and even killed them. The latter charge is doubtful. Dead Indian ladies were no use to Estebánico.

It all went to the head of the temporarily emancipated slave. Estebánico began to get such large ideas that, in the end, he was traveling with a retinue of admiring warriors, "besides many women."

Part of the trouble that followed was the fault of Fray Marcos, who sent the Negro far ahead, all by himself, to look for "some inhabited and rich country," and to send back secret reports on the land as he passed through. The code was ingenious. Ordinary writing would have sufficed, since the Indians could not read, but the Negro probably could not write. Oral messages, transmitted by Indian runners wouldn't do—they were sure to leak. Estebánico was instructed to send back crosses, whose size would indicate the magnitude and importance of his discoveries. If he found "something moderate," he was to send back "a white cross a span [nine inches] in size." If he thought his discovery important, he was to send Fray Marcos a cross two spans in size. If he found a land better than Mexico itself, he was to send "a large cross."

Four days later, Estebánico sent back a cross as high as a man. The country naturally seemed good to Estebánico, for Estebánico was having a fine time. A few days later he sent another cross of equal size. The land Estebánico had now found was "the best and greatest that had ever been heard of." He was, in other words, having a better and better time, the farther he went.

Fray Marcos devoutly gave thanks to God and hurried forward, encouraged by still a third large cross that Estebánico had left by the way. Everything the reverend father found was encouraging—"good lodging, excellent reception, and many turquoises, hides of the cattle [buffalo], and the same information regarding the country." Estebánico sent back more word about "the greatness of the country"—which meant chiefly that it was a great country for Estebánico; but the friar didn't know that.

Farther on, Fray Marcos passed through a valley "settled by attractive people and so bountiful in food that it could provision more than three hundred men and horses. All is irrigated; it is like a garden." In came more news from the enthusiastic Estebánico, "more certain of the riches of the country than before." Fray Marcos himself saw Indians "wearing turquoise necklaces, some with five and six loops." No gold as yet, but surely, it was a rich country.

Then, suddenly, like a dash of cold water, came bad news. Estebánico was dead. The Indians had killed him.

From various contemporary accounts and modern Zuñi tradition, it is not hard to piece together the story. The slave, after becoming a mighty medicine man, a potent practitioner of magic, had begun to put on far too many airs. Feathers adorned him, even to his ankles and wrists, where magic rattles tinkled. He carried the magic gourd rattle of the medicine man, adorned with "some strings of jingle bells, and two feathers, one white and the other red." With Cabeza de Vaca, he had learned how great was a medicine man's prestige and now he was dressing the part with elaboration and completeness.

A small traveling harem of chosen young women shared the pleasures of this wonderful journey. Other attendants brought the great man's escort up to three hundred Indians—and a dog. By this time he was "laden with a large number of turquoises and with some pretty women which the natives had given him." It was enough to make any friar shake his head. Awed Indians joined the magician's train gladly, "believing that by going under his protection they could traverse the whole country without any danger."

Thus, in ceremonial and state, Estebánico, the transformed slave, triumphantly approached the first "city of Cíbola." It was the flourishing pueblo of Hawikuh, now a heap of ruins near Zuñi. Estebánico, in a regal gesture, sent forward a messenger, bearing his magic gourd rattle.

An elder of Hawikuh dashed the gourd to the ground and bade the messengers get out. "He knew what sort of people they represented." Further, they should not "enter the city or he would kill them all." All this Estebánico, by this time completely self-confident and infinitely complacent, heard from his messengers with equanimity, saying that "those who showed anger received him better."

But Estebánico was wrong for once. As he approached Hawikuh, resolute warriors met him with orders not to try to enter their city. In spite of that, Estebánico made the mistake of demanding more turquoises and more women. It was a false move. The warriors of Hawikuh considered this an affront. They seized him and took away his trading goods, the wealth of turquoises he had already so joyfully amassed, and other things he had obtained from Indians along the way. Then they tossed him into a house outside the pueblo—probably one of the granaries—and refused to give him food, a plain sign of hostility.

By this time, the elders of Hawikuh were seriously disturbed. Possibly tales of the Spaniards' cruelty, which equalled any redskin's, had drifted up from Mexico. Was anybody with this queer, black, menacing creature? A chief asked Estebánico if he had any "brothers." Yes, said Estebánico, many of them, well armed and not far away. To Zuñi ears it sounded dangerous. Then the black man said something that sounded still more suspicious. He told the grave, listening elders that he represented white men, coming after him, "to instruct them in divine matters."

Bad, very bad. Clearly, reasoned the elders, there was something wrong with that story. White men they may possibly have heard of. A black man they could see before them. White and black men were mysterious enough anyhow; but how could a black man be the herald of white men?

The elders of Hawikuh felt no special need of instruction in divine matters, anyhow. Had they not priests of their own? Did they not worship the rain-gods, as their ancestors had worshipped for centuries, as their descendants still worship, even in the twentieth century? Black skin seemed menacing to red men who had never dreamed of such a creature. Who was he, to talk of gods?

Worst of all, Estebánico seems to have been wearing the costume of a medicine man of a hostile tribe and to have sent the Zuñis the kind of medicine gourd used by hostile Indians. Hitherto, among other tribes, these sacred objects had been a protection to Estebánico, but not here!

"He must be a spy or guide of some nations that wanted to come and conquer them." The strange, unknown, black creature was queer. Possibly he was dangerous. Better make sure. They killed him. It was all thoroughly logical.

One morning, "when the sun had risen the height of a lance," Estebánico was allowed outside his hut and Indians began to pour out of the city. Estebánico and some of his Indians ran for it, pursued by Hawikuh warriors. Arrows showered after them. Estebánico was killed and a few of his Indians wounded, probably by accident, since the elders of Hawikuh showed no hostility toward the survivors afterward. The black body was torn "into many pieces, which were distributed among the chieftains so that they should know that he was dead." One of the Hawikuh leaders took for his own, four green plates—very different from the native pottery. These were some of the "plates of various colors" which Estebánico carried about with him as part of his camp equipment. It never seems to have occurred to any of the Spanish leaders to carry metal dishes instead of breakable crockery. Somebody kept the black man's dog for a long time. Then the Zuñis killed that, too.

When news of the Negro's death reached Fray Marcos, he turned in his tracks; gave away everything he had except his priestly vestments, to placate his own Indians; and started for Mexico as hard as he could go, "without seeing more land except what the Indians had told them of."

There was excitement when the news reached Mexico. Fray Marcos was too honest to say he had himself seen gold; but he had heard a great deal about it; and he saw one valley that looked promising: "I was told that there is much gold there and that the natives make it into vessels and jewels for their ears, and into little blades with which they wipe away their sweat."

Worst of all, on his return Fray Marcos visited a barber shop. All he wanted was a shave. But barbers are garrulous. Fray Marcos talked of the wonders he had seen. The barber also talked. The wildest rumors spread from the barbershop through the little Mexican colony of Spain, where there was little amusement save gossip.

More gold than in Peru! Every blue-blooded adventurous ne'er-do-well in Mexico pricked up his ears. They had better reason even than De Soto—whose schemes were watched with jealous interest—to anticipate treasure.

Mexico at that time was full of high-born young caballeros, who had more or less "left their country for their country's good." A good many of them seem to have been shipped off to New Spain by loving Castilian families who just couldn't stand having their offspring around any more. There was nothing for them to do in the colony. Trade, farming, industry were beneath them. But for adventurous exploration and risky, exciting expeditions with treasure at the end, they were ideally suited. There is a strong suspicion that the viceroy, Don Antonio de Mendoza, felt that it would be a great relief to send all of them off to the Indian country for a few years. He appointed young Francisco Vásquez de Coronado, one of his provincial governors, to command the expedition which would take them there.

When he moved his command northward out of Mexico toward Kansas in 1540, Coronado was just thirty years old. The younger son of an aristocratic family of Salamanca, left with a mere settlement while his older brother inherited all the family estates, he had come to Mexico in the train of his friend, the viceroy, Mendoza, five years before, with his way to make. He had gained a reputation by putting down a rebellion of Negro miners in 1537, had been appointed by the viceroy to the council of Mexico City, and had married an heiress who brought with her a large country estate. In 1538 he was made governor of New Galicia, the frontier province from which any expedition to the Seven Cities of Cíbola would have to start.

Having seen Fray Marcos on his way as a kind of godly scout, Coronado himself first set off into northern Mexico to find a country called Topira, where the natives habitually wore "gold and emeralds and other precious stones." He did not find it, returned, and had just been appointed permanent, instead of acting, governor of New Galicia, when Fray Marcos returned with his report.

In January, 1540, Coronado was officially commissioned to lead the expedition to the Seven Cities of Cíbola. By the end of February his army was organized and ready for review—a force of about three hundred Spaniards, a large number of slaves, one thousand horses, several hundred pack animals. Like De Soto, he drove livestock with the army to provide meat on the way. In addition, he had a force of about thirteen hundred friendly Indians.

The arms were of every sort. Only twenty-seven soldiers had arquebuses, nineteen carried crossbows. The rest carried swords, daggers, lances, and "native weapons." Only eleven had full armor. About forty had chain mail. The rest relied on stout leather coats. Coronado himself glittered in gilded armor, his helmet adorned with plumes.

From Culiacán, then the northern outpost of Spanish civilization, Coronado himself struck off through northern Mexico with an advance party of one hundred white men, some Indians, and cattle as an emergency ration. Fray Marcos traveled with him as guide. Ships under the naval officer, Pedro de Alarcón, sailed up the Gulf of California—to support Coronado's march to Kansas!—sublimely unaware that Lower California was a peninsula, cutting them off from the Pacific, not an island. Neither Alarcón nor Coronado knew that the highest mountains on the continent intervened between the lands Coronado was to explore and the Pacific, near which he expected to be marching.

The advance party entered the United States through the San Pedro Valley, which runs north from the Mexican border through eastern Arizona till it reaches the Gila River, not far from the Coolidge Dam. Thence they went up the Gila to an old pueblo which the Aztecs called Chichilti-calli, or Red House, because it was "built of red mud." After the glowing reports they had heard, the Red House was a terrible disappointment: "The famous Chichilti-calli turned out to be a roofless ruined house, although it appeared that formerly, at the time when it was inhabited, it must have been a fortress. One could easily tell that it had been built by strange people, orderly and warlike."

Except for a few Indian nomads, the region was nearly uninhabited, clothed in a growth of squat pines with oddly elongated, upward-reaching arms, which produced many edible pine-nuts, and oaks, which produced "sweet acorns." An unidentifiable plant called "fanonas" yielded a fruit "like that from which coriander preserves are made." The "thorny trees"—prickly pears and cactus—no longer appeared and plants more familiar to the Spaniards—water cress, grapes, pennyroyal, and marjoram—grew wild. Such cornfields as they found were very productive; for, though the stalks were low, they bore three or four ears with about eight hundred grains in each. They had already encountered the Rocky Mountain goats and now began to see bears, "grey lions and leopards," which were probably cougars and wildcats; fish described as "barbels & picones," which may have been catfish and Gila River trout, also the otters which always, in those days, appeared where the fishing was good.

The Spaniards had by this time advanced into Pueblo country. Though they never guessed it, the culture they now encountered was nearly as ancient as their own, going back at least to the time of Charlemagne. Sixty or seventy miles west of them, near Florence, Arizona, lay one of the most impressive monuments of the earlier days of Indian greatness. This was the so-called Casa Grande ruin, a mass of adobe and gravel which in those days before the last four centuries had passed over it, was "a four-story building, as large as a castle and equal to the largest church in these lands of Sonora," according to Father Kino, the missionary priest who finally discovered it in 1694, a century and a half after Coronado.

The large building was only part of what had once been a large walled pueblo with many buildings, the whole settlement extending for two or three miles, with a big irrigation canal running in from a reservoir connected with the Gila River. According to Father Kino, "at the same time, making a great turn, it watered and enclosed a champaign many leagues in length and breadth, and of very level and very rich land." Casa Grande itself, he thought, could still be roofed, repaired, and used, though Father Pedro Font, another missionary, who passed that way in 1775, thought it must be five hundred years old—an estimate which was, of course, pure guesswork. All around, the surface was "scattered with pieces of ollas [water jars], jars, plates, etc., some ordinary and others stained with various colors, white, blue, red, etc.," of a kind unknown to the Pima Indians who then possessed the country. It was mute evidence of a large pre-historic population.

Now a national monument, Casa Grande was almost entirely ignored by the Spaniards. Even if he had known of the ruins, Coronado would have cared little about them, for he had a good many other cares at this point. After the glowing account Fray Marcos had given of the country, the reality was a rude shock. The friar may have been encouraged by the government to exaggerate a bit—it was good propaganda to get men to go on the expedition. But even Coronado was disturbed when he found how wildly popular rumor had exaggerated the friar's statements. Everything was the opposite of what he had told.

Hypothetical reconstructions of Indian dwellings in Chaco Canyon, Arizona. Painted by Robert Coffin.

Montezuma Castle, Indian Ruin, Prescott National Forest, Arizona. Photo by Edgar L. Perry.

When they finally sighted their first inhabited pueblo, the shock was even worse. This was no splendid city gleaming with gold, silver, and jewels. "The curses that some hurled at Fray Marcos were such that God forbid they may befall him," wrote one of the soldiers.

The friar had declared the sea—that is, the Gulf of California—was only about fifteen miles from Chichilti-calli. His fifteen miles turned out to be about a fifteen days' journey overland! Coronado learned that the Indians had sighted Alarcón's ships in the Gulf of California; but it was now evident that at such a distance the fleet would be of no help to his army.

Still hopeful, he moved off into the uninhabited desert, somewhere along the southern part of the Arizona-New Mexico boundary, finding no grass whatever for his horses for several days. Then he came to "cool rivers and grass like that of Castile," nut and mulberry trees, and a growth of flax along what was probably the Little Colorado. His route north must have been more or less in the vicinity of the Arizona-New Mexico line, for it brought him to Hawikuh, a pueblo near the modern American town of Ojo Caliente, New Mexico.

The Zuñis, who had killed Estebánico here, were still hostile. They attacked before Coronado was in sight of their city, but were beaten off. In the night, Zuñi signal fires flared and were answered by others—"a method of communication as good as we could have devised ourselves," Coronado observed. He pushed on quickly to the village, for his food was almost exhausted. A small party went forward to make peace if possible. They were answered with arrows. Coronado and the troops arrived to find the Indians drawn up in the plain. When the Spaniards did not attack, the Indians closed in with showers of arrows, until a Spanish charge drove them into the pueblo.

There was food in the pueblo, food that the Spaniards had to have. Crossbowmen and arquebusiers opened on the Zuñi warriors on the roofs; but the strings of the crossbows broke and the arquebusiers "had arrived so weak and feeble that they could scarcely stand on their feet." The Zuñis therefore had little to fear as they stood on their flat rooftops, hurling down "countless great stones." Coronado's elaborate gilt armor made him a chief target. He was hit in the foot with an arrow and twice knocked down with stones. In the end the Spaniards secured Hawikuh and its store of corn, while the Zuñis fled to their stronghold on Thunder Mountain.

There was an attractive modesty about Coronado. He wrote Mendoza: "The Indians all directed their attack against me because my armor was gilded and glittering, and on this account I was hurt more than the rest, and not because I had done more or was farther in advance then the others; for all these gentlemen and soldiers bore themselves well, as was expected of them." It is not the attitude of every commander.

With the victory came more disillusionment. There was no gold or silver here. The cities the Spaniards had expected to find were only "little villages." The pueblos were not decorated with turquoises, though the Indians were using them, for personal adornment. There was at least plenty of maize and some turkeys, which the Zuñi had long since domesticated, both for food and for feathers, and—a cheerful culinary note—Coronado thought the Zuñis made "the best tortillas that I have ever seen anywhere," an opinion which an expedition forty years later enthusiastically endorsed. There was some cotton cloth and a supply of buffalo skins besides deerskins and rabbitskins.

Normally, the Pueblo Indians had all the food they could possibly use. One expedition, some years later, repeatedly either sent surplus gifts of edibles back to the Indian donors, or told them not to send so much. At the Hopi pueblo of Awatobi, these travelers had hardly pitched camp "when about one thousand Indians came laden with maize, ears of green corn, pinde, tamates, and firewood, and they offered it all, together with six hundred widths of blankets small and large, white and painted, so that it was a pleasant sight to behold."

"They brought so much food that we told them not to bring it as it was going to waste." But the Indians brought venison and dried rabbits, just for good measure, and along the road to the next pueblo, the Spaniards found waiting for them "many large earthen jars with water and much food, all very surprising facts." Other villages were equally generous.

The country round about Zuñi—that is, western New Mexico and eastern Arizona—was in 1540 very much what it is today. "There are no fruits or fruit trees," wrote Coronado. "The country is all level and is nowhere shut in by high mountains, although there are some hills and rough passages. There are not many birds, probably because of the cold and because there are no mountains near. There are not many trees fit for fire-wood here, although they can bring enough for their needs from a clump of very small junipers four leagues distant. Very good grass was found a quarter of a league away, both for pasturage for our horses and for mowing for making hay."

Just where Coronado was, he had no very clear idea. One of his men later hazarded a guess that from Arizona and New Mexico, "the land between Norway and China is very far up"! Coronado himself rather thought he was nearer the Pacific than the Atlantic and that the Arctic Ocean "must be much farther away." Actually he was only about fifty miles west of the Great Continental Divide, which he would pass on his next march without noticing it. He can hardly be blamed for that, however. In the flat New Mexico country it can be located only by geographers. Modern tourists would never notice it were there not signs to tell them where it is.

Fifty miles to the west, in Arizona, lay the Petrified Forest, near which one of his reconnoissance parties passed without observing it; and a little farther north lay the amazing medieval ruins of the Chaco Canyon, great buildings and canals, where red men for centuries had built an isolated, peaceful civilization and then, sealing their houses, had vanished quietly, no man knows where or why. These were not to be discovered for many years to come.

The Grand Canyon of the Colorado lay about two hundred miles to the northwest. Coronado didn't miss that, for you can't very well overlook the Grand Canyon. A reconnoitering party of about a dozen men went out under Don García López de Cárdenas to hunt for a large river, said to be somewhere in the West. Though they saw a few villages, they found a large part of Arizona uninhabited and made few notes on the monotonous, flat country where there was really very little to describe. Forty-odd years later an expedition backed by Antonio de Espejo, a Mexican merchant turned explorer, traveling a little farther south, found the Little Colorado, "a fine, beautiful and selected river," admiring its growth of willow and "poplar," which must have been cottonwood. Somewhere near Flagstaff, Arizona,

Espejo found much pasture land and "forests" of piñon and, beyond these, "a warm land in which there are parrots."

Cárdenas troubled with no such observations. He had been sent to find a large river and he paid little attention to anything else. At the end of twenty days' travel, he came to a region "high and covered with low and twisted pine trees," and soon was looking wonderingly down into the Grand Canyon, "from the edge of which it looked as if the opposite side must have been more than three or four leagues away by air." The huge dimensions of the Canyon were hard to believe.

The desert journey across half of Arizona in midsummer had been hot and desperately dry. Water was getting short. Every day, someone had to travel five or six miles to get a supply. Now, before them lay the whole Colorado River—only they couldn't reach it. So distant, so far below them was the stream that "from the top it looked as if the water were a fathom across. But, according to information supplied by the Indians, it must have been half a league wide."

For three days they tried to find a way down the jagged, rocky canyon wall. Each time, they failed. Then someone found a place that looked promising; and three adventurers, "being the most agile," started the long climb down. Eagerly their companions watched the scrambling figures grow smaller and smaller as they swung slowly into the abyss, toward the water far below. (How they hoped to carry water up again, the chronicler does not say. Perhaps each man might have brought back a gourd or two.) On down they went, "within view of those on top till they lost sight of them, as they could not be seen from the top." There was a long, anxious pause. Then, in the afternoon, tiny, distant figures came in sight again, scrambling upward from rock to rock. About four o'clock they swung their legs over the Grand Canyon's rim. Another failure.

"They could not reach the bottom because of the many obstacles they met, for what from the top seemed easy, was not so; on the contrary, it was rough and difficult." "They said that they had gone down one-third of the distance and that, from the point they had reached, the river seemed very large, and that, from what they saw, the width given by the Indians was correct. From the top they could make out, apart from the canyon, some small boulders which seemed to be as high as a man. Those who went down and reached them swore that they were taller than the great tower of Seville." They were thinking of the Giralda, the bell tower of Seville Cathedral, which is 295 feet high.

Cárdenas and his men could go no farther along the canyon for lack of water. Their Indian guides warned there would be no water in the country ahead for three or four days. The Indians themselves could cross it only by leaving buried gourds of water along the trail behind them for the return journey. Already short of water, the Spaniards could hardly do that. Regretfully, they turned back to Hawikuh. Behind them the Grand Canyon lay in majestic peace. No other white men saw it for two hundred years.

Then, in 1776, came Father Francisco Garcés, a priest who had devoted his life to the hard and dangerous work of a missionary among the Indians—who eventually demonstrated their gratitude by clubbing him to death. Approaching from the west, he came first to Cataract Canyon, a tributary of the Grand Canyon. More concerned with the salvation of souls than with anything else and quite indifferent to hardship, Father Garcés says merely that he coaxed his mule into Cataract Canyon along a "difficult road" with "a very lofty cliff" on one side "and on the other a horrible abyss." It remained for Lieutenant J. C. Ives, of the United States Army, engaged in a government survey in 1857–1858, to tell what that ride was really like. Lieutenant Ives was probably the first white man who had passed that way since Father Garcés. The trail the gallant priest had followed was "a slight indentation that appeared like a thread attached to the rocky wall, but a trial proved that the path, though narrow and dizzy, had been cut with some care into the surface of the cliff." After jogging on casually for about a mile, the lieutenant happened to glance down, and discovered that, while his knee almost touched the cliff on one side, his mule was just three inches from a thousand-foot drop on the other. He dismounted hurriedly. Some of his men finished the journey on their hands and knees, so giddy that they dared not stand up.

At the end of this road, what Father Garcés called "another and a worse one" began. Even the fearless priest had to leave his mule here and go ahead on foot until he came to a place where, as he says very simply, he had to "climb down a ladder of wood."

Father Garcés didn't tell the half of it! He had really come to a gigantic stone slab running from one smooth perpendicular wall to the other, blocking the canyon completely, with nothing but a sheer forty-foot drop beyond. Down this he had to scramble on a crude wooden ladder made without nails or a scrap of iron.

When Lieutenant Ives reached the same point eighty years later, he saw no hope of going on at all. Then some one in the party thrust his head far over the cliff and saw the ladder. It seems absurd to suggest that it was the same one Father Garcés had used eighty years before; but in a country where wood is known to last four or five hundred years, the thing is not quite impossible. Whatever its date, the ladder was both aged and infirm. As one of the Ives party set foot on it, the rickety structure began to collapse, just when it was too late for him to scramble back. One upright gave way. Rungs went clattering to the stones below. But the other upright held firm long enough for the eager investigator to slide down, landing on the rocks at the bottom with a mighty bump, but quite unhurt. He had to be hauled up later by fastening together the leather slings of the soldiers' muskets.

The bottom of the canyon was unchanged since Father Garcés had scrambled down. A large spring burst out of the ground, from which flowed a stream, deep blue in color, with the inevitable border of willows and cottonwoods, and a narrow strip of reddish bottom land. Cataract Creek is still so heavily charged with lime that it encrusts everything on which it dries. The fronds of maidenhair fern growing near it are often sheathed in limestone, as if petrified.

Farther along the creek, Father Garcés found the Havasupai Indians, cultivating their four hundred acres of arable land at the canyon's bottom several thousand feet down, building cliff dwellings for refuge in the ancient style. They are still there, cut off from the world and glad of it—"content with their half-underground lot, and only anxious to be let alone," says a modern visitor.

Even Father Garcés did not want to return by the hair-raising trail along which he had come and, finding an easier way out, emerged

The Grand Canyon of the Colorado River (6,200 feet deep). From *Exploration of the Colorado River of the West,* by J. W. Powell, published in 1875.

The Grand Canyon. From *Exploration of the Colorado River of the West,* by J. W. Powell, published in 1875.

between Cataract Canyon and the Grand Canyon, itself. "They cause horror, those precipices," he noted placidly, as he emerged to level ground. Another day's travel brought him to the Grand Canyon somewhere near Canyon Spring—"the most profound caxones which ever onward continue; and within these flows the Rio Colorado. There is seen a very great sierra [that is, the Canyon wall, not, in this case, a mountain], which in the distance looks blue; and there runs from southeast to northwest a pass [the Canyon itself] open to the very base, as if the sierra were cut artificially to give entrance to the Rio Colorado into these lands."

True child of the eighteenth century, the good father had no romantic feeling for the wild grandeur of the Canyon. Neither he nor Cárdenas even mentions the glowing splendor of the colored rocks. The Canyon to them was not a thing of beauty. It was just something that an explorer ought to report, so that it is hardly surprising that for another fifty years after Father Garcés, it was unvisited by white men. The first Americans seem to have regarded this marvel of nature mainly as an annoying obstacle to travel along the Colorado River.

It is a curious fact that none of these parties mention cougars or mountain lions, which swarmed in the Grand Canyon area. A modern United States government trapper is said to have killed five hundred of them in four years! Neither did the very earliest travelers have trouble with the savage herds of wild swine, or peccaries, though Coronado passed directly through their range, which ran from Arkansas and Texas into Mexico. Probably Coronado escaped the peccaries as De Soto escaped the alligators—because his force was so large. In later years, smaller parties often had to climb trees and stay there to escape the long, sharp tusks of these aggressive little beasts. There are still enough of them about to be troublesome upon occasion; and early nineteenth century American trappers were frequently attacked and treed. Some were particularly disgusted by the "odor not less offensive than our polecat," produced by a fetid gland in the creature's back. This spoiled the pork for everyone except a few Indians who had a special way of cooking it in a pit, drawing off the offensive emanations with a tube, and scorned ordinary domestic pork entirely.

The Grand Canyon was not the only incidental reconnoissance which Coronado's expedition undertook. Far behind his main body, a patrol sent out from his base troops, under Captain Melchior Diaz, discovered the lower reaches of the Colorado; found buried letters left there by the naval commander, Alarcón, before he turned back downstream; met giant Indians—probably the Seris, who are still noted for stature—crossed the river and pushed a little way into lower California, until they were blocked by "sandbanks of hot ashes which it was impossible to cross without being drowned as in the sea. The ground they were standing on trembled like a sheet of paper, so that it seemed as if there were lakes underneath them. It seemed wonderful and like something infernal, for the ashes to bubble up here in several places."

While Coronado was marching inland, Alarcón had gone up the Colorado for some distance in small boats, without finding anything of much importance, except fruitful fields and Indians who were mostly friendly. There was really not a great deal to find, and the lower Colorado was troubled by no more white men until, in 1700, Father Kino visited the valley, finding everywhere "pleasant lands." One area on the west bank of the Colorado he thought "a veritable champaign of most fertile lands, of most beautiful cornfields very well cultivated with abundant crops of maize, beans, and pumpkins," and "with very large drying-places for the drying of pumpkins, for this kind lasts them afterwards all the year." Again and again the hospitable Indians loaded him down with more food than an escort of two hundred men could carry.

While Coronado's reconnoissance parties were out, there arrived at Hawikuh visiting Indians from the pueblo of Pecos, which Coronado called Cicuye. They bore an offer of friendship to the white newcomers and a present of "dressed skins and shields and headpieces"—the latter perhaps buffalo-horn headgear like that used by some of the plains tribes. The buffalo hides interested the Spaniards. One of the visitors from Cicuye had a picture of a buffalo painted on a hide and,

THE NEW MEXICO HISTORICAL SOCIETY

View of the pueblo of Acoma. From a lithograph in *Notes of a Military Reconnoissance from Fort Leavenworth in Missouri to San Diego in California*, 1848.

SMITHSONIAN INSTITUTION, BUREAU OF AMERICAN ETHNOLOGY

A photograph taken in 1900 of the pueblo of Acoma, New Mexico.

as best they could, the visiting Indians tried to explain what buffalo were. The puzzled white men concluded that "they seemed to be cows, although from the hides this did not seem possible, because the hair was woolly and snarled so that we could not tell what sort of things they had." An Indian artist made a hasty drawing on buffalo hide to be sent back to the viceroy.

Coronado sent Hernando de Alvarado with twenty men to investigate these tales. Alvarado struck east along the Ojo Caliente Valley, a difficult trail including an old lava flow, so bad that no modern Zuñi is known even to have attempted it. Signs of ancient culture met him along the trail—three old "fortresses," and an old city "all in ruins" but with one high wall still standing, "built of very large granite stones, and above this of very fine hewn blocks of stone." Ignoring a branching trail which led to the pueblo of Zia, or Chia, they came at last to Acoma, the oldest structure still in use in the United States. Perched on their lofty mesa—an ascent "so difficult that we repented climbing to the top," said a Spaniard—these Keresan Indians were secure themselves and a terror to their neighbors, "robbers feared by the whole country about."

They were secure because their village stood on an immense mesa, "a rock out of reach, having steep sides in every direction, and so high that it was a very good musket that could throw a ball so high. There was only one entrance by a stairway built by hand, which began at the top of a slope which is around the foot of the rock."

This was, in fact, a huge sand dune which is still there. Some unknown Indian engineering genius, centuries earlier, had carefully secured this single access to his village. Above the sand dune, "there was a broad stairway for about two hundred steps, then a stretch of about one hundred narrower steps, and at the top they had to go up about three times as high as a man by means of holes in the rock, in which they put the points of their feet, holding on at the same time by their hands. There was a wall of large and small stones at the top, which they could roll down without showing themselves, so that no army could possibly be strong enough to capture the village." Starving Acoma out by siege warfare would not have been much use, either.

There was plenty of corn on top of the mesa, rather more than besiegers could carry, and "cisterns to collect snow and water."

Spanish soldiers, who could barely scramble up along the toe-holds, handing their weapons on ahead of them, watched in amazement the ease with which the Indians of Acoma went up and down, "so freely that they carry loads of provisions, and the women carry water, and they do not seem to touch the walls with their hands."

Later explorers coming up from Mexico commented on the "many irrigated maize fields with canals and dams as if Spaniards had built them." This was an ancient art. The mysterious inhabitants of the Chaco Canyon had been skilled in it, and in the Salado Valley alone, it is estimated that 250,000 acres were in cultivation during pre-historic times.

There was no need for the Spaniards to make an attack that would have been hopeless, anyhow. At first the Acoma Indians came down and drew on the ground the sacred lines of cornmeal, which the strangers must not cross. But when it was apparent that the Spaniards meant to cross, ignoring the magic lines, they gave up their hostility and brought out gifts of turkeys, deerskins, piñon nuts, corn, cornbread, and cornmeal.

Alvarado and his men pushed on into the country of the "Tiguex," the country around modern Albuquerque and Bernalillo, New Mexico. They passed "a fine lake, at which there are trees like those of Castile,"—clearly at Laguna Pueblo—crossed the Rio Grande, and soon met Indians from the pueblos ahead, bringing presents and playing flutes. This was the usual greeting, identical with that De Soto had encountered farther east. Sometimes the Indians seem to have left their flutes at home and simply whistled.

There were twelve inhabited pueblos in the country, besides seven in ruins. In addition, the Indians had smaller, flat-roofed stone or adobe houses in the fields, where, in time of peace, they could live close to their crops.

Much cheered by Alvarado's news, Coronado brought his troops to Acoma by an easier northern trail and then on to the Tiguex pueblo of Cicuye, or Pecos, located on the Pecos River about thirty miles southeast of Santa Fé. A good deal of this country had pine forests, and the Pecos River itself was "a medium sized river with exquisite water, surrounded by numerous trees and many vines, roses, rosebush fruit, and much pennyroyal."

VI

Coronado in Kansas

AFTER THEIR ARDUOUS march, the Spaniards found the Rio Grande a welcome sight. Its rough and sandy banks were edged with willows and cottonwoods, just behind which were the Indians' fields of corn, beans, and melons. Pine-nuts grew wild. Later explorers mention "small mesquite plants," too many thistles for comfort, and the odd "mesquite brabo," or "tornillo tree" *(Prosopis pubescens)*, with twisted spiral seed pods. Not only were the pods "like harquebus screws," but the Spaniards also found the wood excellent for making new arquebus stocks. Like other rivers of the Southwest, the Rio Grande had pools beyond the banks, filled with fish and haunted by waterfowl. On some rivers these pools were very large. Father Garcés, much later, could not reach the junction of the Gila and Colorado at all, because of the pools and "tulares"—swamps of tula reed—that cut him off; and near Yuma, Arizona, the cottonwoods were so luxuriant he could not even see the Gila through them, though elsewhere along the river they were often scant and small.

Among the pueblos Coronado's troops were gratified to find "chickens in great abundance"—the chickens being domesticated turkeys, which the Indians raised partly for meat and partly for feathers, from which they made cloaks of great beauty.

Alvarado had met at Pecos "an Indian slave, a native of the farthest interior of the land"—almost certainly a Pawnee. This Indian, whom the Spaniards "named the Turk because he looked like one," told marvelous tales of his native land, which lay far north of the Pueblo

country. At first he was to be used as a guide only "to the cattle"—
that is, the buffalo herds, about which, after seeing so many hides and
hearing so many stories, the Spaniards were becoming very curious.
But the Turk began to tell such marvelous tales about the gold and
silver to be had, that soon "they did not care to look for the cattle,
and as soon as they saw a few they turned back to report the rich
news to the general."

Coronado listened eagerly to the Turk's tales of "a river, flowing
through the plains, which was two leagues wide, with fish as large
as horses and a great number of very large canoes with sails, carrying
more than twenty oarsmen on each side. The nobles, he said, traveled
in the stern, seated under canopies, and at the prow there was a large
golden eagle." Most of this was a fairly accurate description of the
Missouri-Mississippi River system. If the rivers were rarely two
leagues, they were nevertheless very wide. If the fishes were not as
big as horses, Mississippi River cats were certainly very big. And the
canoes the Turk described were just about the sort of thing De Soto
was seeing at just about this time, on the Mississippi.

The Turk, however, embroidered this basis of possible fact with
wild fictions. "The lord of that land took his siesta under a large
tree from which hung numerous golden jingle bells, and he was
pleased as they played in the wind." The table services were silver,
"pitchers, dishes, and bowls were made of gold." The Spaniards
tested the Turk. They showed him tin. "It was not gold," said the
Turk, explaining "that he knew gold and silver very well, and that
he cared little for other metals." He alleged that he had given some
gold and jewels to an Indian known to the Spaniards as "Whiskers"
(*Bigotes*).

When Whiskers denied this and the Turk's other tales of gold and
silver, some of the Spaniards turned one or more of their savage dogs
on him. After the torture, Whiskers still said the Turk was lying.
Coronado put Whiskers in chains and took him along. It was possible
to believe the Turk, but a check on his stories might be useful.

Eventually there was trouble with the Indians of Tiguex. The
chaining of Whiskers and another Indian, woman trouble, seizure of
Indian garments, all caused hostility. It began with a raid on the

horses and mules, which the Indians stampeded so successfully that many were permanently lost. There was some hard fighting, including a fifty-day siege of one pueblo and an unfortunate misunderstanding of orders, whereby about two hundred Indians were either burned to death or butchered with cold steel, after their lives had been guaranteed. By the spring of 1541, however, the Spaniards were in control of Tiguex.

When the ice broke on the Rio Grande, Coronado started for "Quivira," the country which the Turk had described to him. Whiskers and the chief arrested with him, when set free, "gave" Coronado a young Indian named Xabe, supposed to be a native of Quivira. Like Whiskers, he declared the Turk was lying. According to Xabe, "there was gold and silver, but not so much of it as the Turk had said."

But since it was pleasanter to believe the Turk, he became guide of the expedition, and Xabe was left behind. Somewhere or other, they gathered up still a third native of Quivira named Ysopete, probably a Wichita, who agreed with the other Indians that the Turk was just lying.

From Cicuye, the expedition moved toward the buffalo plains, pausing to bridge the Pecos River. As they moved east through New Mexico, they began to see "the cows."

Two days later, near the New Mexico-Texas border, they came upon "people who lived like Arabs and who are called Querechos." It was the first meeting of the whites and the plains Indians, the Querechos being either Apaches or Tonkawas. Not in the least afraid of the Spaniards, they were not in the least hostile, either, merely coming out of their tents to see the strangers. There was no difficulty talking with them since, like all Indians of the Great Plains, they knew the sign language: "These people were so skillful in the use of signs that it seemed as if they spoke. They made everything so clear that an interpreter was not necessary." They told the Spaniards that to the east was a river more than a league wide, with many canoes, along which they could travel through continuous native settlements for ninety days. There was a strong suspicion that the Turk had rehearsed the Querechos in their story, which agreed closely with his;

but they may have been honestly trying to describe the distant Mississippi.

Next day the nomad Querechos, who lived in "tents made of dressed skins of the cattle," struck camp and moved off. "They follow the cattle to provision themselves with meat," says Castañeda. It was a classic picture of prairie life, completely untouched as yet by white influence. There were about two hundred tepees "of tanned skins, white, and built like pavilions or tents." They grew no crops whatever, living wholly on the buffalo herds, which provided almost all their needs: "They neither grow nor harvest maize. With the skins they build their houses; with the skins they clothe and shoe themselves; from the skins they make ropes and also obtain wool. With the sinews they make thread, with which they sew their clothes and also their tents. From the bones they shape awls. The dung they use for firewood, since there is no other fuel in that land. The bladders they use as jugs and drinking containers. They sustain themselves on the meat, eating it slightly roasted and heated over the dung. Some they eat raw; taking it in their teeth, they pull with one hand, and in the other they hold a large flint knife and cut off mouthfuls."

The Spaniards watched with interest as the village prepared to move on to new buffalo hunting grounds. These plains Indians had as yet no horses. Coronado, Narváez, and De Soto had brought to the United States the first since long before the glacial era. Instead, the Indians traveled "with droves of dogs carrying their belongings."

Though the Querechos used the travois, they also loaded some dogs like pack mules, "with little pads, pack-saddles, and girths." If the loads slipped, the dogs had been taught to "howl for someone to come and straighten them." They were big animals, able to carry thirty-five to fifty pounds or to drag the heavy lodge poles after them. Since most Indians are careless with domestic animals, the dogs sometimes had "sores on their backs like pack animals."

As late as 1602 these Indians still had no horses.

Trouble began as soon as Coronado moved out on the plains. Except for the tepee villages of occasional red nomads, the country had no inhabitants. It had no landmarks, no streams, no mountains, no trees, no bushes, not even stones, for the deep, grass-grown prairie soil covered everything. As far as the strangers could see, there was only a flat expanse of grass, studded with buffalo bones, stretching illimitably away until it met the sky in a huge ring that closed the white men in.

There was no way to find directions. Men got lost. Sometimes wanderers from the column had to wait for the sun to go down before they could tell east from west. Nor could a lost Spaniard follow the track of his comrades, for the stunted prairie grass, when trampled, rose again quickly. American travelers in the early nineteenth century say the grass was about four inches high and make the odd observation that it was "very injurious to the hoofs of animals that travel over it." A man could not even follow his own trail back to camp, nor could a rescue party trace him. Even the marks of the whole army's passage were quickly obliterated, leaving "no more traces when they got through than if no one had passed over." "Although the grass was short," says Castañeda, "when it was trampled it stood up again as clean and straight as before."

When men were missing, artillery boomed, horns blew, and bonfires blazed to guide them in. Some men found their way back only after two or three days. Some never found it. Thirst, exhaustion, starvation claimed them—or perhaps wolves, which were bolder in primitive America than they were later, when they had learned about steel traps and firearms.

The flat monotony of the plains—"a vast level area of land more than four hundred leagues wide"—was a grave problem. It was like being on a ship at sea. The Spaniards had seen mountains on the plains' western edge, but "the opposite cordillera could not be seen, nor a hill or mountain as much as three estados high, although we traveled 250 leagues over them. Occasionally there were found some ponds, round like plates, a stone's throw wide, or larger. Some contained fresh water, others salt. In these ponds some tall grass grows. Away from them it is all very short, a span long and less. The land is the shape of a ball, for wherever a man stands he is surrounded by the sky at the distance of a crossbow shot. There are no trees except along the river."

There were other tepee camps of wandering Indians. Then there were still larger buffalo herds—"such large numbers of cattle that it now seems incredible."

"Traveling over the plains, there was not a single day until my return, that I lost sight of them," Coronado later reported to the king.

The Spanish horses shied violently at the strange sight and scent of the huge beasts: "At first there was not a horse that did not run away on seeing them, for their faces are short and narrow between the eyes, the forehead two spans wide. Their eyes bulge on the sides, so that, when they run, they can see those who follow them. They are bearded like very large he-goats. When they run they carry their heads low, their beards touching the ground. From the middle of the body back they are covered with very woolly hair like that of fine sheep. From the belly to the front they have very heavy hair like the mane of a wild lion. They have a hump larger than that of a camel. Their horns, which show a little through the hair, are short and heavy. During May they shed the hair on the rear half of their body and look exactly like lions."

There must certainly have been antelope, deer, elk, and wolves on the prairie. A late American description, after stray horses had mated to produce the herds of wild horses (which did not exist in Coronado's time), gives some idea of the number of wild things that roamed the ancient West. The American trapper, Pattie, notes: "As far as the plain was visible in all directions, innumerable herds of wild horses, buffaloes, antelopes, deer, elk, and wolves fed in their wild fierce freedom."

When the Spaniards frightened the buffalo, they saw for the first time the crazed fury of a stampede. The herd dashed toward a ravine. "So many cattle fell into it that it was filled and the other cattle crossed over them. The men on horseback who followed them fell on top of the cattle, not knowing what had happened. Three of the horses that fell, disappeared, with their saddles and bridles, among the cattle, and were never recovered."

Equally startling was their first experience of a prairie mid-summer hailstorm, a "whirl wind" that caught them resting in a ravine. The hail came down with such violence that it tore tents to pieces and dented helmets. Pottery and gourds were shattered. The hailstones were "as large as bowls and even larger, and as thick as raindrops," covering the ground in some places to a depth of about a foot. The bruised and terrified horses stampeded, except two or three held by stout Negroes, wearing steel helmets. Coronado might have lost all his mounts but for the fortunate accident that when the storm struck they were in a ravine where they could not scatter, as they would have on the open plains. These sudden hailstorms were not unusual incidents of prairie travel. Lewis and Clark were caught in one in Montana in 1805, and another army expedition had almost the same experience as Coronado, near the Colorado River in 1846.

After a little more travel, the Spaniards were delighted to find a stretch of country—presumably in Texas or Oklahoma—"densely populated" by Teyas, or Texas, Indians, and producing quantities of turkeys ("chickens of the variety found in New Spain"), beans, mulberries, nuts, plums, wild grapes and roses. Strange to say, these Indians grew no corn; but they were mighty hunters. The Spaniards were surprised to see one warrior drive an arrow clear through a buffalo bull from side to side—by no means an unusual shot for a skilled Indian hunter, though the white men thought it "a good feat for a harquebus." For a really good hunter such a thing was mere commonplace, and some Indians made a habit of dashing around the staggering animal and pulling the protruding arrow on through, so that it would not be broken as the buffalo fell.

It was disturbing to find that none of these Indians confirmed the Turk's glowing tales of gold and silver and of stone houses many stories high. The Teyas knew nothing about gold and silver in Quivira. They did know all about the lodges there, which were not stone palaces, but just "straw and hides"—and so they told Coronado.

It was doubtful if there was even enough food for the army in the land of Quivira, they added. That, too, was serious. Coronado had already used up his corn supply. Corn was very scarce in Quivira, said the Teyas. Water might also be a problem. Already Coronado had found the stagnant fluid in the prairie water holes "more like slime than water."

The situation called for a quick dash forward, but this was impossible for a large body. Regretfully Coronado ordered his troops back to the Tiguex pueblos. Regretfully the troops obeyed. His soldiers loved and admired this leader and wanted to be with him at the finish.

With thirty mounted men and six on foot, he started forward toward Quivira. Somebody was a most appalling liar, and Coronado would have to find out for himself who it was. He took Ysopete, who had always said the Turk was a liar. He also took Teyas guides. The Turk went along, too—in chains.

The army stayed where it was long enough to kill meat for the return journey. Hunters brought in buffalo in large numbers, sometimes sixty or seventy in a day. Within fifteen days they had killed five hundred bulls, either because they could find no cows or because they did not realize how much more palatable meat from yearling cows was than the beef of tough old males.

Then skilled Teyas hunters guided them back by a more direct route than the way they had come, reaching Cicuye in twenty-five days instead of the thirty-five of the outward journey. Nearing Cicuye they feasted on wine, marjoram, and a "fruit which tasted like muscatel grapes." They watched prairie dogs for the first time. "In those plains were large numbers of some animals resembling squirrels, and many of their holes."

They were interested in an Indian woman slave from Tiguex, who had recently been in "the possession of some Spaniards from Florida"—Florida at that time being a vague term for the whole southern United States. If the woman was telling the truth, she had passed over from De Soto's men to Coronado's. Rumor among the soldiers was that she had fled from De Soto's expedition only nine days earlier and that she was able to repeat the names of his officers.

One of the remarkable things about North America in those days was the astonishing way in which, under primitive conditions, news got around. Coronado's men picked up news of De Soto. Coronado got news of Alarcón and the ships that were naïvely trying to support him—from the Gulf of California. Alarcón, when he finally went up the Colorado River, got a detailed report of Estebánico and also learned that Coronado had reached Cíbola—"at Cíbola there were bearded men like us who said they were Christians." They rode on horses. Alarcón thought for a time of sending a messenger overland but finally gave it up.

At about the same time, Juan Rodriguez de Cabrillo, early explorer of the California coast, had news of Coronado repeatedly. One Indian told him of "Christians who were journeying" about a week's journey inland. Spanish sailors, filling their water casks, met Indians who "made signs that they had seen other men like these, who had beards and who brought dogs and cross-bows and swords." These Indians signed that the Spaniards were only five days' journey distant. To them Cabrillo gave a letter for Coronado, which was, of course, never delivered. Later, near San Pedro, the ships met Indians who "had passed people like the Spaniards in the interior." Still others "made gestures with the right arm as if they were throwing lances, and went running in a posture as if riding on horseback. They showed that many of the native Indians had been killed, and that this was the reason they were afraid." The whole California coast was buzzing with the news.

It is no wonder the Indians reported the horses, animals they had never seen, which were, inevitably, a great sensation. The early Aztecs, when they first met Cortez, had at first supposed that horse and man were a single creature—a kind of centaur. Though the Pueblos knew better than that, they got the idea that the horses killed and ate Indians. As late as 1700, Father Kino found little Indian boys glad to gather grass for his horses, "delighted that they ate it and did not eat boys." Kino also found the Indians doubtful that a horse could outrun a man. He had to stage a race, Indian against horse, to prove his point. For a long time, all Indians regarded these extraordinary animals with awe. Red raiders approaching a Spanish camp in Arizona forty years later fled in terror when the horses whinnied, "as they found the sound unfamiliar." In one of the pueblos Espejo's men found a sorrel nag, left behind by other, earlier Spaniards, carefully tended by the Indians. "They had built a manger for it and gave it a large quantity of mesquite and talked to it as if it were a person." When Espejo claimed the horse, the Pueblos gave it a final meal of mesquite and took formal farewell of the wonderful being.

Coronado, with his small group of picked men pursued his journey, "turning always to the north from here," with increasing misgivings, for the plains went on and on. They seemed to be illimitable. The Spaniards "traveled always among the cattle, some days seeing larger numbers than others, depending on the watering places."

On across the monotonous prairie they went, north, always north, for about thirty days. The days' marches were short—the infantry had to keep up and they had to hunt. There was no road except the "cattle paths," the buffalo trails which for centuries had been beaten criss-cross into the soil of North America from the Atlantic to the Rockies.

The Turk, in chains, was still with them, though everyone was beginning unwillingly to believe, by this time, that Ysopete was the better guide. More and more doubts assailed Coronado. True, the land had a "good appearance." "Indeed it was fine," says one of the travelers—and no wonder, for it was to become some of the best farm land in the United States. But there was still no sign of the great Indian cities, the gold and silver, with accounts of which the Turk had long regaled them. The Turk and Ysopete had quarrelled from the start. Coronado kept them apart, now, marching the Turk with the rear guard and lodging him at night so that the two would not meet.

Finally, they met Indians, hunting buffalo on foot, who fled as they saw the column of strange men and stranger beasts, but approached without fear when Ysopete called to them in their own language. Probably they were Wichitas.

It was the end of the journey. The Spanish had now come 950 leagues, 2,500 miles, from Mexico—a figure that can be depended on, for weary Spanish infantrymen had been specially detailed to trudge along, counting their paces, all the way. At last they knew that every one of those weary paces was useless. They had reached the land of Quivira, or Kansas—and complete disillusion. It was a fine country, likely to be "very productive of all sorts of commodities," as indeed it is. The Kansas soil was "rich and black" and after the dry plains the Spaniards noted that Quivira was "well watered by arroyos, springs, and rivers" producing "plums like those of Spain, nuts, fine sweet grapes, and mulberries." But it was not the wealthy, civilized land of their dreams, and of the Turk's lying stories. There were buffalo, "as large as anyone could imagine," in enormous numbers. In this very country, three hundred years later, a battalion of the First U.S. Cavalry, caught in the path of a stampeding herd, saved themselves only by concentrating all their fire on the center of the frenzied rushing mass of beasts for almost half an hour. Even that did not stop the herd but merely split it to right and left so that the troops and their hastily corralled wagons escaped. "That torrent of brown wool went right on without any perceptible check in its speed," said one of the troopers, long afterward.

But of gold and silver there was not a trace, save for a single trinket, which a local Indian seems to have secured from one of the Spaniards themselves. Neither were there any cities—only villages of the Wichitas, close relatives of the Pawnees, the tribe to which Ysopete and the Turk probably belonged. These Indians lived in round huts thatched with grass or, as the Spaniards said, "straw." They can be identified as Wichitas, because no other tribe built such shelters. Their lodges were begun by setting forked posts in a circle, lashing horizontal logs on them, and then building a cone around this framework. On this the squaws wove the tough, long bunchgrass of the Kansas prairies, "in and out in such an ingenious manner that each bunch of grass overlaps the bunch below." The result was a warm, waterproof shelter. Sometimes the Spanish found two hundred of these huts in a single village.

Beyond their country, the Wichitas told their white visitors, there was nothing except a district called Harahey, which was probably in eastern Kansas along the Kansas River. In response to Coronado's request, the chief of Harahey came with two hundred warriors, "all naked, with bows, and some sort of things on their heads." These Indians were friendly enough but their description of the country was the knell of Coronado's hopes. It was clear that only more buffalo plains lay ahead. The Teyas guides and the Indian Ysopete had been telling the truth all the time. The Turk was an unmitigated liar.

What to do with him? In a jangle of iron fetters, that unfortunate redskin faced a grim group of Spanish officers. He had lied? There was no use denying, any longer, what had been growing increasingly evident for several hundred miles. Yes, he had lied. Why? The Turk ended his career of mendacity in an outburst of veracity. He had made a last effort to persuade the Wichitas to massacre the little party of Spaniards. The Wichitas refused. Now there was no hope any more, and the Turk told what was clearly the truth for once.

He had played the same trick other Indians had, about the same time, been using against De Soto. "The people of Cicuye had asked him to take the Spaniards out there and lead them astray on the plains. Thus, they themselves would become so feeble that, upon their return, the people of Cicuye could kill them easily and so obtain revenge for what the Spaniards had done to them. This, the Turk said, was the reason that he had misdirected them, believing that they would not know how to hunt or survive without maize. As to gold, he declared that he did not know where there was any. He said this like one in despair."

He had good reason to despair. As Spanish conquistadors went, Coronado was a mild man and a just one. But this was too much. The Turk was strangled on the spot, while his enemy, Ysopete, who had been right all along, was rewarded by being restored to his own country.

Exactly where Coronado was, will always be a matter of dispute. No one doubts he had reached Kansas. Hammond and Rey say simply "central Kansas." Hodge says he was on the north bank of the Arkansas River, crossing near Dodge City and going downstream till he was approaching the Great Bend of the river. Winship suggests that he was between the main forks of the Kansas River. Others think he approached the Nebraska boundary.

Wherever the Spaniards were, the expedition had failed in its main object—to find treasure. Disconsolate, with his dreams of wealth completely crushed, Coronado gathered up his scattered forces and marched back to Mexico, to receive a very cold welcome from a disgusted viceroy, and to face many legal troubles.

VII

Cartier Comes to Canada

Two LITTTLE FRENCH sailing vessels, hardly more than yachts, hove to while they were still some leagues off the grim Newfoundland coast. It was late spring or early summer of 1534, and Jacques Cartier was just beginning his adventurous exploration along the St. Lawrence, which other and later Frenchmen were to carry inland across the continent, for more than two hundred years.

Of Cartier the man almost nothing is known. He was a Breton, of the stout seafaring breed. He was born at St. Malo in 1491. He could command enough capital to outfit an ambitious expedition. He was a skilled and fearless navigator. Beyond that practically nothing is known of his early life, before the moment when he steered out of St. Malo for a new world, brave and strange and perilous.

From the decks of their low-riding craft, neither of more than sixty tons burden, with gunwales that barely cleared the rolling waves, Cartier and some sixty bearded sailors gazed in amazement at what they saw. The new world they had sailed from France to explore was beginning to reveal its expected wonders already—while they were still far from shore.

Birds. Sea birds.

Sea birds swarming over and around one lonely rocky island, far at sea, in such numbers that "all the ships of France might load a cargo of them without once perceiving that any had been removed," while at the same time in the air and round about fluttered other birds till they seemed "an hundred times as many more as on the island itself."

The numbers were "so great as to be incredible unless one has seen them"—in fact, a Jesuit father who tried to land on the same island a few years later found that "if you do not obtain a good foothold, they rise in such numbers that they may knock you over."

Not all the birds on this marvelous, seagirt rock—the modern Funk Island—could fly. The French sailors, who had been living on salt meat all the way from Normandy, looked hungrily at queer, large, black and white fowl, obviously and appetizingly edible, as big as geese and "so fat that it is marvelous." Some of them were settled comfortably among the rocks, others swimming along shore. None of them were flying, for, as the sailors could see when they came closer, the birds had "only small wings about the size of a man's hand."

These were the great auks, a species completely extinct for the last hundred years, but common in primitive North America along the coast from far north in Canada to Cape Cod and probably a good deal farther south. There were plenty of them in this whole range, in 1534 and they were especially numerous on this lonely island, far at sea, for here they were perfectly safe. No Indian was foolish enough to paddle his canoe over thirty miles of sea, just to lay in a stock of eggs and poultry, when both were to be had for the taking, along the river near his *wiggiwam*.

On their wave-beaten cliffs, none of these birds had ever encountered any human enemies. It is doubtful if any of them had so much as seen a human being, until the fatal day when two big longboats put off from the French ships. Within half an hour, the capacious craft were loaded down with fat birds, "as with stones." Each of the ships could salt down four or five casks of them for future use, while the crews feasted on fresh poultry.

Though the great auk was helpless on land, so that it could be caught and clubbed with no effort at all, the sailors found to their dismay that other birds, especially the gannets, fought back, and "bit like dogs." They were even more surprised by a huge white polar bear, "as big as a calf and as white as a swan that sprung into the sea in front of them." Apparently the bear had also come to feast on birds and birds' eggs. The big white beast escaped from this first encounter; but next day, as the ships went on toward the coast, they found him swimming desperately for shore; caught up with the fugitive by lowering away the longboats—the ships themselves being too clumsy to maneuver as the brute twisted and turned in the water; and were soon feasting on red meat as well as poultry. "His flesh was as good to eat as that of a two-year-old heifer," says Cartier, with all a Frenchman's gastronomic enthusiasm, heightened a little by a long voyage on ship's diet.

(One of the amusing things about French explorers is how very French they were. Amid all their hardships and dangers, whatever else they noted down, they never missed good food, the prospects of good food, or a chance to make wine. Some of the missionary French priests, who had given up for their cause almost everything else that makes life worth living, nevertheless took along a little stock of savory herbs.)

Today, polar bears would not ordinarily be found so far south, but in the sixteenth century they were not uncommon around the gulf of the St. Lawrence, and a few may even have come down as far as what today is the United States. Their meat was not always so wholesome as Cartier found it. Much later French explorers, who killed an enormous specimen in Hudson Bay, ate ravenously of the fresh meat, and immediately became so ill that they expected to die, though they were able to save themselves with medicine and Indian sweat-baths. Just what was wrong is by no means clear, for other explorers ate white bear's meat with much satisfaction. Probably Radisson's hungry men had simply gorged themselves and were suffering nothing worse than a stomach-ache, though a friendly Indian explained to the sufferers that the white bear had poison in his liver.

Until white men reached North America with firearms, the polar bears had little to fear. Originally—like the grizzly, which white men would not encounter for two centuries to come—the white bears had no great fear of human kind. Indian arrows were no real danger, and at first the huge animals treated the white man and his arquebus with equal indifference. An English observer notes in 1578 that "the beares also be as bold, which will not spare at midday to take your fish before your face."

Rejoicing that his first landfall on the mysterious shore had been so auspicious, Cartier and his sixty men sailed on up the Newfoundland coast, passed its northern tip, and then turned southwest, through the Strait of Belle Isle, until the Gulf of St. Lawrence began to open out before them.

Here they came to another "Isle des Ouaiseaulx," or Bird Island, now identified as the Greenly Island of modern days, on which they noted with interest as many birds as ever, including a new species, the red-beaked puffins, burrowing into the earth under the flat rocks to make their nests. The steep sides of the island were perforated with their burrows—as they still are. Leaving the ships and going on in longboats, Cartier and some of the men camped for the night on another island, where they were delighted to find the eggs of eider ducks "in great quantity."

Though the first to leave a record, they were by no means the first white men to visit these waters, a fact of which they had evidence the next day when they ran into a large fishing vessel from La Rochelle. Frenchmen had been fishing here for at least thirty years, together with Basques; and it is by no means impossible that they knew all about them long before Columbus, though—like all fishermen—they kept their choicest fishing grounds a secret. Certainly Bretons were off the Newfoundland coast and in the St. Lawrence by 1504, and as early as 1508 a Norman sea captain had ascended the St. Lawrence for more than two hundred miles, bringing Indians back to France, though no record of his adventurous voyage has come down to us.

Feeling their way cautiously and recording soundings of these unknown waters when they could, Cartier's two little ships crept down the west coast of Newfoundland, delighted to find that they could catch a hundred cod in an hour. Whatever else this new land might yield, it was proving endlessly rich in things to eat. Half way across the bay they had new proof of this. They came upon more islands, covered with sea birds, the modern Bird Rocks.

"These islands," Cartier noted, "were as completely covered with birds, which nest there, as a field is covered with grass." Like the bird islands they had already seen, these were—and are—perfect natural refuges. Great Bird Rock rises sheer for 105 feet, offering a landing place to small boats only in the calmest sea, with only one or two difficult routes to the top. "The birds sit there as thicke as stones lie on a paved street," wrote a visitor in 1597. When Audubon visited the rocks in 1833, he found the nests still so thick that they were "almost touching each other." A scientific bird census made in 1870 showed 100,000 gannets.

Although Funk Island, the first Cartier had seen, was a little too far out to sea for birchbark canoes, the Indians swarmed to these more accessible islands whenever they craved a change of diet. It was not really hunting. They killed a supply of wild poultry with clubs or, if that was too much trouble, trampled them to death, bringing back canoes "filled with sumptuous food acquired without price." No slaughter ever seemed to diminish the supply of birds in those days, for it was, as a Jesuit historian wrote as late as 1710, "impossible to count their numbers."

All along the shores of the St. Lawrence, waterfowl were nearly as numerous and there were more along the chains of lakes that stretched west and north, and still more, west and west, and then great flocks in the Columbia and north and south along the coast of the Pacific. "Everywhere," says our Jesuit, "may be seen sporting in the water, geese, ducks, herons, cranes, swans, coots, and other birds whose habit it is to seek their living from the waves." Even in the twentieth century, something like this may still be seen in the protected area of the Missouri River, near Great Falls, Montana.

The ornithological Jesuit is perhaps the first to put on record a queer old story about a strange sea bird, probably the great auk: "One of its feet is armed with hooked claws, the other has webbed toes, like those of a duck; with the latter it swims, with the former it seizes and disembowels fishes." This zoological fantasy seems to have been widely believed, mainly because no one thought of anything so simple as examining a few specimens.

The safety of the upper rocks was inaccessible to the auks. Unable to climb or fly, they had to nest on the lower levels, where their enemies could reach them. So long as only Indians hunted them there, they could survive, but when the wasteful, ruthless white man came, the great auk was doomed, though even so it bred rapidly enough to maintain itself for three hundred years after Cartier.

Cartier's sailors, who had by this time pretty well eaten up their casks of salted wild poultry, landed again—this time to kill about one thousand wildfowl, leaving regretfully when their longboats were full, for "one might have loaded in an hour thirty such long-boats."

Cartier's Frenchmen had at first been horrified by the barren, rocky shores past which they sailed, "stones and horrible rocks," with a little sour earth, in which grew nothing but moss and stunted shrubs. Cartier, as he gazed at it, rather wondered whether this might not be "the land God gave to Cain," so grim was the first impression it produced.

Now the land began to improve, for they were approaching the rich alluvial meadows of the St. Lawrence River. Landing on Bryon Island, almost in the middle of the Bay, they were delighted to find it "covered with fine trees and meadows, fields of wild oats, and of pease in flower, as thick and fine as ever I saw in Brittany, which might have been sown by husbandmen." There were also wild roses, strawberries, "gooseberry" bushes, which may have been merely chokecherries, "parsley and other strong-smelling herbs."

Most astonishing of all were the walruses, "great beasts like large oxen, which have two tusks in their jaw like elephant's tusks and swim about in the water." The sailors tried to catch one they found asleep near the water, "but as soon as we drew near, he threw himself into the sea." It is perhaps just as well that he did, for walruses were often just as willing as grizzly bears to stand and fight it out. An English crew, passing the Bird Rocks some years later, rashly annoyed the "Sea Oxen" they found sleeping by the water's edge; and "when we approached nere unto them with our boate they cast themselves into the sea and pursued us with such furie as that we were glad to flee from them."

Cartier's men, as they cruised slowly around the gulf, continued to encounter the giant, tusked beasts, but seem to have kept at a respectful distance. There were also whales and belugas (small, white whales). All three animals have since vanished from these waters.

Coasting along Prince Edward Island, Cartier was so impressed by the primeval forest that he landed four times to examine the trees— cedar, yew, pine, elm, ash, willow, and still others whose identity he could not even guess at, with wild pigeons and other birds fluttering in their branches. On the Gaspé Peninsula they were again impressed by the towering trees of the virgin forest, "as excellent for making masts for ships of three hundred tons and more, as it is possible to find."

So far, Cartier had had no real contact with Indians. His men had for some time been catching distant, occasional glimpses of "wild and savage folk," clad in furs, painted "with certain tan colors," wearing feathers in their hair—the Beothucks, a long-since vanished tribe. Once, on Prince Edward Island, they saw Indians crossing a river in canoes. A little later one warrior ran along shore, beckoning them to land, but when the longboats turned in toward him, the man lost his courage and vanished into the shelter of the forest. Leaving a knife and a woolen girdle tied to a branch, to show that the white strangers were friendly, Cartier turned back to his ships.

Then two little fleets, totalling forty or fifty canoes, appeared, the men at the paddles making signs of friendship and calling out a greeting which Cartier wrote down as *Napou tou daman asurtat,* words which were identified four hundred years later as Micmac, conveying an offer of friendship. But Cartier himself could make nothing of them, and there were so many Indians that he was afraid to let them get very close. In the end, he had to frighten them away with light artillery.

Next day, in spite of this bombardment, more Indians appeared, this time in nine canoes, holding up furs, as if they wished to trade. Cartier sent two men ashore, carrying knives and other iron articles. Trade was so brisk that the Indians sold even the furs on their backs and had to go home to their camps completely naked. Next day, the Frenchmen had another friendly meeting with the Indians, and Cartier wrote down the words *cochy* (hatchet) and *bacan* (knife), which identify these Indians as more Micmacs.

On the Gaspé Peninsula they soon met about three hundred more Indians, whom Cartier surveyed without any approval at all—"the sorriest folk there can be in the world, and the whole lot of them had not anything above the value of five sous, their canoes and fishing nets excepted."

Bits of vocabulary, which he again set down, show that these were a new tribe, speaking some kind of Iroquoian language. Perhaps they were Hurons, for Cartier describes them as "wonderful thieves." The French explorers were to become tiresomely familiar with the gift for petty larceny of this talented tribe, who, when they couldn't steal with their light fingers, did nearly as well with their prehensile toes.

Cartier completed his first voyage in the next few days, missing the entrance to the St. Lawrence River entirely, because he sailed up the wrong side of Anticosti Island. Having found nothing but more magnificent forest and beautiful, green, empty meadows, he sailed for Normandy, taking with him two young Indians, whom he had— more or less—kidnapped, though he had tried to do it in a friendly way.

Eight months later, in May of 1835, eager for more North American adventure, he returned from France, bringing back with him the two Indians. During their sojourn in France, they had been studying French, and Cartier hoped to use them as interpreters. He had failed to realize how bitterly they resented the original kidnapping, in spite of subsequent good treatment. Again he halted at the Isle of Birds (Funk Island) to secure two boatloads of wild poultry, before steering into the Gulf of St. Lawrence.

This time he followed the northern coast, a course which brought him directly into the mouth of the river, which was to open the way for French explorers reaching southward from the St. Lawrence Valley to the Susquehanna, the Ohio, the Mississippi, and the Gulf of Mexico, and westward through the Great Lakes almost to the Rockies, during the next two hundred years.

Listening eagerly to what his two Indians, who in eight months had learned a good deal of French, could tell him about the country they were passing, Cartier and his men crept up the river, sometimes in their ships, sometimes rowing their longboats close in to shore. Twice they made complete circles, so as to see both banks. It was slow going, for Cartier was desperately afraid of uncharted rocks and shoals. Any damage to his ships now would be hard to repair; serious damage to their hulls could not be repaired at all.

Animal life was as abundant in the river as it had been in the gulf. Whales were everywhere—"none of us remembers having seen so many." Up the Moisie River were many walruses—"fish in appearance like horses which go on land at night." Soon they encountered more beluga. In a little while the water would grow fresh, the Indians said. They were now entering "the great river of Hochelaga"—a name that the St. Lawrence bore for some time. Yonder was the mouth of the Saguenay River, marked by "lofty mountains of bare rock with but little soil," yet with astonishingly high trees. There was copper (*caignetdazé*) in that country, said the Indians.

Just below the Indian village of Stadacona (Quebec) they met their first large group of Indiana, Hurons, who fled until the two Indians called out to them from Cartier's ship. Then the white men were welcomed with dances and gifts of eels, fish, corn, and melons. Other Indians came swarming in as the news spread, and next day came the great Huron chief, Donnaconna himself, paddling out to the ships with twelve canoes.

Taignoagny and Agaya, Cartier's Indians, explained to the chief that they had been well treated by the French chief, in other words, the King of France, and translated willingly enough. Cartier himself ventured into one of the canoes, and the Indians for the first time in their lives tasted French wine and wheaten bread.

The ships went cautiously up the St. Lawrence as far as the St. Charles River, just below Donnaconna's village, where Cartier looked about him with approval: "This region is as fine land as it is possible to see, being very fertile and covered with magnificent trees of the same varieties as in France, such as oaks, elms, ash, walnut, plum-trees, yew-trees, cedars, vines, hawthorns, bearing fruit as large as a damson, and other varieties of trees. Beneath these grows as good hemp as that of France, which comes up without sowing or tilling it."

Cartier describes at some length the village which was to become Montreal: "The village is circular and is completely enclosed by a wooden palisade in three tiers like a pyramid. The top one is built crosswise, the middle one perpendicular and the lowest one of strips of wood placed lengthwise. The whole is well joined and lashed after their manner, and is some two lances in height. There is only one gate and entrance to this village, and that can be barred up. Over this gate and in many places about the enclosure are species of galleries

The Great Auk, from the engraving of Audubon's painting.

The St. Lawrence River and Montmorency Falls, from Ile d'Orléans. Engraved in 1809.

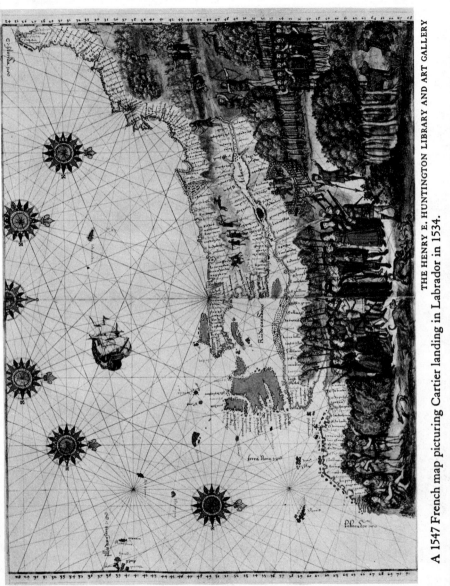

A 1547 French map picturing Cartier landing in Labrador in 1534.

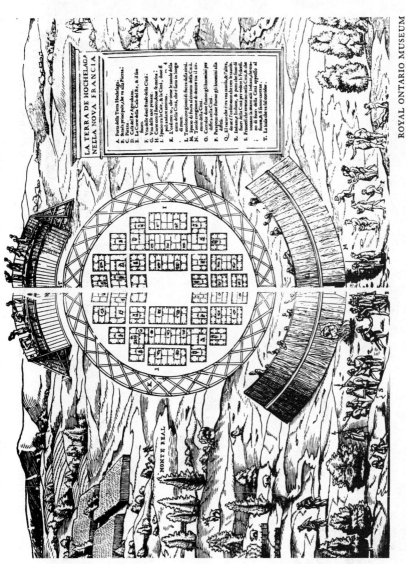

A map which accompanied an early edition of Cartier's narrative showing Hochelaga (Montreal) in 1556. Mount Royal is indicated to the left of the town.

A nineteenth-century representation of Cartier's meeting with the savages at Stadacona, May, 1536.

with ladders for mounting to them, which galleries are provided with rocks and stones for the defence and protection of the place. There are some fifty houses in this village, each about fifty or more paces in length, and twelve or fifteen in width, built completely of wood and covered in and bordered up with large pieces of the bark and rind of trees, as broad as a table, which are well and cunningly lashed after their manner. And inside these houses are many rooms and chambers; and in the middle is a large space without a floor, where they light their fire and live together in common. Afterwards the men retire to the above-mentioned quarters with their wives and children. And furthermore there are lofts in the upper part of their houses, where they store the corn of which they make their bread."

Though friendly enough outwardly, Donnaconna had suspicions of his own. He refused to allow these mysterious strangers to go on up the river to the village of Hochelaga (Montreal). First he offered some Indian children as presents, to persuade Cartier to stay where he was. When that failed, his Hurons made a naïve effort to scare their visitors. Down the river came a canoe with three natives "dressed as devils," one of whom "made a wonderful harangue," after which there was much aboriginal uproar from the deep woods along the bank.

After some other futile efforts to delay him, the stubborn Cartier with one ship and the two longboats caught the turn of the powerful St. Lawrence tide and started upstream, admiring as he went "the finest and most beautiful land it is possible to see, being as level as a pond and covered with the most magnificent trees in the world." Better still, to a Frenchman, was the abundance of grapes.

Beginning with the Northmen, all the early explorers along the Atlantic coast, west to the Mississippi and beyond, and down the Mississippi to the Gulf commented with equal enthusiasm upon the grapes, plenty of which still grow wild in North American woods, though not in the abundance of this early day when their bunches seem to have dangled from every branch. It is no wonder the European visitors usually liked American grapes, for they were the wild ancestors of the Concord, Isabella, Catawba, Scuppernong, and many other varieties, now the pride of American vineyards.

As they reached the Richelieu Rapids, rocky, narrow, swift, and dangerous, canoes put out from shore to warn the Frenchmen of their danger, and another chief came aboard. The number of grapes grew even larger as they pushed on up the river. "The sailors came on board with their arms full of them." Cartier was equally delighted with the trees and with the numerous birds—"cranes, swans, bustards, geese, ducks, larks, pheasants, partridges, blackbirds, thrushes, turtledoves, goldfinches, canaries, linnets, nightingales, sparrows, and other birds, the same as in France, and in great numbers." Though there is no mistaking his enthusiasm, Cartier's ornithology is a little faulty. There are no "nightingales" in North America; he probably heard songsparrows, or thrushes. His "canaries" must have been goldfinches, or perhaps yellow summer warblers. His "cranes" were almost certainly great blue herons, his "turtledoves" the passenger pigeons, now extinct, which, until the white man wiped them out, swarmed in such numbers that their weight broke off the limbs of trees in which they roosted for the night. All the French explorers talk of "bustards," by which they seem to have meant one of the larger species of wild geese.

Cartier was a keen enough observer to distinguish the redwing from other blackbirds, though he describes its shoulder as tipped with "orange." Actually it is a brilliant red, bordered with orange. His "thrushes" were probably robins—the veery, olive-back, hermit, and wood thrushes are not birds likely to be seen casually from ships coming up river; but Cartier was correct enough in his taxonomy all the same, for the American robin is also a thrush, as the speckled breasts of its nestlings show. John Josselyn, the English writer on New England, describes the American robins that he found there as *"Thrushes* with red breasts, which will be very fat and are good meat." Muskrats were another of Cartier's discoveries that created an odd enthusiasm—"large as rabbits and wonderfully good to eat."

Near Hochelaga, soon to be renamed Montreal, he landed and went on afoot, still admiring the country, "the finest and most excellent one could find anywhere, being everywhere full of oaks, as beautiful as in any forest in France, underneath which the ground lay covered with acorns." As for the cultivated fields around the village, it was "fine land with large fields covered with the corn of the country, which resembled Brazil millet, and is about as large or larger than a pea. They live on this as we do on wheat. And in the middle of this is situated the village of Hochelaga, near and adjacent to a mountain, the slopes of which are fertile and are cultivated, and from the top of which one can see for a long distance. We named this mountain 'Mount Royal.'"

Before leaving, Cartier climbed Mount Royal and looked longingly ahead, into the land he knew he would not be able to explore. "We had a view of the land for more than thirty leagues round about. Towards the mouth there is a range of mountains, running east and west [the Laurentian Hills] and another range to the south [the northern slopes of the Adirondacks in New York and the Green Mountains in Vermont]. Between these ranges lies the finest land it is possible to see, being arable, level and flat. And in the midst of this flat region one saw the river extending beyond the spot where we had left our longboats. At that point there is the most violent rapid [Lachine] it is possible to see, which we were unable to pass. And as far as the eye can reach, one sees that river, large, wide and broad, which came from the southwest and flowed near three conical mountains [St. Bruno, Beloeil, and Rougemont], which we estimated to be some fifteen leagues away."

At such a moment it was tragic not to be able to talk with the Indians, who stood about the eagerly gazing Frenchmen and who knew all about the country that lay at their feet. But the interpreters, seized with one of those unaccountable Indian fits of the sulks, had refused to come to Hochelaga at all. Before Cartier lay the land he had come so far to find. Around him were the red hunters and canoemen, who knew its every inch and all its streams.

Cartier did the best he could—and very bad it was—with signs. Some of the information that he got was reasonably correct, however. There were three more rapids ahead, the Indians indicated. Beyond them one could "navigate along that river for more than three moons." The Great Lakes, about which the natives were trying to tell him, were not rivers, but Cartier went home with a clear idea that there was a great waterway leading west, far into strange lands—

an idea that in the long run helped to stimulate the later French explorers. The Indians, pointing to metal objects worn by the whites, were understood to say that there was gold in the country ahead. They were not very good metallurgists, however; and it is likely that, when they pointed to the gold ornaments of the Frenchmen, they were trying to describe the nuggets of copper that lay about on the shores of Lake Superior.

Paying no attention to the vivid foliage of a North American autumn, now blazing about him (which delighted Burgoyne's officers as they moved down from Canada in 1777), Cartier turned back downstream, regretfully. At Hochelaga on his way back he saw, with horror, five scalps which the Hurons were proudly displaying, "stretched on hoops like parchment," an incident which ought to end, once for all, the tale that it was really the white man who taught the innocent redskin the evil art of scalping.

He noted with interest the use of tobacco, which among the Hurons of that day only the warriors smoked "in a hollow bit of stone or wood." A good many of these early American tobacco pipes looked more like enlarged cigarette holders than the modern pipe, with its turned-up bowl. The bowl was simply an enlargement of the stem, with its opening in front instead of above. Such pipes were still in use for ceremonial purposes on top of the Rocky Mountains as late as 1805, when Lewis and Clark smoked them in solemn council, though the modern form of pipe with a bowl opening upward was also in use.

Cartier examined the pungent tobacco the Hurons used and reported: "At frequent intervals they crumble this plant into powder, which they place in one of the openings of the hollow instrument, and laying a live coal on top, suck at the other end to such an extent, that they fill their bodies so full of smoke, that it streams out of their mouths and nostrils as from a chimney. They say it keeps them warm and in good health, and never go about without these things. We made a trial of this smoke. When it is in one's mouth, one would think one had taken powdered pepper, it is so hot."

This was probably the white man's first experiment with tobacco, some fifty years before Sir Walter Raleigh began to popularize smoking in Queen Elizabeth's London. Not all Indians smoked such pungent tobacco as the Hurons. Lewis and Clark nearly strangled the isolated Selish Indians, in the Rockies, by giving them pure Virginia tobacco.

Almost as astonishing as tobacco-smoking to the French newcomers was the extraordinary indifference of the Indians to North American winter cold. Almost stark naked, they walked through ice and snow in apparent comfort.

As the winter wore on, Cartier began to have more trouble with his two sullen interpreters and Indians in general. For a short time it looked as if it might come to hostilities, but, seeing how Cartier strengthened his fort and kept his men on the alert, the Hurons soon renewed their friendship.

In December "the pestilence," in reality scurvy, broke out among the Stadacona Indians. Their gums rotted away, letting the teeth fall out, legs became swollen and inflamed, "blotched with purple-coloured blood," and the affliction mounted slowly to the thighs, shoulders, arms, and neck. Fearing contagion, Cartier forbade Indians to come to the fort, but their disease soon "spread" to the white men. By mid-February, not ten out of 110 men had escaped the disease.

It had not, of course, really been caught from the Indians, for scurvy, a mere deficiency disease, is not contagious. Both Indians and whites were living on a restricted winter diet which did not contain the proper vitamins. Fearing an attack, if the Indians learned how helpless his men were, Cartier explained that they were all at work below decks—a statement which the sick men supported by a mighty hammering with sticks and stones, which was about all their strength permitted. Then Cartier would have two or three healthy sailors follow him ashore—after which he would make great show of driving them back on board to "work."

Though these dramatics deceived the Indians easily enough, they did not stop the disease. Twenty-five sailors died. It looked as if forty more were going to die. Then one day, Cartier met the interpreter Agaya—whom he had seen dreadfully ill ten or twelve days before. Suddenly restored to perfect health, the man told Cartier "that he had been healed by the juice of the leaves of a tree and the dregs of these, and that this was the only way to cure sickness."

Cartier, admitting that *one* of his men had the disease, asked where he could find these miraculous leaves.

Agaya sent two squaws to help the Frenchman gather some. When they came back with branches, the Indians showed him how to grind the bark and leaves for boiling. The sick men at first refused to try the brew resulting, but the one or two who finally did try it "recovered health and strength and were cured of all the diseases they had ever had." The others, drinking too, were likewise cured. One or two enthusiasts even asserted they had been cured of venereal disease!

Within eight days, the French had entirely used up a large tree, which "produced such a result that had all the doctors of Louvain and Montpellier been there, with all the drugs of Alexandria, they could not have done so much in a year as did this tree in eight days." Considering the state of the medical science of the time, Cartier was probably right. The sailors were now receiving the vitamins they needed from some kind of evergreen known to the Hurons as *Annedda,* probably hemlock, perhaps pine.

With his crew still weak, Cartier again became alarmed at the arrival of numerous strange Indians at Stadacona. Having already decided to take Donnaconna to France to repeat his stories of "gold, rubies and other rich things," he decided to forestall any possible attack by seizing the chief at once. The next time Donnaconna visited the fort, he was captured and hurried aboard ship together with the two interpreters. This brought a horde of Indians to the rescue; but Donnaconna, who had been talked into a good humor in spite of the kidnapping by promises to bring him back from France within a year, appeared on deck to make a speech that quieted the uproar. Squaws came aboard with native provisions for him—the Indians did not think much of the white man's diet—and Cartier stood down the river for St. Malo.

He just missed meeting the English vessels, *Trinitie* and *Minion,* commanded by a certain "Maister Hore of London, a man of goodly stature and of great courage, and given to the studie of Cosmographie," which had sailed at the end of April, 1536 and were visiting Cartier's Isle des Ouaiseaulx (Funk Island) toward the end of July, just after Cartier had put into St. Malo. Captain Hore's crew paused to lay in a stock of poultry—it grew to be a habit among explorers passing there —and found some "store of beares both blacke and white, of whome they killed some, and took them for no bad foode."

After that, as food ran short, some of their number were rather more than suspected of cannibalism, while others hit on the extraordinary expedient of watching an osprey's nest, from which they stole "greate plentie of divers sorts of fishes," as fast as the poor hawk brought them to its hungry nestlings. It was something less than sporting, for the little ospreys had to go hungry; but Hore's party were on, or over, the verge of cannibalism. When things were at their worst, they sighted a stray French vessel, probably a fishing boat, seized it, and got home by using its stores. Beyond getting home alive, Hore's expedition accomplished nothing.

Cartier came back to the St. Lawrence again in 1541, but this voyage added little to what was already known of the country. In the meantime, Chief Donnaconna and the other Indians taken to France with him had died. Examining the country briefly, he turned back to France.

Cartier had seen the craggy, wooded St. Lawrence for the last time. He was well into his fifties now, an advanced age for that period. He settled down in France, an ancient mariner home from the sea and the great wilderness, giving sage advice to those who asked, on nautical matters, occasionally serving as a Portuguese interpreter, until he died in 1557.

How often, one wonders, did he stroll down to the harbor of St. Malo, looking west to the setting sun, remembering the wild land where the sun would soon be shining.

VIII

Champlain Goes Farther

FRENCH EXPLORATION IN Canada lagged, thereafter, for nearly sixty years. Breton sailors continued to fish for cod. Occasional vessels sailed half-heartedly a little way up the St. Lawrence. But there was no resolute effort to penetrate to the interior, partly because Cartier himself, in spite of his original enthusiasm, had begun to feel, after his struggles with scurvy, that this was a land where white men could not live without heroic struggles.

The next really great French explorer of North America, the first to enter what is today the United States, was Samuel de Champlain. An old soldier under Henry of Navarre, later Henry IV of France, he had also sailed in the Spanish merchant service to the West Indies, Mexico, and Panama. Brouage, the town near Rochefort where he had been born in 1567, the son of a naval officer, was in those days a busy seaport, though the sea has since withdrawn, leaving it ten miles inland. Here young Champlain grew up, eagerly listening to seamen's tales of the brave new world.

The voyage to the Spanish possessions in America was an extraordinary bit of luck, since the jealous Spaniards usually excluded all foreigners. Champlain seized the opportunity to make a detailed written report of what he saw, illustrated with elaborate drawings. Such information was just what Henry IV was looking for. The result was a patent of nobility, a pension, the permanent favor of the king, and royal persuasion to join the voyage of 1603, commanded by François Gravé, Sieur de Pontgravé.

Champlain cannot have required much persuasion, for his first sight of the Pacific, at Panama, had fired him with the ambition to find a western route to China, by way of the St. Lawrence—a vain hope that was to haunt French explorers for many an arduous year. Friend of the king though he was, and thus assured of fat governmental appointments and an easy courtier's life, Champlain nevertheless preferred the danger, hardship, and adventure of the wilderness.

Under Pontgravé's command, he began by exploring about the same area as Cartier. In 1604, 1605, and 1606 he explored the New England coast from Maine to Woods Hole and thereafter pushed forward the exploration of the Great Lakes and New York. On his first voyage (1603), Champlain wasted very little time in the Gulf of the St. Lawrence but drove straight up the river to Tadoussac.

In some way he had found in France two Indians, brought back by some fishing vessel or some unrecorded explorer. Certainly they were not Cartier's Indians, all of whom had died in France by 1541 at the very latest. Their presence helped him to make friends from the start, for his French-speaking red companions were able to describe to the Canadian Indians "the faire Castels, Palaces, Houses, and people which they had seene, and our manner of living," and to convey offers of French aid against the Iroquois. All this was "heard with so great silence, as more cannot be vttered." Though this seemed alarming, it was in fact merely the reserve which Indian diplomatic etiquette demanded during a council. The Indians turned out to be friendly enough, eagerly accepted French assistance, and gave them a great feast, of which Champlain noted down a description:

"They began to make their Tabagie or Feast, which they make with the flesh of Orignac [moose], which is like an Oxe, of Beares, of Seales, and Beuers, which are the most ordinary victuals which they haue, & with great store of wilde Fowle. They had eight or ten Kettels full of meate in the middest of the said Cabaine, and they were set one from another some six paces, and each one vpon a severall fire. The men sat on both sides the house (as I said before) with his dish made of the barke of a tree; and when the meat is sodden, there is one which devideth to euery man his part in the same dishes, wherein they feede very filthily, for when their hands be fattie, they rub them on their haire, or else on the haire of their dogs."

As he went on up the river to Quebec, Champlain shared Cartier's enthusiasm for the country, but he sniffed with botanical skepticism at certain trees which, he was told, were walnuts. They had, he thought, "the same smell: but I saw no Fruit, which maketh me doubt." He was probably being shown butternut trees, for he later notes that the nuts were "as long as a mans Thumbe."

At the Lachine Rapids, just above Montreal, Champlain's men left their heavy pinnaces and tried to push on in a skiff. They had the mortification of getting stuck on a rock in the first few hundred yards, while "the Canoa of the Sauages passed easily." It was Champlain's first experience with that curse of the canoeist, rapids. "I neuer saw any streame of water to fall downe with such force," he wrote, adding: "It maketh a strong boyling with the force and strength of the running of the water." Ordinary ship's boats, he was soon to realize, were useless in the wilderness. "But he that would passe them must fit himself with the Canoas of the Sauages." Then he could "trauell freely and readily into all Countries; as well in the small as in the great Riuers."

He asked the Indians to "draw with their hand" a map of what lay ahead. They told him of more rapids and open river lying ahead until one reached a lake "which may containe some eighty leagues in length." This was Lake Ontario, which is actually 197 miles long. Between this and Lake Erie, they told him, was a "somewhat high" falls, "where little water descendeth"—certainly the least adequate description of Niagara Falls ever given. Other Indians, more accurate, though still not very explicit, described Niagara as "a Fall that is a league broad, and from whence an exceeding current of water descendeth." Champlain got the impression that it was just another rapid, though missionaries describe it as "celebrated," in 1640, and as "a waterfall of dreadful height," in 1647.

Though they had never seen its western shore, the Indians Champlain met knew of Lake Huron. Its water they said—or Champlain thought they said—was "excessively salt, to wit, as salt as the Sea water." The Indians were by this time probably describing Hudson

Bay, which to them must have seemed just another big lake, but their story, told through the fog of dubious interpretation, made Champlain "beleeue that this is the South Sea." Had he located the long-sought passage to the Pacific at last?

His next voyages took him along the New England coast. Not until June 18, 1609, was he able to start for the Lakes and the Iroquois country—which had roughly the same boundaries as modern New York State, though the rule of the Five Nations stretched far beyond their own boundaries. On the way, Champlain met a band of two or three hundred Indians, Huron, Algonquin, Montagnais, coming to join him. To his dismay, they insisted on seeing the white man's wonders at Quebec, before starting on the warpath against the Iroquois. There was nothing for him to do but return to Quebec and gratify their curiosity. After several days of dancing and festivity at Quebec, the Indians were ready at last. Champlain made his second start, July 3, having rashly undertaken to aid the warriors against their Iroquois enemies. Unconsciously, he was helping to provoke the permanent hostility of the powerful Five Nations against the French and providing the future English colonists with a valuable red ally.

As far as the Richelieu River, he was traversing country the French already knew; but, as he turned into the broad, deep, and beautiful mouth of the Richelieu, he was striking off into territory no white man had ever seen. Other white men were closer than he thought, however, for at that very moment Henry Hudson's *Half Moon* was running down the Atlantic coast, probably not more than two or three hundred miles away.

The lower stretches of the river were easy going, but at the first rapids Champlain found himself handicapped by his heavy white man's shallops. They were too clumsy to be dragged up through the rapids and too big to portage among the thick set trees on shore.

Finding that his men were already losing heart, Champlain left them all behind, except two volunteers, and set off with the Indians in their light bark canoes, which would float on a few inches of water and which one man could carry easily over the winding wilderness portages. By nightfall they had reached country in which Iroquois war parties might be expected at any moment. The Indians built a barricade of logs around rude bark shelters, improvised for the night. Three canoes with nine men reconnoitered several miles ahead; but when they came back to report all clear, the entire party—to Champlain's horror—prepared to go to sleep, in the enemy's country, without posting even a single guard.

When the experienced European soldier protested, his red friends told him "that they could not keep watch, and that they worked enough by day in hunting." It was needless, anyhow, for in a medicine lodge, that night, a medicine man had consulted the spirits—"the devil," in the opinion of the devout Champlain. It was the ordinary performance of the "chisuki" in his "chisukahn," or medicine lodge, characteristic of the Algonkian tribes. The little tent shook and swayed in the grip of supernatural powers, as it does in some of the wilder country along the Canadian border to this very day. From within came the voice of the spirits in a strange language, unknown to the Indians themselves. (Some of the sacred formulas which still survive are also unintelligible to the Indians who use them—probably because the rituals have been recited with little change for centuries, while the dialect of everyday life has changed enormously.)

The outcome was very satisfactory. All would be well, said the spirits. This supernatural form of military intelligence was infallible, the warriors assured him, but Champlain had his doubts. He would have preferred a few scouts or patrols and, above all, some kind of outguard.

But luck was with them. There was no night attack. Next day the war party was off again, winding among "many pretty islands, which are low, covered with very beautiful woods and meadows," where game was so abundant that they could kill all they needed as they went along. The animals in the area were not much disturbed, for the Richelieu River was a no-man's-land, a war road where no one dared to live, as were the four large islands in Lake Champlain, which they entered a day later.

As the canoes slipped silently down the lake, Champlain looked about, enraptured by this unspoiled, primitive landscape. Woods came down to the shores. There were many chestnut trees, which he had not theretofore encountered. The vines, he thought, were the most beautiful he had ever beheld, anywhere, and he was astonished by a huge fish—"five feet long, as big as a man's thigh, with a head as large as two fists, a snout two and a half feet long, and a double row of very sharp and dangerous teeth." Silvery grey in color, this astonishing creature was "armed with scales so strong that a dagger could not pierce them."

While the infinite expansibility of fish is well known, Champlain undoubtedly did see either a gar pike or a muskellunge, rather larger than any modern fisherman is ever likely to see. Being a war road, the lake was as little fished as its shores were hunted, and even the occasional fishing by a war party in search of its supper was done with primitive nets and tackle. The fish had a chance to grow to their maximum size, which intensive modern fishing rarely allows them to attain. "Causar," the Indians called this monster, whose size Champlain may not have exaggerated. Larger fish were known in American inland waters, and one of the Jesuit fathers describes the same creature as "eight feet long, sometimes ten."

There were plenty of other big ones in the lake. Even in the eighteenth century, Charles Le Beau saw four-foot lake trout in Lake Champlain, and elsewhere he caught twenty trout in a quarter of an hour. He does not say how big they were, but remarks that these were only the largest. He could have taken sixty trout in the same time if he had condescended to small ones. These must have been more lake trout, for he says: "Leur chair etoit rouge, ferme & delicat."

The Indians told Le Beau that in Lake Superior the same species would be five and a half feet long and a foot through.

As his war party slipped watchfully down the lake, hugging its west shore, Champlain, looking off across the water, saw "some very high mountains on the east side, with snow on the top of them." He must have mistaken outcrops of white rock for snow, but there is no doubt that he was seeing the Green Mountains. To the south, he could see other mountains, quite as high, but without snow—the Adirondacks.

Both ranges were in Iroquois territory where, his Indians told the Frenchman, "there were beautiful valleys and open stretches fertile in grain, such as I had eaten in this country, with a great many other fruits." The Adirondacks were thickly peopled, continued his red mentors. To reach them one must pass through "another lake, three or four leagues long"—which was, of course, Lake George. From the lower end of the lake, a trail led to "a river which empties on the coast of the Almouchiquois," that is, the Hudson.

As they were now getting close to the enemy, the warriors began moving only at night, halting at dawn, and bivouacking in the thickest woods they could find during daylight. When Champlain dreamed that he saw Iroquois drowning in the lake, his Indian companions were delighted. It was a favorable omen.

At ten o'clock the next night, as they were creeping toward the cape of Ticonderoga, the encounter came. Down the lake something moved. Distant canoes are hard to distinguish from clumps of sedge, snags, swimming animals. At a great distance, it is not always easy to tell whether they are moving, or whether the movement of your own craft makes them seem to move. Champlain and his companions must have watched with painful attention for several seconds. Then there was no doubt. An Iroquois war party—in these waters certain to be Mohawks—were approaching with equal caution, paddling up the lake toward them.

The two warrior bands detected each other's presence at almost the same time. As neither side cared to risk a night engagement, both turned in to shore, where the Iroquois hastily built log barricades, while Champlain's Indians lashed their canoes together with poles, so that they would not get separated if they fought afloat, when the morning came.

Then two canoes paddled over toward the enemy to inquire formally if they wanted to fight. The Iroquois replied ceremoniously that the light was bad. Why not start at dawn? Both sides then wasted the night in dances, songs, and mutual taunts. More prudent commanders would have made their men rest; but to the Indian mind, war was quite as much a sport as anything else, and the ceremonial that attended it was vital.

Carefully concealing their white allies, complete with armor and arquebus—the smooth-bore shoulder firearm of the period—in three

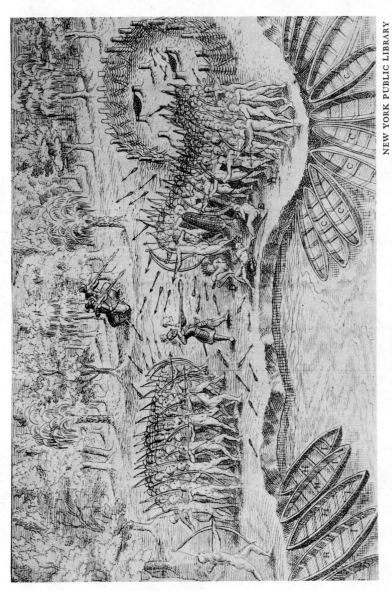

Champlain's illustration showing himself firing at an Iroquois war party. His allies, the Hurons, stand behind him. From the *Voyages*.

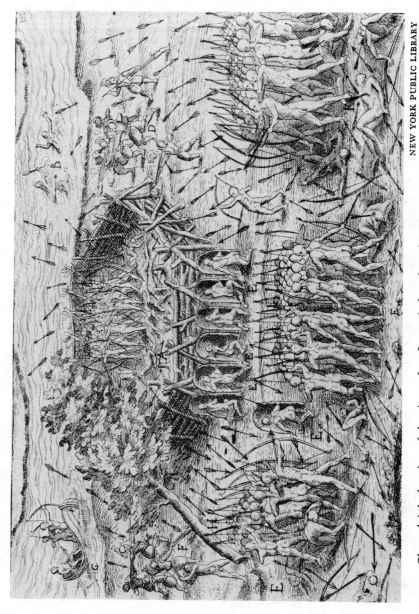

Champlain's drawing of the siege of an Iroquois fort, from his *Voyages*.

different canoes, Champlain's Indians approached the shore. As they reached it, the white men slipped out. The Iroquois do not seem to have noticed them and Champlain, concealing himself behind the warriors, contrived to get his two men, unobserved, under cover on the Iroquois flank.

Champlain himself came through the line of warriors and advanced ahead of them until he was only thirty paces from the two hundred Iroquois—"strong and robust to look at, coming slowly toward us with a dignity and assurance that pleased me very much." The Iroquois must have been amazed at the figure that approached them so fearlessly, clad in gleaming corselet and carrying no weapon save the apparently harmless arquebus. This did not really give the white man so much advantage as later and better firearms. The trouble was that if you didn't hit an Indian at the very first shot, he was likely to put half a dozen arrows into the arquebusier, while the latter was reloading. But its bang was highly impressive.

The Iroquois halted, and there was a moment's pause while the enemies looked each other over. Then, as the bows were drawn, Champlain let drive, with four balls, at one of the three Iroquois chiefs, easily distinguished by their plumes. He got three hits, which astonished the Iroquois, secure in wooden armor that was supposed to be proof against all weapons. As Champlain was reloading, his men opened fire from the woods on each flank, and in a moment the last of the three chiefs was killed. Throwing away their arms, the Iroquois scuttled for the forest, with Champlain banging away behind them, while his delighted Indians gave chase with knife and tomahawk, until they had killed several more and had captured about a dozen alive.

That night, Champlain saw what happened when hostile Indians caught you. In horror, he proposed killing the first victim of the torturers, who by that time had been burned, scalped, and had his nails and sinews torn out. Somewhat puzzled by their valued white ally's incomprehensible scruples, the Indians let Champlain finish the agonized wretch with a single shot—which he did "without his seeing it at all." On the way home, he continued to marvel at the stoicism of the other prisoners, who answered his questions about the Iroquois country cheerfully enough and "always went along singing without any hope of being better treated than the other." It was the traditional behavior of a captive brave.

Champlain's effort to end the horrors of the stake is one of the few cases in which a French officer tried to interfere with Indian torture. After Braddock's defeat, the French garrison at Fort Duquesne calmly went about their ordinary military duties, while British captives were being burned to death within sight and hearing. Champlain was a chivalrous gentleman of different standards. He saved one other Iroquois prisoner from torture in 1610, after a skirmish on the Richelieu.

He left for France soon afterward, first sending a very youthful companion to live with the Indians of the interior, where no white man had yet penetrated, to learn the language, himself taking an Indian boy to spend the winter in France. He would thus have two interpreters, when he returned.

He was back in Canada by the beginning of March, 1611, and was soon in eager conference with the youngster he had sent to winter with the Indians. The lad "explained to me all that he had seen in the winter, and what he had learned from them"—not a word of which did Champlain ever trouble to write down. Not even the name of this youth is known, though he was the first white to penetrate so far into the lake country. What a tale he might have told!

As Champlain had now completely won the confidence of his Indian friends, they offered to show him their country and anything he might want to see there. Champlain hurried back to France, hoping to get a force of forty or fifty men for the proposed journey. When he returned in 1613, Champlain was met by a certain Nicolas de Vignau, who had in the meantime been living with the Indians of the interior. Quite unaware that Vignau was "the boldest liar that had been seen for a long time," Champlain was exalted by the man's tale that he had journeyed far into the interior and even to Hudson Bay. He rushed the good news back to Paris and himself started off up the St. Lawrence. The widening of the river called Lake St. Louis pleased him—"filled with beautiful large islands consisting of meadows only, where it is pleasant to hunt, deer and game being abundant.

There is also plenty of fish. The country surrounding it is full of big forests."

Having lost two Indians by drowning only a short time before, he observed the roaring rapids with trepidation: "We passed some small rapids by rowing, which cannot be done without sweating. It takes great skill to shoot these rapids and avoid the whirlpools and breakers which are in them, and the savages do this with a dexterity that cannot be surpassed, looking for side passages and the easiest places, which they recognize at a glance." Anyone who has watched a red canoeman coaxing his craft through tricky water will recognize the accuracy of the description. However adroit, the most skillful white canoeman is clumsy when compared to his red brother.

Champlain himself nearly drowned trying to drag a canoe through one of these rapids. He fell, was caught between two rocks (where it is very easy to be held under the water by the force of the current and drowned), and could not get the line loose from his wrist. Just as it seemed that his hand would be torn off, the plunging canoe floated into a backwater, and the strain eased.

Admiring picturesque islands and the Rideau Falls, noting vines and walnut trees, and groaning—as has every woodsman since—at the "amount of trouble caused by portages," he pushed on. Once he notes a root "which makes a crimson dye, with which the savages paint their faces"—the first mention of bloodroot *(S. canadensis),* one of the most beautiful of American wild flowers, though Champlain seems never to have noticed the blossom. Few explorers were much interested in such things.

At the Des Chats Rapids, rushing down with "a marvelous noise" through pine- and cedar-covered islands, the country became so wild that they had to cut down their duffle to an absolute minimum, abandoning reserve food and taking with them only "arms and lines, to afford us something to live on." Champlain carried three arquebuses— a useful way of getting in several shots before reloading the cumbrous weapons.

Wearily they paddled, with aching arms, through an area of burnt-over pinelands—the most depressing of all landscapes—suffering the tortures of muskeg mosquitoes, whose persistence was "so remarkable that it is impossible to give a description of it." Some modern writers say that mosquitoes were not really bad in North America until the white man cut down the forests, but the plaints of the early explorers hardly bear this out. Champlain himself remarks elsewhere that "it was wonderful how cruelly they persecuted us." On the Pembina River, a branch of the Winnipeg, Alexander Henry found mosquitoes "in such clouds as to prevent us from taking aim." One agonized victim called them "vexatious, glory-minded, musical winged, bold denizens of the shady forest." Along the Susquehanna River, a Moravian missionary complained: "Muschgetters tormented us all night," and in the wild swamps of primitive Florida, John Bartram groaned: "they bite sharp and sting like nettles." Father Sagard in the Huron country feared they might blind him. Strange to say, one hears very little of black-fly and "no-see-ums," probably because the early travelers lumped all insect pests together as mosquitoes.

The well-screened modern, protected by the constant war of his health department against the mosquito, can hardly appreciate the torments of the first travelers, unless he ventures into the muskegs which remain in modern wilderness. I have myself often looked up, in camp, under a good safe net, and counted three or four mosquitoes to the square inch, looking hungrily in at me; and it is still possible to find marshy islands where the deep 'cello tone of millions of mosquitoes —much deeper than the shrill note of one mosquito—can be heard a hundred yards or more away.

In spite of their sufferings, the early explorers did singularly little to protect themselves. The Illinois Indians along the Wabash slept on a framework of poles, lifted far enough above the earth floors of the lodges to let the smoke pass under them. They must have been half-strangled, but at least they escaped the insects.

Strange to say, none of the first explorers except Father Sagard seems to have thought of taking a mosquito net along. Not until 1727 does one hear of anything so sensible. The Jesuit, Father Poisson, after describing his torments on the lower Mississippi, remarks that one could escape them by sleeping under a strip of canvas, carefully tucked under the mattress, "and in these tombs, stifling with the heat, we are compelled to sleep." Though the Lewis and Clark expedition had "mosquito biers," its members sometimes suffered. The famous Indian baby that went all the way with the expedition was bitten till its whole face swelled and Lewis' Newfoundland dog was so bitten that he howled with pain. Even in the middle of the nineteenth century, the young German artist, Rudolph Friedrich Kurz, sketching along the Missouri depended entirely on smoke: "Unless one makes a Hades of one's room every evening with the smoke of sweet sage, one cannot possibly sleep at all." Kurz thought Indians were less troubled because the insects preferred "the blood of a white, unsmoked body."

Though accounts of later white life on the frontier abound in descriptions of "the shakes" and "the ague," one hears nothing, in these early days, of malaria. It is possibly true, therefore, that the malarial parasite had not yet been brought to America in the bloodstream of some infected white man; and though some of the American mosquito species must have been potential disease carriers, they were harmless (however annoying), because there were as yet no malarial parasites for them to carry.

Champlain's party finally reached Muskrat Lake, where a chief called Nibochis "was surprised that we had been able to pass the rapids and bad roads that it was necessary to traverse to reach them." Here, in 1867, was found a bronze astrolabe—an instrument now superseded by the sextant—which was probably dropped by Champlain himself on this very journey. At least, it is hard to think of anyone else who ever had occasion to carry an astrolabe to Muskrat Lake.

The next chief, Tessoüat on Lake Allumette, was the first to reveal the mendacity of De Vignau. Champlain now discovered that the man had never visited Hudson Bay nor even gone so far as Lake Nipissing. He had, in fact, spent the entire winter with Chief Tessoüat himself! Eventually, De Vignau admitted everything. He had lied to Champlain solely because he thought his tales would induce Champlain to bring him back to Canada.

In disgust, Champlain returned to his base and thence to France.

After various political vicissitudes, he returned to the Indian trading place at the Rapids of St. Louis in 1615, to find his red friends again begging for help against their Iroquois enemies. This time he traveled along the Ottawa River, regarding that landscape with disgust, instead of his usual enthusiasm for wild nature: "an unattractive country full of firs, birches and some oaks, a great many rocks." The Indians did not like it either and had left the area almost uninhabited.

"It is true that God seems to have wanted to give to these frightful desert regions something in its season to serve for the refreshment of man." In this case, God's gift was the blueberry, about which—although he never knew what a really good Yankee cook could do in the way of blueberry muffins or pies—Champlain was appropriately enthusiastic: "a small fruit very good to eat," which, with other berries, "the inhabitants dry for their winter as we do prunes in France for Lent." He was soon to find that the blueberry could, on occasion, be an almost indispensable wilderness food as well as a delicious one.

Spending only two days with the Indians on Lake Nipissing, the party went on to Georgian Bay, on Lake Huron. Food ran short, and they might have gone hungry save for the abundance of blueberries and wild raspberries—the latter probably identical with the purple-flowering raspberry which still grows along American lanes and byways. On Lake Huron Champlain met for the first time Indians carrying buffalo-hide shields, though he does not seem to have seen the buffalo themselves. Looking out over Lake Huron and questioning his Indians about it, Champlain named it "The Fresh Sea." He gives its length as 750 miles instead of 250—probably because he gathered from the Indians the idea that Lakes Huron and Superior were one.

Whites and Indians together soon reached Carhagouha, a Huron village in modern Tiny Township, near La Fontaine, Ontario, with triple palisades thirty-five feet high; and here, finding that the warriors he was to accompany had not yet assembled, went on to the village of Cahiagué, near modern Orillia, the principal Huron village in Ontario, which had two hundred of the long, bark cabins used both by the Hurons and the Iroquois.

Corn, squash, sunflowers, vines, plums, raspberries, strawberries, and nuts grew everywhere. There were "little wild apples"—probably the American crab—and "a kind of fruit which has the form and color of small lemons, about the size of an egg. The plant that bears it is two and a half feet tall and has three or four leaves, at the most, of the form of the fig-leaf, and each plant bears only two apples."

Quite obviously Champlain is here describing, with fair accuracy, the common May apple, which grows so thickly (where it grows at all), and with such exquisite white flowers, that it forces itself on the attention of explorers. A good many of them mention it. Some Indians ate it and one white man—an optimist if there ever was one—even thought it tasted "like apricocks." One does not hear much of its use as food, however. The Indians may have agreed with the Harvard botanist, Asa Gray, who describes it as "slightly acid, mawkish, eaten by pigs and boys."

Champlain thought the whole country "very beautiful and attractive. Along the river bank it seemed as if the trees had been planted there in most places for pleasure." Other Frenchmen passing in 1673 along the banks of the St. Lawrence as they approached Lake Ontario thought this "the most agreeable country in the world, the river dotted with islands on which were nothing but oaks and *bois francs* of excellent height. The shores, too, both North and South are no less beautiful, the woods very clear and tall and forming *futtayes* like the finest forests in France. The two sides of the river are nothing but prairies, with good grass, in which are beautiful flowers infinite in number. From Lake St. Francis to the rapids there is no more agreeable country in the world than this would be, if it were once cleared."

Champlain saw "many cranes, as white as swans," which must have been either little blue herons—almost pure white when young—or egrets ranging north from Florida as, to the surprise of ornithologists, they did again in 1948.

Rambling idly about the forests as he waited for the war party to get ready, Champlain noted abundant oaks, elms, and beeches, interspersed with whole "forests of firs, which are the common resort of partridges and rabbits." The soil seemed to him a little sandy, but he could see that it grew good corn for the Indians. Lakes Couchiching and Simcoe yielded plenty of fish, which the Indians caught in nets and weirs and cured for the winter. Bear and stags were driven along by a line of four or five hundred Indian beaters until they could be forced out upon points projecting into the river, where the line of hunters closed in upon them while other hunters in canoes killed those that tried to escape by swimming. The Indians were amazed to see what Champlain's arquebus could do as a sporting arm; but one warrior clumsily managed to get himself shot and had to be pacified with a present.

Hunting as they went, Champlain and the war party worked along the north shore of Lake Ontario, crossing at the eastern end, which is the source of the St. Lawrence. As they were now approaching the western edges of Iroquois territory, they hid their canoes and started cautiously forward into western New York, on foot. It was "very agreeable and beautiful country crossed by several little brooks and two small rivers which empty into this lake; and a great many ponds and meadows, where there were an unlimited amount of game, many vines, and beautiful woods, and a great number of chestnut trees, of which the fruit was still in the burr." Champlain tasted them. The nuts were small, he thought, in comparison to the large European chestnut but, like De Soto's Spaniards, he was pleased by the new flavor, which he thought "good." The American chestnut is—or was, in the days before the blight destroyed all chestnut trees—far sweeter than its European congener. The Indians did a lively business selling chestnuts to the settlers in New England, where John Josselyn called the nuts "very sweet in taste."

Hearing that there was a tribe to the south of the Iroquois who were friendly to his Hurons, Champlain sent his daring lieutenant, Étienne Brulé, with a message asking these unknown Indians—apparently Susquehannocks or Andastes—to join him with five hundred warriors. It was a desperate mission, for Brulé would have to move straight through Iroquois country, emerging somewhere near the New York-Pennsylvania border, on the headwaters of the Susquehanna.

Meantime, Champlain moved overland across New York until on October 9, 1615 his Hurons captured three Iroquois men, four squaws, three boys, and a girl—all out fishing. Champlain was horrified when the Hurons seized one of the women and cut off her finger. Actually, this was merely a bit of Huron playfulness, intended to give the prisoner a slight foretaste of the real tortures that lay ahead. When the humane Champlain protested, the Huron chief—willing to humor his white friend's queer ideas—replied that this was no more than the Iroquois did to Hurons. However, since Champlain objected, he would allow nothing more to be done to the women, "but he certainly would to the men." Champlain, realizing that this was the limit of Huron concession, asked for no more.

On October 10, they reached the Iroquois fort—probably located at Fenner, Madison County, New York, and certainly somewhere in that vicinity. As they heard the report of the arquebus and the whistle of the bullets, the Iroquois scuttled for the shelter of their palisades, carrying their dead and wounded along to save them the disgrace of being scalped. However, the five hundred allied warriors for whom Brulé had been sent, never arrived, and after the first skirmish the assailing Hurons withdrew "about a cannon shot out of sight of the enemy."

Champlain finally talked them into building "mantelets"—wood shields long used in European warfare, which could be pushed forward to protect advancing troops—and a "cavalier," or large, moveable platform with walls all around it, built high enough to overlook the Iroquois palisades. Within four hours, everything was ready. Two hundred brawny warriors pushed forward the cavalier, with four arquebusiers firing from its top. This soon drove the Iroquois warriors off the platforms used for shooting arrows from inside the palisades. But the Hurons got excited, left the protection of their mantelets, started shooting uselessly into the logs of the fort, and set fire to them at the wrong place, so that the wind carried the flames away.

"They must be excused," wrote the disgusted veteran of the wars of Henry IV, tolerantly, "for they are not soldiers and, besides, they do not want any discipline or correction, and only do what seems good to them."

Champlain yelled orders till he was "like to burst my head with shouting"—he had apparently learned a little Huron—but it was quite impossible to get the excited redskins to carry out his plan of attack. Taking advantage of this confusion, the Iroquois poured water—which was always kept standing inside the palisades—into the wooden troughs of their fire defense system. It gushed out over the blaze that had been kindled against the palisades "in such abundance that one would have said that it was brooks which flowed through their spouts; so much that in less than no time the fire was all out." Champlain was again wounded by arrows, this time severely and with two hits.

Before long, the Hurons had had enough. Like most Indians, they had no taste for siege warfare. Though the wind was favorable, they refused even to try to fire the Iroquois palisades again, while they waited in vain for the expected five hundred re-enforcements. When they got the worst of it in small skirmishes outside the palisades, Champlain and his men always had to go to the rescue with arquebuses, and the Iroquois always withdrew at sight of these dreaded weapons, though with much objurgation. The white men, they yelled, ought to keep out of Indian quarrels.

The Hurons finally retreated, carrying in improvised baskets their wounded, including Champlain, who could not even stand on his wounded knee. The only good thing he could say for Huron tactics was that "they make a retreat with great security, putting all the wounded and aged in the centre, with well-armed men in front, on the wings and at the rear, and they keep up this arrangement until they are in a safe place."

They found their canoes undisturbed and, having put enough space between themselves and the Iroquois, paused to hunt. Champlain, who had been carried for days, trussed up like an infant, helpless, on the back of a sturdy warrior, was doubtless glad to get the relative freedom of a canoe-bottom. As deer were not to be found, they lived on geese, "swans," white cranes, ducks, small birds, "trout and pike of immense size."

Meantime, the Indians set to work to get some venison. They built a stockade in the form of a triangle, open at the base and 1,500 paces on the side, its apex opening into a small, enclosed yard. Just at dawn, a line of beaters began driving deer into the stockade, striking sticks together and howling like wolves. Forced into the little yard at the apex of the triangle, the deer were easily killed. Hunting thus, every other day for thirty-eight days, the war party killed 120 deer. Champlain was astounded to find that these Indians refused to roast any of the meat or let any fat or bones fall into the fire. He was encountering for the first time the varied superstitions about the disposal of game, especially the bones.

What you did with the bones, both of fish and game, determined success in future hunts, though some free-thinkers daringly asserted that it did not matter much what you did with the vertebrae, so long as the other bones were treated respectfully. Indians along the Saguenay never let their dogs gnaw the bones of game animals, since if they did they would never kill any more game. It must have been hard on the dogs.

The Montagnais kept from the dogs the bones of animals taken with nets, including birds. As for beaver, it was always best to throw their bones into the river, because the souls of dead beaver invariably visited the camp of the men who had killed them, to see what had been done with their bones. If they found the dogs gnawing them, they went to tell the other beavers of the outrage. "But they are very glad to have their bones thrown into the fire, or into a river; especially the trap which has caught them is glad of this."

When a skeptical Jesuit ventured to question these well-known facts, he was crushed with the rejoinder: "You don't know how to catch beavers yourself, and yet you presume to talk about it." Fish, the Hurons agreed, objected to having their bones burned, but would come willingly to the nets if they were reassured on this point. None of this was really much more foolish than the beliefs of a good many modern hunters and fishermen.

Eager though he now was to get back to the French settlements, Champlain had to settle down to life with the Indians for some weeks. In December he set out for the country of the Petun, or Tobacco Nation, who lived southwest of the Hurons in what are today Dufferin and Gay counties. Unused to travel on snowshoes with his duffle dragged on a birch toboggan, Champlain suffered severely from the Canadian winter, even though his personal load weighed only twenty pounds, while the Indians carried a hundred. A thaw added to their troubles, as they went splashing through evergreen woods, never knowing when they would break through ice or packed snow. Tangles of fallen trees, always common in the North American forests, made snowshoeing difficult and blocked their toboggans. But in spite of his troubles Champlain was pleased by the wooded country, "full of hills and little fields, which make the landscape pleasant."

The Petun Indians were friendly, as were the Ottawa, whom he next visited. "They are the cleanest savages in their households that I have seen, and they work the most industriously at various patterns of mats, which are their Turkish rugs."

From tribe to tribe he passed, on the best of terms with all Indians except the Iroquois, and so came to Montreal and to the end of his career in exploration. He was captured when English raiders seized Montreal, returned to France, and came back at last after Canada had been restored to France, as governor, in 1633. He died at Montreal on Christmas Day, 1635.

IX

"We Were Caesars"

IN SPITE OF Champlain's adventures, the Iroquois country in New York State was still largely unknown. Champlain had barely approached its eastern borders and then, traveling west through Canada, had penetrated only a little way from the west. The next advance in French exploration was made by the daring Canadian, Pierre Esprit Radisson, who first explored central New York and then, with his brother-in-law, penetrated far into the Great Lakes district and probably beyond the Mississippi.

Toward the end of his life, Radisson wrote down his own story—wrote it in some of the wildest syntax that has ever masqueraded as English. He had had little formal education to begin with, and probably did not write very good French. He had gathered his earliest information largely in Mohawk, or in the related Iroquoian dialects which anyone who spoke Mohawk could understand. During his later adventures Radisson was among middle western tribes, speaking various languages, which he had to pick up as best he could. All might yet have been well had he been content to tell his tale in his native French, though he sat down to write with a wild jumble of native names and half-understood native languages in his head. But, being in English service when he set down his story, he insisted on writing English—another language that he did not understand very well.

The literary results are somewhat startling; but the story is important, and the wild, free flavor of Radisson's style is in itself amusing. Most of the time—though not, by any means, always—the reader can see what he means. At other times the reader can guess, with some hope of correctness. In other passages, there is no hope at all.

Captured by the Mohawks, Radisson had the good luck to be adopted by a famous and extremely good-natured warrior, whose whole family became devoted to their new white kinsman. He thus had a unique opportunity to see the still unspoiled way of Iroquois life in eastern New York and eventually left a full account of what he had seen.

Radisson, then sixteen, was captured in the spring of 1652. He had gone out from the fortified frontier settlement of Three Rivers, then his home, to hunt ducks with two French companions. After going about a mile, the trio met a white herdsman, who warned them to keep away from the hills, where he had seen "a multitude of people which rose up as it weare of a sudaine from of the Earth." These were Iroquois, who constantly lurked about the French settlements, hoping to scalp just such incautious wanderers from the fort as the three young men. When, after killing a few ducks, the others wanted to return, Radisson recklessly went on alone.

Loaded with three geese, ten ducks, crane, and some teal, he finally started home. Alarmed by a sudden sound in the woods—not even an Indian can move quite so silently as some writers aver—he reprimed one pistol, searched the woods without seeing anything suspicious, and went on.

Just as he was about to fire at some more ducks, he stumbled upon the bodies of his two companions, naked, one with three bullet and two tomahawk wounds, the other with several stabs and the marks of the tomahawk. In his excitement, says Radisson, "my nose begun'd to bleed, wch made me afraid of my life."

Making for the river, he saw twenty or thirty heads bobbing up out of some long grass. Dropping a bullet on top of the light birdshot already in his fowling piece, he suddenly found himself surrounded by Iroquois, rising on all sides—from the grass, the rushes by the river, and the bushes. He got in one shot from his fowling piece and one from his pistol before he was seized and dragged off by the Iroquois, "laughing and howling like so many wolves." Once they had Radisson safely in the woods, they showed him "the two heads all bloody." Presumably this means scalps, which the French woodsmen often described as "têtes." One of the most dismal experiences of Indian captivity was recognizing the scalps of your family or friends. Kentucky prisoners, for example, recognized the scalp of Colonel Richard Callaway, one of Daniel Boone's associates, "by the long black and gray mixed hair," when Shawnee warriors brought it gleefully into camp.

Radisson's life was saved by his boldness, which made a good impression on the Iroquois from the start; and this impression he confirmed a few days later when, prisoner though he was, he gave a terrific pummelling to a young warrior who insulted him. Though stripped naked and tied up for some time after his capture, he was soon given his clothes again and fed "meat half boyled, mingling some yellowish meale in the broath of that infected stinking meate."

Indians never worried much over infected meat, ptomaines, and food poisoning. Like Europeans of the same period, they had no refrigeration, and where white men tried to forget the ill savor of their meat by drowning it in spices, the Indians simply learned to like it that way.

What Radisson got was just a war party's usual emergency ration. The fact that game killed some time before was rather "high" did not disturb the warriors in the least; but, seeing that Radisson could barely force himself to swallow it, they made a new mess, not much better, some of which he managed to eat. Meantime, they combed and greased his hair, painted his face red and gave him a mirror to admire the results. As they started their return journey—passing "300 wild Cows together" as well as moose, beaver, and "an infinit of fowls"— the Iroquois gave him more and more liberty, occasionally remarking "Chagon!" (Cheer up!), giving him a knife, and even letting him shoot at a stag.

As usual, Radisson is not very clear as to the route followed, beyond saying that they went down the Richelieu River. Probably they followed Champlain's route to Ticonderoga and then went down Lake George and over to the Hudson. As they approached the Mohawk villages, twenty squaws appeared, bringing dry fish and corn, who, after the warriors had eaten, loaded themselves "like mules wth our baggage."

In spite of all their friendliness, as they entered the village, the Iroquois prepared to make him run the gantlet. There was no special hostility in this. It was as a warrior once explained, "a sort of how do do," besides being a convenient and entertaining way of seeing which prisoners were sturdy enough to be worth adopting. Daniel Boone, surrendering to Blackfish, war chief of the Shawnees, in 1778 stipulated that his men were not to run the gantlet but forgot to include himself in the agreement. When Boone butted down with his head a Shawnee warrior who stepped into his path to get in an especially hard knock, the woods rang with Shawnee laughter, and he was then enthusiastically welcomed into the tribe, and adopted by Blackfish, himself.

As Radisson, already stripped for the ordeal, sat looking apprehensively at "women and men and children wth staves and in array," prepared to belabor him, an old squaw came up and threw a covering around him, while the young men with her led him away. Taken to their cabin he was fed roast corn, clothed, and had his hair greased and combed once more. Thereafter, he lived the life of a carefree young warrior: "I tooke all the pleasures imaginable, having a small peece at my command, shooting partriges and squerells, playing most part of the day wth my companions." The two daughters of the lodge —"wch weare tolerable among such people"—dutifully greased and combed his hair each morning, calling him by the name of their dead brother, "Orimha" (Stone), and carried his hunter's "bundle," or pack, for him when he started on a hunting trip. The new name happened to correspond with his Christian name, Pierre.

Hunting with three Mohawk companions, Orimha found game so plentiful in eastern New York that in a single day they killed three bears, a beaver, and a stag. When they had to cross a wide stream, the skilled red woodsmen improvised a canoe in two hours.

All would have gone well, had they not met an Algonquin prisoner, also from the vicinity of Three Rivers, who was by this time trusted to go hunting alone. Speaking Algonquin, a radically different language which the Iroquois could not understand, this man persuaded Radisson to help him tomahawk the three hunters, as they lay sleeping that night. Radisson, "loathsome to do them mischief y^t never did me any," nevertheless quieted his conscience by reflecting that "they weare mortall ennemys to my country, that had cutt the throats of so many of my relations, burned and murdered them." In the night, he and the Algonquin killed the three sleeping hunters and escaped to the St. Lawrence. Here, chased by lurking Iroquois, they threw overboard the incriminating scalps, but they floated long enough for the pursuing Iroquois canoes to pick them out of the water.

The Algonquin having been killed, Radisson was dragged back to his village with other prisoners. His story that the dead Algonquin was responsible for the murders and he himself had been the Algonquin's prisoner was not very convincing, and with the other captives he was put to torture. This time he had to run the gantlet, beaten with "staves, hand Irons, heelskins wherein they putt half a score bullets," while other Iroquois belabored him with fire brands and rods of thorn. His Iroquois father and mother, much distressed, finally rescued their erring but still beloved son and took him to their bark cabin.

The Indian father, torn between wrath and affection rebuked his wandering boy. "You senseless," he cried, "thou was my son, and thou rendered thyselfe enemy, thou lovest not thy mother, nor thy father that gave thee life, and thou notwthstanding will kill me. Bee merry; Conharrasan [a sister] give him to eate." It is a wonder that the wording is not even more mixed up than it is, since the rebuke was delivered in mixed Iroquois and Huron, neither of which the French-speaking Radisson understood much better than the English in which he later tried to write.

His Mohawk family were determined to save him. Perhaps they even believed his story that it was the Algonquin alone who had killed the sleeping hunters by the campfire; but others of the tribe were not so credulous. For the third time Radisson was taken back to the scaffold and thereby enabled to write a unique account of Indian torture from personal experience, a tale few survived to tell:

"That day they pluck^t 4 nailes out of my fingers, and made me sing, though I had no mind att that time. I became speechlesse oftentimes; then they gave me watter wherin they boyled a certain herbe that the gunsmiths use to pollish their armes. That liquour brought me to my

speech againe. The night being come they made me come downe
all naked as I was, & brought to a strang Cottage. I wished heartily it
had ben that of my parents. Being come, they tyed me to a poast,
where I stayed a full houre w^{th}out ye least molestation.

"A woman came there wth her boy, inticed him to cutt off one of
my fingers wth a flint stoan. The boy was not 4 yeares old. This [boy]
takes my finger and begins to worke, but in vaine, because he had not
the strength to breake my fingers. So my poore finger escaped, having no other hurt don to it but the flesh cutt round about it. . . .

"The next morning I was brought back againe to the scaffold, where
there were company enough. They made me sing a new, but my
mother came there and made [me] hould my peace, bidding me be
cheerfull and that I should not die. Shee brought mee some meate.
Her coming comforted me much, but that did not last long; ffor heare
comes severall old people, one of which being on the scaffold, satt him
down by me, houlding in his mouth a pewter pipe burning, tooke my
thumb and putt it on the burning tobacco, and so smoaked 3 pipes
one after another, wch made my thumb swell, and the nayle and flesh
became as coales."

Still on his scaffold, he watched several others, including a pregnant
Frenchwoman, burned alive. One Mohawk, to show his courage,
tied his own leg to Radisson's and thrust a burning brand between
them. As he had failed to observe that it was burning hard on his
side and scarcely at all on Radisson's, the torturer injured himself severely without doing much additional damage to the prisoner.

Radisson was then taken down and brought before the village council with other prisoners. In despair, he watched while one woman and
two little children were killed and thrown outside; but the pleas of
his Mohawk father, mother, and brother saved him for the second
time. After he had been nursed back to health, he managed to escape
to the Dutch settlement at Albany, whence he was sent to France.

Most men would by this time have had enough of life beyond the
frontier; but Radisson was of the breed to whom something in the
wilderness calls. He was one of those who had to go and see. There
were other and stronger motives among most of the early explorers,
but in men like Radisson and Champlain this one was dominant. The

Jesuit fathers, often loathing wilderness life, were led by the desire to snatch Indian souls from damnation. Everyone else wanted to make money from the fur trade—a consideration to which neither Radisson nor Champlain was wholly indifferent, though it was always secondary. There was also the hope of gain and glory won through extension of the French dominions—usually a vain hope, for though the Most Christian King cheerfully accepted all his heroic explorers could do for him, his rewards, whether in cash, titles, or decorations, were pitifully thin. But there was always something more.

It was the lure of the great woods, the wild, free life, the strange, new peoples, the satisfaction of going where no white man had been, the hunt, still lakes at dawn, new plants, strange animals, the silent overarching trees, the spice of danger. For these unreasonable causes— incomprehensible to smug and thrifty townsmen, safe at home—the coureurs de bois, like the British, American, and Spanish explorers, risked their lives and salted North America with their bones for three centuries, until at last they had seen it all, there was no more left to explore, and the whole continent was white man's country at last.

Of these was Radisson. Reaching France early in 1654, he was off to Canada again a few months later. Another man might have been content in the French settlements along the St. Lawrence. Not Radisson. There is little doubt that he and his brother-in-law, Médard Chouart, Sieur des Groseilliers, were the two young Frenchmen who, in 1654, traveled more than five hundred leagues to Green Bay on Lake Superior, and into Wisconsin, "in little Gondolas of bark." They found that Indians speaking the Huron-Iroquois language extended far to the south of the Lakes, those speaking the various Algonkian languages—Cree, Ojibway, Ottawa—equally far north. In those northern lands there were "many Lakes which might well be called freshwater Seas, the great Lake of the Hurons, and another near it, being as large as the Caspian Sea." The second lake was probably not Lake Superior, which was then considered part of Lake Huron, but Lake Winnipeg, far to the northwest, half way across the Continent. The two young explorers at least knew of a lake called "Ouinipeg, that is, 'stinking water'" and of the Indians unfortunately called "Puants" (Stinkards) because they lived on its shores. They had also learned of the Nadeoesiouek (Sioux), who had forty villages, the Crees, who wandered from the Lakes to the "North Sea," and other tribes.

The two young men, whoever they were, returned in triumph in 1656, with an Indian fleet of fifty canoes, "propelled by five hundred arms, and guided by as many eyes, most of which had never seen the great wooden canoes of the French,—that is to say their Ships." These strange Indians, from various tribes around the Great Lakes, "asked for some Frenchmen, to go and pass the winter in their Country," and for Jesuit missionaries.

They had to wait. The Jesuit fathers were already starting out in another direction—into the wilderness near Syracuse, New York, where the hostile Iroquois were showing signs of friendship at last. They had asked for Frenchmen to live among them, and an advance party had already gone to build a fort.

A second party was to follow. Radisson, after twice escaping from the Iroquois, joined up to go back into their power again with the missionary priests. Why, with all North America still to explore, he chose the part most dangerous to himself, there is no explaining. The expedition was going into new country, and that was usually enough for Radisson. He hoped for safety, so long as he was among the Onondagas, not the Mohawks who had adopted him. He would not be recognized unless a visiting Mohawk from his own village passed that way—a chance he would have to take.

With an Iroquois escort, they approached the American boundary by way of that widening of the St. Lawrence known as Lake St. Francis—"a delightfull & beautifull country"—shooting deer, "auriniack" (moose) and waterfowl as they went. As for the fish, wrote Radisson, "what a thing it is to see them in the bottom of the watter, & take it biting the hooke or lancing it wth lance, or cramp iron."

It turned out to be a desperate and bloody journey. The Iroquois, after making peace with the French and with their Huron allies, had persuaded a group of trusting Hurons to return with them and settle in Iroquois country. On the way something happened to change the minds of the Iroquois. Perhaps some incident of the trail irritated them. More likely, they had just changed their fickle, aboriginal minds and felt like killing somebody. At any rate, they murdered the Huron men, sparing only the squaws and one old man.

Placidly, the Iroquois put a kettle on the fire for supper and called a council. The priest was summoned to hear what Radisson calls "their wild reasons." Some Iroquois had been drowned by accident. It was necessary to revenge that upon the Hurons! Further, they wished "to certifie the ffrench of their good will." There was nothing for the horrified white men to do but sit down with the murderers for supper, hoping for the best and keeping their arms handy.

In spite of everything, Radisson was enchanted by the game they saw as they passed into New York State. Deer were so plentiful that the party hunted as much for sport as for food. Once, driving a deer into the water they paddled up beside it and hung a bell to its neck. "What a sporte to see ye rest flye from that y^t had y^t bell!"

Once, at dusk an incredible number of bears passed the camp—"a very remarquable thing. There comes out of a vast forest a multitude of bears, 300 att least together, making a horrid noise, breaking small trees, throwing the rocks downe by the watter side." The creatures paid no attention to shots and, in the gathering dark, no one cared to leave camp to investigate, since it "frightened us that they slighted our shooting." Radisson doubtless exaggerated the number of bears—the woodsman today usually sees a single black bear and counts himself fortunate to see even that—but the Iroquois agreed that "they never heard their father speake of so many together."

Although modern zoologists scoff at this tale (which clearly needs some toning down), it is not so utterly incredible as is sometimes asserted. Bears in primitive America were not always solitary. Alexander Henry, the Younger, the eighteenth century explorer and trader, speaks of seeing seven drinking at the same time and found their dung as thick as buffalo chips. Lewis and Clark found grizzlies together, and tourists still see a good many in company in the Yellowstone. Writers who want to subtract 299 bears from Radisson's figure are going too far.

It is just possible that this curious assemblage was an incident of the mating season. In New England, at about the same time, John Josselyn remarked that when in rut, the black bears would "walk the

Country twenty, thirty, forty in a company, making a hideous noise with roaring, which you may hear a mile or two." Nothing of the sort occurs today, perhaps because there are not so many bears or because they have grown timid.

As Radisson's party moved toward Lake Ontario, the St. Lawrence became "a beautifull river, wide one league and a halfe"—with no portages for stretches of fifty or sixty miles at a time. An Indian shot an eagle for its feathers. Ospreys and "other birds"—probably kingfishers and herons—were snatching fish from the river. The canoemen could kill salmon with clubs and they hauled a sturgeon up from six fathoms. The water was so clear that, even at five fathoms, bottom could be clearly seen, with fishes moving above it. The travelers caught eels and killed "a great bigg and fatt beare." A returning Mohawk war party who recognized Radisson, showed no resentment at his escape, asking only "when should I visit my friends." Soon, said Radisson diplomatically, and sent gifts to his Mohawk family.

Lake Ontario being deceptively calm, Radisson ventured too far out and was caught in a storm. The rest landed but Radisson rode it out, with a bag of corn hanging in the water to steady the pitching bow of his canoe, and his gunwales "5 fingers or lesse" above the tossing water.

As they approached the village of Onondaga, passing along the Oswego River and Lake Onondaga, Radisson thought the central New York country around Syracuse "a most pleasant country, very fruitfull." It was "smooth like a boord, a matter of some 3 or 4 leagues about. Severall fields of all sides of Indian corne, severall of french tournaps, full of chestnutts and oakes of accorns, wth thousand such like fruit in abundance." The wild fowl were everywhere. "Ringdoves," that is, the now-extinct passenger pigeon, were "in such a number that in a nett 15 or 1600 att once might be taken. So this was not a wild country to our imagination, but plentyfull in everything."

The Jesuits have left a further description of the same area. The village of Onondaga, which was moved every few years as the soil wore out or the filth and vermin became intolerable, was then south of Manlius, New York. It was not unlike the Huron village at Hochelaga, which Cartier described, or the Iroquois village that Champlain had seen—a palisade, a fortified gate, inside the "long houses" of bark, primitive apartment houses, in which dwelt many families.

The French were already established in a fort of their own, some miles distant from the village and not very far from Syracuse, a district which one father thought would be "one of the most commodious and most agreeable dwelling places in the world, without excepting even the levee of the River Loire, if its inhabitants were as polished." Plums and grapes grew there and other fruits "which excel ours in beauty, fragrance, and taste." Heroic devotees though they were, the Jesuit fathers were also Frenchmen, who, even in the wilderness of central New York, never quite lost their Gallic interest in good food. Among the fruits were "stoneless cherries," called *atoka*—in other words, cranberries. There were also fruits "of the color and size of an apricot, whose blossom is like that of the white lily, and which smell and taste like the citron." This was the May apple again, which Champlain and others had already seen. There were also different apples as large as a goose egg—the paw-paw—delicate in flavor, with a sweet smell, and a wonderful tree called "the universal plant"— which is quite plainly common sassafras. Its pounded leaves would heal all wounds. Its leaves had "the shape of a lily as depicted in heraldry." Its roots had the odor of laurel and gave dyes of various colors.

The salt springs yielded brine so strong that they were surrounded with a crust of crystals. The water itself was a brine strong enough to salt and season meat. There were magnesium and sulphur springs. At the salt springs the passenger pigeons gathered—you could take seven hundred of them in a single morning. A still more wonderful spring had water which ignited; and toward the country of the Cat Indians was "heavy & thick water" which burned like brandy, bursting into "bubbles of flame" when fire touched it. The Indians used it to oil their hair and bodies. Some of this flame was sulphureted hydrogen. The oil was a petroleum leakage—the once-famous "Seneca oil." From it must have come the "bituminous flame" which the Indians— spearing fish by night—used to make torches for the bows of their canoes.

A few years later, in 1669, Father de Galinée gave a better description of "une fontaine extraordinaire," which may have been the same oil spring. "Bursting out of a high rock, it forms a little rivulet. The water is very clear but has a bad odor, like that of Paris mud when one stirs it with the foot under the water." Someone thrust in a torch and "instantly that water took fire like brandy and would not go out till it rained." Father de Galinée was mightily mystified.

Matters went so ill in this earthly paradise, however, that at length, finding the Onondaga increasingly unfriendly, the handful of Frenchmen decided on flight, while there was still time. They made a great feast for the Indians—one of the "eat all feasts," at which it was a point of honor for the guests to swallow every morsel set before them. While the Indians were sleeping off the orgy—some astute Frenchman may have thoughtfully added a touch of laudanum to the food, as later traders often did when their red customers grew obstreperous—the French slipped silently down the river. A hog tied to a bell made noise enough inside the fort to convince the Indians that the white men were still there. It was a week before their departure was discovered.

After about a month safely back in the Canadian settlements, Radisson was again eager to "travel and see countries." He joined his brother-in-law, Des Groseilliers, who had already been on Lake Huron, and who was now just starting "to discover the great lakes that they heard the wild men speak off." These were not necessarily the Great Lakes as we know them. Radisson defines them very obscurely as "the Great and filthy Lake of the Hurrons, Upper Sea of the East, and Bay of the North"—the latter, perhaps, Hudson Bay, into which the innumerable lakes, west of Superior, drain.

With them were going two priests, "to convert some of those foraigners of the remotest country." With them also were going a mixed group of about 140, part white, part Indian, hoping for profit from furs. Radisson called this, for reasons no one has ever been able to guess, "the Auxoticiat voyage."

Up the now-familiar St. Lawrence they went. Radisson began to survey his new associates dubiously. Canoemen ought to keep quiet and they ought to keep together. These fellows let their canoes straggle for six or eight miles along the river, landing casually to kill game. Radisson knew that Iroquois war parties were pretty sure to be lurking somewhere along the St. Lawrence or the Ottawa River, on the lookout for just such incautious human prey. What did these amateurs know about the big woods or the dangers of wilderness rivers? Some of them could not even swim.

It began to seem to Radisson that these people might better have stayed home. They seemed the type that is happier "when one sees his owne chimney smoak, or when we can kiss our owne wives or kisse our neighbour's wife wth ease and delight." Did they realize the hardships they were approaching? "It is a strange thing when victualls are wanting, worke whole nights & dayes, lye downe on the bare ground, & not allwayes that hap, the breech in the watter, the feare in the buttocks, to have the belly empty, the wearinesse in the bones, and drowsinesse of ye body by the bad weather that you are to suffer, having nothing to keepe you from such calamity."

That kind of toil was some time in the future but the Iroquois danger was immediate. Radisson and his brother-in-law warned the greenhorns and were laughed at for their pains. These men had never stood the torture, watched the slaughter of the helpless, hidden with a red war party while they waited their chance to destroy a doomed village. "They laughed at us, saying we weare women; that the Iroquois durst not sett on them."

The attack came, of course. Thirteen men were killed before the Iroquois were beaten off. After the battle, the dismayed greenhorns started home. Radisson and Groseilliers went on with the Indians, determined to "finish that voyage or die by the way."

And die, they very nearly did. Food, except for an occasional bear, ran short. Swimming in the river, the bears were easily killed and when caught on islands the Indians first frightened them into the river, then killed them swimming. But there were not many bears. The travelers boiled some berries, not yet ripe, and gathered that last resort of the voyageur, tripe de roches, which they mixed with some fish.

Now, tripe de roches is the most nauseating food known to man; but it has the advantage of growing thickly on every rock along all the northern lakes, so that the traveler, even when game and fish both fail him, can never quite starve. It is a lichen, which looks enough like bits of tripe to justify its name. Boiled, it turns into a viscid mess, something like glue, with a bad taste and worse smell, whose sole advantage is that it is slimy enough to go down quickly. The Indians called it *windigo wakon*—which shows their opinion of this dubious vegetable, for a windigo is a horrible woods spirit so mad with hunger that it has already eaten off its own lips! "Like starch, black and clammie & easily to be swallowed," says Radisson, adding dolefully, "I think if any bird had lighted upon the excrements of ye said stuff, they had stuck^t to it as if it weare glue." Later wilderness travelers, who also had to eat tripes de roche or starve, were even less enthusiastic. Boiled down to a mucilage about as thick as white of egg, Alexander Henry, the Younger, found it "bitter and disagreeable," though a "hearty meal." There was doubt even about that. Father Ménard and his party at Keweenaw Bay in 1660–1661, thought the nauseous mess was "feeding their imagination more than their bodies." Father Sebastian Rale, after trying tripes de roche both boiled and roasted, decided they were better roasted—that is, they were "less distasteful."

Probably the only human being who ever was enthusiastic about the stuff was a young squaw on one of Alexander Henry's expeditions. Food ran short, hunting was bad, and her red compatriots decided that they would have to use the lady as an emergency ration. Just at that moment they found enough tripes de roche to make cannibalism unnecessary, and the squaw survived.

As Radisson and Groseilliers went on up the Ottawa River, the going grew harder. "The most parts there abouts is so sterill that there is nothing to be seen but rocks & sand, & on the high wayes [paths or portages] but deale trees that grow most miraculously, for that earth is not to be seene that can nourish the root, & most of them trees are very bigg & high." Shoes and leggings gave out, and there was no chance to replace them till they could kill moose or deer to get leather. The sixty portages they had to cover were overgrown so that "feet & thighs & leggs weare scraped wth thorns, in a heape of blood."

It was an immense relief when the canoes shot out into the chill, clear waters of Lake Nipissing (Lac des Castors), where they opened a cache that Indians of their party had left on the way down. They killed bear and deer.

The lake was full of fish, "seene in the water so cleare as christiall." Those who have never looked deep into an unspoiled wilderness lake, lying in a rock basin without swamps, within the deep woods, will think Radisson's comparison merely conventional. In fact, the word "crystal" is literal. This was pure rain water, fallen through dustless woodland air upon bare, clean rock or upon a forest floor, where every bit of soil was firmly held by roots, so that the falling rain, as it ran off, took scarcely a particle of earth with it. Such water produces what are still called "clearwater lakes," like rocky basins of distilled water. They are especially clear when they are so cold that micro-organisms cannot grow to cloud the water. Through twenty feet of such water in sunlight, you can see pebbles on the bottom or moving fishes, as if they swam in liquid nothing, the pure, clear water being all but invisible. When the wind is still and these lakes are smooth, they take the color of the sky, so that the canoes seem to be moving through the air itself. Once it has flowed through warm and sluggish muskeg swamps, the clear water loses this quality—changing the flavor of some fish—and flows at last into the lower lakes as the ordinary dull lake water that is all most white men travel far enough to see.

Where there were so many fish, as Radisson found, there were certain to be otters, playful creatures so swift that they could catch a fish by swimming under water. Despite their priceless coats of soft brown fur, they had been little hunted; and so many were about that Radisson suggested "all gathered to hinder our passage." The animals did delay the Frenchmen, for their Indians paused to hunt. Shy though the otter has since become, Radisson's Indians could shoot these with arrows. They did not dare to risk the sound of firearms, for they had found suspicious footprints in the sand.

These, the Indians said, had been left by hostile warriors, for the tribes of those days "all knowes there one another by their march, for each hath his proper steps, some upon their toes, some on their heels, wch is natural to them, for when they are infants the mother wrapeth them to their mode."

Traders though they were when occasion favored, the two white men seem to have been little interested in fur just then. They were still on the outward journey, with hostile Iroquois, or hostiles of another tribe, somewhere about. No one wanted the extra burden of bales of fur, though the canoe-run down French River from Lake Nipissing to Georgian Bay on Lake Huron was quick and easy.

The fishing again delighted Radisson. On the offshore sandbanks there were "such an infinite deal of fish that scarcely we are able to draw out our nett." Some of the fish were "as bigg as children of 2 years old." The Indians speared them through the ice, watching through a little hut built over a hole, using a painted wooden fish for decoy, and judging the direction of a big fish's approach from the minnows, fleeing in the opposite direction. In autumn they speared the fish by torchlight. One warrior speared half a ton in a single day, and in 1846 a white man caught, in twenty minutes' use of hook and line, more than he could eat in a fortnight.

The sturgeon Radisson could identify—so many that a later Frenchman said he caught them *"à confusion."* There is even record of one canoeman who killed a sturgeon with an axe. Other species Radisson could not even guess at.

"The coast of this lake is most delightful to the mind," he wrote. "The lands smooth, and woods of all sorts." Particularly it was "delightful to goe along the side of the watter in summer where you may pluck yᵉ ducks," which even two hundred years later were still there—in "incredible numbers."

Just where he went after passing Lake Huron, no one knows. Radisson's own geography is vague. He may have gone as far as the vicinity of Lake Pepin on the Mississippi. Certainly during the course of their wanderings Radisson and Groseilliers penetrated six days beyond the lake, to the southwest, where they found "a beautiful River, large, wide, deep, and worthy of comparison, they say, with our great River St. Lawrence." Goit.g on, they met a tribe called "Nadwechiwec"—obviously the Nadowessiek, or Sioux. Later Radisson mentions a tribe who wore long hair and were called the "Tatarga, that is to say, buff." Now the Sioux, in ancient days, always wore long hair, their word for buffalo is "tatanka," and there is a division of the tribe calling themselves by that name. Probably Radisson met them in Minnesota, along the northern edge of Sioux country. In their country, wood was scant and the Indians had learned "to make fire with coal from the earth and to cover their cabins with skins." Other Indians made "buildings of loam, very nearly as the swallows build their nests." Clearly these are plains Indians of some kind. Those with skin tepees and fires of buffalo chips—which were not coal but did come "from the earth"— were probably Sioux. The Indians with earth lodges would be the Mandans and Arikaras, living along the Missouri.

The travelers probably knew the Mandans only by report, for Radisson does not mention them by name in his *Voyages,* though he told a Jesuit about them on his return.

For months on end, Radisson and Groseilliers wandered about the Great Lakes, crossing Michigan and Wisconsin and probably entering Minnesota, but the narrative which Radisson wrote in England years afterward is not very clear as to just where he was. It is not to be wondered at. He had no maps. He had no means of keeping a journal—even if he had had time and energy. The rivers and mountains he saw had no names. Distances were vague. The Indian tribes had appellations that cannot always be identified today; and even those tribal names that are still familiar do not always help, for the tribes were always moving.

Radisson loved the beautiful, unspoiled, lake-and-forest country. "The further we sejourned the delightfuller the land was to us. I can say that [in] my lifetime I never saw a more incomparable country." Traveling one of the great inland lakes, he admired "the beauty of the shore of that sweet sea. Here we saw fishes of divers [sorts], some like the sturgeon & have a kind of slice att the end of their nose some three fingers broad in the end and 2 onely neere the nose, and some 8 thumbs long, all marbled of a blakish collor. There are birds whose bills are two and 20 thumbs long. That bird swallows a whole salmon, keeps it a long time in his bill. We saw alsoe shee goats very bigg [antelope?]. There is an animal somewhat lesse than a cow whose meat is exceeding good [caribou?]. There is no want of Staggs nor Buffs. There are so many Tourkeys that the boys throws stoanes att them for their recreation."

The trees were large but no longer grew in the dense clusters of the

Canadian forest—in other words, the country he is describing is on the edge of the Great Plains. Vines grew by the riverside and the grapes—no French explorer ever fails to note them—were "very bigg, greene." The "lemons" were "not so bigg as ours, and sowrer." Probably this means May apples once more. If Radisson bit into a green one he certainly got something sourer than any lemon.

As he looked upon unspoiled North America, Radisson became philosophical: "The country was so pleasant, so beautifull and fruitfull that it grieved me to see y^t ye world could not discover such inticing countrys to live in. This I say because that the Europeans fight for a rock in the sea against one another, or for a sterill land and horrid country." In his newfound middle western Eden, all this was changed: "Contrarywise those kingdoms are so delicious & under so temperat a climat, plentifull of all things, the earth bringing foarth its fruit twice a yeare, the people live long & lusty & wise in their way."

Buffalo, which then ranged pretty well north, greatly impressed him: "As for the Buff, it is a furious animal. One must have a care of him, for every yeare he kills some Nadoneserenons [Sioux]. He comes for the most part in ye plaines & meddows; he feeds like an ox. . . . The horns of Buffs are as those of an ox, but not so long, but bigger. & of a blackish collour; he hath a very long hairy taile; he is reddish, his haire frized & very fine. All the parts of his body much [like] unto an ox. The biggest are bigger then any ox whatsoever."

At last, in the spring of 1660, the two came out of the lake country, "4 moneths in our voyage wthout doeing any thing but goe from river to river"; but they brought with them a great store of beaver skins. As they approached the French settlements, they had to fight their way as usual through the perpetually lurking Iroquois, but they came through safely.

In June of 1661 Radisson and Groseilliers were off again, through the usual Iroquois blockade and then following their earlier course up the Ottawa River to Lake Nipissing, then down French (River of the Sorcerers) River to Georgian Bay. This time they coasted along the north shore, and portaged around the Sault Sainte Marie. Game was scarce except in Lake Nipissing, and on Lake Huron they had to subsist on "small fruit," except when an Indian dived into the lake and dragged a beaver out with his bare hands. As they started off along the south shore of Lake Superior, matters improved. They made "good cheare of a fish that they call Assickmack, wch signifieth a white fish." Westward, they began to take "sturgeons of a vast bignesse, and Pycks of seaven foot long." Game began to appear. "The beare, the castors [beaver], and ye Oriniack shewed themselves often, but to their cost; indeed it was to us like a terrestrial paradise."

When Radisson went hunting farther west in Lake Superior he found a pool where "bustards" (wild geese?) were nesting. Creeping up to keep from frightening the birds, he found to his amazement that the fearless creatures were trying to frighten him!

"I began to creepe though [that] I might come neare. Thought to be in Canada, where ye fowle is scared away; but the poore creatures, seeing me flatt uppon the ground, thought I was a beast as well as they, so they come neare me, whishing like gosslings, thinking to frighten me. The whistling that I made them heare was another musick then theirs. There I killed 3 and the rest scared, wch nevertheless came to that place againe to see what sudaine sicknesse befeled their comrads. I shott againe; two payed for their curiosity."

Five days' food supply in almost as many minutes! He thought he could have killed a winter's store of meat in one month's hunting. They "Made good cheere" and found the admiring Indians docile. "We weare Cesars, being nobody to contradict us."

Radisson, the Frenchman, was exultant. The Spaniards in Mexico—of whom vague rumors passed from tribe to tribe until they reached the northern Indians—had not as yet monopolized all the best parts of North America. France, too, should win a part of the strange new continent. Radisson knew that he had found "yett more countreys as fruitfull and as beautifull as ye Spaniards to conquer, wch may be done wth as much ease & facility, and prove as rich, if not richer, for bread and wine; and all other things are as plentifull as in any part of Europ."

The Indians showed him bits of Lake Superior copper lying about on the forest floor and a mountain made "of nothing else," but told him not to burden himself with specimens, since there was plenty more of it ahead. Sandbanks along the lake shore were so high that an

Indian, climbing to the top "did shew no more than a crow." At other places along the shore were "meddows that weare squared, and 10 leagues as smooth as a boord," beaver dams with pools behind them covering twenty leagues, and old beaver pools which had silted up and became "trembling ground," or muskeg. In this "if you take not great care you sink downe to yor head or the midle of yor body. When you are out of one hole you find yourselfe in another. This I speake by experience, for I have been catched often. But the wildmen warned me, wch saved me; that is, that when the mosse whould breake under I should cast my whole body into the watter on sudaine. I must wth my hands hold the mosse, and goe soe like a frogg, then to draw my boat after me." It was an awkward and undignified method of progress but it was safe.

He saw also the rock Nanitoucksinagoit, a "likenesse of the devil," where the Indians flung away "much tobacco and other things in its veneration." This was clearly just another of those shrines of Matchi Manitou which can still be found in the Canadian woods with fresh sacrifices lying about, even in these modern days. The figure which Radisson thought a representation of the devil may have been what is now called "The Ghost," a human figure in a long garment, with outward pointing hand and, of the face, an eye and the nose alone visible. Painted in yellow, bright sunlight makes it look phosphorescent.

Father Galinée and Father Dollier, in an access of missionary zeal, destroyed a similar figure between Lake Erie and Lake Huron, a few years later. On a natural rock formation which had, according to the indignant priest "no more relation to a human figure than the imagination gives it"—the Indians had painted a kind of face in vermilion. The priests smashed this with hatchets, carried the larger pieces out into the river, and dumped the rest in the water along the shore. They had just lost their altar vessels, in an accident for which they felt sure the idol was responsible; and when they presently met with good hunting, they felt equally sure that—however twentieth century archeologists might later feel about it—heaven had blessed their pious deed.

Near "The Ghost" in Radisson's day, was the "Great Portal," a natural bridge of rock with some six acres of land above it, the opening "bigger in the going up" so that a five-hundred-ton ship could have passed through. Water rushing in and out of neighboring caves made a "most horrible noise, most like the shooting of great guns." Near it were rocks pictured in copper stain. The "Portal" was still standing about 1900, when it collapsed.

The winter was desperately hard. Game vanished. White and red alike grew gaunt from hunger.

Just where all this happened is not quite clear—certainly somewhere on the western end of Lake Superior and perhaps on Lac Court Oreille. During the winter a Sioux delegation visited them to request "miniskoick," "a thunder"—that is, a gun. Presents, including three hundred beaver skins, were showered on the Frenchmen by various tribes.

Toward the end of the winter, they went to visit the Sioux in their own country—probably Minnesota, perhaps at the village of Kathio, southwest of Mille Lacs, where Father Hennepin had been held prisoner. They were surprised by the big buffalo-skin tepees of the Sioux—"great cabbans most covered wth skins and other close matts," which the squaws could pitch in less than half an hour.

Spring and summer of 1663 they spent with Cree, north of the Lakes, but they were now growing so used to the country that they give no description of it. Once they chased a party of Iroquois, who had wandered all the way from New York "to discover somewhat." Slowly they worked their way back to Lake Nipissing, fought their way through the Iroquois war parties who still hung about the St. Lawrence, and reached Montreal.

Here a painful shock awaited them, after all their hardships. They had gone into the woods without a government license. The French governor confiscated the entire stock of furs that they brought with them out of the wilderness. All their gains were swept away at once. Furious, they left Canada, and entered the service of the English King, Charles II. All of Radisson's subsequent exploration was far to the north, along Hudson Bay; and though he went back into French service a few years later, he returned for a second time to English service, dying in England.

X

Vérendrye and His Sons

STILL THE LURE of the Western Sea tormented the French. About 1738 one of the greatest and least known of North American explorers began to feel it. This was the French subaltern—he never rose to be better than a captain—Pierre Gualtier de Varennes, Sieur de la Vérendrye. To the modern inhabitants of the American states he explored, he is little more than a name. To most Americans he is not even that, though the Canadians have a juster appreciation of his achievements. He had served in Europe as a lieutenant in the Régiment de Bretagne, fighting at Malplaquet, where he received four sabre cuts, and was shot through the body. In all, he was wounded nine times, during his European service.

Finding eventually that, without private means, he could not live on a French officer's pay, he gave up his lieutenancy; returned to his native Canada; took the inferior rank of ensign in the colonial forces; married and settled down, for the only quiet years of his arduous life, on his property near Three Rivers. Here were born the four sons who were to share his adventures.

As his family grew larger, Vérendrye began to look for something more remunerative than his own little trading post. He secured command of the extreme, advanced posts on Lake Nipigon, immediately north of Lake Superior. Though French canoemen had already pushed two or three hundred miles beyond this to Rainy Lake and Lake of the Woods, the Nipigon posts and Fort Beau, the post among the Sioux, were the westermost establishments thus far made permanent. Except for the canoe routes along what are now the "border lakes," between the United States and Canada, there was no real knowledge of what lay beyond; but always there were rumors of a route to the Western Sea. Eagerly Vérendrye questioned the Indians who emerged from the lake-and-forest country westward, to barter with him.

Yes, the red men told him, there was a great river flowing west. "Ge-e-getz" (yes). It flowed at last into the sea. The simple children of the forest were sincere enough, and what they said was true, but it was extraordinarily misleading.

The drainage basin of the Rainy Lake–Lake of the Woods–Lake Winnipeg system is peculiar. Once you are over the height of land dividing it from Lake Superior at Grand Portage, lakes and rivers do flow west—at first. The early French—who had no idea of the immense breadth of North America and no suspicion that the Rockies and Sierras barred the way to the Pacific—reached the only reasonable conclusion. Here was a height of land—obviously the Continental Divide. Lake Superior water flowed east. The border lakes and their connecting rivers all flowed west. Follow these westward currents and you would certainly come to the Pacific Ocean—the long-sought Western Sea. From there to China it could not be far.

It is an extraordinary fact that although the true dimensions of the earth had been correctly calculated by that time, none of these early explorers westward seem to have had any idea of western distances. Considering that they knew something about distances in Asia and all about distances in Europe, across the Atlantic, and westward as far as the Lake of the Woods—which is after all nearly half way across Canada—a little addition and subtraction ought to have given them some idea how far it was, westward to the Pacific and on around the globe to China. Magellan and Drake had long since crossed the Pacific, so that the distance from America to Asia was known. But for some reason, no one ever attempted to figure out the distances, so that, for two hundred years, explorers continued to push westward, absurdly hoping to sight the Pacific at any moment and so find the new route to the Orient.

In 1728 Vérendrye, already bubbling with enthusiasm for western discovery, visited Michilimackinac, where he met Father Gonner, one of the two missionaries working among the Sioux at Fort Beau-harnois. The priest had seen enough of that redoubtable tribe to feel sure that there was little hope of passing through their territory to the Western Sea. He was, therefore, quite prepared to share Vérendrye's enthusiasm for a route along the border lakes. Vérendrye, who had already prepared a written outline of his plans, entrusted them to Father Gonner, who offered to take it to Quebec and urge it upon the governor. He even supported it with a memoir of his own, "Relation d'une grande rivière qui a flux et reflux."

Vérendrye went back to Lake Nipigon, where he continued to ques-tion the Indians. Tacchigis, a Cree chief, told the eager Frenchman that he had traveled as far as "the lake of the great river of the west." Other Indians had told Vérendrye the same thing. Eagerly he con-tinued to question his Cree friend. Did Tacchigis know of any more great rivers? Yes. From a height of land sloping to the southwest—which must have been somewhere in Minnesota—he had seen four great rivers. He was pretty clearly referring to the Red River of the North, the Saskatchewan, Big Elk River (a stream of no great impor-tance, which flows into the Rainy River), and the headwaters of the Mississippi—though of course these cannot all be seen from any one point.

Another Indian, a slave held by the Cree, told Vérendrye that the western lands were full of tribes who "raise quantities of grain, fruits abound, game is in great plenty and is only hunted with bows and arrows; the people there do not know what a canoe is; as there is no wood in all that vast extent of country, for fuel they dry the dung of animals." The slave added that he had seen "the mountain the stone of which shines night and day, and that from that point you begin to notice a rise and fall of tide." This was probably a reference to the Rockies and perhaps even to the Columbia estuary—"more than three leagues in width," according to the slave, "at the place where the ebb and flow begins."

The guide whom Vérendrye picked for his journey, an Indian named Auchagah, or Ochagah, obligingly drew a map of the country from Kamenistiquia (near modern Fort William, Ontario) on Lake Superior, all the way to Lake Winnipeg. Auchagah probably drew on birch bark, which has long since crumbled; but luckily a copy has survived. It shows the "Montagnes de Pierres Brillantes"—the Rockies were at first called the "Shining Mountains," and it is a pity the name was ever changed—standing close to Lake Winnipeg, which is mistakenly shown due west of Lake of the Woods. Actually it is almost due north. Other Crees drew still another map, meantime telling Vérendrye wonderful stories of western lands rich in minerals, teeming with game, so filled with beaver that the Indians living there threw their beaver-skin robes away every spring, "not being able to sell them."

With all this information, Vérendrye returned to Quebec in 1730. Reminding the French governor that "the English have every interest in getting ahead of us, and if we allow them time they will not lose the chance of doing it," he got permission to build a new fort in the West, as a base for further exploration toward the Western Sea. But thrifty French officialdom would not provide a sou toward expenses. Instead, Vérendrye was offered a monopoly of the fur trade in the new regions—which was of no use to anyone else—and forced to run into debt to equip his expedition. "Some means had to be found of indemnifying him," says a government report, "and no more suitable means is in sight than to let him enjoy the fruit of his own labours." Officialdom changes little with the centuries. It was not long before Vérendrye was under bitter official attack for engaging in the fur trade—the very thing he had been authorized to do, and his only possible means of supporting the expedition he had undertaken for the government.

By the end of August, Vérendrye had reached the Grand Portage on the northwestern coast of Lake Superior, which led into the border lakes. Here there was trouble with his men, mutinous when they saw what ardors and endurances lay before them. Vérendrye compromised by sending three men—including one of his sons, and his nephew (who was also his trusted lieutenant), Christophe Dufrost, Sieur de la Jemeraye—on to Rainy Lake, while he himself wintered with the others at Kaministiquia. In the spring he pushed on, joined La Jemeraye, with whom he paddled down the short Rainy River, its banks bordered by oaks, with abundant beaver, into Lake of the

Woods, where he built Fort St. Charles. This was a really strong wilderness fort with a double palisade, fifteen feet high and a hundred feet square with four bastions, houses, a chapel, and a powder magazine.

The lakes supplied an abundance of muskellunge, bass, lake trout, wall-eyed pike, and pickerel. These were really big fish. Fishing in the transparent Lake Superior waters, the Indians built huts over holes in the ice. Looking from darkness into the water, they could see down forty or fifty feet and as late as 1860 are said to have been spearing fish with thirty-five and forty foot poles.

One of Vérendrye's fishing parties caught four thousand big white fish, besides trout, sturgeon and other species. Cadillac mentions sturgeon, pike, "carp," "hareng," and "poisson doré." The shallow water was full of wild rice, which attracted waterfowl. It was impossible to go hungry; but Vérendrye made haste to burn the trees and underbrush off a tract large enough for a wheat field, which he seeded at once. Exultantly he reflected that the Indians' maps of his route thus far had been perfectly correct. The rest of their stories of the country farther west must be equally true. He talked to twenty Cree, taking them separately, one by one. Their stories all agreed.

For the next few years, Vérendrye stayed at his fort. So far as he could, he kept down tribal wars. He had trouble making friends with the Assiniboins, who were alarmed because they heard that the French had come to eat them. He listened to marvelous stories of a strange tribe, the "Sioux who went underground"—really the Mandans or Arikaras, both of whom lived in earth-covered lodges. Some of these Indians, he learned, had light hair, chestnut or red, as well as the usual Indian black hair, and were "white in color." The light hair was probably just premature greyness, which afflicted a good many youthful Mandans; but there is no doubt their skins were lighter in color than those of other Indians, a fact which helped along an endless series of tales about "Welsh Indians" and "White Indians," which it took a hundred years to end. Their chief sent Vérendrye an invitation to visit him.

Vérendrye hoped to start out for the Mandan country by the spring of 1735. Meantime, he sent two men to make friends with the Indians on Lake Winnipeg. In May, 1734, one of his associates—another Cartier—took ten men to Lake Winnipeg and built a fort there. A Cree chief adopted one of Vérendrye's sons, who went off with the Cree and Indians to Lake Winnipeg.

Vérendrye himself, with a cargo of peltry, was back in Montreal, in August of 1734. Though the government had from the start refused to pay him or even provide supplies, it now objected to his effort to pay for the expedition by fur trading. The problem was finally settled by allowing him to farm out his fur-trading posts to merchants, while he himself devoted himself entirely to exploration—still at his own risk and his own expense.

He returned to the wilderness and to tragedy. His nephew, La Jemeraye, was killed on the Roseau River, west of Lake of the Woods. Soon afterward, hostile Sioux—catching his son, Jean-Baptiste, Father Aulneau, and about twenty of their men on an island in Lake of the Woods—killed them all. As the bodies were found lying in a circle, Vérendrye concluded they had been treacherously attacked while in council. The Sioux had amused themselves by cutting off the heads and wrapping them in the beaver skins for which the Frenchmen had been so eager. It was a typical bit of grim, sardonic Indian humor. Fifty years later, dead Americans were sometimes found with their mouths filled with earth—because they always wanted land!

Questioning the Indians on Lake Winnipeg carefully, he began to hear more stories about the "tribe of whites that we are so desirous of getting in touch with"—the Mandans. He now learned that the river on which they lived—the Missouri—did not run west but turned south, entering the ocean at a place "where there are white men, towns, forts, and cannon, and where prayer is said, there being priests in the country." The Indians, he felt sure, must be talking about the Spanish settlements on the Pacific coast. Actually, they were trying to give him a fairly accurate description of the Missouri, from the Dakotas to St. Louis, and of the Mississippi to the Spanish settlements along the Gulf coast.

In October, 1737, he was again at Quebec, laying in supplies and rather more than hinting to his obtuse superiors that he would like promotion to a captaincy—he was now in his early fifties!—plus the

Cross of the Order of St. Louis, in recognition of his nine wounds. Maurepas, the comfortable official at Versailles, was very indignant because Vérendrye had not accomplished more exploration and alluded to the massacre of the twenty-one men beheaded by the Sioux as "most annoying."

The governor, Beauharnois, at Quebec, being a little closer to wilderness realities, defended Vérendrye in letters to Versailles. To his face, however, he blamed the explorer for leaving his post, warning that if he came down to the settlements again, he would not be allowed to return to the wilderness. Vérendrye promised he would visit the Mandans that very winter. Bewigged, perfumed, and lace-ruffled, Versailles maintained its grievance against the skin-clad explorer—"considerably surprised at the little progress that officer has made towards the discovery of the Western Sea."

With fresh supplies, again bought at his own expense, Vérendrye hurried back to Fort Maurepas, on Lake Winnipeg, which he reached September 22, 1738. His son's earlier effort to reach the Mandan country had failed because he could not get canoes for the first part of the journey. Spurred on by the nagging criticism of Quebec and Versailles, Vérendrye prepared to go himself. The local Cree were lugubrious about his prospects. The water in the Assiniboin River was low; Vérendrye would ruin his canoes. The Assiniboin Indians, through whose country he would have to pass, were at best a queer lot. They did not know how to kill beaver, like proper Crees. Their only clothing was buffalo skin—outlandish garments which were not what the French wanted anyway. They were "people without intelligence" who would not get along with the French. It sounds very much as if the Cree were trying to keep the profits of the French trade in their own hands.

Paying no special heed to all this talk, Vérendrye pushed up the Assiniboin River, hitherto unseen by white men, as far as he could go. There had been no rain all summer, it was now the end of September, and the river was very low, with many shallows and yet with a strong current—about as bad canoe water as can be imagined. Trees lined the banks, but Vérendrye noted that there were no conifers. That meant that there would be no gum or resin to repair his bark canoes if anything went wrong; and if his canoes were completely wrecked there would be no way to calk new ones. Beyond the river lay only "a boundless stretch of prairie in which are multitudes of buffalo and deer."

Leaving his men to bring on the baggage in the canoes, the leader himself struck off overland for six days into more new country, meeting increasing numbers of friendly Assiniboins, until he came to the portage leading from the Assiniboin to Lakes Manitoba and Winnepegosis—at the modern Canadian town of Portage La Prairie. Here he built a new fort, farther west than any Frenchman had yet traveled. A few days later the trader, Charles Nolan, Sieur de la Marque, caught up with him, bringing nine more men.

On October 18, with La Marque and twenty men, Vérendrye struck off southward on foot, following an ancient Indian trail used by agricultural Mandans, who sold their surplus corn as far north as Rupert's Land. In Manitoba, sections of the Mandan traders' trail can still be seen. The party were much delayed by a leisurely Indian guide, who, like most Indians, traveled only when he felt like it, and by hospitable Assiniboins, who insisted on being visited. On the third day an Assiniboin chief, accompanied by his whole village of forty lodges, delayed them for a day "that he might have the pleasure of seeing and entertaining us." Vérendrye had hardly got his party started again when the guide insisted on a detour of sixty or seventy miles to visit still another Assiniboin village. Here each warrior put his hand on Vérendrye's head, taking him for his father, and then on the other Frenchmen's heads, taking them as brothers, meantime weeping copiously. It was an old Assiniboin custom, which earned them the nickname of "Weepers" among the French. At least, Vérendrye had established French influence and French trade with one more tribe.

When he got started again, the whole Assiniboin village set off for the Mandan villages with him, explaining volubly that these people were white, were in fact Frenchmen like their newfound friends.

After crossing the "first mountain" (probably Pembina Mountain) the route was over rolling prairie, a perpetual succession of small hills and valleys with "magnificent plains" ten or twelve miles in extent. The prairies were almost wholly grass, with only occasional clumps of trees—called by the French "islots." So infrequent were these little groves that the Assiniboins often carried firewood with them, loaded on their dogs, though they could in emergencies make fires of dry buffalo chips, known to the French as "bois de vâche."

Old soldier that he was, Vérendrye observed with respect the march discipline of the Assiniboins—scouts ahead, detachments on each flank in contact with a strong rear guard, women, children, dogs, the aged and infirm in the middle. Women and dogs carried all the baggage, for these Indians had no horses. The moment a buffalo herd was sighted, the scouts yelled the news and all the most active men rushed forward to join the hunt. Killing buffaloes on foot is risky business, but no one was hurt and there was soon plenty of meat.

Assiniboin runners, sent ahead, brought the Mandan chief and some of his men to a prairie rendezvous at some distance from the Mandan village. Poor Vérendrye, who had "expected to see people quite different from the other savages," was at once disillusioned. These Indians might be lighter in coloring than other tribes and their hair might not always be black, but they were just more Indians—"they do not differ from the Assiniboin, being naked except for a garment of buffalo skin carelessly worn without any breech cloth."

The Mandan chief was hospitality itself toward the Frenchmen (who brought valuable trading goods), but he cast a jaundiced eye upon the horde of Assiniboins. It would be expensive feeding them all, as Indian hospitality demanded, and the chief promptly got rid of a large proportion by what Vérendrye thought "a sharp trick."

He was especially glad to see his Assiniboin friends, the Mandan chief explained, as hostile Sioux would soon attack his village, and he needed help. Well aware that the Assiniboin lived in mortal terror of the Sioux, he was deliberately trying to scare them off. His trick worked fairly well. The moment they heard of the alleged war scare, most of the Assiniboins wanted to halt in their tracks. Their crafty host had almost succeeded in getting rid of his unwelcome guests entirely, when an inconveniently heroic old Assiniboin warrior jumped up to declare that it would be shameful to abandon their father—that is, Vérendrye. The moment their courage was called in question, the Assiniboin warriors decided to go on. The Mandans at least escaped a visit from most of the women and children, who were left behind with a small guard, but they still had to feed six hundred warriors, who went gallantly—and hungrily—forward, to help in their defense against wholly imaginary Sioux.

Seeing that they had only in part achieved their purpose, the Mandans tried the same trick again. When they reached their village, they began again to "spread the report that the Sioux were not far away; that several of their hunters had caught sight of them." While the Assiniboins in great alarm were preparing to decamp, a Mandan chief slyly told Vérendrye to stay where he was. By signs, he explained that the Sioux alarm was false—designed only to get rid of the hungry Assiniboin visitors. Unfortunately the Assiniboin squaw of whom Vérendrye's Cree interpreter was enamored departed with the rest, and there was no holding back the interpreter after that. Even with his assistance, interpretation had at best been sketchy. Vérendrye had spoken French to his son, who had spoken Cree to the interpreter, who had spoken Assiniboin to any Mandan who happened to understand it.

"I made myself perfectly understood," Vérendrye noted in his journal, but he was probably too confident. This round-about interpretation had certainly been better than the signs with which he had to get along for the second half of his visit; but there must have been a good deal of misunderstanding in any conversation which had to pass through so many intermediaries. This multi-lingual translation was by no means unusual; Lewis and Clark often had to do very much the same thing.

From the Mandan village, Vérendrye examined the new country as far as he could. The Missouri River was muddy "rather brackish" from the salt and sulphur marshes and pools which he had noted during the latter part of his journey—"not of the best quality for drinking." In fact, when the Lewis and Clark expedition passed that way in 1804, Meriwether Lewis was poisoned by minerals in the river water.

Broad, muddy, filled with shoals, studded with snags and tangled masses of trees, its swift current swept past Vérendrye, flowing from the unknown into the unknown—to the Western Sea, he hoped. It was hard to get any idea from the Indians, so eager to talk that one interrupted another when they tried to speak. Often, too, they failed to understand his questions. Asked one thing, they gave a totally irrelevant reply, obviously "through failure to comprehend." Vérendrye thought the river might turn west or southwest before it reached the sea, where, the Mandans told him, there were men like himself, dressed in cloth instead of skins. Again the Indian accounts began to sound as if he were on his way to the Spanish settlements on the Western Sea.

The exact spot Vérendrye had reached is not easy to determine. He had crossed from modern Ontario into North Dakota and was certainly not very far from Bismarck. Probably he was at the Mandan village near Armistead, North Dakota, and some fifty or sixty miles above the state capital, where Lewis and Clark would spend the winter of 1804-1805. But at the time Vérendrye arrived,—before the great smallpox epidemic, a result of white traders' visits, which nearly destroyed the tribe—Mandan villages were scattered for many miles down the river. Lewis and Clark, on their way up the Missouri, passed the ruins of one abandoned village after another. All of these were occupied in the eighteenth century and Vérendrye may have been in any one of them.

The landscape was very much the same, wherever he was. All around him were the rolling Dakota prairies, not very different from what they are today.

The Mandans were a sedentary, agricultural people. Vérendrye looked with surprise at their large, warm, earthern lodges, made with a framework of logs as large as modern telegraph poles, over which earth was piled to a thickness of several feet, the whole dome-shaped structure being quite unlike the flimsy and chilly bark, grass, or skin shelters of other Indians. They were big houses. One of the Mandan ceremonial chambers could accommodate two hundred Indians, and the lodge of an ordinary warrior had room for forty or fifty people, at need—not to mention horses. The central fire, smoke from which escaped through a hole in the roof—no Indian ever thought of a chimney—made the dwelling comfortable enough, even in the grim Dakota winter. Planks divided the dwelling into small apartments. Personal belongings were neatly stowed in leather bags, hung on the posts. Beds, raised about two feet from the ground, were made of green buffalo hides, which tightened as they dried. In fair weather, the rounded earth roofs made comfortable places for the men to loaf, while they smoked and watched the squaws at work.

The village was laid out in streets and squares, and had about 130 lodges, enough so that "often our Frenchmen would lose their way in going about." The streets were kept clean—something unique in Indian villages.

The whole settlement was surrounded by a palisade, from which bastions jutted out to give defenders a flanking fire along the wall. The whole was surrounded by a ditch fifteen to eighteen feet wide and about as deep. Entrance was possible only on wooden steps, which could be removed in time of danger. "If all their forts are similar, you may say that they are impregnable to savages. This fortification, indeed, has nothing savage about it," wrote Vérendrye.

Outside the palisades, scattered here and there, were smaller forts, each containing only forty or fifty lodges, for use in the summer when the squaws were busy in the fields. And all around was the prairie, rolling green in spring and summer, rolling brown in autumn, rolling sheets of white in winter, with the Missouri River—muddy and full of snags, then as always—rolling out of mysterious lands no white man knew into others equally mysterious.

Secure in their villages, well supplied with buffalo beef and corn, the Mandans were high livers, rarely troubled by the famine that was a perpetual menace to the northern Indians. Though buffalo meat and corn were a staple diet, they varied it with antelope, deer, bear, beech-nuts, squash, and pumpkins. His hosts set more than twenty dishes before Vérendrye every day.

The Mandan corn crop would hardly impress a modern farmer. The ears must have been even smaller than the dwarf corn which horticulturists have recently developed for modern suburban gardeners. They are described as no bigger than a man's thumb. But the Mandans made up for small ears by the quantity in which they raised them. Like all Americans, they enjoyed "green" corn, and they stored the dried kernels in pits dug six or seven feet deep into the ground. These were the "many cellars for storing things," which Vérendrye mentions. Here also were stored meat, fat, and skins. No wonder the Mandans were "great eaters" and "strong on feasts."

La Marque and Vérendrye's sons "went continually" to Mandan dinners. Since they could not talk with the Indians, the next best way to make friends was to feast with them. The Indians ate from earthen pots, with spoons and ladles of buffalo horn. The later use of similar utensils by white pioneers led to one of the quaintest of native American oaths, "by the great horn spoon."

Mandan cooking was better than most native efforts. They could boil meat properly by hanging their earthen kettles directly over the fire, instead of by clumsily dropping hot stones into a bark kettle as the Assiniboins did. Most tribes had to wait for the coming of the white man with his iron and brass kettles before they could do anything of the sort. So much importance did the Mandans attach to their earthenware, that the first Mandan chief who traveled with Lewis and Clark refused to move without an abundant supply of crockery.

For the time being, Vérendrye had gone as far into the unknown interior of the mysterious continent as he could go. December, 1738, was already partly gone. He could return overland on foot to the Assiniboin River, but beyond that he would have to travel by canoe. To do that, he would have to get back before the spring floods began.

Leaving two men behind to learn the Mandan language, he started back over the windswept, bitterly cold prairie. Beyond the wide Missouri,—they seem not to have crossed to the other bank—he and his sons could see small hills and undulating prairie, unexplored, endless, unknown, tantalizing—calling, calling to those adventurous, eager spirits. Somewhere beyond lay the Shining Mountains and the Western Sea. Into that land the Vérendryes must go.

By February they were back on the Assiniboin, Vérendrye himself sick and exhausted. "Never in my life did I endure so much misery, pain and fatigue as in that journey." The two men he had left among the Mandans rejoined him in September. They had talked with strange Indians who had come overland from Spanish territory, with still more detailed descriptions of the white men there, who "prayed to the great Master of Life in books," with pages that looked "as if made of leaves of Indian corn," and who "sang holding their books

Canyon of Rapid Creek, in the Black Hills. From Reynolds' *Exploration of Wyoming and the Yellowstone,* 1859-60.

Two drawings from *Exploration of Wyoming and the Yellowstone,* 1859-60. Above: Bear Butte in the Black Hills. Below: Citadel Rock on the upper Missouri.

in great houses where they assembled for prayer." One of these strange Indians wore a cross and "pronounced often in talking to them the names of Jesus and Mary."

The distant white men, the Indians said, had firearms, horses, and cattle. Their women were "very white and handsome, wearing their hair in a coil and ear-rings of brilliant stones, with bracelets and collars of very light yellow; and by imitating the movements he showed them that they played the harpsichord and the bass viol."

Vérendrye sent one of his sons to the Mandans to inquire further, but no account of his journey survives. The young man brought back cotton cloth and porcelain beads, obviously of Spanish manufacture; but he had been unable to get a guide to take him beyond the Mandan country. He also brought two horses—the first seen by white men on the western plains.

At last, in 1742, Vérendrye pushed his exploration beyond the Missouri. The Indians of the border lakes were at war with the Sioux, and he was too busy trying to keep them quiet to go himself; but he sent his sons. Starting from the Assiniboin River, April 29, they made a quick journey to the Mandan villages, being now thoroughly familiar with the route. Here they expected to wait two months for the arrival of a visiting tribe, whom they describe only as the "Gens des Chevaux," or "Horse Indians," probably Cheyennes.

When these Indians failed to arrive, two Mandans offered to serve as guides. With these Mandans and two other Frenchmen, the Vérendryes set off.

The fascinating journey which followed, through primitive, unspoiled Dakota plains, and perhaps into Nebraska, Montana, and Wyoming, is reported in one of the most exasperatingly inadequate journals ever penned. There were, of course, no maps. The Vérendryes could indicate their route only by compass bearings, without even rough guesses at the length of each day's march. Worse still, they failed to learn the real names of the tribes they met, identifying them only by French names which today are meaningless. Worst of all, they kept no daily log but waited until their return to write down what they could remember.

For twenty days they moved on foot, west-southwest, a course which took them across North Dakota and into (or across) the northwest corner of South Dakota. One gets an idea how empty North America was in those days from the fact that they saw no Indians in all this distance—only "plenty of wild beasts." Almost certainly they passed through the colored Bad Lands along the Little Missouri, for the journal describes "earths of different colours, as blue, a kind of crimson, grass-green, shining black, chalkwhite, and ochre." Much interested, they wanted to bring back specimens but, traveling afoot, did not dare risk the extra load.

It was early August before they reached the "Mountain of the Gens des Chevaux"—perhaps what is now known as the "Cannonball." As Indians were likely to do when they went too far from home, one Mandan guide began to get nervous, hesitated, and soon would go no farther. After some months of travel, the Vérendryes had failed to find Indians, just as the Lewis and Clark party, traveling along the Missouri River north of the Vérendrye route, failed to find them, sixty years later.

The Vérendryes halted, built a lodge, and "lit fires on all sides as signals," hoping the Gens des Chevaux would come, but determined to trust themselves "to the first tribes that might appear." At the end of the month, the homesick Mandan started back.

In mid-September, to their joy, they saw a smoke. It was an encampment of the "Beaux Hommes" Indians—who may have been identical with the Crows. Whoever they were, they were good-natured and cordial. Though the second Mandan guide now went home too, leaving the white men without a translator, they learned enough about the language of their new friends to get along pleasantly with them. After some weeks camping together, both whites and reds set out south-southwest, passing from one now unidentifiable tribe to another. These new Indians were well supplied with horse and even had mules and jackasses. Some Indians began to speak a little Spanish. With a war party of the "Gens de l'Arc,"—who may just possibly have been more Cheyennes—the Vérendryes went on "through magnificent prairies where wild animals were in abundance," until they saw distant mountains, from whose summits they hoped soon to behold the Western Sea. The chief of the Gens de l'Arc had promised: "You will be able to see the Sea which you seek." They pushed on till they were at the very foot of the mountains, which were "well wooded with timber of every kind and appear very high."

At this unlucky moment, the Gens de l'Arc suddenly became alarmed. They feared that the Gens du Serpent (who were probably not the relatively peaceful Snake, or Shoshone, Indians) might attack their home villages. They decided to return. There was nothing for the Frenchmen to do but return with them, "très mortifiés de ne pas monter sur les Montagnes." They did not even have the faint consolation of knowing that there was, in fact, no sea whatever beyond the mountains they had scanned so hopefully.

They could console themselves with the thought that they had penetrated westward farther than any other white men, though the Spaniards had already come about as far in the opposite direction. Coronado had brought his mounted column from Mexico to Kansas two hundred years earlier; a joint Comanche and Spanish expedition, en route for the Illinois country had reached the Missouri River before getting itself wiped out in 1721.

Just where the Vérendryes went will always remain a mystery. Since the tribes they met cannot be identified and since they recorded only days of travel and directions, without distances, it is impossible to trace their route with any accuracy. Perhaps they had reached the Black Hills, in the southwest corner of South Dakota. Perhaps they had gone as far as Casper, Wyoming. They can hardly have reached the Rockies or they would have commented on their snow-capped summits. When they turned back they were still a long, long distance from the Pacific, though they did not know it.

Fortunately, one important point in their return journey is definitely fixed. They paused at the junction of the Bad River with the Missouri, directly opposite Pierre, South Dakota. Here, on March 15, 1743, they found a band whom they called the "Gens de la Petite Cerise." These were certainly Arikaras, who occupied this area until the Sioux drove them out in 1797.

The elder Vérendrye had long since left with the Mandans a lead plate, such as other French explorers had buried here and there, claiming the country for France. The sons, too, had carried a lead plate through all their burdensome journey. This, they decided, was the place to leave it. On a hill overlooking the river, they built a pyramid of stones, where they placed "a tablet of lead with the arms and inscriptions of the king."

There it remained, undisturbed, from 1743 until one Sunday afternoon in February, 1913, when some schoolboys in Pierre took their girls out for a walk. One of the girls saw, projecting from the ground, an inch or two of dull metal. She loosened it with some difficulty and picked it up. As the others clustered around to look at it, one boy made out the "number" 1743. They very nearly threw it away, but one girl hazarded the guess that it might be "Moses' tablet"; whereupon, deciding that it might be "worth something," if only a few cents as old lead, they took it home. It is now the chief treasure of the South Dakota Historical Society.

The Vérendrye marker is a thin plate, eight and a half by six and a half inches and about an eighth of an inch thick. On one side is the official inscription:

ANNO XVI REGNI LUDOVICI XV PRO REGE
ILLUSTRISSIMO DOMINO DOMINO MARCHIONE
DE BEAUHARNOIS MDCCXXXXI
PETRUS GUALTIER DE LAVERENDRIE POSVIT

On the other side someone, probably the two engagés, tried to correct the more obvious misstatements. Pierre Gualtier de la Vérendrye had not himself deposited the tablet and this was not the year 1741; but it was the only plate they had, and they did the best they could. Rudely they scratched what seems to be

POSE PAR LE
Chevalijet de LAVR
Toſt Louy la Londette
A Miotte
le 3od mars 1743

Part of the inscription is obscure and there has been dispute as to the correct way of deciphering it. Probably the best effort both at decipherment and translation is that of the late Louise Phelps Kellogg:

"Placed by the Chevalier de LVR (La Vérendrye) Lo Jos (Louis Joseph, his brother) Louy La Londette A Miotte (the two employees) the 30th of March, 1743."

Since the explorers feared the Indians might regard the placing of the tablet as bad medicine—as indeed it was—the whole thing was done secretly. The Indians "did not know about the tablet of lead that I had put in the ground," wrote one of the Vérendryes in their journal.

In the following month (April), the four Frenchmen, accompanied by three Indian guides, returned to the Mandan village, passing a group of friendly Sioux without adventure. From the Mandan village they went on to the Assiniboin, after one minor skirmish with another band of Sioux—hostile, this time. They rejoined their father July 2, 1743. It was the end of the Vérendrye explorations in the United States, though the adventurous family was still to add a little to its exploits in Canada.

XI

The English in Virginia

IT IS ASTONISHING how Europeans swarmed about the great, empty land of North America, as the middle of the sixteenth century was approaching. Almost simultaneously, De Soto was exploring the South, Coronado the Southwest, Alarcón the Gulf of Mexico, other Spaniards the California coast, while Cartier was carrying forward in the Gulf of St. Lawrence those French explorations that would eventually reach half way across the continent. The Spaniards would have been exploring the St. Lawrence, too, had Cabeza de Vaca been willing to lead an expedition thither to forestall the French. But Cabeza de Vaca, who thought the whole scheme "a very doubtful business," went off to South America instead.

The English had been slower than their competitors, despite the early start in North American exploration that the Cabots gave them; and it was not until the century was approaching its close that they made their first serious efforts at colonization. Then two bold and brilliant subjects of Queen Elizabeth began to meditate schemes of their own for adding to her dominions.

When, in 1565, the ferocious Spaniard Menendez butchered the Huguenot colonists in Florida, a handful of the Frenchmen had the luck to get safely away into the forests and, after that, the extraordinary luck to be picked up by a passing English vessel.

One of them was Jacques Le Moyne, or Le Moine, an artist who had gone with the colonists to make pictures of the newfound world. In London, whither his English rescuers bore him, his paintings of strange plants, strange animals, and Indians, who were strangest of all, interested the half-brothers, Sir Humphrey Gilbert and Walter Raleigh,—already eminent though not yet a knight—and also the gallant soldier-poet, Sir Philip Sidney. Le Moyne's originals have, with a single exception, long since vanished; but they had at once attracted the attention of a Flemish artist, Theodore de Bry, whose engravings from them were used to illustrate a queer little book by the expedition's carpenter, Nicolas Le Challeux, another of the little group who survived the Menendez massacre. Le Moyne's pictures were extremely vivid. Even from the copies that have survived one can see how they must have stirred the eager Elizabethan imagination.

To add to English interest, just about this time Sir Francis Walsingham, chief of Elizabeth's secret service, chanced upon a really gifted liar, in whose extraordinary yarns a substratum of exact truth, though undoubtedly present, is today discouragingly hard to identify.

This was the sailor, David Ingram, of Barking, Essex, one of a group of 114 men whom Sir John Hawkins had put ashore in the vicinity of Tampico in 1568. According to Ingram's own story, the place was somewhere near the River Camyna, or Rio de Mynas, which was about 140 leagues west and by north from the Cape of Florida. If the exact spot was not Tampico, it was certainly somewhere in the western part of the Gulf of Mexico.

Finding themselves entirely too close to the Spaniards for comfort, with no sign of an English relief expedition, some of the bolder spirits started to walk across North America, in the desperate hope that an English vessel might happen along and pick them up on the Atlantic coast. Most of them vanished, of course—killed by Indians, dead of hardship, starved, exhausted, or perhaps absorbed into Indian tribes as extraordinary strangers, too wonderful to kill. It is just possible that their blood may account for some of the queer stories about "white Indians," or Indians with blue eyes and blond or chestnut-colored hair that haunted American exploration till the days of Lewis and Clark.

Of them all, only Ingram and two companions survived on the long way northeastward. Ingram said they reached the Atlantic at "Cape Britton," which has usually been interpreted as meaning Cape Breton Island, in Nova Scotia. As the French ship of a certain "M. Champaine" (not, of course, Champlain, who was then a mere boy) picked him up and accommodatingly brought him home, Ingram naturally picked up French place names. It may well have been that Cape Breton was the only point on an uncharted coast for which he knew any name at all, and that he simply used it as the easiest way of explaining himself to Sir Francis. After all, Ingram was only a poor sailor, who had to tell the powerful minister of state what he wanted to hear.

In 1582, after his two companions were dead, Ingram told Walsingham that the trio had made the journey in eleven months. Though that certainly cannot be true, it did not disturb the Elizabethan statesman, who had no conception of American distances. As a matter of fact, Ingram himself may have thought it was true. Anyone who has traveled the wilderness knows how hard it is to estimate distances, how soon the calendar ceases to have meaning, and how time becomes mainly a matter of hours to the next camp, food, or rest. Ingram may have meant that their actual traveling time was eleven months, without counting long intervals for hunting, or for rest. Certainly, considering the directions they had to find for themselves, the rough trails they had to travel, the hunting they had to do by the way, the dangers which they had to escape, either eleven months is far too short or they did not go as far as they thought. There is little room for doubt, however, that Ingram did go on foot from somewhere in the Gulf of Mexico to somewhere on the eastern coast.

The sad thing is that all three men were merely illiterate adventurers. Wonderful yarns they doubtless spun in many a tavern, so long as anyone was willing to stand a drink. But by the time Sir Francis Walsingham got hold of Ingram, that adventurous tar had for so long been embroidering a heroic story (which would have been even more remarkable with no adornment) that he had probably forgotten what the truth really was.

Be that as it may, his story, in spite of its wild congeries of impossible "facts," has many a glimpse—not all of them faint ones—of something not altogether unlike the truth. It is at least an interesting light on what a pedestrian, strolling diagonally across most of the eastern

Indians killing alligators. From an engraving by Theodore De Bry, based on a drawing by Jacques Le Moyne, one of the Huguenot colonists in Florida 1562–66. From *The New World* by Stefan Lorant.

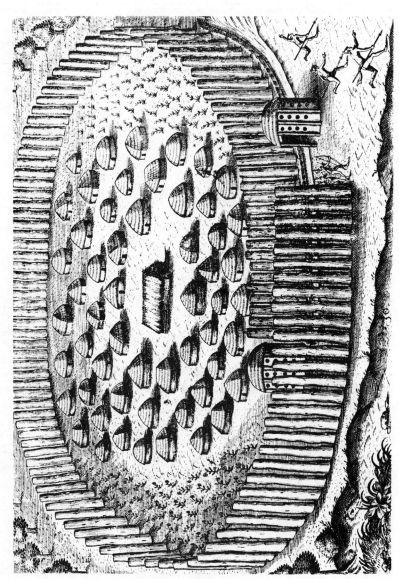

A fortified Indian village. From De Bry's engraving based on Le Moyne's drawing. From *The New World* by Stefan Lorant.

half of North America about the middle of the sixteenth century, thought (or could make others think) he saw.

Ingram claimed to have gone "from beyonde terra florida extendinge towardes the Cape Britton about eleaven monethes in the whole"; and he is quite evidently thinking of the contrast between the Florida Peninsula and the prairies when he says: "The grounde and Countrye is moste exelent fertill and pleasunte, and specyallie towardes the Ryvar of Maii [in modern Florida], for the grasse of the reste is not soe grene as yt is in those partes, for the other is brente awaye wth the heate of the sonne, And as all the countrye is good and most delycate havinge great playnes as large and as fayer in many places as maye be sene, beinge as playne as a boarde. And then greate and huge wooddes of sundrye kynde of trees." He describes how grass in "the lowe growndes there be soe rancke, that the grasse growethe faster then yt canne be eaten, wherby the olde grasse lyethe whithered thicke, and the newe grasse growinge thorowghe yt." That is just about how the early southern prairies must have grown, especially if some of Ingram's "grass" was canebrakes, which flourished along all the southern rivers.

He gives a fairly good description of the buffalo, though he exaggerates their size: "There is very great store of those Buffes wch are Beastes as bigge as twoe Oxen in lengthe almost twentye foote havinge longe eares like a bludde hownde, wth long heares aboute there eares, there hornes be Crooked like Rammes hornes, ther eyes blacke, there heares longe, blacke, roughe and hagged as a Goate, the Hydes of these beastes are solde verye deare." This would hardly satisfy a mammalogist. Buffalo's ears don't look like a bloodhound's; but the great beasts do have shaggy hair, which might easily make a man, observing from a respectful distance, think their ears longer than they are. And buffalo probably did look twenty feet long when you had to walk defenseless through a herd.

Ingram is more accurate when he describes "Deare boathe redde, white, and speckled"—in other words, ordinary red deer, deer in their grayish white winter coat, and fawns.

His "Beares boathe blacke and white" are correctly described. He might have seen polar bears as far south as Cape Breton Island, but he is probably simply the first white man to describe the grizzly, whose greyish hair was called "white" by explorers even later than Lewis and Clark. This becomes almost certain when he describes "one other straunge Beaste bigger then a Beare"—a grizzly was indeed bigger than any bear white men had ever seen. Further, "yt had nether heade nor necke, his eyes and mouthe weare in his brest," and the creature was "full of sylver heare." In other words, observing from a good, safe distance—which shows he was a wise man—Ingram saw a big "silver tip" with his mouth open in a snarl and his head sunk well below his shoulders, so that his head did seem to emerge from his belly.

It was, of course, somewhere in the modern state of Florida or along the Gulf coast, that he saw "a birde called a flaminge, whose feathers are very redd." He must have been much farther north when he observed what is plainly the great auk: "There is alsoe another kynde of fowle in that Countrye wch haunteth the Ryvers neare vnto the Islandes, they are of the shape and [size] of a goose, but there wynges are couered wth small callowe feathers and cannot flye. you may dryve them before you like Sheepe, they are excedinge fatte, and very delicate meate. they have white heades." People who insist on doubting everything Ingram reports should note the accuracy with which he describes these two birds—one of the extreme South, one of the North.

Unfortunately, he also says that he saw "boath Eliphantes and Uunces." As nobody knows what an "Uunce" is, nobody can contradict Ingram about that. Probably he meant an "ounce," or panther, of which he might easily have seen any number. Elephants he could not have seen; but there is a remote chance that he may have been the only white man who ever saw a live American mammoth. After all, two hundred years later Thomas Jefferson was assured by Indians that mammoths still survived in the interior.

Remembering also that a river looks pretty big when you have to cross it in a frail canoe, Ingram's description of enormous rivers fits well enough with the Mississippi, the Hudson, and the headwaters of Delaware and Chesapeake bays, all of which he may have seen.

In some places where Ingram is plainly wrong, he is not necessarily lying. He certainly did not, as he says, see Indians habitually using iron; but he may have seen them with bits of meteoric iron; and he could have seen plenty of copper, which was used to some degree all the way from the big Lake Superior deposits to the New England coast and New York, where Henry Hudson found copper tobacco pipes in general use in 1609. The great "ruby" which Ingram says he saw an Indian "king" wearing cannot have been a real ruby. But make it a big piece of turquoise used for the adornment of a Pueblo Indian (Ingram must have passed through or near Pueblo country) or any kind of red agate, and it is fairly credible. Ingram didn't pretend to be a mineralogist, and, anyhow, he probably had never seen a real ruby in his life.

Believe them or not, however wild some of his other tales may have been, they had one virtue: They were exactly what Elizabethan adventurers and capitalists, with money to spend in exploration, wanted to hear. Nothing could have been better calculated to stimulate English interest in North America, the more so because success would be another triumph over the hated Spaniard. It was all valuable information to Sir Humphrey Gilbert, who was one of those present when Ingram was examined.

Sir Humphrey died at sea in 1583, cheerfully shouting across the water to another vessel, as his own ship went down, that the way to heaven was "as near by sea as by land." That ended the royal patent granted to him for American exploration, but it did not end the undertaking. The American patent was transferred to Raleigh, who sent out his first expedition in the following year. The obstinate efforts to settle Virginia which followed the voyage of 1584 are especially well reported, since they were under literate commanders who had to send the news back to London, where Raleigh took a strong scientific interest in what they found, as well as in the merely commercial aspects of the venture. Hence the story is far better recorded than most early ventures, both in written reports and in the pictures of fish, vegetation, natives, and insects, made on the spot by John White, one of the early leaders, who was also a competent draughtsman and painter.

In July of 1584, the two ships sent out by Raleigh and commanded by Philip Amidas and Arthur Barlow reached North Carolina, not far from Cape Lookout. Coasting north, they slipped through New

Inlet into Pamlico Sound and made their first landing on one of its southern islands. Delighted with its fertility, the crews celebrated their arrival by firing their muskets in salute, and as they did so, "a flocke of cranes, the most white, arose by us, with such a cry as if an Army of men had shouted altogether." The white "cranes" were, of course, either egrets ranging pretty far north, or very young little blue herons, which, before they reach full growth, have pure white plumage. It was the newcomers' first glimpse of the vast plenty of waterfowl that haunted creeks, marshes, and rivers all over North America. The marshy ground was full of woodcock, plover, and snipe; and in the streams were beaver, otter, muskrat, and "minxes," as they were soon to discover.

Except in one or two favored spots there is nothing quite like it today. In those days there was nothing to disturb the herons, ducks, and wild geese, which nested freely where they wished, waded or paddled in streams whose banks are now thickly populated, and feasted on frogs, tadpoles, and fish which have long since been driven from polluted waters. The Indians to be sure, killed freely; but no Indian wastes game; and the numbers they could kill with bows and arrows made no inroads at all upon the huge flocks that came and went each spring and fall.

Enraptured, these first English visitors, accustomed to the trimly domestic English landscape, gazed about upon the primitive luxuriance of their first small sample of wild North America. The "goodly tall Cedars" seemed "the highest and reddest Cedars of the world, bettering those of the Assores, Indies, or Libanus [Lebanon]." Red cedars in modern times are usually cut down untimely for the manufacture of pencils or fence posts; but the huge cedars upon which all the early explorers comment had had a century or more to live out their natural lives and reach—however slow their growth—a size undreamed of by modern Americans, who know only the small cedars of neglected pastures. "Cypress," apparently swamp cedar, grew eighteen feet in circumference and reached a height of fifty to eighty feet of straight trunk before the branches began.

Except along the rivers, which the newcomers had not yet seen, the land was wholly forest—pine, oak, "cypress" (which was merely more cedar), and sassafras, the latter always of interest to early visitors who could not quite conquer the interest in spices and aromatic barks which had prompted the first ventures westward. Besides, sassafras had been selling at twenty shillings a pound in London.

Like the air which blew seaward from it on each land breeze, the forest itself was fragrant. The trees were "of excellent smell and qualitie." In all, Virginia had "about 14. severall sorts of sweete smelling tymber trees." All North American woods must have been far more fragrant then than they are today.

Though the attention of the Virginia adventurers was mainly centered on useful plants, the more striking wild flowers soon caught their eyes. Robert Beverley, one of Virginia's first historians, notes that "the Cardinal-Flower, so much extolled for its Scarlet Colour,—is in almost every Branch; the Moccasin Flower, and a Thousand others not yet known to English Herbalists." In far-off Canada, a priest was admiring the brilliance of the cardinal flower at about the same time. (It is, incidentally, interesting to note the characteristically southern word "branch" for "brook" appearing so early in America.)

One good reason for the fragrance of Virginia woods is given in Beverley's further observation of "the fine Tulip-bearing Lawrel-Tree which has the pleasantest Smell in the World, and keeps Blossoming and Seeding several months together." Presumably this was a magnolia.

Seamen's eyes were quick to note professionally the oaks "far greater and better" than any in England—as was natural since they, too, had grown for centuries without danger of the lumberman's axe. Captain John Smith estimated, a few years later, that Virginia oak could be trimmed to single timbers two and a half feet square and sixty feet long! The pines, which grew thick along the sea coast, were so tall that, unless their trunks were cut specially short, it was hard to load them on board a ship of three hundred tons.

As in most of North America, wild grapes ran everywhere, covering not only the trees and the treetops, but—when there was no longer room there—the forest floor as well.

Going on a little farther, the first English arrivals established themselves on Roanoke Island, where the hospitable Indians feasted them with tea of wild ginger and sassafras, and "wine" made from the native grapes. This is one of the few cases on record of Indian wine-making—one suspects it was nothing but fresh grape juice gone a little alcoholic. The natives added to their hospitality with venison, roast fish, melons, boiled roots, and fruits of various kinds.

Someone asked the name of the country and received the reply "Wingandacoa." As there was no translator and conversation was wholly by signs, the warrior addressed did not understand the question. Feeling that he had to say something, this extremely polite red-skin thought it tactful to remark: "What pretty clothes you are wearing." As a result, the name of the new land was officially reported as "Wingandacoa"; and there would be a state of that name in the Union today, if Queen Elizabeth's vanity had not led to an order to call the new country Virginia in her honor.

When this first expedition returned to England with glowing accounts of what they had seen (explorers never underestimate their own discoveries), Raleigh made haste to send out in 1585 another ship, commanded by one of the greatest of Elizabeth's seamen, Sir Richard Grenville—soon to be famous for his battle to the death with the Spaniards. This time settlers came, and with them Thomas Hariot, eminent man of science, friend of Raleigh and of the poet Marlowe—obviously sent out to make a reliable scientific report on the country and its resources.

This time the Indians were not so friendly—probably because they began to realize that these white strangers had come to stay. There was some fighting and much difficulty in getting the natives to share food supplies.

The white men did not understand how to live off the country, rich though it was. Food ran short. One party exploring the interior ate two mastiff dogs "boyled with Saxefras leaves." Later, they made a meal on "soup made of sassafras leaves, a food which nobody had ever tried before"—and, it may be added, a food that nobody has ever cared to try since. At intervals other parties had to leave the island and go over to the Virginia coast "to live upon rootes and Oysters." Despite the excellence of Virginia oysters and the usual English enthusiasm for them, they seem to have regarded this as rather a hardship, though the local Indians depended almost entirely upon shellfish during the period when their crops were ripening.

Just as matters were becoming desperate, in sailed Sir Francis Drake, with a fleet of twenty-three ships. With the backing of Sir Philip Sidney, he contemplated establishing another colony, plans for which had to be given up as the danger of Spanish invasion at home grew more threatening. The fact that Raleigh's men were rivals of his own proposed settlement deterred that generous mind not a whit. Drake first offered them supplies and then a vessel of 170 tons burden to take them back to England. He had recently captured twenty Spanish ships and was well able to spare one from his fleet. The colonists were safely back in England by July, 1586.

Scarcely had they gone, when Grenville sailed up Pamlico Sound, with supplies from England. Bewildered at finding no trace of the men he had left he landed supplies anyhow; and with them he put ashore a small group of new settlers, under the impression that the settlers of 1585 must still be somewhere about. So far as he knew, they had had no opportunity to leave and there were no signs that they had been attacked.

When, in the following year, 1587, three more ships arrived, they found that this colony, too, had vanished. Weeds growing about the cabins showed that the settlers had been gone for some time. Grenville left more men but when, in 1589, another little fleet put in at Roanoke, these settlers, also, were missing. Grass grew over heavy metal objects that they had abandoned. Various chests had been buried and then dug up again by someone. John White, their returning leader, found his books, maps, and pictures mouldering on the ground.

Searching, they found the bark stripped from a tree and the word "CROATOAN" carved. Later, on another post, they found the letters "CRO." Neither inscription included a cross, which they had agreed on as a sign of distress. The relief ships started for Croatoan Island, about twenty miles to the south, but were driven off by a storm. White could not persuade the sailors to further search: "And thus we left seeking our Colony, that was never any of them found, nor seene to this day 1622."

Years later, Indians told the Jamestown settlers that the abandoned colonists had lived in native villages until medicine men instigated the murder of all except four men, two boys, "and one yonge mayde"— who may have been Virginia Dare, the first white child born in the United States.

There the mystery rested until, in 1937, a stone was discovered on the east bank of the Choman River, in North Carolina, with the carved directions, "Anye Englishman shew John White Govr Via." This told briefly of the party's fate; but it now appears to be just one more of the surprising number of fraudulent inscriptions with which practical jokers, at great expense of time and labor, have strewn North America.

In spite of disasters, the English kept sending settlers to Virginia. It was not long before they had settled on the mainland and were pushing explorations inland, up the James River as far as "that cataract or fall of water, which the Indians call Paquachowng," i.e., the falls at Richmond, 110 miles from the mouth of the James. Beyond this part of Virginia's "fall line," they presently penetrated "as the river led them," some forty or fifty miles farther—in other words about as far as Columbia, Virginia, half way between Richmond and Charlottesville.

Not too far beyond this point, they hoped to find the Pacific Ocean. William Strachey, in his *First Booke of the Historie of Travaile into Virginia Britannia,* thought that one branch of the James River came from "high hills afar of, within the land." From Richmond he thought it would be about ten days' march, not over 160 miles, to these mountains, "from the topps of which hills, the people saie they see another sea, and that the water is there salt." John Stephenson, in 1651, was just as positive that "New Albion" on the Pacific, of which Drake had taken possession in 1577, was only ten days "from the head of Jeames River, over those hills and through the rich adjacent valleyes, beautyfied with as profittable rivers which necessarily must run into that peacefull Indian sea." The only thing wrong with these ideas was the presence of the Mississippi River and the Rocky Mountains.

Above the fall line, the land was wooded everywhere, save for marshes and a few open fields. So thick were the woodlands that many of them were still uncut at the Revolution. Even the fields which farmers did work were often still covered with gaunt, dead trees that had been girdled and left to die. Around and among these, crops grew as best they could.

As the first English explorers pushed inland through Virginia, they found waterfowl growing scarcer, though wherever there was a pond they reappeared. But there were wild turkey "of an incridible Bigness, partridge, pigeons, deer, rabbit, fox, raccons, bear, panther, elk, wild-cat, buffalo, possum, wild hog." Some wild turkeys had been found earlier, near the sea, for one account of events in 1605 mentions "store of Turkie nests and many Eggs." The raccoons, according to Raphe Hamor, were "as good meat as lamb."

In some places rainfall left glistening minerals along the banks of streams so thickly "that the grownd in some places seemeth as gilded." A stream near Jamestown "wash'd down with it a yellow sort of Dust-Isinglass, which being cleansed by the fresh streaming of the water, lay shining in the bottom of that limpid Element." This raised hopes of finding gold and other precious minerals, but the glistening objects by the shore were only bits of quartz, mica, or iron pyrites, though the Jamestown people sent two ships back to England with "this gilded Dirt," before they found out their mistake.

They were not the only ones to make it. Bartholomew Gosnold, explorer of the New England coast, eagerly eyed worthless but "glistering mineral stones" on an island off Cape Cod, and many a load of "ore" was sent back to Europe, only to be found worthless. The early French along the St. Lawrence took home so many shining crystals, of no value at all, that "un diamant de Canada" became a proverb for anything worthless.

The marshy lowlands below Virginia's fall line naturally had more fish and fowl—certainly more waterfowl—than the uplands, which had "more number of beasts." There was an exception to this rule in the black bears which haunted the coast, where the Indians hunted them "most greedily; for indeed they love them above all other their flesh." Much to the irritation of the English settlers, who also liked it, the Indians usually refused to sell bear meat. They kept it for themselves

—"very toothsoome sweet venison, as good to be eaten as the flesh of a calfe of two yeares old." Farther up the coast, John Josselyn, seventeenth century writer on New England, noted that the animals were "very fatt in the Fall of the Leaf with feeding upon Acorns, at which time they are excellent Venison," and the meat of black bears, well fattened for winter hibernation, continued to be a favorite diet among the settlers as long as the old frontier endured.

Most of the open country was along the rivers, where marshes might occupy from twenty up to two hundred acres. In some of these swampy areas, wild onions grew in patches an acre or more in extent. The wild "leeks" occasionally reported were probably just more of these same wild onions. The Indians scornfully refused to eat them, but the newcomers from England, though disappointed by their small size "not past the bignes of the toppe of one's thumb"—thought that "they eate well sod or otherwise in sallets and bakt meats."

"Grass there is little or none," says one early report, "but what groweth in low Marishes: for all the Countrey is overgrowne with trees." The southern coast, though sandy, was "thick sett with woodes of divers sort," and the "mould and sword of the earth" was two feet thick.

Everything seemed to grow readily. The settlers brought from the West Indies, "the plants of orange trees, which, put into the ground carelessly, and neclected, have yet prospered." Garden seeds from England did quite as well. Everyone wondered at the dimensions of the Indians "potatoes." "English," or "Irish" potatoes the settlers knew already, but these tubers, either red or white in color, were "as big as a Boy's Leg, and sometimes about as long and as big as both the Leg and Thigh of a young Child, and very much resembling it in shape." The description is both apt and accurate, but none of this was so remarkable as they thought—you can grow sweet potatoes or yams as large as that even in the North.

Unlike such great western torrents as the Missouri and Mississippi, the Virginia rivers below the fall line were not swift enough to carry down many large trees in the spring floods. Hence they were not blocked with snags in midstream or great "barrages" of tangled timber stretching out from the shore, as were the western rivers, and from the beginning they were navigable far inland.

Not realizing that most of the rivers were tidal, the colonists were surprised to find "within the shoares of our rivers, whole bancks of oysters and scallopps, which lye unopened and thick together, as if there had bene their naturall bedd before the sea left them." Englishmen accustomed to their own small bivalves, are always surprised at the size of American oysters. Everyone knows Thackeray's complaint after his first experience with a Cape Cod halfshell that he felt as if he had "swallowed the baby." In those early days, however, oysters grew to enormous sizes. "I have seene some thirteen inches long," says William Strachey. Virginia oysters grew, Strachey explains, "in whole bancks and bedds, and those of the best." John Pory describes Massachusetts oysters "as broad as a bushell," while John Josselyn says they were nine inches long and had to be cut in three pieces before they could be swallowed, "very fat and sweet" and "delicate breakfast meat."

The Indians boiled them with mussels, thickening the mixture with cornmeal, the result being "a good spoone meate." Smoked oysters were an ancient Indian invention, which in recent years have become popular at white men's cocktail parties.

Strachey noted that the tide ebbed and flowed "well nigh unto the heads of all the rivers (I meane to the falls, unto the high land)," so that the water was naturally salt enough for shellfish pretty far up stream. The Virginia shore had evidently been sinking rather rapidly not long before the English settlement, for they found great expanses of oyster shells on land along the river banks—in one case for a stretch of three miles. These, they noted, would be a convenient source for lime. Plaster made of shells instead of limestone was, in fact, used all along the Atlantic coast for the next two centuries. You can still find some of it in very old houses.

The Virginia explorers were about the only ones who paid any attention to the insect life about them, though some of the French kept a sharp eye on the possibility of silkworm raising. Partly this was due to the lucky fact that John White was a really skillful painter and draughtsman, with a keen interest in botany and zoology, and partly to the fact that they stumbled upon some trees, on whose foliage the fat green larvae of some species of the big American Saturnid moths were feasting. Hariot calls them "fine, large silkworms, as big as walnuts." He was disappointed because "we did not find them in such abundance as we heard that they existed in other parts of the country, yet since they grow so naturally there, a successful industry could be established." Though he was primarily a mathematician and astronomer, not an entomologist, Hariot was not far wrong. Silk *can* be made from the cocoons of the American Saturnid moths, but like all other sericulture in the United States, this has never been commercially successful.

Just about this time, interest in the silkworm was developing in England, and James I was making every effort to encourage it. The English colonists, delighted to find Virginia mulberries growing wild, in "many pretty copsies or boskes," imported some "seed"—that is, eggs—after which "there was an assay made to make silke, and surely the wormes prospered excellent well, till the master workeman fell sicke, During which time they were eaten with Rats."

White also noted the big, yellow Tiger Swallowtail butterfly which floats so gracefully about modern flower beds all summer long. He even made a life-size drawing in color of the beautiful creature, which probably caught his fancy because there is nothing like it among English lepidoptera. His drawing is remarkably accurate, even the venation of the wings being rather well indicated. Though he fails to catch some details of shape and coloring, there is no doubt about the black and yellow markings and the "swallowtails," which give the butterfly its popular name.

Though the Tiger Swallowtail's gleaming wings may be seen fluttering all over eastern North America and though a closely related species, indistinguishable to the unpracticed eye, is equally numerous in the West, White is the only man who, down to the eighteenth century, thought it worth recording.

He also drew in color a quite recognizable gadfly, an insect he could not very well escape noticing since it bites so fiercely and so freely. More interesting are four colored drawings of the firefly, "A flye which in the night seemeth a flame of fyer." John Josselyn, who also

Map of the coast of Virginia, showing the island of Roanoke. Entitled "The Englishmen's Arrival in Virginia," it is Theodore De Bry's engraving copied from John White's water color. From *A Brief and True Report of the New Found Land of Virginia*, by Thomas Hariot, published in 1588.

De Bry's engraving, based on a water color by John White, showing the Indians' manner of fishing with crude spears and nets. From *A Brief and True Report of the New Found Land of Virginia.*

noted the fireflies, exclaims: "Glow-worms here have wings, there are multitudes of them insomuch that in the dark evening when I first went into the Countrey I thought the whole Heavens had been on fire seeing so many sparkles flying in the air."

In spite of all their hardships, the Virginia colonists were delighted with "the mildnesse of the ayre, the fertilitie of the soyle, and situation of the rivers." Hariot, making a kind of scientific survey of the country, carefully listed all natural resources—herbs, nuts, fish, birds, and dye-woods like sumac, most of which he could not identify, though he learned the Indian names of eighty-six different birds. He also preached to the Indians and was at pains to learn their myths and religious beliefs, as well as he could.

Most of the fruits and plants pleased the colonists. They found "cherries," which were "much like a Damson." There is not much doubt that these were beach plums, "but for their taste and colour we called them Cherries." Strawberries seemed "much fairer and more sweete then ours." Some fields were "full of fine and beautifull Strawberries, foure times bigger and better then ours in England." Some of the omnipresent wild grapes were nearly as big as English cherries—which is not incredible if we remember that most of the cultivated fruit of that day was smaller than the highly developed products of twentieth century horticulture.

William Strachey thought it wonderful "to behold the goodly vines burthening every neighbour bush, and clymbing the toppes of highest trees, and those full of clusters of grapes in their kind, however dreeped and shadowed soever from the sun." And he adds, "I can saie yt, that we have eaten there, as full and lushious a grape as in the villages betweene Paris and Amiens, and I have drunck often of the rathe [early] wine, which Doctor Bohune and other of our people have made full as good, as your French British wyne."

Not all the fruit was so satisfactory. One account says that the few wild crab apples they found were "very small and bitter," but Hamor declares: "Crabbes great store, lesse, but not so sower as ours, which grafted with the *Siens* [scions] of English aple trees, without question would beare very good fruits."

There was also a berry, "very much like unto Capers," which grew in moist valleys. This must have been the cranberry, which in its wild state ranges south to Virginia. The settlers thought that "they differ not much from poyson," unless boiled, though a little later the Massachusetts colonists thought them so good they sent ten barrels home for Charles II to taste. Colonel James Smith, captured by Indians just before Braddock's defeat in 1755, found cranberries agreeable enough when well sugared, "though rather too sour of themselves." Cranberry sauce was well known to Americans as early as 1675, when John Josselyn tells how: "The Indians and English use them much, boyling them with Sugar for Sauce to eat with their Meat; and it is a delicate Sauce, especially for roasted Mutton." The berry itself, Josselyn adds, was "of a sower astringent taste."

Other wild fruits which interested the English were "raspises" (wild blackberries and dewberries, and probably some native American raspberries), "hurts" (apparently blueberries), and "Marecocks," which are described as "a pleasant wholesome fruit much like a Lemond"—presumably the fruit of the passionflower, though possibly the May apple.

The Virginians' greatest botanical shock was their first experience with persimmons. The inexperienced Englishmen mistook them for plums (the Spaniards seem to have done the same thing), tried to eat them before the frost had touched them, and immediately wished they hadn't. As William Strachey complained, "when they are not fully ripe, they are harsh and choakie, and furre in a man's mouth." However, another Englishman remarks of the persimmon, "if it be not ripe it will draw a man's mouth awry with much torment, but when it is is ripe, it is as delicious as an Apricock."

The real enthusiast was a much later Englishman, Elias Pym Fordham, a nineteenth century settler in Indiana, who thought persimmons tasted "like raisins dipped in honey." It is amusing to note the date of this observation. Fordham ate his persimmons on December 16. There had been plenty of frost in Indiana by that time!

The English newcomers also noted violets, purslane, and sorrel—edible plants now usually regarded as mere weeds, though the colonists found them "good for brothes and sallets" and the two last are still occasionally used as food. There was nothing unusual to the Elizabethan about eating the young violet leaves, which at home in England were not only used as a salad but were also fried in batter, the result being, according to Sir John Evelyn, "one of the most agreeable of all the herbaceous dishes."

There was a certain danger in experimenting with unknown American plants. A group of Virginia soldiers who, a little later, gathered a mess of young Jimson weed "for a boil'd Salad" were dangerously affected. A contemporary account says that they suffered from amnesia and temporary insanity for eleven days; and though that may be an exaggeration, there is no doubt that Gray's *Botany* lists the weed as "narcotic-poisonous." The fact that there was enough of it at so early a date to produce such a serious effect suggests that it is a native American plant and not, as sometimes suggested, an Asiatic importation.

The Virginia colonists were not quite so painfully surprised by strange plants and strange fruit as was John Josselyn, who went out for a walk in the wild country near Scarborough, Maine, about 1638. On a tree, he "chanc't to spye a fruit as I thought like a pine Apple," which was "of an Ash Colour." It was a queer-looking fruit, to be sure, and remarkably big; but Josselyn had seen so many strange things in this new country that he was not greatly surprised. He grasped it—only to be stung by an emerging swarm of furious hornets, so severely that his companions could hardly recognize his swollen face. When he recovered from his stings, Josselyn pondered on the odd substance of which the big grey nest was made. It was, of course, paper, but Josselyn did not realize that: "Of what matter its made no man knows; Wax it is not, neither will it melt nor fry, but will take fire suddenly like Tinder."

American nuts met with instant favor. Like the Spaniards, both French and English appreciated the superior flavor of the American chestnut, "whose wild fruit equalize the best in France, Spaine, Germany, or Italy." The chinquapin nut interested the English, when they found the Indians regarded it as "a great daintie." The "walnuts" they found must have been hickories, for they describe the "Pawhiccora," or "hickory milk" which the Virginia Indians, like those farther south, made by pounding up the nuts, shell and all, in water and then letting the shell fragments settle.

Curiously enough none of the early explorers mention poison ivy, though some of them must have suffered from it. Probably, among the multifarious ills of the wilderness, they did not quite realize what caused its itching, biting, spreading rash, though it is also likely that this ill-omened plant has spread rapidly since the white man has opened fields and roads. It cannot flourish in the shade, and eastern North America in the beginning was mostly shade. The earliest mention of it appears to be that in the journal of Jeremy Belknap, a parson who, traveling from Boston to Oneida in 1796, on his way encountered "the poison of bushes and plants which usually affect the skin." The remedy of that period was the root of wake-robin, bruised in milk.

The English in Virginia had a surprisingly quick eye for birds, probably because of the keen interest of Hariot and of White. The latter made surprisingly good paintings of them. They noted the wild turkey, "partridges"—presumably ruffed grouse or Bob White quail—which were "little bigger than our Qualles," the red-winged blackbird, "divers sorts of small Birds, some read, some blew," which were presumably cardinals and bluebirds. George Percy in 1605 saw "Black Birds with crimson wings, and divers other Fowles and Birds of divers and sundrie collours or crimson, Watchet, Yellow, Greene, Murry, and of divers other hewes." Except for this mention of yellow birds, goldfinches escaped notice in Virginia, but Gosnold's men in Massachusetts saw them, "like canary birds." The "Parrats, and Pigeons," which they found everywhere seem strange to modern Americans, who are used to finding in their woods only a few shy wood doves and no parrots at all; but these were the now-vanished Carolina parroquet, which in those days ranged north to Canada, and the passenger pigeon, whose immense numbers all travelers describe for the next two centuries, though ruthless pot-hunting wiped it out long ago.

The parroquets were beautiful little birds: "Yet be they a fowle most swift of wing, their winges and breasts are of a greenish cullour, with forked tayles, their heades, some crymsen, some yellowe, some orange-

Carolina parroquet and Passenger pigeon, from Mark Catesby's *Natural History of Carolina, Florida and the Bahama Islands,* 1754.

"Sioux Moving Camp," a pencil sketch by George Catlin from *Souvenir of North American Indians*, 1850.

tawny, very beautiful." Strachey also describes the immense numbers of the passenger pigeon, fearing he will not be believed in England "yf I should expresse what extended flocks, and how manie thousands in one flock, I have seene in one daie, wondering (I must confess) at their flight, when, like so many thickned clowdes, they (having fed to the norward in the daye tyme) retourne again more sowardly towards night to their roust; but there be manie hundred witnesses." Hamor says: "wilde Pigeons (in winter beyond number or imagination, my selfe haue seene three or foure houres together flockes in the aire, so thicke that euen they have shaddowed the skie from vs."

The rivers were full of fish which the Indians took by netting, spearing, angling, and even by shooting them with arrows tied to a long line. Shad were in "great store, of a yard long, and for sweetnes and fatnes a reasonable good fish." But since the peculiarly American art of boning shad had not yet been discovered, the English writer concludes sadly: "he is only full of small bones." You could take five thousand at one haul of the net as late as the eighteenth century, according to the Reverend Andrew Burnaby—and who would accuse a clergyman of telling fish stories?

Captain John Smith notes: "We had more Sturgeon, then could be devoured by Dog and Man." George Percy, one of his men who later wrote a little *Discourse on Virginia* (1606), exclaimed: "As for Sturgeon all the World cannot be compared to it." Smith claimed to have taken fifty-two sturgeon at a haul on one occasion and sixty-two at another. This was extra good fishing; but it was not unusual for a single net to take seven or eight of the great fish in four or five hours; and the Indians did not always bother with nets. A really bold red fisherman thought nothing of slipping a noose over a big sturgeon's tail and then simply hanging on, drawing breath when he could, no matter where the fish dragged him. As the sturgeon did all the struggling, it wore out its strength in the end, and its captor— himself often half-drowned in the process—hauled it ashore. Now and then a sturgeon simply jumped into the canoe.

Raphe Hamor tells how he helped take at a single haul of the net "a frigots lading of Sturgion, Base and other great fish," adding: "if we had beene furnished with salt, to have saued it, wee might haue taken as much fish as would haue serued vs that whole yeere."

The fish themselves were enormous, much larger than any taken today. From the latter part of May to the end of June, young sturgeon not more than three feet long ran up the rivers; but from that time to mid-September sturgeon six and even nine feet long were taken. Smith's tales are by no means incredible. Six-foot sturgeon are not unknown even now in modern Minnesota, and there seems no doubt that even these huge fish are smaller than their ancestors. The fresh-water sturgeon of the middle western and Canadian lakes today are declining in size since dams have cut them off from the sea. Sixteenth and seventeenth century fish certainly reached a larger growth than they ever get a chance to attain in our much-fished modern streams. In fact, John Josselyn mentions sturgeon sixteen feet long.

Smith's story gets an odd mid-continental confirmation from an oral tradition still extant among the Seine River band of modern Ojibway in northern Ontario. These living Indians say that their forefathers in ancient days feared to take their canoes out on Lake Manitou, some fifty miles north of the border, lest the great fish upset the canoes. Sturgeon do have a habit of sleeping near the surface on sunny days, and a light birchbark colliding with one of them might easily be overset. Josselyn also mentions this odd fact. The sturgeon, he says, "are in some Rivers so numerous, that it is hazardous for Canoes and the like small Vessels to pass."

Where there were so many fish, the ospreys were sure to be. The English newcomers watched in surprise as the great birds plunged into the river, and were still more surprised, no doubt, as they observed that bold pirate, the bald eagle, forcing unhappy ospreys to give up their fish.

As time passed and more settlers came, Virginia became a prosperous, civilized colony. Settlement was spreading in the middle eighteenth century as far as Charlottesville and the eastern foothills of the Blue Ridge. Most of the Indians sullenly vanished—though a few remain to this day. Bold, eager, curious, and greedy men, looking at the sun as it sank behind the Blue Ridge, began to wonder what lay beyond the mountain.

XII

The Finding of New England

SUCH RECORDS AS were left behind by the first explorers who sailed along the North American coast, from Florida to the St. Lawrence, give little idea what the land beyond the coast itself was like. The fact is, they didn't know themselves. Most of them merely ran along the mysterious new continent—at a safe distance, to make sure of having deep water under their keels—and then turned back to Europe. It is true that Gaspar Corte Real, a native of the Azores who visited North America in 1500 and again in 1501, went ashore long enough to capture and send back sixty wretched Indian slaves; but he cannot have gone very far inland and he left no account of what he found. When he disappeared, his brother, Miguel, went out in 1502 to find him and also disappeared. A much obscured inscription on a rock at Dighton, Massachusetts, apparently containing the name Corte Real, perhaps may show that one of the brothers passed there before he died.

After that, from the Norsemen to Raleigh's colonists, no one except the Florentine, Giovanni da Verrazano, ever penetrated so much as five miles beyond the North Atlantic shoreline. Even Verrazano ventured inland only in Rhode Island and that only on one or two occasions in 1524.

None of these men saw much of the country itself, and the little they did see was very sketchily reported. These early voyagers were sadly handicapped by the clumsiness of their vessels, which made it difficult and dangerous to attempt exploration ashore.

As yet, European naval architects had not developed ships that could sail easily into the wind. As a result, the early sixteenth century explorers simply hurried on along the strange coast looking for the mythical Northwest Passage as long as the wind was favorable. They could not pause to examine the country and describe it in detail, for they did not know when the wind would change.

Moreover, they had to be extraordinarily cautious all the time, for the coast was wholly uncharted, and there was no way to repair serious damage to their hulls. Bringing his tiny *Half Moon* into New York harbor—which is deep enough for the whole United States battle fleet—Henry Hudson crawled along cautiously, keeping a small boat ahead, taking soundings most of the way. Cartier was equally circumspect in the Gulf of the St. Lawrence, where the biggest modern liners can enter with ease—since they know the channel. Precautions like these took time that might otherwise have been spent on exploration inland.

To make things still more difficult, the mouths of many of the big northern rivers were blocked with sand dunes or with wooded peninsulas and islands, which at a little distance blended with the wooded shore, concealing the rivers entirely. Sebastian Cabot probably sailed past New York harbor without ever guessing it was there. Verrazano ran 150 miles south of North Carolina without finding a harbor. Hudson seems to have suspected there was a river somewhere up New York Bay, not because he could see it, but because he felt the current against his hull. Even when great expanses like Chesapeake Bay and Delaware Bay or the Gulf of St. Lawrence opened invitingly inland, a ship's master, thousands of miles from any possible dockyard, thought twice before he ventured in.

So many troubles beset the first adventurers, that it is no wonder they spent no time writing landscape descriptions. Ocean currents, of which these early mariners had no very clear ideas, upset their reckoning. Often, they did not know quite where they were. The ship's run for the day was often hard to calculate. (Columbus himself was uniformly wrong. The extra-short day's runs, with which he tried to fool his crews, turn out to have been nearer right than the "correct" figures which he kept secret!) In northern waters, fogs and icebergs added to the difficulties.

Even when the first explorers did go ashore, the wretched Indians and Eskimos whom they met did not suggest the prospect of much profit in the new country. The Pilgrim Fathers themselves got a very bad impression of Massachusetts at their first glimpse, in the middle of a New England November. "What could they see but a hidious and desolate wilderness, full of wild beasts and willd men?" wrote William Bradford. "And what multitude ther might be of them they knew not." It was natural to feel that way, "for summer being done all things stood upon them with a weatherbeaten face; and the whole countrie, full of woods and thickets, represented a wild and savage hiew." When they did land, they found "shuch thickets as were ready to tear their cloaths and armore in pieces." Their letters home led Oliver Cromwell to describe New England as "that desert and barren wilderness."

Confronted with such country, it is no wonder hopeful sea captains usually thought it wiser to keep running along the coast—particularly as astute Indian chiefs soon learned to get rid of their unwelcome visitors by finding out what they were looking for and then explaining that they would find it just a little farther on—in another tribe's territory. At any moment the Northwest Passage to Asia, fame, and wealth seemed just about to open out ahead. It never did, but exploration lives on hope.

The first real description of the North Atlantic coast is that of Giovanni da Verrazano,—sent out by Francis I, King of France,—who, on March 7, 1524, saw land in what he thought was latitude 34° North. Though errors of one or two degrees were by no means impossible in the navigation of that period,—Columbus even "shot" the wrong North Star—it is probably safe to say that Verrazano was somewhere to the south, rather than the north, of Cape Fear, not far from the general vicinity of Wilmington, North Carolina.

Running to within half or three-quarters of a mile of the low-lying coast, Verrazano saw "great fires built on the shore of the sea" and knew that the land was inhabited, though he did not meet Indians. When, after running 150 miles south, he could find no harbor, he turned north again; so that, when he finally anchored and sent a boat ashore, he seems to have been back off the coast of North Carolina.

The rather advanced southern Indians along the coast, amazed by the white skins of their strange visitors, were hospitable. Verrazano managed at first to convince himself that they looked like Chinese—which is not quite so absurd as it sounds, for Indian children are often distinctly Mongolian in appearance, and Verrazano had probably never seen a real Chinese in his life. The natives were certainly strangely colored and very foreign-looking in Italian eyes.

The shore was covered with sand dunes. Rivers or arms of the sea cut into the coast. The white men admired "the spacious land, so high that it exceeds the sandy shore, with many beautiful fields and plains, full of the largest forests, some thin and some dense, clothed with various sorts of trees, with as much beauty and delectable appearance as it would be possible to express." There were palms, laurels, "cypresses," and other trees, "unknown in our Europe," at which Verrazano could only guess.

These trees, he notes, "for a long distance, exhale the sweetest odors"—an odd and pleasant phenomenon which a good many other early explorers noted and which, when the wind is right, still occasionally greets the eager nostrils of modern mariners. In primitive days, when the virgin North American forests were in blossom, the Atlantic coast was so redolent, spring and summer, that its fragrance was perceptible miles at sea. Raleigh's colonists, off the coast of "Florida"—which then meant almost anything south of modern Virginia—"felt a most dilicate sweete smell, though they saw no land, which ere long they espied." This was in July of 1584. One of the voyagers says it was "so strong a smel, as if we had bene in the midst of some delicate garden abounding in all kinde of odoriferous flowers, by which we were assured, that the land could not be farre distant." Verrazano also sniffed fragrance while still at sea. The trees, he says, "for a long distance, exhale the sweetest odors," adding in some MSS., "we smelled the odor a hundred leagues. and farther when they burned the cedars and the winds blew from the land."

Even as far north as Massachusetts, Bartholomew Gosnold's crew, when still one day's sail off the coast, in 1602, "had smelling of the shore, such as from the southern Cape and Andalusia, in Spain." And John Winthrop, approaching Mount Desert Island was pleased by "a smell off the shore like the smell of a garden."

In the South, the fragrance of North America was stronger still. Columbus, as he led his little fleet through Crooked Island Passage on October 19, 1492, just a week after the great discovery, sniffed eagerly at an offshore breeze, on which "there came so fair and sweet a smell of flowers or trees from the land, that it was the sweetest thing in the world." At the same place in 1940, his biographer, Mr. S. E. Morison, shared the same experience almost five hundred years later.

As they landed in New York Harbor from the yacht *Half Moon*, in 1609, Henry Hudson's men were pleased by the grass and flowers on the New Jersey side of the Narrows, "and very sweet smells came from them," although this fragrance did not reach out to sea.

It is sometimes suggested that all these early travelers were obsessed with the idea of finding a passage to the spice islands, and so merely imagined the fragrance they report, but this idea seems wrong. For one thing, they never report spicy odors. Then, too, independently of each other (most of them were keeping their discoveries as secret as they could), for more than a hundred years, they tell the same story of the very fragrance that still rolls out to sea in parts of the Gulf of Mexico.

Occasionally, in very early days, masses of flowers floated in the water. A ship running in past Cape Anne toward Gloucester, in 1629, passed through a film of floating blossoms, "sometymes scattered abroad, sometymes joyned in sheets 9 or 10 yards long, which we supposed to be brought from the low meadows by the tide."

Probably in the blossoming time of that ancient, primeval, undisturbed wilderness—such as no man today can quite imagine—fragrance ran along the whole eastern coast from New England to the Gulf. Woodlands which had not yet been turned into factories, towns, golf courses, concrete roadbeds, farmlands, and town dumps, were full of fragrant flowers in numbers which the poor modern remnants of ancient forests barely suggest. Flowering plants and flowering trees in ancient days were many thousand times as numerous as their contemporary descendants. It was a wilderness so large that things like this could happen; whereas in modern days the only fragrance even hinting at the intensities of early times is to be found in the redolent pine forests of the North or the great expanses of chaparral in the West—to which, curiously enough, the discoverers never allude.

Except perhaps in Florida, few of the Atlantic coastal forests presented the hopeless tangle of vegetation to be found on the Pacific. "Their density is not so great but that they are entirely penetrable," said Verrazano.

Along the coast, Verrazano noted only "stags, deer, hares" among the game animals and "various numbers of birds, adapted and convenient for every pleasure of the hunt." Though the woods buffalo then ranged the eastern forests—as they were to do for at least two centuries more—they do not seem to have approached the sea, except perhaps along Chesapeake Bay. None of the early explorers mention them. Few even saw the hides that were occasionally brought from the interior. There were, of course, many other animals in the coastal forests, but sticking close to their ships, Verrazano's sailors had no chance of seeing them.

Coasting slowly north, Verrazano found "an isthmus a mile in width and about 200 long, in which, from the ship, was seen the oriental sea between the west and north. Which is the one, without doubt, which goes about the extremity of India, China and Cathay." His description is far from accurate, but it is clear enough he was looking, across intervening lowlands, at either Chesapeake or Delaware Bay. Though Verrazano himself soon came to doubt that he had really seen the Pacific, he failed to cut this comment out of his manuscript, with the unfortunate result that map-makers began to put a huge and entirely imaginary "Gulf of Verrazano" where the extremely solid substance of Canada, Oregon, Washington, Montana, the Dakotas, and most of the Middle West actually lay. It made the Northwest Passage and the mythical "Strait of Anian" seem plausible, and thus amazingly mixed up the exploration which followed.

Going about 150 miles farther, he came to "another land which appeared much more beautiful and full of the largest forests." These also were open, "but not of such fragrance, on account of being more north and cold." There were "wild roses, violets and lilies, and many sorts of herbs and fragrant flowers different from ours."

It is not hard to guess at the wild flowers Verrazano must have seen. The ordinary pink wild rose would be blooming in the meadows, and the Canada lily would be nodding its clusters above them, while almost anywhere in the woods the white strangers could have seen the innumerable species of North American wild violets, purple, white, and yellow. Either Verrazano or some early Spaniard was quick to notice the flashing red bee balm—also called Oswego tea, or square-stalk—for it is pictured in a book by the Spanish medical botanist, Nicholas Monardes, in 1574.

He must also have seen the brilliant Turk's cap and Philadelphia lilies, for John Josselyn later remarks that "Red-Lilly growes all over the countrey amongst the bushes." Josselyn also notes a good many other plants, of which the most interesting is the "yellow bastard daffodill," whose "green leaves are spotted with black spots"—obviously the dog's-tooth violet, or trout lily, though the leaf spots are actually brown instead of black.

Since Josselyn and some of the Jesuit explorers often had a quick, if not very scientific, eye for wild plants, one is at first puzzled by their failure to mention some of the commonest and most striking American wild flowers. Queen Anne's lace, ox-eye daisy, bouncing Bet, celandine, and the common black-eyed Susan, for example, are never listed. There is, however, a good reason for that. All of these, except the black-eyed Susan, are later importations from the old world. The black-eyed Susan is a western wild flower, unknown along the Atlantic coast until, in modern times, it was accidentally brought East in shipments of seed—some say clover seed. Without these flowers, now wide-spread, prehistoric American meadows made an appearance very different from that of today.

Presently—Verrazano says three hundred miles farther on, but many of his distances are obviously wrong—the ship blundered into New York Harbor "in the midst of which flowed to the sea a very great river, which was deep within the mouth." Apparently Verrazano kept his ship in the Lower Bay—at least that is the only way to explain his remark that he remained "anchored off the coast in good shelter."

He then took a small boat, "entering the said river to the land." If he
entered the river, he must surely have come as far as Manhattan
Island and perhaps beyond.

New Yorkers being ardent "greeters" even then, the local Mohicans
swarmed down to the shore "clothed with the feathers of birds of
various colors." They showed the white men a good landing place;
and, as the news of these strange beings spread, thirty canoes put out
"with innumerable people, who passed from one shore and the other
in order to see us." Verrazano had just begun to admire "a very beautiful lake with a circuit of about three leagues," which was probably
some part of the harbor near Manhattan Island, when a gale sprang up
and he hurried anxiously back to his ship.

So brief was his visit that it made no great impression on the Indians.
There seems to have been not even a lingering tradition of Verrazano's passage when Henry Hudson arrived seventy-five years later,
though Indians' stories about Hudson were still being told after twice
that time. Verrazano, however, had his moments of vision. He reflected, as he surveyed the site of the future metropolis, that "it was
not without some properties of value"!

As they sailed on up the New England coast, they passed Block
Island, hilly and tree-covered, though John Winthrop, a century later
did not think much of the trees. The island, he said, was "all overgrown with brush-wood of oak,—no good timber in it." Not much
interested in lumbering, Verrazano noted from his quarter-deck that
the country must be thickly inhabited. After dark, fires gleamed all
along the shores. These were the villages of Mohican and other Long
Island and Connecticut tribes, soon to fall if not already falling, under
the ruthless domination of the fierce Mohawks, whose home was
farther up the Hudson River, which Verrazano had just left.

Without landing, he pushed on to Newport, anchoring in Narragansett Bay. Not far from his anchorage up the Taunton River, near
Dighton, Massachusetts, lay Dighton Rock, covered with innumerable
inscriptions, among which a serious modern scholar believes he can
discern a carved inscription left by Miguel Corte Real. But this is at
best a dubious clue to his mysterious fate, since the great boulder at
the water's edge has other inscriptions, both Indian and white, so

numerous that they overlap each other; and even the most cautious deciphering is just a little questionable.

Untroubled by such archeological misgivings, enchanted by the beauty of the place, Verrazano lingered fifteen days, making friends with the Indians and platonically admiring their squaws' "beauty and charm; very graceful; of comely mien and agreeable aspect." New England Indian girls seem to have merited his enthusiasm. John Josselyn, 150 years later, expatiates on the attractions of the "Indesses." "The Indesses that are young are some of them very comely, having good features, their faces plump and round, and generally plumt of their Bodies, as are the men likewise, and as soft and smooth as a mole-skin, of reasonable good complexions, but that they dye themselves tawnie, many pretty Brownettos and spider-finger'd Lasses may be seen amongst them."

Those Verrazano met were much more discreet than most Indian women, or perhaps the Narragansett warriors were simply more jealous than most Indian husbands and fathers. They refused to let the squaws come aboard the ship at all and even sent some of them off to a distant island. Unlike the Iroquois and western tribes, who freely offered their women to visitors, the New York and New England Indians were models of propriety. Hudson later commented on the prim decorum of the native damsels of Manhattan, though later white arrivals found them quite otherwise.

During their stay at Newport, Verrazano's men went fifteen to eighteen miles inland, much impressed by wide fertile fields, "open and devoid of every impediment of trees, of such fertility that any seed in them would produce the best crops." Among later white settlers, the Narragansett Indians had the reputation of being the best farmers on the Atlantic seaboard. They had made wide clearings around Narragansett Bay, though not all of this was for farming. Part of it was to attract the deer, which liked the green shoots sprouting from old stumps or young trees. A description of 1634 says that the country here was "champain for many miles."

Verrazano found plums, "filberts" (presumably hazel or beech nuts) as well as some fruits he could not identify, and "apples worthy of Lucullus" (*pomi luculliani*). The alleged excellence of this fruit is a little hard to understand, for the wild American crab was usually small and sour, but as the Ohio, Illinois, and Indiana tribes had flourishing apple orchards in the eighteenth century, there may have been other and better native American species than the wild crab. More likely, almost any fresh fruit looked "Lucullan" after months at sea. There was a great deal of game, which the Narragansett Indians of Rhode Island hunted with bows and arrows, the latter "worked with great beauty," and tipped with heads of "emery, jasper, hard marble, and other sharp stones."

Verrazano anticipated the views of the United States Navy, observing that the bay could shelter "any numerous fleet, without fear of tempest or other impediment of fortune."

The Indians had thus far been uniformly friendly, in spite of the fact that somewhere near New York the white sailors had tried to kidnap a young squaw "of much beauty and of tall stature." When they found this impossible "on account of the very great cries which she uttered," they contented themselves with stealing a little boy. News of these crimes evidently did not spread, for Indian confidence in their white visitors remained undisturbed.

This friendly, unsuspicious attitude changed rapidly, however, when Verrazano reached Maine, "a high land full of very thick forests, the trees of which were pines, cypresses and such as grow in cold regions," on the whole a country that seemed too sterile for farming, especially as these Indians seemed to depend mainly on the chase. (There were actually a good many cornfields which Verrazano from his ship failed to see.)

Though Verrazano set down no detailed description, we know that primitive New England was almost entirely forested, except for Indian clearings and occasional meadows. It was part of the great pine and hardwood forest that stretched across the northern United States, growing thinner as it approached the Mississippi. Sometimes there are descriptions of particular districts, but they are all pretty much the same. James Rosier, an English voyager who later turned author, says, for instance, that Monhegan Island was "woody, grouen with Firre, Birch, Oke, and Beech, as farre as we saw along the shore; and so likely to be within." Sudbury, Massachusetts, was a forest of pine, oak, walnut, without much chestnut, the forest relieved by extensive meadows. Plymouth County, Massachusetts, had rather larger oak, maple, walnut, white pine, cedar, and pitch pine than the rest of Massachusetts. Some of the cedar swamps ranged from two hundred to one thousand acres of nearly solid growth. The rest of New England was very much the same, explorers being especially impressed by the huge size of the "stately timber"—which they unfortunately failed to measure. On the higher mountains, the size of the trees slowly dwindled until they stood only about two feet on the timber line.

Though the New England forests were not always dense, they seem to have had rather more underbrush than those farther south. James Rosier, going inland in Maine, found "Oke like the stands left in our pastures in England, good and great, fit Timber for any vse. Some small Birch, Hazle and Brake. . . . In many places are lowe Thicks like our Copisses of small young wood. And surely it did all resemble a stately Parke, wherein appeare some old trees with high withered tops. and others flourishing with living greene boughs. Vpon the hills grow notable high timber trees."

Verrazano found the local Indians rather aloof and unwilling to have him visit their villages. They wanted no close association with the whites. They were willing to trade, but only by letting their own goods down over the cliffs on cords to the ship's small boats waiting below, "continually crying on land that we should not approach." They would accept in exchange nothing but knives, metal fish hooks, and "sharp metal." When Verrazano tried to send an armed party ashore, the Indians attacked it, and when the red men were tired of trading, they "made all the signs of contempt and shame which any brute creature could make"—the American Indian never having been remarkable for delicacy in such matters. It is clear enough that these Maine Indians had met white men before—probably in fishing vessels—and had no illusions left.

Though he says nothing of Cape Cod and Massachusetts Bay—perhaps because he cut straight across the Bay—Verrazano seems to have sailed along the whole New England coast and some distance beyond. He himself says that he went as far as 50° N. and—the manuscripts do not agree—sometimes says 54°. He admired the islands that now provide a summer playground, "all near to the continent, small and of pleasing appearance, high, following the curving of the land, among which were formed most beautiful ports and channels, as are formed in the Adriatic Gulf, in the Illyrias and Dalmatia." Some places were "open and bare of forests."

With that Verrazano turned his bow toward Europe and vanishes from history. It is believed that he made one trip more and was killed while serving as pilot to later American travelers. According to an eighteenth century authority, "Verrazan was taken by the Savages, who butchered and eat him."

No more visitors are recorded on the New England coast until 1602, though there must have been a good many French, English, or Basque fishermen from time to time. As St. Lawrence and Newfoundland waters had been fished for at least a century, it was only natural for an occasional fishing vessel to try its luck in the teeming waters farther south. Indeed, though records are lacking, there is no doubt that this happened. The attitude of the Maine Indians toward Verrazano would be sufficient evidence of that, but there is more and better evidence.

As Bartholomew Gosnold, first skipper to sail straight across the Atlantic from Europe to New England, and Bartholomew Gilbert, son of Sir Humphrey, drew in toward the southern coast of Maine in 1602, they beheld approaching "a Biscay shallop with sail and oars." Supposing these were white men, they hove to, and then discovered, to their amazement, that the craft was manned entirely by Indians! All but two were naked, or nearly so; but one was wearing blue cloth breeches; and "one that seemed their commander wore a waistcoat of black work, a pair of breeches, cloth stockings, shoes, hat and band, one or two more had also a few things made by some Christians." (The voyagers' guess about the leader was undoubtedly right. An Indian chief always took the best white man's clothes when he could get them. Even the great Blackfish, war chief of the Shawnees, did not hesitate an instant to demand in 1778 that his adopted son, Daniel Boone, should turn over at once the clothes that a sympathetic English governor had given him.)

These Indians, who "spoke divers Christian words," gave every sign of friendliness. But what were they doing in that shallop? Their possession made it plain enough that white men had recently met disaster of some sort—shipwreck, massacre, looting, or all three—upon that coast.

The English newcomers cleared out immediately. Pausing only to note that the country was a "land somewhat low, certain hammocks of hills lying into the land, the shore full of white sand, but very stony or rocky" with trees which were "very high and straight," they steered south as fast as they could.

Their experience was not really so remarkable as they thought. Other voyagers shortly after found two parties of Indians in "bisken" shallops and Indians who were able to "use many french words" and even broken English.

But Gosnold and his men were not much interested in such matters. They had come for sassafras root, which in England was in demand as a medicine—such demand that at times the London price reached twenty shillings a pound. The most fantastic medical virtues were attributed to the tree. In 1574, Nicholas Monardes, botanist and "physician of Seville" describes cures "with the water of this merveilous tree." It was supposed to be good for "large importunate fevers . . . it comforteth the liver and the Stomacke . . . it dooeth make fatte . . . dooeth cause lust to meate," and was also beneficial to "Tertian Agewes, griefes of the breast caused of cold humors, griefes of the head," and might be prescribed for "them that bee lame and creepelles and them that are not able to goe."

It was also regarded as a specific for "the French poxe," in other words, syphilis. Columbus' crew were supposed to have brought the scourge back with them from America, and here was an American plant that would cure it.

The winds must have been favorable that night, for next morning the ship was "embayed with a mighty headland" formed of "a white sandy and very bold shore." Plainly Gosnold was somewhere inside Cape Cod, which he named after making a mighty haul of codfish there. He went ashore—it was the first recorded landing in Massachusetts—"and found the ground to be full of pease, strawberries, whortle-

berries, &c., as then unripe, the sand also by the shore somewhat deep."
The trees were mainly "cypress," birch, witch-hazel, and beech.

Just what the Englishmen meant by "whortleberries" is hard to
determine. Perhaps they saw cranberries, but more probably a few
early blueberries, still green. Elsewhere the blueberries were plentifully in blossom. On one island they found "the outward parts all
overgrowen with low bushie trees, three or four feet in height, which
beare some kinde of fruits, as appeared by their blossoming." These
can only have been blueberry bushes, which in New England are in
blossom just about the time the wild strawberries are ripening.

Of strawberries also they found a great many, "as sweet and much
bigger than ours in England." The frequency of delighted comment
on the strawberries, as white men pushed farther into North America,
is surprising. The first white visitors to Maine and its coastal islands
mention them. The Pilgrim Fathers were gratified to discover "great
store" at Plymouth. The Reverend Francis Higginson lists "ripe
strawberries and gooseberries, and sweet single roses" among the
attractions of Gloucester Harbor. Two hundred years after the Pilgrims, adventurers were equally pleased to find them growing lavishly
west of the Mississippi.

As Gosnold's crew rounded Cape Cod and coasted south, they found
open country along the shore—"all champaign and full of grass."
Martha's Vineyard they named because of the immense quantities of
grapevines, which wreathed the trees and made the forest floor a
tangle through which a man could hardly walk—"being stored with
such an incredible nombre of vynes, as well in the woody parte of the
island, where they runne upon every tree, as on the outward parts,
that they could not goe for treading upon them."

Martha's Vineyard was "full of wood, vines, gooseberry bushes,
whortleberries, raspberries, eglantines, &c. Here we had cranes,
stearnes, shoulers, geese, and divers other birds which there at that
time upon the cliffs being sandy with some rocky stones, did breed
and had young." It is impossible to guess what most of these birds
were. It is a pity, for the English visitors had a unique opportunity
to observe the heath hen, a common bird in those days and for many
years after, now utterly extinct, though one bird, the last known in-

dividual of the species, did not disappear until recent years. Occasionally the sailors killed "penguins"—an interesting bit of evidence that the great auks, in those days, ranged far south along the New England coast, where Champlain also found them.

Another list describes mainly waterfowl. There was likewise "great store of Deere, which we saw, and other beasts, as appeared by their tracks, as also divers fowles, as Cranes, Hernshawes, Bitters [bitterns], Geese, Mallards, Teales, and other fowles in great plenty; also, great store of Pease, which grow in certeine plots all the Island over."

Even these experienced seamen were astonished by the fishing. "The abundance of Sea-Fish are almost beyond beleeuing," says the author of *New England's Plantations*. Says another early observer: "Sculles [schools] of mackerall, herrings, Cod, and other fish that we dayly saw as we went and came from the shore were woonderfull." If they had not been intent on digging sassafras root, the Englishmen could have loaded their ship with fish "but in seven faddome water, and within lesse than a league of the shore, where, in New-found-land they fish in fortie or fiftie fadome water and farre off."

One English crew in 1605, three years later, caught cod three to five feet in length "so fast as the hook came down." Off Nantucket they "saw many Whales" and again found "great store of excellent Cod fish." Other crews, approaching the coast in 1607, says James Rosier, the obscure author of a "Relation" of their adventures, "tooke great stor of cod fyshes the bigeste & largest that I ever Saw or any man in our Ship." No wonder the name that Gosnold had given to Cape Cod clung to it forever, in spite of the efforts of other explorers to give it other names.

Rosier also tells how his ship, sailing up the Sagahadoc (Kennebec) River a little later, found itself surrounded with "abundance of great fyshe in ytt Leaping aboue the Watt^r on eatch Syd of us as we Sailed." This was the characteristic leaping of sturgeon, mentioned as late as 1760–1770, which continued for years afterward, though today the great fish are nearly gone from these waters. As the sturgeon of those days were six to nine feet long at least, they must have hit the water with a resounding smack.

Flounders, which the first adventurers identified as "plaice," were everywhere. "They (at flowing water) do almost come ashore, so that one may stepp but halfe a foote deepe, and pick them vp on the sands." There were also rockfish and "lumpes," a delicious morsel, now nearly exterminated; and, says the author of *New English Canaan,* "we generally observed, that all the fish, of what kinde soeuer we tooke, were well fed, fat, and sweet in taste."

Equally satisfying were "divers sorte of shell-fish, as scollops, muscles, cockles, lobsters, crabs, oyster, and welks, exceeding good and very great." All these, though no better in flavor, seem to have been much larger than they are today. One voyager was told of twenty-five pound lobsters and actually saw sixteen-pounders. There are at least two reports of lobsters weighing twenty pounds. There were so many that an Indian could catch thirty in an hour and a half. A boat's crew of white men took fifty, in one hour, in three feet of water, using a big hook fastened to a stick. One writer says that "the least Boy in the Plantation may both catch and eat what he will of them. For my owne part I was some cloyed with them, they were so great and fat, and lussious." Near Plymouth, says John Pory, another obscure voyager, the lobsters of those happy days were "so large, so full of meate, and so plentifull in number, as no man will believe that hath not seene. For a knife of 3 halfe pence I bought 10 lobsters that would well have dined 40 labouring men; and the least boye in the shippe, with an houres labour, was able to feed the whole companie with them." The Indians liked a lobster dinner as much as anyone, but there were not enough Indians on Cape Cod to make serious inroads on the numbers of the crustaceans.

It is just possible that Cuttyhunk, where Gosnold intended to found a permanent settlement, was the original of that magic isle which Shakespeare used as his setting for *The Tempest.* Though most Elizabethan scholars accept "the still-vex'd Bermoothes" as the original, it is worth noting that Shakespeare's patron, the Earl of Southampton, was also Gosnold's. The dramatist certainly knew all about the voyage, though there is no real proof it influenced him.

The settlement had to be given up because so few men were willing to be left behind, in the wilderness. Eventually, the whole crew returned to England, with a cargo of sassafras root—and the first description of Massachusetts.

Explorers now came thick and fast to the coast of New England. Martin Pring, a Devonshire sea captain, was briefly in Massachusetts Bay in 1603, but his descriptions add nothing to those of Gosnold's expedition. After him came Champlain, who though not the actual leader of French explorations along the New England coast, was the only man to leave an account of them.

However suspicious Verrazano had found the Maine Indians eighty years before, the French—except for one or two small skirmishes—now found them uniformly friendly, both in Maine and Massachusetts. The new generation of red men that had grown up since Verrazano's visit had seen enough of occasional fishermen to realize that the white men's acquaintance was worth cultivating for the sake of the metal knives and axes they brought with them.

New England was still in the Stone Age. To clear fields for their crops the Indians had to peck down the huge trees of the primeval forest with their stone axes and then, by burning them where they lay, get rid of the waste timber, thus unconsciously fertilizing the crops with wood ash. Sometimes they seem to have built fires around the trees and brought them down by burning through the trunk. With their crude stone tools, Indian carpenters found fire of great assistance in making dugout canoes. Burning the upper side of a log, they scraped the charred wood away; then lit their fire again, alternately burning and scraping until the canoe was finished. Birch and other barks made lighter canoes but they could not stand the rough treatment that a dugout would endure. Since they had not learned to split planks and could not saw them for lack of tools, the New England Indians lived mostly in shelters made of reed mats or oak bark. They do not seem to have used birch bark for shelters as the Indians of the Great Lakes did, and their use of the conical *wiggiwam* of tradition is very doubtful.

The French explorers found many clear fields, producing bountiful crops, especially as they approached Massachusetts. Even in the North, however, some of these Indian farms were fairly large. One tract of cleared land near the St. Croix River was fifteen or twenty acres in extent. Crops were the usual native corn, beans, pumpkins, and squashes.

The islands scattered along the coast, which had delighted Verrazano, still lay just as he had seen them—covered with pine, fir, birch, and aspen, haunted by the great auks, which Champlain like Gosnold, describes as "penguins." All of the coastal explorers missed the "great store of wild Turkies" that the later permanent settlers found as they went farther inland.

The "loups marins," as the French called the seals, swam about or sunned themselves on the rocks. Porpoises rushed by the little French vessel in numbers that were almost a nuisance: "There was not a day or a night when we did not see and hear pass by our boat more than a thousand porpoises, which were chasing the smaller fish." Though there were a good many whales, few mention them before Captain John Smith. Like Gosnold and many others, Champlain noted the abundance of fish—herring, cod, salmon, bass, halibut. He mentions the virtues of New England oysters with typical French gastronomic enthusiasm, but seems just a little disgusted because the Indians also ate "a shell-fish which is called the clam."

As they crossed the Bay of Fundy, the land did not seem very promising—"nothing but rocks" and "not especially fertile," though well covered with pine and birch. Running on down the coast they reached Mt. Desert Island, September 5, 1604—"very high with notches here and there, so that it appears, when one is at sea, like seven or eight mountains rising close together. The tops of most of them are without trees, because they are nothing but rock. The only trees are pines, firs, and birches. I called it Isle des Monts Déserts." The trees must have been enormous. In the early twentieth century one could still find, here and there, the rotting stumps of giant, ancient pines. Governor Bernard, who sailed from Boston to Mt. Desert in 1762, comments especially upon the fine timber, wonders at the "artificialness" of a beaver dam, and notes the wild meadow grass of the island, which grew "high as a man."

Guided by local Indians, Champlain went up the "beautiful and delightful" Penobscot as far as Bangor, stopping at the falls. The country was "pleasant and agreeable. The oaks there seem to have been planted for pleasure," but there were practically no Indians. The Etchemin tribe visited the Penobscot only to fish and hunt during the summer. It was one of those empty areas not uncommon in North America, which sometimes lay completely uninhabited for a century or two before the hunting became so easy that neighboring tribes were attracted to it. Kentucky, when Daniel Boone and the Long Hunters entered it, was another such area, inhabited by no tribe, though claimed as a hunting ground by both Cherokees and Shawnees.

At the mouth of the Choüacoet River, on the site of Saco, Maine, stood a permanent Indian village, well palisaded with tree trunks and surrounded by pleasant meadows and fields of pumpkins, squashes, tobacco, corn and beans, the latter twisting around the cornstalks in lieu of poles—it is still a good lazy man's way to grow pole beans.

Though Champlain does not mention them, the New England Indians were clever enough to grow watermelons, something few modern New England gardeners succeed in doing. John Josselyn describes them in 1675: "Water-Mellon, it is a large Fruit, but nothing near so big as a Pompion, colour, smoother, and of a sad Gras green rounder, or more rightly Sap-green; with some yellowness admixt when ripe; the seeds are black, the flesh or pulpe exceeding juicy." Pennsylvania grew just as good watermelons, for one of the Swedish writers expatiates upon "a most beautiful and excellent fruit, which we call, in Sweden, *water-melon*. It grows on rows like pompions, and some of them are so large that three tankards full of liquor may be extracted out of one melon. When they are cut, the inside is of a beautiful flesh colour; the taste is delightful, and it melts in the mouth like sugar." Not all of these early watermelons had the characteristic red pulp. Some in the Southwest had a pulp "white in color, mixed to a greater or less degree with traces of red," which gave the fruit "a very pretty appearance."

Grapevines had been unaccountably absent as Champlain sailed along the northern coast of the state, but they sprawled through the forests on the Saco. The thirsty Frenchmen crushed the grapes to produce "a very good verjuice." No wonder Champlain wrote that "this place is very pleasant and as agreeable as any one could see."

The birds were both interesting and edible. Passenger pigeons flew about in "infinite number." It is hard today to realize just how great those numbers were. John Josselyn, who also saw them in New England, says there were "millions of millions." In view of what trained ornithologists observed elsewhere in America even two hundred years later, we know Josselyn was not exaggerating when he wrote: "I have seen a flight of Pidgeons in the spring, and at *Michaelmas* when they returne back to the Southward for four or five miles, that to my thinking had neither beginning nor ending, length nor breadth, and so thick I could see no Sun, they joyn Nest to Nest, and Tree to Tree by their Nests many miles together in Pine-Trees." There were so many that it did not pay to shoot them. Instead, they were taken in nets in such quantities that they soon began to diminish in New England, though flights so large that they literally darkened the sky continued in the Middle West until the latter part of the last century.

Though Champlain does not mention the hummingbird, it was first noted in Canada and New England about his time. The Jesuit fathers wondered at the swift, graceful, ruby-throated and iridescent creature, puzzled because it seemed to take no food at all. They believed that it must live solely upon the fragrance of the flowers. Many of the "hummingbirds" the good fathers thought they saw were probably not birds at all but large insects—hawk-moths or clearwing moths, which still haunt flower gardens as do the hummingbirds, deceiving all but expert eyes.

John Josselyn was probably the first Englishman to mention "the *Humming Bird,* the least of all Birds, little bigger than a *Dor,* of variable glittering Colours, they feed upon Honey, which they suck out of Blossoms and Flowers with their long Needle-like Bills; they sleep all Winter, and are not to be seen till the Spring." A "dor" is an iridescent English beetle, aptly compared to a hummingbird, since it gives off a buzzing drone as it flies. The migration of these tiny birds was so hard to detect that the legend that they sleep all winter was firmly believed for many years.

Father Paul Le Jeune, a Jesuit to whose carefully written "relations" we owe a good deal of our knowledge of early North America, says in 1634 that the ruby-throat is "called by our French the fly-bird, because it is scarcely larger than a bee; others call it the flower-bird, because it lives upon flowers. It is in my opinion one of the great rarities of this country, and a little prodigy of nature. God seems to me more wonderful in this little bird than in a large animal. It hums in flying, like the bee; I have sometimes seen it hold itself in the air and stick its bill into a flower. Its bill is rather long, and its plumage seems to be a mottled green. Those who call it the flower-bird would, in my opinion, speak more correctly if they would call it the flower of birds."

Already stuffed specimens had been sent back for European collections. Efforts to keep the little birds in cages, feeding them with honey or sugar mixed with water, did not succeed. They rarely lived more than two months.

Among the islands of Boston harbor, Champlain found a number of friendly Indians, who danced for him by way of acknowledgment of a gift of knives and beads. Much of the land along the shore had been cleared for cornfields and the whole area was "very pleasant and agreeable, with a great many beautiful trees," including oaks, "very beautiful cypresses, which are reddish and have a very good odor" (obviously red cedars); and "walnuts" (which were probably hickories). He saw what must have been the mouth of the Charles River but made no effort to ascend its sluggish current into the wilderness site of Harvard University, which was to be founded only thirty years later. All he would have seen in Cambridge and greater Boston was a forest of pine, fir, spruce, oak, maple, birch, with the usual New England elms, a good many beaver, and swamps along the Charles River and up and down the shore of the harbor. But there was "as fat black Earth as can be seene anywhere."

Coasting along Cape Cod, Champlain noted the flat, sandy terrain familiar to this day, with "a great many cabins and gardens," and finally put into Plymouth Harbor, where he found Indians fishing for cod with hooks made of bone barbs fastened into wooden 'shanks and tied to fishing lines made of "Indian hemp"—in other words, the fibre of the swamp milkweed. Like their white successors, these red New Englanders were mighty fishermen. "The Salvages compare the store in the See with the haires of their heads," wrote Captain John Smith a few years later. The squaws made the hemp fishing lines and "she is very old that cannot spin a threed to make Engins to catch a fish."

It is curious to reflect that Massasoit and Squanto near Plymouth, and Samoset in Maine—all three staunch friends of the Pilgrim Fathers—must have been going quietly about a redman's daily concerns as Champlain's party passed in 1604 and John Smith's in 1614. None of these white men seem to have met them, nor did the Indians think the earlier white visits worth mentioning to their Pilgrim friends, though they must have known all about them.

Plymouth Harbor soon became the best known on the New England coast. Martin Pring had been there in 1603, a year before Champlain. John Smith put in and gave it its modern name in 1614. In 1620 came the Pilgrims, and it is reasonably certain that a good many fishing smacks passed that way and sailed away again leaving no record. From some of these casuals of the sea, Samoset learned the words, "Welcome, Englishmen!" with which he electrified the Pilgrim Fathers as he stalked into their new settlement. He "spoke to them in broken English, which they could well understand but marvelled at it." Samoset was not a Massachusetts Bay Indian but came from down East, "wher some English-ships came to fhish, with whom he was acquainted, and could name sundrie of them by their names, amongst whom he had gott his language." Squanto, or Tisquantum, a Plymouth Indian, had actually visited England.

Perhaps as a result of Champlain's voyages, the New England Indians began trading with the French. The Pilgrim Fathers were mightily surprised when they found that a flight of hostile arrows had brass arrowheads instead of the usual stone. The only possible source was French traders from the St. Lawrence. Because they rusted away while stone arrowheads were indestructible, metal arrow heads of this sort are now little known, though traders supplied a good many of them. Few museums have even a single specimen, though iron arrowheads were still being sold to western Indians around 1800 and perhaps later.

When Gosnold, Pring, and Champlain visited the Massachusetts Indians, however, they were still using stone arrowheads, as they had in Verrazano's day. Stone knives were sometimes supplemented by the sharp, cutting edge of a reed, and stone arrowheads by the sharp, thorny tail of the horse-shoe crab—the only use ever discovered for that curious creature, except by a few Virginia Indians who occasionally, and rather reluctantly, ate it. There was much agriculture, the squaws raising the usual crops and storing their corn in the sand: "they make trenches on the hillsides in the sand, five or six feet, more or less, deep; put their corn and other grain in big sacks made of grass, and throw them into the trenches and cover them with sand three or four feet above the surface of the earth. They take from their store at need, and it is as well preserved as it could be done in our granaries."

It was one of these stores that the Pilgrim Fathers found in an hour of need—"heaps of sand newly paddled with their hands, which they digging up, found in them diverce faire Indian baskets filled with corne, and some in eares, faire and good, of diverce colours." Indian ears of corn often had kernels of various colors, a variety now grown only rarely and for ornament.

Cape Cod's shores have not changed very much in appearance. "This coast consists of lofty sand dunes, which are conspicuous as one comes from the sea," wrote Champlain, and again: "There is a great stretch of open country on the shore before one enters the woods, which are very agreeable and pleasant to see." Captain John Smith said very much the same thing about Cape Cod: "Onely a headland of high hils, overgrowne with shrubby Pines, hurts [probably blueberries] and such trash." He also notes: "This Cape is made by the maine Sea on the one side, and a great Bay on the other in forme of a Sickell."

The French explorers crept around the Cape without noting the lakes of Plymouth County, of one of which Gosnold left a charming little picture: "neere to the seaside, they found a standing lake of fresh-water, almost three English miles in compasse, in the midst whereof stood a little pretty plott or grove of wood, an acre in quantity, or not much above; the lake full of tortoises, and exceedingly frequented with all sorts of fowle, which bredd, some lowe on the bancks, and others on low trees about the lake, in great aboundance, whose younge ones theye tooke and eate at their pleasure."

English explorers were again upon the coast at about the same time the French were returning to Canada, and a series of small fleets put out for the New England coast until at last the Pilgrims made their permanent "plantation" at Plymouth, Massachusetts. Some of these voyagers were lost, few stayed any length of time, and fewer still, alas! left any very detailed description of what they saw until the redoubtable Captain John Smith arrived. But the English had now learned to sail directly westward, instead of first heading south for the West Indies, where the Spaniards jealously noted their passage, and then creeping northward up the coast. Though Philip II's ambassador in London operated a first-class intelligence service, which kept a close eye on what was going on, reporting to Madrid every bit of information about English exploration it could get, including at least one map, there was no longer any way for the Spaniards to interfere with these northern voyages.

About the time Champlain's party of Frenchmen were returning to the St. Lawrence, Captain George Popham (nephew of the Lord Chief Justice of England) and Raleigh Gilbert (another son of Sir Humphrey's, nephew and namesake of Sir Walter Raleigh) made a landfall at Monahigan, or Monhegan (Barty's Island) in May, 1606. Once they had established a Maine settlement, they and their colonists met with little but hardship and went mournfully back to England in 1608—"the Country esteemed as a cold, barren, mountainous, rocky Desart."

At about the same time, Captain Edward Harlow sailed for Barty's Island, did a little fishing, had a few brushes with the Indians, and returned. His chief accomplishment was to take back with him an Indian named Sakaweston, "that after he had lived many yeeres in England went a Souldier to the warres of Bohemia." (One would give a good deal for the autobiography of that particular redskin!)

Undismayed by discouraging reports, Captain John Smith came to Massachusetts Bay in 1614. Smith was a daring individual who, finding even Elizabethan England too dull for his tastes, had gone off to Hungary to fight as a soldier of fortune against the Turks. Captured and enslaved, he had won the favor of a pasha's wife—no ordinary achievement in a Moslem country—and had been sent for his own safety to the Caspian–Black Sea area. Here he killed his Turkish master and escaped, making his way back to Hungary and arriving in England in 1604, with his thirst for adventure not at all sated. He joined the Virginia colonists in 1606 and had an extraordinary career, sometimes in disgrace, once sentenced to be hanged, eventually rising to be President of the Council, and returning to England in 1609. Though historians have scoffed at his escape from death through the intervention of Pocahontas, no less an authority than the *Dictionary of American Biography* soberly remarks that the episode was "quite in accord with the customs of Indian life and there is nothing inherently improbable in the story."

In the beginning he and his companions engaged in whaling, but soon "found this Whale-fishing a costly conclusion," for they "saw many and spent much time in chasing them, but could not kill any." Abandoning whaling, Smith set to work mapping the coast, while the others traded in furs. They went home after six months, not wholly disconsolate, for they took with them a cargo of furs and fish.

Smith's description more or less agrees with Champlain's, for of course there had been no change in the few years that lay between the visits. In a small boat with only eight men he went "from point to point, Ile to Ile, and Harbour to Harbour," trading, exploring, mapping, and naturally getting a much closer view of the country than had been possible for Champlain in his larger sailing vessel. When the wind failed, Smith could get out the oars and take his small boat where he wished.

"This Coast," he wrote, "is mountainous, and Iles of huge Rockes, but over-growne for most part, with most sorts of excellent good woods." Ending his travels at the Penobscot, he looked eastward along the coast, seeing only more "high craggy clifty Rockes and stony Iles." Nowhere did there seem to be much soil and yet the trees were enormous. Smith was amazed that "such great Trees could grow upon so hard foundations."

Always appreciative of his own exploits (though he seems to have been far more accurate than many of his critics have been willing to believe), Smith left copious accounts of his travels, descriptions of the country, and a map. His descriptions were a little too glowing. They read like a real estate agent's brochures, which in fact they were; for, backed by London merchants, Smith was writing to attract capitalists to support expeditions and settlers to hold the land. Certainly no one else has ever found New England, charming though it can be, quite so perfect as the land that Smith depicts. But in general, the tales of the exuberant Elizabethan are confirmed by the more restrained statements of his predecessors, French and English.

He was the first and last chronicler who ever grew enthusiastic over the New England climate, but the fisheries impressed him most of all. New England cod and hake were two or three times as big as those from Canadian waters and the fishing season was much longer. Mullet were two to four feet long. Salmon were easily taken as they ran up the rivers in the spring. The Indans, "young Boies and Girles Salvages, or any other bee they never such idlers" could take them easily with crude native tackle, and fish like these were worth money.

"Is it not pretty sport," asked the captain, "to pull up two pence, six pence, and twelve pence, as fast as you can hale and vere a line; hee is a very bad Fisher cannot kill in one day with his hooke and line one, two, or three hundred Cods."

Nor was the fishing confined to salt water. In September, eels began to come up the rivers from the sea. As cold weather approached, they burrowed into the river bottoms, "being bedded in gravell not above two or three foote deepe." The Pilgrims looked on in amazement when their new Indian friend, Squanto, felt for eels in the mud with his toes, trod them neatly out of the ooze, and in a short time had all he could carry.

After they had learned the trick from Squanto, the early Massachusetts settlers caught plenty of them. John Winthrop tells how two or three boys "brought in a bushel of great eels at a time, and sixty great lobsters." The eels, John Pory remarks, were "passing sweete, fat, and wholesome, haveing no taste at all of the mudde," and "as greate as ever I saw anie." Pory, who was at one time assistant to the great geographer, Richard Hakluyt, must have been a bit of a gourmet, as such things went in the seventeenth century in North America, for he also comments on the virtues of the bluefish, of which he says: "In delicacy it excelleth all kind of fish that ever I tasted." Modern restaurateurs would do well to remember his further observation that it is "of a taste requireing noe addition of sauce," its natural flavor being "as sweete as the marrow of an oxe."

In April the "old wives," ran up the rivers to spawn. Nothing could stop them. "Yea, when a heape of stones is reared up against them a foot high above the water, they leape and tumble over and will not be beaten back with cudgels." The Puritan settlers took them up in hogsheads and when they could not eat them all, followed Massasoit's advice and dropped two or three into each hill of corn, for fertilizer. Pory thought them good eating, too: "At their going up they are very fat and savory, but at their comming downe, after they have cast their spawnes, they are shotte, and therefore leane and unwholesome."

At the stream near Plymouth which is still called Smelt River, flowing from Smelt Pond, Pory saw "the greate smelts passe up to spawne likewise in troupes innumerable, which with a scoupe, or a boule, or a peece of barke, a man may cast upon the bank." The same thing happened in other wilderness rivers, but Nature had accommodatingly placed this stream close to the Pilgrims' settlement.

Later New Englanders saw that there would have to be some limit on the fishing, but their ideas were generously expansive. Plymouth set the limit between five hundred and one thousand barrels for the town as a whole. By the Revolution this had come down to two hundred barrels. In 1730 each household was limited to four barrels. In 1763, the towns of Plymouth and Wareham took 150 barrels from Agawam Brook alone. Sad to say, in the Merrimac River, salmon, shad, and alewives were growing less abundant as early as 1753.

But in the very beginning, when the white man first came, the streams simply boiled with fish. You didn't have to ply net or line. The Indians found it simpler to shoot them. "Their Boyes will ordinarily shoot fish with their Arrowes as they swim in the shallow Rivers," says *The Wonder-Working Providence of Sions Savior in New England*. It was very simple—"they draw the Arrow halfe way, putting the point of it into the water, they let flye and strike the fish through."

There were so many shellfish that, no matter how lavishly the Indians feasted, they could not exhaust the immense supply. The settlers took advantage of this to fatten their hogs on what they could not eat themselves, turning their swine out on the beaches to find mussels and clams for themselves and crush the shells in their powerful jaws.

Henry Hudson's men, who passed that way during the interval between Champlain's visit and Smith's—leaving no trace save the stump of one tree, which they cut down to make a new mast—took equal delight in that early New England institution, the shore dinner. They put lobstering parties ashore whenever they felt inclined. Lobster-fishing somewhere in Maine three days out of four in July, 1609—one day was too foggy—they caught 130, which was certainly an adequate supply, considering that there were not more than twenty in the crew. A day or two later, evidently weary of lobster, they took twenty big cod and a big halibut—rather more than they could eat—in two hours' fishing.

Smith concluded that if a man couldn't make a good living in this miraculous country, "worthy is that person to starve," for "one hundred men may in two or three houres make their provisions for a day." He thought that thirty or forty practical men, properly equipped, ought to be able to provide two or three hundred people "with as good Corne, Fish, and Flesh as the earth hath of those kinds, and yet make that labour but their pleasure."

When the Pilgrim Fathers very nearly did starve amid all this food a few years later, their plight only moved the hard-bitten old soldier to scorn. Quite plainly he intimated that these were, after all, only hare-brained religious cranks, "Brownists," who didn't understand wilderness life. He might have been more tolerant if he had paused to remember the "starving time" of the Virginia colonists; though that, too, was mainly due to ignorance of the right way to live in the big woods. North America always did provide abundant food, but you had to understand how to get it and also how to preserve it. The frequent winter famines of the Indians were largely due to improvidence, and those of some settlers to ignorance.

It was a matter of some years before there was any effort to describe the country farther back from the coast. The interior of New England was a tangled wilderness, with the added disadvantage that all the stones that now make stone walls, were then scattered through the forests, where the last glacier had dropped them. Settlement at first clung to the coast and only gradually crept inland, but early explorations of the White Mountains give a pretty clear idea of inland New

England in primitive times. Mt. Washington, being clearly visible for many miles, early aroused curiosity and in 1632 a certain Darby Field, otherwise unknown, visited "the tops of the White hill," including Mt. Washington. He saw some kind of "shining stones," which roused hopes that they might be diamonds.

In the autumn of the same year, Thomas Gorges, deputy governor of Maine and Richard Vines, councillor, went up the Saco River and clambered up Mt. Washington—"about 7 or 8 miles upon shattered rocks, without tree or grass, very steep all the way. At the top is a plain about three or four miles over, all shattered stones, and upon that is another rock or spire [Sugar Loaf], about a mile in height, and about an acre of ground at the top." They found no diamonds and returned disappointed.

The going must have been rough, indeed, for the sturdy Major Robert Rogers, commander of Rogers' Rangers, could not get more than half way up and returned, reporting thick beech, hemlock, and some white pines for four or five miles, then six or seven miles of black spruce, covered with "white moss," and beyond that "scarce any thing growing." The Indians having no interest either in diamonds or mountain climbing, there were no trails; and even about 1800 the hemlock and spruce boughs were so interlaced that climbers had to go almost on hands and knees and even then had their clothing nearly ripped from their backs. Optimists who took horses to the mountains in 1804 gave one look and sent them back.

The Notch, two perpendicular rocks only twenty-two feet apart, had been an important pass for war parties of Canadian Indians raiding New England. But after the war parties ceased, it was forgotten until its rediscovery by hunters in 1771. John Josselyn, who had been the first to use the name White Mountains, says of the country beyond, "daunting terrible; being full of rocky hills, as thick as mole hills in a meadow, and clothed with infinite thick woods." But in the long run, New Englanders conquered that country, too.

XIII

The Manitou at Manhattan

THOUGH VERRAZANO HAD, in 1524, actually entered New York Harbor, he had made no effort to go on up the Hudson River, and he had left a very scant account of what he found. It is just possible that one year later, in 1525, Estevan Gómez, a Portuguese in Spanish service, also dropped anchor in the Bay.

The visits of the white men made little difference to the native red New Yorkers. The strange, pale creatures, in their canoes with wings, had come, lingered a day or two, vanished again over the big sea water, soon to be entirely forgotten by busy men intent upon the whirl of Manhattan life—hunting, fishing, and clamming.

The Indians of Manna-hata knew nothing of the other white men in other winged canoes, who had for more than a hundred years barely managed to miss the greatest harbor of the eastern coast. No doubt keen black eyes had noted Sebastian Cabot as he sailed blithely past in 1498, but Staten Island and Long Island conceal the Hudson and the Upper Bay from an observer only a little way out to sea; and from Cabot's distant ship, the Lower Bay must have seemed just another indentation in the hundreds of miles of monotonously wooded shores. For safety's sake, he had to keep well off this unknown shore, and he certainly had no idea of the tremendous opportunity he was missing. The Indians of 1498 could hardly have signalled him, even if they had wanted to.

Other explorers had never even tried to reach the middle Atlantic states. George Waymouth in 1602, Martin Pring in 1603, Champlain in 1604 and 1605, Captain George Popham in 1606, Captain John Smith in 1614, and many a fishing vessel now forgotten had crept along the Massachusetts coast, but they had gone little farther. Probably none of them came so far south as Rhode Island.

From the West Indies and the Gulf, Spaniards had sent vessels into the unknown North. The Bay of Santa Maria, which the Spaniards found early in the sixteenth century may have been the Chesapeake. Possibly they tried to settle there in 1556. "Axacan," a Spanish settlement of 1570, was almost certainly on Chesapeake Bay, where in 1573, Pedro Menéndez Marquez also put in. Clearly, however, there was no gold in this country, and the Spanish went no farther north—unless the mysterious "Pemaquid Pavements" and other relics found with them are evidence of a transitory Spanish settlement in Maine, of which no written record has ever been found.

When the first Virginia settlers followed in the Spaniards' wake, they had too much trouble in their own settlements to venture much farther along the coast. Even the daring Captain John Smith did not go beyond Chesapeake Bay and the lower waters of the Susquehanna, so long as he was based on Virginia; and during his later explorations, he never left New England waters.

Hence, while the frozen North and sunny Florida were being ardently explored, New York and the middle Atlantic states—the greatest prizes of all, midway between—remained unknown longer than any other part of the Atlantic coast. In the West, rumors of the white men in Mexico and their doings spread far and wide across the plains. In the North, the Indians of the Great Lakes and far beyond soon learned about the French. But through the dense forests of the central states news of the newcomers did not spread so easily; and so these Indians had no contacts either with the French on the St. Lawrence or the English in Virginia.

Such happy isolation could not last forever. It would soon have been ended by Frenchmen coming overland and down the Hudson, if Henry Hudson had not sailed up the river when he did, clearing the way for his Dutch employers. At the very moment when Hudson was running south along the New England coast, Champlain, far inland, had already begun this movement. The French failed to colonize New York, only because Hudson got there first.

That is why Manna-hata Island, what is now known as The Bronx, Brooklyn, Queens, Long Island, and the Jersey shore still lay green, forest-clad, unspoiled, and peaceful on September 3, 1609. The forest that covered most of their surface was mainly giant oaks—"the finest oaks for height and thickness that one could ever see"—poplars, hickories, and quantities of plum trees which in September were blue with fruit, especially on Manna-hata and along Sandy Hook, where passing voyagers paused to gather it.

Manhattan Island itself was "indented with bays, coves and creeks." Much of it was "very good woodland," not very thick with trees, however, for grass grew in the woods and also in occasional little valleys. There were "many brooks of fresh water running through it, pleasant and proper for man and beast to drink, as well as agreeable to behold, affording cool and pleasant resting places." It is said that at least a hundred of them still flow, shut from the air forever, beneath modern Manhattan's asphalt, steel, and concrete. Northward, the trees diminished and the land was partly clear, while a great meadow of about 150 acres, watered by "a very fine stream," stretched along the East Side until the forest closed in again farther up the East River. In some places there were wild cherries and, soon after the white man's coming, peach trees, escaped from his orchards, began to grow plentifully. Wild flowers were so fragrant that Jasper Danckaerts tells how, walking down Manhattan Island, he and a companion "sometimes encountered such a sweet smell in the air that we stood still, because we did not know what it was we were meeting."

The southern end of the island was more pointed than it is today (the white man has done a good deal of filling), and there was a canoe landing here. Northward across the island ran a trail with various branches, and it is probable that Broadway and some of the other irregular northward-reaching streets of today follow Indian paths of incredible antiquity. The strange curving of modern Pearl Street is simply due to the fact that it marks the winding margin of the ancient East River.

There was a stream and marsh at Canal Street, a hill called Ishpatena (now Richmond Hill) at Charlton and Varick, while the land between Fifth and Eighth Avenues was under water or very swampy. On the West Side, the waters of the Hudson reached to Greenwich Street. Above Fortieth Street the island was all forests and glades, "useless except for hunting." Though this land eventually came under cultivation it was not built up for centuries. George Washington, cursing like a madman, met his retreating troops in a cornpatch near the corner of Fifth Avenue and Forty-second Street and steadied them long enough to hold the British off.

Along the shores gulls flapped and screamed as they do now, but there were many other birds, long since disappeared from the modern wilderness of steel and concrete. So numerous were the birds in these vanished woodlands that, says an early account, "men can scarcely go through them for the whistling, the noise, and the chattering. Whoever is not lazy can catch them with little difficulty."

Songsparrows, vireos, warblers filled the brighter edges of the forest, though they shunned the dark interior. Deer stamped along Fifth Avenue. Occasionally there was the bright scarlet flash of a tanager in passage. Hawks floated in the sky, soared, swooped, and chased their small winged prey into the security of thickets and tangled grapevines under the great trees. Kingfishers plopped into the streams. Now and then a bald eagle soared over, less dangerous to other birds than one might think, since the royal creature had a most unkingly appetite for the offal the Indians left lying about, or for dead fish lying along the shore. Above the schools of fish that packed the Hudson soared the ospreys, plummeting down into its current occasionally to emerge, flapping mightily, with a salmon or sturgeon (unknown now in those waters), shad, or mullet firmly clutched in their talons.

The Narrows were high wooded points, with a few Indian cornfields. Governor's Island was a beautiful grove of nut trees—probably hickories—which gave it the name Nut Island. Coney Island was a mere tangle of brush, almost without trees.

Eastward stretched Long Island, remarkable for "many fine valleys, where there is good grass," elsewhere forested with elm, oak, nut trees, cedar, evergreens, maple, sassafras, beech, birch, hazelnut, and chestnuts, "which yield store of Mast for Swine." One early observer even mentions holly. The middle of the island was an open plain, about four by sixteen miles, "upon which plain grows very fine grass." The Hempstead area was never forested. Otherwise, "the greatest part of the Island" was, according to a Jamaica resident of the middle seventeenth century, "very full of Timber."

It was attractive country, as he described it: "The fruits natural to the Island are Mulberries, Posimons, Grapes great and small, Huckelberries, Cramberries, Plums of several sorts, Rosberries and Strawberries, of which last is such abundance in June, that the Fields and Woods are died red: Which the Countrey-people perceiving, instantly arm themselves with bottles of Wine, Cream, and Sugar and instead of a Coat of Male, every one takes a Female upon his horse behind him, and so rushing violently into the fields, never leave till they have disrob'd them of their red colours and turned them into the old habit."

Like Manhattan the island was filled with "divers sorts of singing birds, whose chirping notes salute the ears of Travellers with an harmonious discord, and in every pond and brook green silken Frogs, who warbling forth their untun'd tunes strive to bear a part in this musick." In May the woods and fields were "curiously bedecke with Roses, and an innumerable multitude of Flowers."

Staten Island was well wooded and watered, the whole south side a large plain with much salt meadow and marsh, while the western part of the island was also flat, with a good deal of marsh. Like Manhattan, it had many irregular projecting points and bays or creeks penetrating inland. The woods were so thick as to obscure the sky, and in them and along the jagged shore were wild turkeys, geese, snipe, and "wood hens"—presumably ruffed grouse. Menhaden, the little fish now caught for oil and fertilizer, rotted on the beach by thousands, with eagles gorging on their carcasses. Deer moved about in herds of twenty-five or thirty at a time. A great sandbank edged the shore.

Beyond, in New Jersey, the reaches of the lower Raritan made wide swamps, with willows instead of factories on their margins. On Manna-hata, too, there were swamps and pools, notably at Washington Square, where Minetta Water attracted flocks of waterfowl. The

t' Fort nieuw Amsterdam op de Manhatans

Hartgen's View of New Amsterdam, the earliest known picture (c. 1626).

A view of the Palisades or steep rocks on the west side of the Hudson River opposite upper Manhattan. From the *New York Magazine*, June, 1791.

entrance to the Hudson River and Newark Bay were likewise thick with geese and ducks, which wintered here between September and April, returning to the Canadian lakes to breed each summer. "Swans" haunted the fresh water farther inland. "White and gray" herons were everywhere. Wild turkeys in New Jersey weighed thirty to forty pounds and, when exhausted after their short flights, could be caught with the hands. Migrating passenger pigeons were "so numerous, that the light can hardly be discerned where they fly"—the foxes chased them "like fowl."

Daniel Denton, a Long Island settler, describes how, above the swamps, both sides of the Raritan River were "adorn'd with spacious Meadows." Most of New Jersey was "a rich Champain Countrey, free from stones [the writer had grown up in Connecticut!], and indifferent level; store of excellent good Timber, and very well watered, having brooks or rivers ordinarily, one or more in every miles travel." The grass, in the open "champaigns," was "as high as a mans middle."

A few miles inland were the beautiful Passaic Falls, unknown to the first white New Yorkers and not described until 1680. There was only one Indian family in the neighborhood, which today is the centre of Paterson. Here the Passaic River struck "a large blue rock, which is broken in two obliquely with the river." Through the crevice between the two a stream eight or ten feet wide tumbled down through smooth, blue, precipitous walls—from a height of eighty feet, according to a European visitor, though the real height is nearer fifty.

The visiting English clergyman, Andrew Burnaby, who saw them in the middle of the eighteenth century, thought the Passaic Falls very beautiful: "The river is about forty yards broad, and runs with a very swift current, till coming to a deep chasm or cleft, which crosses the channel, it falls above seventy feet perpendicular in one entire sheet. One end of the cleft is closed up, and the water rushes out at the other with incredible rapidity, in an acute angle to its former direction." He saw two rainbows at once in the spray and thought the smaller waterfall, just upstream, "a most beautiful one, gliding over some ledges of rocks each two or three feet perpendicular, which heightens the scene very much."

The enormous Jersey swamps beyond Hopoghan (Hoboken) must

have been even wider than they are today—a convenient source of supply for squaws in search of rushes for the mats that made the earthen floors of Manhattan "apartments" a little more comfortable. These marshes and streams were full of muskrats, which some of the first white men thought a very palatable roast.

Not too far away were beavers, whose skins, when stitched together, made good warm robes, while their large flat tails made excellent eating, enjoyed by both white and red. "The Tail boiled, proves exceeding good meat, being all Fat, and as sweet as Marrow," wrote a seventeenth century Englishman. Fur traders soon found that old Indian beaver robes, saturated with the oils which the redskins smeared on their bodies, were better than new skins. The aboriginal owners were sometimes contemptuously amused to find the prices their old clothes would bring. Young beaver tamed easily. There was one in seventeenth century Boston which "would run up and down the streets, returning home without a call." Neighboring Connecticut, especially around New Haven, had beaver dams in almost every stream.

In New Jersey, up the Hudson, and out through suburban Connecticut, ranged deer and black bear, with perhaps an occasional, southward-wandering moose. The North American black squirrel—now almost unknown, though there are a few on the uptown campus of New York University—shared the treetops with his chattering red and grey cousins.

Porcupines ranged all the eastern forests, and the legend that they could shoot their quills had developed as early as 1675. "A very angry Creature and dangerous," says John Josselyn, "shooting a whole shower of Quills."

Sea food as everywhere along the coast was easy to procure. The pure sea waters of the harbor and the brackish waters of the lower Hudson—a mysterious, tidal river, which to the Indian mind seemed to flow alternately in both directions—were filled with fish, biting greedily at crude baits impaled on rough bone fishhooks, taken easily in weirs or in nets woven of the fibres of the swamp milkweed— "Indian hemp." Across the Hudson the Indians spread these nets, between stone weights and floats made of small sticks, with a carved "figure made of wood, resembling the Devil," which bobbed about in the water to signal a catch. Sturgeon ran up the stream as far as Albany, and up the Mohawk as far as the Cohoes Falls. A wandering parson as late as 1796 saw seven-footers, which at an earlier date would not have been really large fish.

Oysters, clams, mussels, lobsters, crabs were to be had for the gathering, just as they were in New England. New York oysters were of the generous size common up and down the coast, sometimes eight or ten inches long and three or four inches across, so that one oyster made "several mouthfuls." As late as the Revolution, Gowanus oysters, "the best in the country," were reported to be a foot long, growing in clusters of ten to sixteen.

It seems to be quite true that at the Revolution all the lobsters left New York Harbor and did not come back until after 1800. Local legend attributed this crustacean exodus to the cannonading at the battle of Long Island; but it was probably just one of those queer movements of aquatic fauna that no biologist wholly understands.

Whales also went as far inland as Albany. "Rensselaerswick" had scarcely been established when there appeared in the Hudson off its shores, "a certein fish of considerable size, snow-white in color, round in the body, and blowing water out of its head." This ancestor of Moby Dick was soon followed by a forty-footer of normal dark coloring, which grounded at the mouth of the Mohawk. There were always whales in the Lower Bay and off Long Island. Stragglers turn up even today.

Over all of Greater New York was the quiet of the wilderness, broken only by the occasional calls of birds and the rare cries of the usually silent wilderness beasts. At night, above the still, bark villages, boomed the whoo-whoo of the great horned owl. Wolves may have howled occasionally but there cannot, even then, have been many of them—the Indian population was too thick, scattered here and there along the shores and among the islands.

In the spring and occasionally in summer, the little creeks and swamps resounded with a deep, menacing boom—astounding to the unaccustomed ears of white men. It was only "the dreadful frogs, in size about a span [9 inches] which croak with a ringing noise in the evening." Birchbark canoes and hollow log dugouts, instead of freighters, liners Europe-bound, tugs, barges, and ferryboats, plied busily across the quiet waters, tossing a bit when a brisk wind blew up the Bay. A palisaded Indian fort stood somewhere near Castle William but there is no record that it was ever besieged by hostile bands.

When the pitch-black of the wilderness night came down on quiet New York City and scattered villages about the harbor and along the Sound, campfires twinkled fitfully here and there. No need to conceal them. The imperial Five Nations guarded their subject peoples. But most campfires were hardly visible, for the red man has a marvelous knack of building tiny fires yet keeping them alive. Only occasionally was the silence broken by the sound of revelry on Manna-hata Island. Then there was a rattle of gourds along Broadway, the boom of deer-skin drums, the shouts of dancers, wild native songs, and the shuffle of moccasined feet on hard-trodden earth.

On the morning of September 3, 1609, all that centuries-old life changed forever, though no one—not even Henry Hudson and the mixed Dutch and British sailors of the yacht *Half Moon*—realized that a new world metropolis was being born. The towering buildings that thrust aside the sky, the bustle in the streets, the reek of gasoline, the buses, taxicabs, motorcars, the subways boring through the granite foundations of Manna-hata or forcing their earthworm way beneath the Hudson's ooze, the rushing-about of human ants, intent upon their small affairs, the blazing, parti-colored lights of midtown Broadway, the pinnacles of lower Broadway, the stately castles of Fifth Avenue— all these were implicit in a little two-masted yacht, its bright paint now a little dulled by salt spray, whose clumsy bow and pointed bow-sprit poked uneasily into strange waters.

Little enough is known of the man who looked eagerly from his quarterdeck toward the forested shores. Henry, or Harry, Hudson (no one ever called him Hendrik except his Dutch employers) was a bold and capable seaman, who appears in history for the first time, on April 19, 1607, "proposing to goe to sea foure dayes after, for to discover a Passage by the North Pole to China." That voyage failed, as did another the following year. He was now on his third voyage of exploration, this time in the employ of the Amsterdam Chamber of Commerce.

Black eyes in painted faces watched the Dutch ship come. Far down the Bay, something strange, something enormous to Indian eyes—however small it might now seem to a white man's eyes looking down from a liner's deck—crept upon the surface of the water. At first it seemed dark with huge white wings, then as it drew closer to the land it appeared brightly colored with wings that seemed to grow ever whiter as the sunlight struck them.

Long afterward, aged warriors told the story to the Moravian missionary, John Heckewelder. Their stories can hardly—after a lapse of 150 years—have been very accurate, but they got the main points right and they preserved the wonder of that historic moment.

The arrival of the *Half Moon* was a tremendous event, which made a great impression on the Indians; and though the story handed down by the campfires was embroidered as the years went on, the tale checks fairly well against the day-to-day entries that one of Henry Hudson's officers noted down upon the spot. It checks also with a very early Dutch story, based on conversation with Indians who were living when the *Half Moon* arrived and published less than fifty years after the event. Heckewelder was right when he said the Indian account was "as authentic as anything of the kind can be obtained."

According to this semi-historical legend, a few Indians were fishing in their dugout canoes "where the sea widens"—in other words, somewhere in the Lower Bay. Far out on the waves they "espied at a great distance something remarkably large floating on the water, and such as they had never seen before." Paddling hastily back to shore, they called companions to see this wonder. More Indians came tumbling down to the shore.

There it was, sure enough! Everyone could see the strange thing, but no one knew what it could be. Mighty was the speculation, "some concluding it either to be an uncommon large fish or other animal, while others were of opinion it must be some very large house." Soon they could see that the queer thing, whatever it might be, was drawing closer.

Clearly, it was time to warn other Indians, in villages scattered about on the mainland and the islands. Runners dashed over the forest trails. Canoes splashed hurriedly about the Bay. More Indians came rushing down to the shores. There was no doubt that the strange object was moving toward them, and it now seemed to be "a large canoe or house"—so large and so magnificent that only a Manitou of some sort could possibly inhabit it. Perhaps the Great Spirit, the Master of Life himself, was coming to visit his red children. In that case, what to do? How should the red men receive visiting divinity?

A council of the chiefs met hastily to decide on etiquette for this unprecedented occasion. While medicine men conjured frantically and squaws prepared a feast, the chiefs—somewhat at a loss—decided that the best thing to do was to commence dancing. A dance was a religious ceremonial sure to be appropriate to almost any great occasion.

As the dance commenced "in some confusion," more messengers came rushing to the council with news that the strange thing was indeed a floating house of various colors—Dutch ships of the *Half Moon's* period were gaily bedizened—and that, whether it carried a Manitou or not, it was now easy to see that it was full of living beings. More runners brought more news. These creatures were very strange indeed. The watcher on the shore could now see that the unknown beings were "of quite a different colour." Their dress was also odd. One was brilliant red all over—that must be the Manitou himself. It was, in fact, Captain Henry Hudson in formal attire: a red coat, gold-laced.

As the floating house drew nearer, the Indians could hear the strange creatures on it shouting across the water to them in a strange language. No one knew what they said but the Indians shouted back. It seemed only good manners. Some of them wanted to run for shelter in the woods. Others feared this might give offense to the newcomers, who would then surely seek them out and kill them. Better to stand their ground and see what was to come. Was not courage a warrior's chief glory?

Seen close at hand, the floating "house" began to appear more and more like a large canoe. Finally it halted, its white wings flapping strangely. Then a smaller canoe put off. Old New York tradition says that Henry Hudson first stepped on shore at Coney Island, opposite Gravesend, Long Island. He was all in red and his clothing glittered in a way the Indians could not understand. Hudson had, in other words, gotten out his best clothes for the occasion and was covered with gold lace.

As the Indians watched, a large "hockhack," or gourd—in other words, a bottle or decanter—was brought to the red Manitou by one of his servants. From it he poured a strange fluid of which he drank, and which he then offered to the grave chief, who sniffed it cautiously. Wiser than they knew, all feared to drink, until one warrior bolder than the rest, drank, staggered, and fell to the ground. But presently he arose to declare that nothing had ever given him such a feeling of happiness as the strange fluid. Then they all tried it and they all got drunk. Hence, says tradition, the island was named "Manna-hata," or "place of drunkenness." It is a very dubious tale, for the island seems to have had its name long before Hudson, and the name does not appear to refer to drunkenness at all, while the incident—itself sufficiently historical—took place some time later near Albany.

From these native sources, it is better to turn to the day-by-day log of Robert Juet, of Limehouse, an English officer of the Dutch ship, the commander's own log of the trip, except for one or two accidentally preserved fragments, being now wholly lost. The yacht *Half Moon* had originally been sent out for exploration in the arctic north of Europe by Dutch speculators, who had employed the veteran seaman, Hudson, to command it. Finding passage beyond Nova Zemlya impossible, he turned west instead of east and ran down the North American coast from Newfoundland as far as "the King's River in Virginia, where our Englishmen are." It is strange that they did not put in, for Hudson's friend, John Smith, who had furnished him with information for the voyage, was still there. But without revealing his presence, Hudson turned north again for more careful examination of the coast. Unfortunately, he left no description, though he seems to have entered both Chesapeake and Delaware bays. On the northward voyage he saw in latitude 38° 9′ "a white sandy shore and within it an abundance of green trees" somewhere in Maryland. He suspected the presence of a big river running into Delaware Bay from the numerous "sands and shoals" and "from the strength of the current that set out."

As the ship came up the Jersey coast in the early morning, the crew "saw a great fire, but could not see land." At dawn, they made out

Sandy Hook, "all like broken islands," and eventually came into "a great lake of water," where they felt the current of the Hudson, pouring seaward, "a great streame out of the bay." Looking northward, as they anchored about five in the afternoon, they saw "high hils"—the Navesink highlands on the Jersey shore and Harbor Hill on Long Island. Even from so far down the Bay, the site of the American metropolis made a good impression—"a very good land to fall with, and a pleasant land to see." When the morning mists cleared about ten o'clock on the morning of the third, Hudson sent a small boat ahead to take soundings while the *Half Moon* crept cautiously in, the sailors noting as they went that there were "many salmons, and mullets, and rayes, very great." After further sounding on the fourth, they went farther into the harbor and then, for the first time went ashore to catch mullet and one huge ray, "as greate as foure men could hale into the ship."

Juet makes no mention of the Indians' excitement or of giving them liquor, saying only "the people of the countrey came aboord of us seeming very glad of our comming, and broughte greene tobacco, and gave us of it for knives and beads." There was much trading. Here they had a fight with the Indians and lost one man, with an arrow through his throat.

After that there was no more hostility for some time and Hudson gradually worked his ship into the inner harbor and slowly up the river, doing a great deal of sounding—as all the explorers had to do when they were close inshore in these totally unknown waters. On the twelfth they "turned into the river two leagues and anchored," being presumably somewhere off West Forty-second Street. Indians brought "very good oysters" and beans aboard and as the tide came in each day, Hudson went with it a little farther up the river, noting that "the land grew very high and mountainous" near Peekskill. Sometimes the crew seined for salmon, sturgeon, and other fish. The *Half Moon* passed West Point about the fourteenth, and ran on up the river noting "high mountaines"—the Catskills—and suffering from the characteristic hot weather of New York State in mid-September.

By the eighteenth the *Half Moon* was near Albany and here, Juet says, took place the incident that oral Indian tradition misplaced. Hudson took some chiefs into the cabin and gave them so much wine and aqua vitae "that they were all merrie" and "in the ende one of them was drunke"—apparently the incident preserved by native tradition.

By this time, they were certainly among the Mohawks, though the crew—no anthropologists—seem to have observed no differences among the tribes they met. On the twenty-fourth they started back down the river, admiring the forests on the bank "great store of goodly oakes, and walnut-trees, and chest-nut trees, [y]ewe trees, and trees of sweet wood [sassafras?] in abundance." One of the few fragments of Hudson's log that have been preserved contains his note that this was "as pleasant a land as one can tread upon," and "the finest for cultivation." Since the chestnuts were already ripening, the sailors took a "great store" of them. Passing through the Highlands they noted that "the trees that grow on them were all blasted" and some of the mountains were entirely barren, in sharp contrast with the forested country round about. There was some pilfering by the Indians on the way downstream and a little fighting; but by early October they were again at Manhattan. By noon of October 4, the *Half Moon* was again at sea on her way to Europe.

Hudson sailed once more in 1610, discovered the great Bay that bears his name, was frozen in throughout the winter, and in the spring was seized by mutinous sailors led by the mate, Robert Juet, who had been with him in New York. Set adrift in a small boat by his own crew, who did not quite dare to kill him, he vanishes from all human record on June 23, 1611.

XIV

Into Pennsylvania

Verrazano and Hudson had not attempted any thorough exploration of Delaware Bay, probably fearing its uncharted shallows and ever-present sandbars. Since other early voyagers shared their fears, Dutch interest was for some years concentrated on New Netherlands, later to become New York. In the meantime, interest in America had spread to Sweden, especially after Peter Minuit, dismissed by Holland, had entered the Swedish service. Swedes and Dutch soon became rivals along the Delaware, or South River, which was to lead the white man into one of the richest parts of North America, though before the century was over, it was in British hands.

There is no doubt that a few obscure English adventurers had preceded the Dutch along the Delaware. A squaw told Dutch explorers in 1632 that, some time before, her tribe had killed the English crew of a shallop in what is now Big Timber Creek, Gloucester County, New Jersey. No one knows who the victims were, but when the Dutch found the Indians wearing jackets of English make, they knew the story must be true.

In 1631 the first Dutch colonists arrived, with a cargo of brick and cattle to help them get a start, and began a settlement at Swanendael, near Lewes, Delaware, on the western coast of the bay. Here they built a brick house, surrounded by a palisade. They had high hopes of profitable whaling, for they had heard, quite correctly, that "many whales kept before the bay, and the oil was worth sixty guilders a hogshead." But the only oil they got was from a dead whale, washed up ashore.

Dutch vessels sailing for Swanendael the next year had to stop for repairs in England, then narrowly escaped a fight with a Turkish corsair off Madeira, and then a Frenchman off St. Christopher. In spite of these piratical perils, they were within sniffing distance of North America by December 2. Eagerly they "smelt the land, which gave a sweet perfume, as the wind came from the northwest, which blew off land, and caused these sweet odors."

This was not the natural scent of flowers, which others mention. One of the Dutch travelers wrote: "It comes from the Indians setting fire, at this time of year, to the woods and thickets, in order to hunt; and the land is full of sweet-smelling herbs, as sassafras, which has a sweet smell. When the wind blows out of the northwest, and the smoke is driven to sea, it happens that the land is smelt before it is seen."

There was a melancholy landing at Swanendael. Indian raiders had wiped out the settlement completely. Human skulls and bones lay intermingled with heads of horses and cows, the Indians having apparently carried off both beef and horsemeat for a feast.

The full horror of the victims' fate does not seem to have dawned on the Dutchmen. Not until 1646 do we get a description of scalping, a practice which seems to surprise the Dutch writer. The Indians, he says, "first struck the person on the head, so that he either died or swooned, after which they took off the skin of the head, after which some persons might revive again. This is called scalping, and is still in use among all the American Indians, and the skin of the head is called a scalp, which is their usual token of victory. An old Swedish woman, called the mother of Lars Buré, living at Chinsessing, had the misfortune to be scalped in this manner, yet lived many years thereafter, and became the mother of several children. No hair grew on her head again, except short down."

The Dutch explorers' first trip inland along the Delaware showed that, however unsuccessful their original efforts at whaling had been, they still had brilliant opportunities. William Penn later observed that "mighty Whales roll upon the Coast, near the Mouth of the Bay of

Delaware." The Dutch explorers, passing two whales in the bay, on their initial journey up the Delaware, found another at the river's mouth and were astonished to find a fourth spouting in fresh water, about twenty-five miles from the bay, above Wilmington.

The Delaware River was choked with ice then, as it was to be later when Washington made his famous Christmas crossing to surprise the Hessians. The Dutch, who had arrived at just about the same season, were frozen in for a fortnight, and several times their boat was nearly smashed by floating ice.

But there were compensations. Even in winter, they could see so many grapevines that they called the place Wyngaert's Kill, though they had no idea what kind of grapes the vines might produce. It remained for the Quakers, fifty years later, to begin making wine from clusters white, red, and black.

There was no trouble shooting wild turkeys weighing from thirty to thirty-six pounds. But, though these birds were much larger than the few surviving wild turkeys found in American woods today, they were not nearly so large as those William Penn's colonists were to find fifty years later. Though twenty-five pounds would be a big wild turkey now, there are numerous fifty-pound records from colonial times, far too many for all to be dismissed as merely hunters' optimistic guesses. John Josselyn reports forty- to sixty-pound birds in New England and himself saw one that weighed thirty pounds "when it was pull'd and garbidg'd."

The difference is probably due to the fact that the turkeys of the primitive American wilderness ranged the most fertile parts of the country, getting all they could eat and waxing fat accordingly, while their modern descendants are crowded back into mountain wastes, where food is harder to find.

The wild turkeys seem to have survived longer in Pennsylvania than in New England. In 1645, one observer in New England saw sixty broods of young turkeys—which must have totaled several hundred individuals—"on the side of a Marsh, sunning of themselves in a morning betimes." But within thirty years these wild birds had been pretty well wiped out in New England, though the settlers now had them as tame barnyard flocks.

The site of Washington, D. C. Engraved from an early 18th-century painting.

An early English engraving of the Falls of the Passaic River, New Jersey.

The earliest Swedish settlers got their first clue as to what the rest of the country might be like from the numbers of waterfowl passing overhead. They could not themselves explore very far. Nor could the Indians themselves give much information, since the average redskin does not usually travel very far out of his own bailiwick. They could tell the Swedes only that "as far as they have gone into the interior, the country is inhabited by other wild nations of various races."

But the waterfowl swept north in spring and south in autumn in such numbers that it was clear there must be an enormous stretch of country inland. The wild geese which appeared in October would pause briefly and "afterwards proceed southward, with great cries, and hopping along with an almost incredible swiftness; at the same time there came also swans, cranes, herons, ducks, and various other kinds of birds and fowls." This was just the ordinary autumn migration, which had led Columbus to a landfall; but it was an astonishing thing to the unaccustomed eye.

The valley had other attractions. One early visitor thought the Delaware "the most healthfull, fruitefull, and commodious River in all the North of America, to be planted." In fact, as Lewis Evans, the eighteenth century geographer, was later to record, "before the arrival of the Europeans, the whole County was a Wood, The Swamps full of Cripple & Brush; and The Ground unbroke."

Travel overland between the Delaware and the Hudson was difficult. Even at the end of the seventeenth century, there was nothing but a footpath for men and horses, which ran through an oak and hickory forest with a few chestnuts, with more shrubby undergrowth than usual. Then came "large plains, beset with a few trees, and grown over with long grass and so at length to the Falls of the Delaware," near Trenton. The "falls" disappointed most newcomers, being only "a place of about two English miles in length, or not so much, where the river is full of stones, which are not very large, but on consequence of the shallowness, the water runs rapidly and breaks against them, causing some noise, but not very much." The thunder of falling water impressed Europeans, who had heard nothing like it at home.

Even in mid-February, the Dutch travelers found the Delaware had "a great plenty of fish," which included perch, roach, pike, and sturgeon, the presence of the latter in fresh water at that season being rather surprising. One haul of the net brought in enough for thirty men. Early travelers discovered, to their delight, that the sturgeon stayed in the Delaware "all the sommer time, which are in such aboundance in the upper parts of the River, as that great benefitt might be raysed by setting up a fishing for them."

William Penn and his Quakers, arriving fifty years later, found a good many other fish, such as herring, "Rock" [bass?], eels, trout, and shad—the latter, of course, having been out in salt water during the winter exploration of the Dutch.

Brook trout, the finest of American game fish, and catfish, the worst of American coarse fish, attracted no attention at all from any of the early eastern explorers. That nobody paid any attention to the small eastern catfish is easy to understand; but it is strange to find a careful geographer like Lewis Evans saying that in Pennsylvania there were "scarce any Trout, except in a few remote Runs."

The fact is, there was remarkably fine trout fishing in both eastern and middle western states. Pennsylvania streams are reported as late as 1809, "full of fine trout," and John Josselyn wrote of early New England: *"Trouts* there be good store in every brook, ordinarily two and twenty inches long."

Fish like that would cause a sensation nowadays, but in primitive America and for many years after white settlement began, they were not at all unusual. Around Lake Superior brook trout of four to four and a half pounds, with a maximum of five and a half pounds were frequently taken about the middle of the nineteenth century. A fisherman wrote in 1847, "You may take a boatload of them which will average 3 to 4 pounds in weight." Scientists of the Minnesota Geological and Natural History Survey saw one in 1879 that measured twenty-four inches and weighed five and three quarter pounds.

Fish of other kinds were easy to take. Shad ran up the Delaware and other eastern rivers in the spring in enormous numbers. In the Delaware, according to William Penn himself, one settler "drew 600 and odd at one Draught; 300 is no wonder; 100 familiarly." They were quite as numerous in the Susquehanna. The first settlers were sternly practical folk, no epicures. It is painful to record that they had no conception of the ineffable virtues of planked shad—so little, indeed, that they ate the most delicate of American fishes "Pickled or Smokt'd, as well as boyled fresh," which is no way to treat fresh shad. The early Pennsylvanians' culinary barbarity with sturgeon was almost as monstrous. They simply boiled them, as they did nearly everything else. No one seems to have heard of smoked sturgeon, and as late as 1685, William Penn was still lamenting that "a good way to Pickle Sturgion is wanting."

"Rock" were salted down in barrels for winter use, as old-fashioned Yankee farmers used to do with shad, even in the later nineteenth century. As for the teeming schools of herring, said Penn, "they almost shovel them up in their tubs." No wonder that, as Penn also reports, Indian boys, however young, rushed off to "go a Fishing till ripe for the Woods, which is about Fifteen." And no wonder, either, that little white boys were sometimes rather reluctant to be rescued from Indian captivity.

Along the Delaware and its tributary streams, there were some beaver, whose pelts the Dutch and Swedes eagerly bought from the Indians. One English enthusiast remarks that the whole Delaware Valley "aboundeth with beavers, otters, and other meaner furrs, which are not only taken upon the banks of the main river, but likeways in other lesser rivers." One tributary, the Lehigh, was almost choked with beaver dams, which must have helped produce what was known as "the Great Swamp," between Easton and the Poconos, on its head-waters. Later settlers were to discover that beaver filled the inland rivers, creeks, and ponds all the way to the Rockies.

The Pennsylvania, Delaware, and New Jersey woods had the usual American fauna, wolves, raccoons, red and grey foxes, fisher, beaver, otter, muskrat, "minx," lynxes, wildcats, bear and deer. Occasional reports of "elk" may mean that the moose ranged a good deal farther south than zoologists have suspected; but there were genuine elk in the colony. On the West Branch of the Susquehanna, around Williamsport, a good man· were still being killed in the early nineteenth century.

In New York, one hears a good deal about "lions," that is the American cougar, panther, or "mountain lion"; but it is never mentioned by Dutch or Swedish writers, who seem to have kept close to the river, rarely venturing far into the forests or on visits to the Indian villages. The Quakers and Pennsylvania Germans, who got on much better with the Delaware and other Indians and so ventured farther inland, often report the presence of "panthers," but from the beginning these animals seem to have been rather rare. This was natural. Carnivora are never so numerous as the animals on which they prey.

There are no reports of panthers' attacks on cattle, only too frequent elsewhere, and, of course—in spite of many legends—it is doubtful if the cougar ever attacks mankind. There is, however, one Missouri record of wandering hunters who found a deer, a cougar, and a man, lying dead together.

Panthers were usually as timid as other wild animals. The famous scout, Christopher Gist during his westward journey in 1752, caught in a snowstorm near Pittsburgh, simply "scared a Panther from under a Rock where there was Room enough for Us, in it we camped & had good Shelter." This particular panther, obviously one of the meekest beasts of prey that ever lived, had chosen its lair with such excellent judgment that the Gists made themselves at home in the poor beast's den four days, resting till the weather moderated.

Panthers lingered for a long time in Pennsylvania, though even before the white man came they had been much hunted, since they were not the totem animal of any clan and no Indians spared them. The white man's rifles and hunting dogs wiped them out almost completely. A locally famous hunter, Aaron Hall, is reputed to have killed fifty of them in the Juniata Valley between 1845 and 1870. Hall used to amuse himself by setting up frozen panthers and bears in front of his cabin door, to the consternation of timid visitors. In spite of the slaughter, a few may still linger. A track-walker saw one calmly sunning itself within sight of the New York Central tracks in Centre County as recently as 1910.

The eastern cougars, though all one species, varied a good deal in color. They were sometimes dark, sometimes almost red, more often slate-grey with orange and fulvous tinges at the ears, throat, and nose, or along the belly. A very few really deserved to be called mountain "lions," for they developed manes like those of the African and Asiatic lions, though not nearly so luxuriant. One such animal was killed in the Bald Eagle Mountains in 1797.

Three American animals which always surprised Europeans attracted special attention in Pennsylvania—the opossum, the flying squirrel, and the skunk. De Soto's men had probably seen possums, and in 1699 Le Moyne d'Iberville, exploring the lower Mississippi had killed eight. His description leaves no doubt of what they were: "an animal which has a head like a sucking pig and of about the same size, hair like a badger, grey and white, the tail like a rat, the paws like a monkey, which has a purse beneath its belly, where it produces its young and nourishes them." Early Pennsylvanians were quick to notice "that strange creature, the Possam, she having a false Belly to swallow her Young ones, by which means she preserveth them from danger."

The external pouch in which the living young are carried after birth—characteristic of all marsupials—completely puzzled Europeans. Like D'Iberville, most of them supposed that the young were born in the pouch; and a queer story grew up that they were not produced like ordinary embryos in the uterus, but developed like buds on the female's nipples, and then broke off! This seemed plausible because young possums are only about half an inch long at birth—a British Army surgeon thought them "as small as a large bean"—and immediately after birth are placed in the mother's pouch, where they remain, clinging to the nipples, as if they really did grow there.

Extraordinarily adaptable to modern conditions, the possum is still with us. It even lives and breeds in the wild state in Flushing Meadows, within the confines of New York City and in sight of the deliberations of the United Nations, and is believed to be moving north into states where it was never seen before.

Nearly as mysterious was "that Remarkable Creature the Flying-Squirrel, having a kind of Skinny wings, almost like those of a Batt, though it hath the like Hair and Colour of the Common Squirrel, but is much less in Bodily Substance; I have (myself) seen it fly from one Tree to another in the Woods, but how long it can maintain its Flight is not yet exactly known." Virginia colonists had also noted those "assapanick"—the "ick" being just the usual plural ending in the Algonkian Indian language group.

It is a queer fact that few of the early English explorers mention skunks, though it is hard to see how novices in the forest could escape disaster at their first meeting with this deceptively beautiful and apparently harmless little animal. The skunk, like the rattlesnake, is a gentleman: he always signals before he attacks. Besides, neither animal wants to waste its defensive fluids. But newcomers from Europe did not know what the "woods pussy's" characteristic stamping of the earth portended, until the woods pussy whirled about and, stern first, went into action. Then it was too late.

"The Squnck," says John Josselyn, feelingly, is "an offensive carrion," and "of so strong a scent, that if it light upon anything, there is no abiding."

The Indians knew enough to give skunks a wide berth, though the Ohio mound builders established what was almost a world's record, by eating them. Some hundreds of years later, Canadian boatmen on the Missouri River occasionally ventured upon the same fearsome repast.

The first written mention of this troublesome little beast is by missionary priests. The description given by one of them—"these devil's brats"—suggests that the good father had learned some North American zoology by sad experience. Father Paul Le Jeune, S.J., in 1634 is very emphatic about the noisome mammal: "It is more white than black; and, at the first glance, you would say, especially when it walks, that it ought to be called Jupiter's little dog. But it is so stinking, and casts so foul an odor, that it is unworthy of being called a dog of Pluto. No sewer ever smelled so bad. I could not have believed it if I had not smelled it myself. Your heart almost fails you when you approach the animal; two have been killed in our court, and several days afterward there was such a dreadful odor throughout our house that we could not endure it. I believe that the sin smelled by sainte Catherine de Sienne must have had the same vile odor."

There were still skunks on Staten Island in 1794, when an English traveler sailing past wrote: "Our noses were suddenly assailed with a most disagreeable stench, and before I could speak of it, the people on board cried out, 'A Skunk;' it seems this nasty animal may be smelt at a mile distance, if the wind sets that way."

The settlement of Pennsylvania proceeded in a semi-circle, gradually widening outward toward the Susquehanna. It was reaching into some of the best farm land in the world. "The land is very good, fruitful, and withal very healthful," wrote Captain Thomas Young, an early arrival from England. "The soil is sandy, and produces several sorts of fruits, especially grapes, which grow wild in great quantities, of which I have eaten six several sorts. . . . The earth being fruitful, is covered over with woods and stately timber, except only in those places where the Indians have planted their corn." The low ground, then full of beaver and otter, he thought would make excellent meadows, presumably when the beaver and otter were gone.

Within a surprisingly short time, the rich farmland of Bucks, Berks, and Lancaster counties was pretty well cleared of trees—though not so completely as to drive off the game. By the time of the Revolution there were few oaks thicker than six inches in southeastern Pennsylvania. The landscape was assuming the appearance of lush agricultural fertility for which it is famous today, though Pennsylvania farming still had a long way to go. Stumps dotted the fields. In Mifflin County, along the Juniata, some years later, every man convicted of drunkenness, had to work off his penalty by digging up one stump. A local legend says that the pile thus painfully extracted by inebriate settlers at Lewistown was of prodigious size.

The enormous barns and fat pure-bred cattle of the agricultural counties were still far in the future. Pigs were turned into the woods to feed themselves on roots and acorns. Cattle ran wild. Since horses were scarce, the farmers plowed with oxen, whose plodding weight was almost a necessity in subduing rank, matted soil that had recently been forest. Animals under these conditions were not very productive. A gallon a day was thought to be a good yield for a milch-cow.

Pennsylvania cornfields were luxuriant even in prehistoric times. Peter Lindström, engineer for the government of New Sweden, on the Delaware, one of the first Europeans to see them, describes the ears of corn as having ten to fourteen rows of kernels, each seed planted returning a thousandfold. Lindström also ought to be famous as the first man to pay literary tribute to the virtues of corn-on-the-cob. "When these are just ripe," he says, "and they are broiled on the hot coals, they are delightful to eat."

There is little mention of insects at first; but as the fields were cleared for cultivation, native American "bugs" joyfully swarmed from their original haunts to feast on tenderer leaves than unassisted Nature could produce. There were not so many insect pests in those days as there are today. The Colorado potato beetle and the Japanese beetle, to take two horrible examples, were still far in the future, and the European corn borer was then a native of central Europe, which had not yet discovered the succulence of an ear of sweet corn. For a time there is no mention of insect trouble in Pennsylvania cornfields, though southern Indians complained that "the worm yowanne" attacked their maize.

Insect pests enough soon appeared, however. The cutworm seems to have attacked American gardens from the very beginning. John Josselyn, in New England, mentions "a dark dunnish Worm or Bug of the bigness of an Oaten-straw, and an inch long, that in the Spring lye at the Root of Corn and Garden plants all day, and in the night creep out and devour them." Jasper Dankers, visiting Virginia and Maryland planters in the seventeenth century, notes that "the Lord sometimes punishes them with insects, flies and worms," thus "causing great famine."

Lewis Evans notes dolefully that "No Imagination can conceive how full this Country is of all sorts of Insects, not a fruit of any Sort escapes their Enquiries." Apples, cherries, and peaches, he thought, would do well "if it were not for the Injury of the Worm." Plums had "The Worm Biting them just as they begin to change Colour." Nectarines, he feared, would never succeed in America "upon account of the Worm." No one seems to have had any idea of spraying the fruit trees. A swarm of the seventeen-year "locust," or cicada—erroneously described as "fourteen year"—was noted near Philadelphia as early as 1749.

Bees brought into the colonies soon escaped to the woods. There were many "bee trees" in the eastern Pennsylvania forests in William Penn's day, but as late as 1753 there were none beyond the West

Branch of the Susquehanna. By the early nineteenth century escaping swarms were across the Mississippi and they seem to have kept about one hundred miles ahead of the frontier, all the way to the Rockies. It is interesting to note how quickly the black bears learned to rob bee trees for their honey. The Indians are said to have regarded the "white man's fly" with dread, for swarming bees in the forest presaged the coming of the white invader.

Fireflies astonished the first Swedish settlers in Pennsylvania as much as they astonished the French missionaries farther north, but both somewhat exaggerated the brilliance of the illumination. It is not really true, as one Swede reported, that the firefly "gives so strong a light, that it is sufficient, when a man is travelling to show him the way." It may be true that "one may also write and read the smallest print by the light which they give"—but it takes a good many fireflies in a bottle to do it. Fireflies were responsible for a panic among the Swedish troops at Fort Christina, who "thought they were enemies advancing towards them with lighted matches." They were thinking, of course, of the "slow matches" carried to fire the clumsy firearms of the period.

A later English traveler was equally impressed and a little alarmed when he saw "the singular phenomenon of fireflies" near Princeton— "a sudden spark of fire appears close to you in various directions, and as suddenly disappearing: it frequently alarmed me, when I saw these sparks among hay, straw, and wood."

There was little Indian trouble in Pennsylvania at first. The Dutch along the North River had for the most part paid for their land, and the New York Indians were consequently well-disposed toward white men. Though the legendary twenty-four dollars paid for Manhattan Island was not a very high price, in the light of subsequent real estate values, the Indians probably thought that they had made a good bargain.

This favorable impression was increased by William Penn's scrupulous fairness in dealing with the Iroquois and their Delaware subjects. Charles II might have granted him the land, but the Quaker conscience is a mighty force. Penn's "inner light" bade him pay the redskins a fair price and he obeyed it.

William Penn was unlike most Englishmen to whom colonial grants were made—he actually came out and lived in his colony, where he saw to it that honest dealing prevailed. The son of Admiral Sir William Penn, who had beaten the Dutch fleet in 1665, an Oxford man, a wealthy young aristocrat, he became a convert to Quakerism and then a frequent preacher at Quaker meetings. It was very embarrassing to everybody when the admiral's son began to be rather frequently arrested for illegal sermons. It was still more embarrassing for Charles II when the admiral died, leaving his heir the creditor of the king for a very large sum, which His Majesty had no way of paying, and no intention of paying, either. But there was an easy way out. Penn was looking for a place where the Quakers would be free from persecution; Charles II claimed most of North America. They made a deal. Penn gave up his claim for money in return for Pennsylvania, where his children remained "proprietors" until the Revolution. (There is a legend that one barren mountain top near WilkesBarre still belongs to them because, in all the years since Charles II, no one has ever wanted it.)

The Indians, punning on his name and the quill pens of the day, called him "Onas," or "Feather"; and so long as "Onas" lived, the Indians were fairly treated and the utmost friendliness prevailed. It was a contrast to the hostility met by the Swedes and the first few wandering English. On one occasion Quakers near Reading were startled by the sudden appearance of Indians painted for war; but it turned out they had heard a rumor that their white friends were in some kind of danger, and had hurried down to protect them! There were a good many conversions among the Pennsylvania Delawares. As early as 1742, the Moravian synod near Reading had three converted warriors as lay-preachers.

Some time after Penn's death, relations changed for the worse, and there was plenty of scalping and massacre up and down the Susquehanna Valley in the Revolutionary War. The famous "Walking Purchase" was particularly resented. The Indians had agreed to sell the land as far as a man could walk in a day and a half. But they had not anticipated that Penn's heirs would prepare the course by carefully clearing a path through the woods; or that the "walk" was to be a kind of Marathon race by specially trained athletes. Some of the warriors officially appointed to supervise the "walk," as a guaranty of fair dealing, dropped out before the course had been finished. It was all they could do to keep pace themselves, and the land the white men thus secured comprised vastly more of their hunting grounds than the honest Delawares had ever contemplated parting with. They solaced themselves later by murdering the entire family of the fastest of the white "walkers," though, luckily for him, they never caught the "walker" himself.

The Susquehanna Valley was the obvious next step for Pennsylvania settlement. Until the middle of the eighteenth century it was almost unknown. The first recorded explorer is Étienne Brulé, Champlain's trusty lieutenant, who in 1615 had traveled its entire length; but—whatever he said in his oral report to Champlain—he left no written record. The Quakers probably never guessed that he had ever passed that way. At about the same time Captain John Smith had found the river's mouth but had gone only a little way upstream. The first real descriptions of the unspoiled valley—which even to this day is as beautiful in its way as a lesser Rhine—come from the Penn's indefatigable interpreter and Indian agent, Conrad Weiser, and the Moravian missionaries, who sometimes traveled with him and sometimes made the trip alone.

Weiser, though little known nowadays to anyone except Pennsylvanians (and not many of them), was one of the remarkable men of his time. Son of a German immigrant to New York, he had come with other German pietists down the Susquehanna to settle in Pennsylvania. Pious, gentle, utterly fearless, skilled in the woods, he had lived among the Iroquois as a boy, thus acquiring a shrewd knowledge of the red man's way of thinking and a thorough speaking knowledge of the six Iroquois dialects. On one occasion when an embassy of Nanticoke Indians could not make themselves understood by the Iroquois council at Onondaga, Weiser obligingly translated for both parties. The Penns found him an invaluable agent and the Iroquois, who trusted him completely, seem to have thought him as much their agent as Penn's.

His enemies were all white. The animosities stirred up by Weiser's ill-advised venture into Pennsylvania Dutch monasticism at the Ephrata cloisters in 1735, as the result of a religious revival, somewhat dimmed his reputation even in his own time. Ephrata was that paradox—a monastery for both sexes! Single women lived together in one building, single men in another, while married couples belonging to the community, though allowed to live together in cottages round about, were enjoined to the strictest celibacy. The results were about what anyone save the devout but wool-gathering wits of the Ephrata eccentrics might have expected. The successive appearance of four additional Weiser children during the period of their father's supposed celibacy led to trouble. The heads of Ephrata felt that, though thoroughly legitimate, so many offspring were hardly compatible with the monastic life. In the end Weiser broke with the Ephrata community entirely, only to become reconciled later and consecrated a member of their special priesthood.

None of this affected his value as an Indian agent, however, and his picture of the Susquehanna and the Endless Mountains at the time of his winter journey to the New York Iroquois at Onondaga is the first real account of this district that has been preserved.

The Susquehanna is really two rivers—at least its modern inhabitants have never been able to decide whether the North Branch or the West Branch is the real river. The Susquehanna is thus like a huge capital "Y" running from New York State to Chesapeake Bay. Into the West Branch runs the Juniata, still the most beautiful river in Pennsylvania, and in primitive times the best hunting ground in the state.

The waters of the two branches come together at modern Sunbury, which was known to the Indians as Shamokin. Since internal peace has come to North America, no one thinks of Sunbury as having strategic importance. In primitive times, however, to control Shamokin was to dominate canoe routes and trails along three big rivers—the very heart of Pennsylvania—that is, the North and West branches, and the Juniata, which enters a little farther south.

All this was perfectly clear to the shrewd sachems of the imperialistic Iroquois League at Onondaga. Slowly they gathered the conquered and tributary tribes—Shawnee, Tutelo, Sapony, Delaware, Nanticoke

Forest scene on the Lehigh River in Pennsylvania. Engraved from a painting by Karl Bodmer (c. 1830).

Indians hunting moose. From a painting by George Catlin.

along the North Branch—the most important center of the subject peoples being the area around modern WilkesBarre, which was called Wyoming or Wajomink. At Shamokin or near it dwelt the Iroquois viceroy, Shikellamy, representing the dominant Iroquois. Another "half-king" on the upper waters of the Ohio, near Pittsburgh, controlled western Pennsylvania and Ohio. Colonial diplomats at Philadelphia dealt either directly with Shikellamy in minor matters or, in great affairs of state, with the supreme Iroquois council at Onondaga.

In mid-winter of 1736, the Penns at Philadelphia had certain matters to lay before the Iroquois council at Onondaga—that is, Syracuse, New York. In the whole colony there was only one man to send, since only Weiser spoke their difficult aboriginal dialects. Between Shamokin and Onondaga lay a wilderness so thick that in many parts even game animals shunned it. Except at Wyoming, the villages were far apart and in winter the Indians were so near starvation themselves that they could do little to help a traveler. There was often a good deal of game along the river, but not enough to be sure of a winter's food supply.

Weiser set off in February of 1737 on the long walk from Philadelphia to Onondaga. From the very beginning it was a hard journey. The path over the mountains to Shamokin was, according to an early map, "scarce passable." He made a dangerous crossing of the flooded river, full of floating ice which threatened at every moment to crush the frail canoe of an Indian trader who consented to ferry him across. Going up the West Branch of the Susquehanna a short distance to the village where Shikellamy was then living, he found that worthy chief absent and the Indians almost without provisions. Iroquois warriors arriving from New York brought news that the snow was six feet deep in the mountains ahead. Weiser managed to buy a little cornmeal and some beans.

About the time Shikellamy returned, there came limping in an Iroquois warrior. He had gone to Virginia with a war party which had found the southern Indians too much for them, and was now trying to get home alone, very much the worse for wear. With this warrior, Shikellamy, and two other companions, Weiser started out up the West Branch. Once they passed the remains of ancient earth-

works, obviously fortifications, but so old that even the Indians had no
idea who had built them. There are a good many of these in the Middle West but they were rare in Pennsylvania and have long since
been leveled by the white man's plow.

The small tributary creeks were so flooded that Weiser's men could
hardly cross. The snow was already three feet deep. As they turned off
from the main stream up Diadachton (Lycoming) Creek, they had to
scramble between "frightfully high mountains and rocks, overgrown
with carell or palmwood" in a valley "not broader than the bed of the
stream." In dismay, Weiser proposed returning; but, when the Indians insisted that the trail would soon improve, they scrambled ahead,
the red men climbing on hands and feet along the cliffs above the
rushing creek, while Weiser used a small hatchet to cut footholds in
the ice for the white members of the party. Now and then, when the
path crossed the icy stream, they had to wade. Then, in their dripping
moccasins, they moved so slowly that their toes were in danger of
freezing, since they had "no space to keep our feet warm by exercise."
The evergreen forests around them were "of the kind called by the
English, spruce, so thick that we could not, generally, see the sun
shine." In three hours, they had gone about a mile. They bunked
that night on evergreen boughs laid on the snow, into which their fire
—as they found next morning—slowly sank a full yard. By that time,
there was nothing to eat for breakfast except "a little Indian corn
and beans, boiled in water."

The Endless Mountains began to live up to the name that weary
and disgusted Indians had given them. Even in summer, without
snow and cold and freezing water, Diadachton Creek was a bad route.
A Moravian missionary in June, 1745, noted: "The forest is so dense
that for a day the sun could not be seen, and so thick that you could
not see twenty feet before. The path, too, is so bad that the horses
were often stuck, and had to be extricated from the bogs; and, at other
times it lay full of trees that had been blown down by the wind, and
heaped so high that we were at loss whether to turn to the right or
to the left." Another writer remarks that in the whole area, now
known as North Mountain and Towanda Mountain, "scarce an Acre of

10" was capable of cultivation. In fact most of the country is still a state forest reserve.

Weary of wading the freezing creek, Weiser and Shikellamy decided to leave the valley and try traveling on the mountain itself. That was not much better. Within a quarter of a mile, Shikellamy slipped at a point where the mountainside was "steeper than the roof of a house." The stone he caught to support himself came loose, and the chief slid to within a few feet of a hundred-foot precipice with "spitzige" rocks below. Here his pack went past one side of a sapling while Shikellamy went past the other. There the dignified old viceroy hung till his companions rescued him. When they reached the valley again, Shikellamy, looking up at the precipice, thanked "the great Lord and Creator of the world, that he had mercy on me, and wished me to continue to live longer."

Presently they had to cut a long pole, which they all held as they waded across, waist-deep. The evergreen woods were still "so thick, that for a mile at a time we could not find a place of the size of a hand, where the sunshine could penetrate, even in the clearest day." Looking about through this redoubled gloom of a dark winter day, Weiser decided that central Pennsylvania could only be described as "die grausame Wüste"—the dismal wilderness. Moravians later echoed him, describing this part of the "Shomoko road" as "the great desert." They soon learned to avoid it entirely by canoeing up the North Branch, after the ice was gone.

Weiser was now on Towanda Mountain. Conditions were nearly as bad on North Mountain, just south of them, over which the Moravian, Martin Mack, groaned in 1742: "Our way lay through the forest, over rocks and frightful mountains, and across streams swollen by the recent heavy rains. This was a fatiguing and dangerous journey."

On one mountaintop, Weiser found two Iroquois skulls fastened to poles. They had once belonged to warriors who, bringing South Carolina Indian prisoners home to New York for torture, grew careless. They failed, when they halted on this spot, to tie up their captives, who snatched up rifles while the victors were busy cooking, and killed them both. Iroquois later explained that the prisoners must have had the help of an evil spirit. No one could do that to the conquerors without supernatural aid. More cautious warriors tied their prisoners to posts every night, carefully fastening their feet in holes dug in the ground beside the stakes. Red painted poles, erected for this purpose, were left along the trail for the convenience of returning war parties.

As they crossed the height of land and began descending Towanda Creek (Iroquois: Dawanta, fretful or tedious), things began to improve. They came out of the dismal evergreens into a pleasant grove of white oaks (leafless at that season) and to Weiser "it seemed as if we had escaped from hell."

The wind grew warmer. They had dry ground to sleep on. After another desperate creek-crossing they reached the North Branch Susquehanna, having eaten their last reserve of food, to find that the Indians were "hungry people, who sustained life with the juice of the sugar-trees," in other words, maple syrup. In many parts of Pennsylvania, there would have been plenty of deer, "yarded up" in the deep snow and easy to kill. But game animals avoided these dense mountain forests. Weiser mentions no sign of deer or other game animals along the trail, though the Moravian bishop Spangenberg going up the Diadachton in June found at a salt lick the tracks of "elk." He describes them as "deer, like horses without a name," and does not make clear whether he means real elk or southward-ranging moose. In spring and summer, passing hunters sometimes left extra meat hanging in the trees, out of the reach of wolves, for anyone who might follow. Spangenberg's party feasted on a cold roast of bear, thus left behind; and other Moravians, having caught a deer swimming the upper Susquehanna and killed it with a hatchet, hung up part of the carcass for friendly Nanticoke Indians whom they knew to be following. But Weiser, traveling in mid-winter, could have no hope of such luck. Spangenberg himself remarks that the mountains, when covered with snow, did not attract animals.

When Weiser and Shikellamy at last reached an Indian village buried in the forest, they found the men were all out hunting, but so far they had not been able to get meat. The travelers kept alive on cornmeal gruel and once enjoyed the luxury of corn flavored with lye made of the ashes. Many Indians liked this mixture—the white men still use lye in making hominy—and some Indians thought that a little powdered woodash lent flavor to a meal. Others preferred the tart flavor of formic acid from a few insects. The Indians explained to Weiser that the lye made the corn "slippery and pleasant to eat," and Weiser himself, in no mood to be finicky, admits that it "was not of a bad taste."

The flavor, however, did not tempt him to linger. Passing Tioga, he turned off up a tributary of the Susquehanna at Owego, finding the few Indians along the way keeping alive on maple-sap, which had at least the merit of being rich in sugar. On maple sugar, says Weiser, "we sustained life, but it did not agree with us." Then the Indians found some wild potatoes or ground nuts, about as big as pigeons' eggs, and matters began to look up. The party finally got a little corn and sent Indian runners ahead to Onondaga to announce their coming.

As Weiser's party pushed on, they were discouraged to meet the runners they had sent ahead, returning with the news that they could not get through the snow in the mountains.

The country between Owego and Syracuse was also desperately hard going. There were mountains, swamps, thickets, cliffs against which the streams rushed closely, while such trail as there was wound back and forth across the streams, chilling the traveler in one ford after another. The worst of it was, there was often no clearly marked trail at all for a stretch of two or three miles. As a Moravian remarked, "where they cannot distinguish it each one runs through the woods according to his own judgment." Finding the right road toward night-fall was no joke. One traveler hopefully followed what he thought was the trail, only to discover that it was the track of a black bear, which fortunately was traveling in the same direction.

Bartram, the Quaker botanist, a few years later, said the mountains were often "great banks of craggy rocks and tremendous precipices." The tops were barren stone, with "mighty rocks tumbled down, and those left appearing as if piled up in a pyramid and hereby preserved from a share in the awful ruin below among their fellows; the soil being so perfectly washed from their root, as evidently no longer to support them."

Bartram felt pretty sure the waters of Noah's flood had done it all, gradually retiring to the St. Lawrence and the Susquehanna, rivers regrettably not mentioned in Holy Writ.

At the very end of Weiser's journey, matters improved. The last great mountain on the New York side appeared to Bartram an "easy and fruitful ascent and descent, in its great width, every where crowned with noble and lofty woods, but above all, in its being intirely free from naked rocks and steep precipices." But Bartram made the journey in July. Weiser, in mid-winter, was interested neither in Noah's flood nor in landscapes. To him, the wintry mountains were "a dreadful thick wilderness," such as even he had never seen. At one point he sat down to die, rather hoping the bitter cold would hasten his demise; but sturdy old Shikellamy, still vigorous, persuaded him to make one more effort and brought him safely to Onondaga.

As they came down out of the mountains on the north side, the heavy forest through which they had been traveling opened up into scattered groves and toward the end they passed through forty miles of sugar maples mingled with other trees, which Bartram later noted. But there was not much comfort in leafless sugar maples, even though the going was easier, and the party reached Onondaga in a state of exhaustion. The Iroquois received them hospitably and urged them to eat and rest, "for you look like Dead Men."

Weiser's hardships give a most unfair picture of what most of this country was like. In winter, the game took refuge elsewhere, but in season it was filled with big, brown elk, which moved in herds of thirty to sixty and other animals were also plentiful: deer, wolves, foxes red, black, and silver. The elk were most abundant in northern Pennsylvania, ranging between the North Branch of the Susquehanna and the Allegheny River. In modern terms one might say that there were elk all the way from WilkesBarre to Pittsburgh. Elk were sometimes tamed so that they came and went with the settler's cows.

The lower New York country through which Weiser passed toward the end of his journey set Bartram, the summer traveler, into ecstasies; and Lewis Evans, who traveled with him, describes the landscape as "varied with pleasant, swelling knobs, brooks and little lakes. In its vegitation it abounds with sweet-maple [sugar maple], linden, birch, elm, white pines in some places; and with goose-berry under-woods on the north side of all the ridges."

The wild currants, or wild gooseberries, interested all early travelers, for they grew freely all over the northeastern part of America, though agriculture has long since forced them back into mountains and wood-lands. There were two kinds, a large black currant, which had a dis-agreeable smell but was "reasonable pleasant in the eating," and a red or purplish "gooseberry," also called a "thorn grape," because of the spines around it. Lewis Evans calls the black currant "a nauseous sort," but others had rather more favorable opinions of it. Similar species grew in the West, where the Lewis and Clark expedition was later to discover them.

Though civilization with the introduction of better horticultural varieties has made these berries rather scarce, they can still be found in wilder country. In fact, they still grow in the very mountains where Evans and Bartram found them. A contemporary biologist, who has gathered and eaten them there, credits the wild berries with "a pro-nounced tang which is more than worth the trouble caused by the spines."

Weiser's return journey, after the winter was over, was much easier. Taking a canoe, his party ran easily down the North Branch of the Susquehanna, now clear of ice. Though there were almost no rapids to worry about, the upper reaches of the river were so swift that, when the water was high, a canoe could run downstream at fifty miles a day. Though the thick forests were almost empty, there was usually game near the river itself and "wild beans along the banks," where they were gathered by the Indians whose local place names still linger by the Susquehanna,—musical ones like Catawissa and Wyalusing and Wyoming, harsh ones like Nescopeck, Wapwallopen, or Shickshinny. Strange to say, the paw-paw, a middle western fruit, grew along the river below Shamokin, transplanted by early Indian horticulturists.

Waterfowl, of which there are still a good many in the migration season, haunted the river, and the omnipresent passenger pigeon haunted the woods, though not in the enormous flocks common in the Middle West. Turtle eggs by the shore eked out the wilderness diet in season, and any canoeist was reasonably sure of a fish dinner if he dropped a line overboard the last mile or so to camp—as he still is in northern Ontario. There were at least some deer, and Moravian missionaries caught five raccoons in a single tree on one of the Susquehanna's tributary creeks. Their journals do not comment on the flavor, but Virginia colonists thought raccoons very good eating. Another Moravian comments on the difference between the mountain and the river route. "In the forest there is no game of any kind," he says. "It is very different from ascending the Susquehanna by water. There is no dearth of food there, game being always abundant," but the hunting seems always to have been better on the West Branch.

There were some wolves all along the river, and occasionally a lucky shot from a passing canoe dropped one. Near Tunkhannock, a Moravian remarks, wolves "made a terrific noise around us during the night," though—misisonary or not—he was woodsman enough not to be afraid of them.

Weiser's canoe party spent little time in hunting, on their way downstream, though they got one shot at a bear, missing him, and bagged a turkey and several wild ducks. By May 1, 1737, they were safely home.

The Susquehanna in those days was a fine stream for fish, though the first travelers seem to have been in too much of a hurry to catch any. There are more records of shad than of anything else, though there must have been just as many fish of other kinds. Two thousand shad were taken in a single night at Wyalusing, Pennsylvania, but that was nothing compared with the celebrated "widow's haul" on the North Branch, which brought in ten thousand at once. Each partner in the enterprise could claim the proceeds of one haul and this sweep of the net chanced to belong to a settler's widow—hence the name. As late as 1798, fishermen at Nanticoke, on the North Branch, caught so many shad that they first sold all the populace would buy, salted some more, gave away all people would take, and then—with their supply of salt exhausted—threw the rest back into the river. But by the 1830's a Nanticoke fisherman could bring in only a few hundred at a time. The Connecticut settlers who just before the Revolution tried to make the country around WilkesBarre into a part of New England, sent home for a net in 1772, when they found how easy Susquehanna shad-fishing was. The 1772 price was from three to six cents (presumably this means British pence) a fish. Shad-fishing became a seasonal industry, and from Berwick and Beach Haven to WilkesBarre and Forty Fort, fisheries lined the river banks.

Fishing was even better in the lower river. Near the Conewago Falls, the worst rapids in the river, where a ledge of rock stretched clear across the current, there were so many shad and salmon that one could look out from shore and see great schools of them swimming. There were also many bass here, as late as the present century; and elsewhere the river had perch, mullet, eels, and suckers.

It is too bad that Weiser scanted his description of the North Branch as he floated down its waters in 1737, and still more regrettable that he kept no diary at all when, in 1742, he accompanied Count Zinzendorf part way up the river to Wyoming, near modern WilkesBarre. The count, who had given up everything to become a simple Moravian missionary, fortunately made up for this by keeping a diary of his own.

The usual trail to Wyoming was not, as one might expect, along the route of the modern roads and railroads that now follow the great curves of the North Branch. Instead, the first travelers saved time by going up the West Branch and then striking overland to the Wyoming villages, on the North Branch. This was a kind of Indian reservation, established by the dominant Iroquois for their subject peoples. Because there were so many tribes in the area, Moravian missionaries often visited it in their effort to make converts.

Zinzendorf found the Susquehanna woodlands varied by occasional meadows of "fine grass," sometimes as high as a man's head. On the Wyoming flats the grass was so tall that a horseman could hardly see over it, for the land of the alluvial plain was extremely rich, as it still is.

The river, uncontaminated as yet by sewage and the waste of the coal mines, was so clear—"beautifully transparent," Count Zinzendorf called it—that when Bartram's party went swimming they "might have seen a pin at the bottom," even where the water was chin-deep.

Since the hills which edge the Susquehanna were thickly wooded with oak, sugar maple, birch, poplar, beech, chestnut, ash, walnut, and "great magnolia" (which must mean tulip poplar), with pine, spruce, and hemlock for contrast, the display of autumn foliage was magnificent. The brilliant reds which the maples gave to the fall landscape always impressed Europeans.

The autumn landscape in New York, New England, and western Pennsylvania was of equal splendor. The traveler, Thomas Ashe, describes how "millions" of colored trees near Pittsburgh were surrounded by millions more, rising as if in successive amphitheatres in the series of mountains. "It appeared as if every tree, though many were of the same class, had shades, hues, and characters, peculiar to itself." There is another description by Thomas Pownall, governor of Massachusetts, 1756–1760, who took a great interest in colonial geography: "If I should persuade the Painter to attempt the giving a real and strict Portrait of these Woods in Autumn, he must mix in upon his Canvass all the Colours of the Rainbow, in order to copy the various and varied Dyes which the Leaves at the Fall assume; The Red, the Scarlet, the bright and the deep Yellow, the warm Brown, the White, which he must use, would give a prismatic motley Patch-work that Judgment would not bear; and yet the Woods in this embroidered Garb have in real Nature an Appearance beyond Conception."

In other words, the color and brilliance of a North American autumn were very much what they are today, except that, when all the world was forest, the resulting spectacle was so much the more gorgeous.

An overland route to Wyoming ran from the area of Pennsylvania Dutch settlement around Nazareth and Bethlehem, across the Pocono Mountains, ending somewhere near modern WilkesBarre. Even today, this mountain route includes some rather wild country with a good many rare birds and plants. Beyond Nazareth, the hills were mostly covered with scrub oak, but red plums grew wild and were very much sought after by the local Indians, who were "very fond of this insipid fruit" and sometimes planted orchards of the wild plum trees. The hills and mountains were populated by bear, deer, elk, and probably moose, besides foxes and wolves which long remained to plague frontier farmers. As late as the Revolution, there was still plenty of game, and a note in the 1828 edition of the Marquis de Chastellux's *Travels* comments appreciatively on the "venison, moor game, the most delicious red and yellow bellied trout, the highest flavoured wild strawberries" to be had at Bethlehem.

Until General Sullivan took his army that way during the Revolution, to crush the New York Iroquois, there was no road across the Poconos, only narrow Indian trails. Even Sullivan's military road was just wide enough for a train of pack horses. The forest was "so thick that the trees almost touch, by their height and their matted branches making a dimness, cold and fearful even at noon of the clearest day. All beneath is grown up in green and impenetrable bush. Everywhere lie fallen trees, or those half-fallen, despite of their weight not reaching the ground.—Thousands of rotting trunks cover the ground, and make every step uncertain; and between lies a fat bed of the richest mould." No wonder these forests were called "The Shades of Death," a name which Pennsylvanians often gave to very thick woodlands. Since the Indians here did little burning of the forests, the closely crowded pines grew tall and slim to eighty and a hundred feet, varied with hemlock and white spruce, intermingled in some places with tamarack. The undergrowth included much mountain laurel. Wild flag grew in the swamps and edged the brooks. Much of the land was swampy—enough of it remains so, to make it a treasure house for botanists in search of carnivorous plants—rare in North America—like Venus' fly-trap and the pitcher plant, which catch, kill, and consume insects. Travelers do not mention these, since they kept as far as possible from the swamps where they grew; but the "Hessian" army surgeon, Dr. Schoepf, could not miss the "purple" lady-slipper (*Cypripedium acaule*), which he calls "the Canadian cypripedium," collinsonia (rich-weed, or stone root), helonias, which Gray lists as "rare and local" in modern times, and the blue lobelia.

He missed the blazing red of the other lobelia, the cardinal flower, and the bloodroot, whose waxen petals make it one of the most striking, yet delicate, of American wild flowers. Other travelers in Virginia and Pennsylvania were quick to note and to observe the red juice oozing from the broken roots, which gives the plant its modern name. This red juice of the "puccoon" provided the Indians with paint for their faces and dye for cane or reed baskets. Thaddeus Mason Harris, a sharp-sighted observer of the very early nineteenth century, thought that "transplanted to our gardens, this would be admired as an ornamental flower." He was right. No wild plant domesticates more easily;

but, for some reason, few American gardeners have ever tried to grow it.

By the middle eighteenth century, Pennsylvania was a flourishing and secure colony, occupying perhaps half of its present territory. Westward, settlement lagged, for there lay Indian lands, which the Penns scrupulously respected. But farther west, near Pittsburgh and along the Ohio River, white men of quite a different sort had long been penetrating.

XV

West to Pittsburgh

THOUGH THERE WERE several other possible routes, travel into the western part of Pennsylvania was very largely along "the Blue Juniata"—which still differs from the Blue Danube by really deserving its name, since its scenery has suffered less than other American rivers from industry and its attendant ugliness. Along its branches, trails led to the foot of the series of Allegheny ridges that barred Pittsburgh off from the rest of Pennsylvania and, having crossed the mountains, wound on through the forests to the rich Ohio Valley and the middle western prairies. Other trails led up the Susquehanna, along its West Branch, overland to the Allegheny River, and so downstream to Pittsburgh; but the Juniata trails were more used because they ran so nearly east and west.

The whole stretch of country in and near the valley was a perfect hunting ground and, as such, much valued by its Iroquois conquerors. Even in the early nineteenth century, wild turkeys could be seen in frequent flocks near Shippensburg. Travelers met them running along the trail. Like wild turkeys elsewhere, they were so well-fed that one traveler on the Allegheny River describes them as being "so over-burthened with fat that they fly with difficulty. It frequently happens, that after shooting one on a tree, you will find him bursted by falling on the ground." An occasional Pennsylvania settler coaxed a wild flock into his barnyard in the winter and kept them there in semi-domestication.

Other game birds were the woodcock, which haunted swampy

ground, much of which has since been drained, quail, grouse, and passenger pigeon. However delicious a tidbit the woodcock might provide, white men soon found that where woodcocks most abounded, there was malaria, too. This was because the woodcock loves to probe for worms by thrusting its long and sensitive bill into soft ground. Hence, where there were woodcock there were swamps; where there were swamps, there were mosquitoes; where there were mosquitoes, there was malaria, though no one in that unscientific age guessed the connection. Easton, on the Delaware, was praised as a healthy place to live, "for its exemption from the fevers of the country, from the fact of there being no woodcock ground within five miles of the Courthouse."

In addition to deer, which were everywhere, there were "black moose," or "black elk,"—presumably moose, which occasionally must have wandered much farther south than most modern naturalists suspect; and "grey elk"—the elk of today, which may have been as numerous on the Juniata as they certainly were on the West Branch of the Susquehanna.

The "black" bears of the Juniata Valley were remarkable for the variety of their color variations. Besides the usual black specimens, some were brown, others "red," and some yellow. The last red bear is said to have been killed in 1912 and the last brown one in 1914. The first white hunters scorned wolves, wildcats, and foxes as "small game," and though there were beaver in Pennsylvania, one hears little about them after the seventeenth century.

There were also woods buffalo, a species distinct from the bison of the prairies, somewhat larger (though reports of one-ton bulls may be an exaggeration), blacker, with shorter hair, no hump, and larger hind quarters. Thus, even after the nineteenth century had begun, the Pennsylvania traveler toward the Ohio could live sumptuously on game shot en route, without taking much time for hunting. Conrad Weiser's sufferings had been due to the peculiar country of the Endless Mountains, through which he traveled, and the lack of game in these rocky forest wastes, in winter.

Just how far east the buffalo ranged in the beginning, there is no telling. The first white explorers did not find them in New England or Virginia. They are reported on the sands of Anticosti Island, in the St. Lawrence, in the sixteenth century, but Parkman believes that these animals were really moose. It is doubtful if buffalo ever existed in any numbers east of Hudson Bay or the Hudson River. There were certainly some along Chesapeake Bay, though they are not mentioned by the first explorers; and buffalo of some kind reached clear to the Atlantic coast in Georgia and Florida and probably in the Carolinas.

In Pennsylvania, they ranged east as far as the Susquehanna and probably beyond, though early settlers along the Delaware and in New Jersey seem to have known nothing of them. Though they seem to have been rare in the valley of the North Branch of the Susquehanna (if they entered it at all), there were a good many along the West Branch and also along the main river between Harrisburg and Sunbury and almost certainly along the Juniata. An old buffalo trail is still pointed out in Union County, Pennsylvania, and at least one tree in the state even now shows marks supposed to have been caused by buffalo, rubbing against its bark.

Efforts to domesticate the animals or cross them with domestic cattle—George Washington was much interested in this idea—soon failed. Some Indians wove buffalo wool with great skill; but white efforts met with little success, though at least one woman spun and knit buffalo wool at Wright's Ferry on the Susquehanna.

These eastern woods buffalo did not move in the vast herds common on the western prairies; but herds of several hundred, which were not infrequently seen east of the Mississippi, seemed enormous to unaccustomed eyes. One group of hunters in western Pennsylvania killed six or seven hundred in two years, taking only the skins, which were worth two shillings apiece, and leaving the carcasses as mountainous piles of rotting beef. Another hunter in the same area boasted of having killed two thousand with his own hands. A farmer near Lake Onondaga, in New York State, who had made the mistake of building his log cabin near a salt lick, saw it literally "rubbed out" in a few hours, by innumerable huge brutes, scratching their shaggy sides against it. The rueful owner, who was himself nearly crushed to death, thought they enjoyed tossing the logs about on their horns.

As late as 1799, a hungry herd of four hundred buffalo descended upon Selinsgrove, on the Susquehanna, to raid the stocks of hay during a severe winter. Amid the excitement, one huge creature burst into a settler's cabin, followed by others in a headlong stampede, which trampled the man's wife and children before the desperate farmers could kill them.

The last buffalo in Pennsylvania is supposed to have been killed at Buffalo Cross Roads, near Lewisburg, Pennsylvania, January 19, 1801. By that time, they had nearly vanished from the Atlantic seaboard.

All of this country was a single gigantic woodland. The great belt of white pine, which swept southwest from Canada and Maine into New Jersey, began to thin out in eastern Pennsylvania, was mingled with hardwoods through most of central Pennsylvania, and vanished near the Pennsylvania–Ohio border. There was a ten-mile circle of pine timber near the headwaters of Tionesta Creek, which flows into the Allegheny, and a pine forest around Carlisle and along the trail from that town to Shippensburg. Much of the Pennsylvania pine grew on mountain tops and on the poorer lands, as the settlers soon discovered when they began to select farms. Some hemlocks usually grew near the stands of white pine.

There were many oaks, especially between Harrisburg and Carlisle, with sugar maples a close second, and many chestnuts. Black walnut and shagbark hickories grew in the river plains and there were some elms, though not so many as in New England, together with wild plum, buttonwood, and tulip poplars, which even so far north sometimes reached a maximum diameter of four feet, with branches starting at sixty feet.

The flowering dogwood shook out its mantle of great white flowers each spring, and the less ornate dogwood species grew less noticeably. Beech and aspen were rather rare and the red maple was a rather poor rival of its relative, the "sugar tree."

The black walnut was at the northeast edge of its range in Pennsylvania. "None of it grows either farther northward or westward than the province or the borders of the Delaware," wrote the geographer, Lewis Evans, describing the Penns' domains. Never very abundant, the black walnut nevertheless grew all over the state, providing one of the most valuable woods in later days for furniture and, above all, for the stocks of that deadly new weapon, "the Pinnsilvania rifle." (It is just the hard luck of the clever Pennsylvania gunsmiths that the products of their exquisite handicraft are chiefly remembered in history as "Kentucky rifles." They made their reputation in the hands of Kentucky hunters, indeed, but they were developed from German models in Pennsylvania and the best of them were made by Pennsylvania gunsmiths.)

In the swamps, "in soil unfit for any other purpose," says Lewis Evans, white cedars grew with a density hard to imagine nowadays. These trees, he adds, "grow very fast, and so close together that there is scarce Room in some places for a Man to squeeze between them, & the Swamps where they grow are the greatest Curiosity in America."

There were more swamps then than now. So many trees have been cut down by the white man that there are now fewer forests to hold back the surface water, which runs off quickly in spring floods. Evans remarks of southeastern Pennsylvania in 1753: "Our Runs dry up apace, several which formerly wou'd turn a fulling Mill, are now scarce sufficient for The Use of a Farm, the Reason of which is this, when the Country was cover'd with Woods & the Swamps with Brush, the Rain that fell was detain'd by These Interruptions." In the first seventy years of white settlement, some creeks ceased to be navigable, and this slow drying up must have proceeded gradually westward with the extension of settlement.

No one lamented the disappearance of the picturesque forests, since there were altogether too many trees for comfort. Even after the Revolution, Dr. J. D. Schoepf, a surgeon attached to the German mercenaries of the British Army, remarks: "What I saw every day and in the greatest numbers was trees." The thickness with which they grew rather got on the German's nerves, and he complains that "from Carlisle it is not only continual forest, but a very monotonous forest, there being little variety."

Other travelers agreed with Dr. Schoepf that there were so many trees, you couldn't see the country. America, complained Elias Pym Fordham, an English settler, was "not a land of prospects. There is too much wood; and, when on the barren peak of some rocky hill, you catch a distant view, it generally is nothing but an undulating surface of impenetrable forest." Even in the Middle West where the woods began to thin out there were no "high, far-seeing places."

These forests, like many others in North America, were so dark under their canopy of leaves, further shaded by the grapevines which ran up the trunks to spread out their foliage in the sunlight above, that there was little underbrush. The forest floor was too dark. Only small, shade-loving wild flowers could grow there.

"The American forests have generally one very interesting quality," wrote Thomas Ashe, "that of being entirely free from under or brushwood. This is owing to the extraordinary height, and spreading tops, of the trees; which thus prevent the sun from penetrating to the ground, and nourishing inferior articles of vegetation. In consequence of the above circumstance, one can walk in them with much pleasure, and see an enemy from a considerable distance."

All North American trees were bigger than most of those today, because they could grow undisturbed for centuries, till they reached their full natural size. In primitive times there was no need to cut them and nobody who wanted to. The Indians used little timber, except for dugout canoes. Bark and a few saplings made their shelters. Fallen branches supplied firewood faster than they could burn it.

In this dense forest mass, the weaker saplings soon died. The big trees that survived stood fairly close together. One early account says you could not shoot an arrow in any direction for more than twenty feet without hitting a tree; but it was not hard to wind in and out among the great trunks. The Indian trails which crisscrossed the continent were only a few inches wide, with just space enough for a runner to pass, or a war party in single file.

The sombreness of the forest, which by day was dark and silent, made travel through it rather gloomy. "In the eternal woods it is impossible to keep off a particularly unpleasant, anxious feeling, which is excited irresitibly by the continuing shadow and the confined outlook," wrote Dr. Schoepf. The constant danger and the stillness of the woods themselves made both the red man and the white man taciturn. The big woods were no place for idle chatter. It scared the game. It warned a possible enemy, where every turn of the trail was a possible ambush. Concealment was easy for an enemy. Daniel Boone used to say you couldn't see an Indian anyway. Why try? Dan'l kept a sharp eye out for the glint of their rifle barrels, instead.

The songbirds which flit in and out of modern woodlands did not live in these dark woods, which offered no food for the seed-eating birds and little enough for the insectivorous birds. There were wolves, panthers, owls, eagles, and the great black raven, now almost extinct. The crow, which has almost driven out the raven, came into these parts of Pennsylvania only after settlement had partly opened up the country. There were also woodcock in many places, the now-vanished Carolina parroquet in the virgin forest, quail in open meadows, partridge and pigeons nearly everywhere.

The various native sparrows—the songsparrow which concertizes along modern roads in spring, the field sparrow, the beautiful redbrown fox-sparrow, often mistaken for a thrush—seem to have come in from the open grasslands, the river valleys, and the coast, after the country was open. Neither did anyone notice the annual warbler migrations, which every spring fill the eastern woodlands with literally millions of tiny, darting, brilliantly feathered creatures. Both the warblers and the sparrows were unobtrusive little birds and the first settlers had no great interest in Nature as such. No one mentions them. Even Indian Nature myths ignore them. The gay black and yellow of the goldfinch, a bold fellow always singing as he flies, no one could miss; but early descriptions even of goldfinches come from the less densely forested areas.

However quiet by day, the forests became unpleasantly vocal at night. Thomas Ashe, benighted on the mountains between Bedford and Pittsburgh, draws a harrowing picture of his perils. "Wolves, panthers, and tiger-cats, were at hand to devour me." Perhaps Ashe really thought he was in danger. More probably this is the exaggeration of a journey's perils common among travelers. Neither wolves, panthers, nor "tiger-cats" (probably lynxes or bob-cats) would attack a human being in midsummer with the woods full of game. It is doubtful if any of them ever would, unless attacked. However, "clouds of owls rose out of the valleys," their evening hunt being naturally accompanied by a good deal of hooting. The hoot of the great horned owl is one of the most menacing sounds of the wilderness. The big timberwolves' howls are more like a factory whistle than anything else and, however harmless the beasts may be, they do not sound harmless. They certainly did not sound harmless to poor Ashe. To make matters worse a "tiger-cat" caught a possum just outside of Ashe's camp and there was a great deal of shrieking on both sides before the possum was finally eaten. As a crowning blow to a tired man, trying to rest, a whip-poor-will began calling from a neighboring tree; and, as there is no known method of silencing a whip-poor-will, Ashe got very little sleep that night. He comforted himself by watching a magnificent display by "lightning-flies." He was no worse off than another traveler in central Pennsylvania, who was kept awake by two panthers which screamed about his camp all night long. Apparently he had accidentally taken shelter in their den—you can hardly blame the panthers.

A slightly grim note was added to wilderness travel by the rattlesnakes, which greatly startled white newcomers in America, though they are in fact the least dangerous of the world's venomous reptiles, since they ordinarily give warning. It is a queer fact that De Soto ignored the big and dangerous southern rattlesnakes, while everyone was horrified by the relatively small and harmless rattlesnakes of the Northeast, especially in Pennsylvania. Most of these innocent ophidians would have been perfectly willing to let the Europeans alone, if the Europeans had only let them alone. From the beginning, however, the evil, flat, wedge-shaped head and the high, shrill whirr of the rattles caused horror.

"Yea there are some Serpents called Rattle-snakes," wrote a New England clergyman in 1630, "that have Rattles in their Tailes, that will not flye from a man as others will, but will flye vpon him and sting him so mortally, that hee will dye within a quarter of an houre after, except the parttie stinged haue about him some of the root of an Hearbe called Snakeweed to bite on."

A belt of rattlesnake skin was supposed to give pregnant women an easy delivery. Almost two hundred years later, Lewis and Clark encountered a similar notion far up the Missouri River. When the famous squaw, Sacagawea, had difficulty with her first baby, a frontiersman suggested that they grind a ring from a snake's rattle to powder and give her that. The baby was born at once and without further difficulty. It was, to be sure, a faith cure, for the rattle was merely chitin without any medical value whatever; but the rattlesnake has always had a medical reputation. Rattlesnake oil is still highly esteemed by some people.

Though rattlers often struck at the first Pennsylvania travelers there were few fatalities. The eastern rattlesnake is not very big and his blow—a rattler does not bite, but literally "strikes," driving his poison fangs into his enemies like any other hypodermic needles—usually failed to penetrate the stout leather leggings frontiersmen wore. Snakes became a much more serious problem after fields had been cleared, when farmers bent down to shock the grain by hand and women began to gather greens, with unprotected hands along the ground.

There were, however, some unnerving episodes. There was excitement during a religious service in the Juniata Valley, when a rattlesnake was discovered crawling about among the ankles of the congregation, but no harm was done. The creature was quickly dispatched, and even the arrival of a second snake, fortunately of a harmless species, did not seriously interrupt the sermon.

Philip Tome, the famous hunter of the Williamsport area, tells how in 1794 two hunters had to anchor their canoes in mid-stream to sleep secure from rattlesnakes, and how the local Indians used to sleep on beds held above the ground on forked sticks, to keep snakes from crawling into their warm blankets. In August, one could see thirty or forty rattlers at a time, lying among the rocks over which Weiser had scrambled in midwinter. Once Tome saw "a pile of rattlesnakes as large as an outdoor bake-oven. They lay with their heads sticking up in every direction, hissing." Prudent white settlers made their houses snake-tight, kept doors carefully closed, and in especially bad snake seasons kept fires burning around the house. The Indians sometimes burned over the underbrush to kill off snakes.

The rattler is a serpent peculiar to the Americas, which developed in this hemisphere during Tertiary times and never spread to other continents. Various other snakes have a habit of vibrating their tails to give warning, sometimes vigorously enough to produce a buzzing sound, even though they have no rattles. The rattlesnake simply evolved one step further and added hard, chitinous "rattles" at the end of its tail. Before the white man came, rattlesnakes were rarely disturbed. The Cherokees and the Hopi thought them sacred; other Indians seem to have let them severely alone. Their prey was everywhere and easily caught, the dose of venom injected being tremendous in comparison to the small bodies of mice and similar animals on which they lived. Hence the rattlers of the primeval forest ate well and were larger and more numerous—consequently more dangerous—than their modern descendants, which in the East have been driven back into the mountains and the few remaining woodlands. The habit of rattling attracted attention and got them killed as soon as they threatened white men, especially since long immunity from danger had made them completely fearless.

The ease with which these overconfident serpents could be killed occasionally made them a convenient emergency food supply. One surveyor observes that the meat "was generally eat with as good relish as any fresh meat we had eat on the road. I can say with the greatest Candor I never ate better Meat." Curiously enough, there has been a modern effort to revive the popularity of rattlesnake meat, this time as a delicacy for cocktail parties. A further culinary use for rattlesnakes was discoverd by dragoons exploring the West who, growing weary of field rations, boiled "a verry huge rattlesnake, of which they made a delicious dish of soup." Understandably, no one since has cared to follow up the idea.

The rocky "dens" in which rattlers, like other snakes, assemble to sleep away the winter, were particularly alarming to white men who stumbled upon them. One hears nothing of snake dens in Canada, where the winters were too cold for snakes to hibernate, and not much about them in New England; but they were common enough in the middle Atlantic states.

It is interesting to note that the familar legend that the rattlesnake can charm squirrels has the respectable antiquity of three centuries, appearing in the early Jesuit relations. In the South, the Cherokees— who referred to the rattlesnakes respectfully as "bright old inhabitants" —carried the story still further, averring that "no living creature moves

A view of the Juniata River. From the *Columbian Magazine*, August, 1788.

Pittsburgh, Pennsylvania, in 1796, the second known view of the city. Fort Duquesne was situated in the angle between the Allegheny and Monongahela Rivers, just to the left of the town. Eighteenth-century travelers were much impressed by the natural beauty of the landscape.

Pittsburgh and Allegheny from Coal Hill, 1849. A notable feature of this view is the large number of river steamers shown.

The Delaware Water Gap, looking south. From *Picturesque America*, 1872.

within the reach of their sight, but they can draw it." But these were semi-sacred rattlesnakes, "kings, or chieftains of the snakes," living somewhere near the headwaters of the Tennessee River in a valley of their own. Though well aware that the big southern snakes were dangerous, the Cherokees objected to having the "bright old inhabitants" killed, and sometimes handled them with impunity, as the Hopi still do. Various herbs were, quite erroneously, believed to cure snakebite.

For some reason, the other venomous snake of the East, the copperhead, is almost never mentioned either by Indians or by the white explorers, though it is still fairly common and must have been far more abundant in primitive times. Only the soldier, Timberlake, refers with horror to the "copper snake," whose bite, he says, is hard to cure while that of the rattler is easily cured. Timberlake, also, found rattlesnake rather good eating.

The westward trail, over the gentle slopes, fresh, clear, tributary streams, and beautiful open forests of the Juniata, was easy to follow, except where it was "greatly encumbered by trees fallen across it, blown up from the roots."

At Huntingdon, Pennsylvania, was an ancient and famous landmark, "the Standing Stone," fourteen feet high and something over a foot square, probably set up by Oneida Indians, for whom certain stones had magic significance. When they left the country, the Standing Stone disappeared, either because they took it with them or because they hid it so securely that it has never since been found. Fragments of a second Standing Stone, set up by white men, are now at Juniata College; and still a third, frankly modern, now stands in the town, near the ancient site.

Farther west, near Bedford, Pennsylvania, the mountains grew steeper and higher, as the traveler drew nearer to the dreaded Alleghenies, but even here the Juniata was still a stream "where warmth and moisture assure a livelier green and the trees luxuriating in a fat soil cast wider shadows," according to Dr. Schoepf. Being something of a botanist, like most early physicians, the German army doctor was impressed by the Juniata's "crooked banks shaded by calamus, cephalanthus, rhododendron, Weymouth Fir, chestnut and beech."

Near Pittsburgh, the traveler encountered the "impenetrable" thickets of scrub oak and laurel on the long, parallel mountain ridges, one succeeding another, which are characteristic of the Pennsylvania landscape in the extreme eastern and western parts of the state. They are old mountains, much eroded through endless geological time, without the towering, jagged peaks of the much more youthful Rockies. None of them were much more than half a mile high, but no woodsmen then had any idea of the tremendous ranges that the western pioneers of the next century would have to cross. Travelers scrambling up one Allegheny ridge with laurel bushes and scrub oak tearing at their garments, only to scramble at once up another just as bad, naturally thought them impenetrable. Worst of all was Laurel Ridge, just west of Pittsburgh. Said Thomas Pownall: "The Undergrowth towards and over this Hill is so abundant in Laurell Thickets that the Traveller must cut his Way through them." But in springtime, when the whole tangle of bushes burst into bloom, even the weariest traveler had to admire.

The entire Pittsburgh area, now a distressing congeries of freight tracks, furnaces, oil tanks, factories, and warehouses, was remarkable for its beauty. The only hint of the ubiquitous murk of industrialism that was to come, was the occasional appearance of veins of coal on the surface of the ground. Coal was often "discoverable in the gullies of the road, and among the roots of trees that have been overthrown by the wind." Along the banks of the Monongahela and in the adjacent hills, its black veins were plainly visible, sandwiched between the rocks. It lay almost perfectly horizontal, appearing and reappearing "on almost every hill and valley."

So remarkably clear was the atmosphere, even after the first manufacturing had begun, that an English visitor, who had heard the eighteenth century village of seven thousand people described as the American Birmingham, actually complained of the *lack* of smoke in Pittsburgh, which he thought unsuitable in a prospective center of industry. But even he enjoyed the idyllic setting of the infant metropolis, "surrounded by all that is delightful, in the combination of the hilly woodlands and river scenery."

Near Pittsburgh itself, there was a magnificent view from the Allegheny Ridge, where today one looks down only on the smoke and fume of roaring modern industry. Looking westward from this point in primitive times, one saw only treetops, gently moving like a still, green sea, or tossing and moving like the sea after a great storm, endlessly to the horizon. This particular view became famous among early white settlers—not wholly on aesthetic grounds. They noted eagerly that, in spite of a few pines and hemlocks, the trees were mostly deciduous, an augury of good agricultural land in the forest floor beneath, if the trees could ever be cleared away. Pittsburgh then seemed clearly destined to be one of the leading agricultural areas of the new America.

This view, though probably the finest of its kind, was typical of the Pennsylvania landscape almost anywhere. The Endless Mountains in the east and the Alleghenies in the west ran diagonally across the state. Between the ridges lay immense forests, and most of the ridges themselves, except in the west, were also tree covered. "The Vales between the Ridges of these Mountains," wrote Thomas Pownall in 1776, "have all one and the same general Appearance, that of an Amphitheatre enclosing, as it were, an Ocean of Woods swelled and depressed with a waving Surface like that of the great Ocean itself. . . . If the Spectator hath gotten a stand on some high Mountain so as to look across any Number of the Ridges which may be less high than that he stands on, he then sees a repeated Succession of Blue and Purple parallel waving Lines behind each other." These he thought "the most picturesque Landscapes that Imagination can conceive."

Some of the mountain intervales, however, were "glades," with no timber worth mentioning. The glade between Allegheny Mountain and Laurel Hill was ten or twelve miles wide, filled with high, thick grass—"fine fertile country of excellent meadowlands."

Approaching Pittsburgh from the south, up the Potomac, along Wills Creek, over the southern boundary of modern Pennsylvania, one came on the upper waters of the Monongahela. Just before reaching them, the trail passed over what were called "the Great Meadows," a broad flat expanse of grassland, sparsely wooded, lying between two ridges. They are of interest chiefly as the scene of George Washington's disaster at Fort Necessity. Open spots like this grew more and more frequent between western Pennsylvania and the Mississippi.

Amid this beautiful country, the site of the village of Pittsburgh stood out, gem-like, with various Indian villages scattered about, more or less in its vicinity. Forested hills rose through the clear air between the pellucid waters of the Allegheny, flowing from the north, and the more turbid waters of the Monongahela, meeting them from the south. Other forested hills stretched away southwest, to form the valley that led these waters, joined in the Ohio, through rich forests, which eventually became plains and savannahs, to the Mississippi.

An early nineteenth century English traveler wrote an exuberant description of the "beautiful vale" that led into the village of Pittsburgh: "It was impossible to behold anything more interesting than this: it extended three miles on a perfect level, cultivated in the highest degree; bounded by a rising ground on the left, and a transparent river on the right; and leading to a well inhabited town, where I meant to repose after a journey of 320 miles, 150 of them over stupendous mountains and barren rocks. Such a sight could not fail of gratifying and enchanting me."

It has been a long time since anybody approaching the city of steel and smoke has been enchanted by the landscape; but all travelers seem to have felt that way about it in those early days.

Through this beautiful, unspoiled, wild country, lying as it had lain since glacial times, unchanged, the first English traders and explorers struggled westward, while French traders and explorers were working their way south. Their paths crossed at Pittsburgh, and empires came to grips.

XVI

The Sieur de La Salle Explores

WHILE WILLIAM PENN and his Quakers were settling Pennsylvania, the French were just beginning to make their way into what was later to become the Middle West. The first white discoverer to leave any real record of the Ohio River country was Robert Cavelier, Sieur de La Salle, a recently ennobled French bourgeois from Rouen. Educated by the Jesuits and probably originally destined for the Society of Jesus, he had returned to secular life before taking the vows, and had come to Canada in 1666 to begin the two decades of intrepid exploration, which took him from Canada to the Gulf of Mexico and led to his death at last, murdered by his own men, somewhere in Texas.

During a brief interlude of peace between the French and the Iroquois, Seneca warriors, wintering at his seigniory, had told him about a stream that rose in their country—that is, western New York— and flowed into the sea at such a distance that it took eight or nine months to travel there. The redskins were thinking of the Allegheny, Ohio, and Mississippi as a single river, which was not so strange an idea then as it seems now.

Eager to see the new country, La Salle secured permission to visit it in company with two Sulpitian missionary priests, Father Dollier de Casson, a former cavalry officer who had entered holy orders, and Father Galinée, chosen because he was a skilled surveyor. With no great difficulty, they made their way in 1669 to the Seneca village near the modern town of Victor, in western New York, where they hoped to find Indians who would show them the route into the new country.

At this moment, by what at first seemed like good luck for the French, a Seneca war party returned, with a prisoner from one of the Ohio tribes. As the captive would make them a perfect guide, the French tried to buy him, but the Senecas preferred to have fun with him, in their own grim way. The horrified white men had to sit by, while their prospective guide was first burned alive, and then eaten.

Seeing that there was no hope of help at this village, the party withdrew to another at the head of Lake Ontario, hearing the roar of Niagara in the distance. The Indians told them the sound came from "one of the most beautiful cataracts or waterfalls in the world," which fell from a rock "higher than the highest pine"; but, traveling in haste, they did not pause.

Suddenly, to their astonishment, Louis Jolliet—later to be Father Marquette's companion on the Mississippi voyage—also appeared in the village, on his way to explore the Lake Superior copper deposits; and the two priests, changing their plans, started off with him, leaving La Salle, as they thought, to go back to Montreal. Father Galinée even hints maliciously that he was frightened out of the country by the sight of three enormous rattlesnakes.

Instead, as soon as his companions were gone, La Salle started off to the Iroquois capital at Onondaga and there, apparently, found an Indian who knew the Ohio country and was willing to go there with him. Perhaps with this man as a guide, perhaps with no guide at all (the records are far from clear), the determined Frenchman struck west again at the head of a small party, reached one of the upper tributaries of the Ohio, and descended to certain "falls," by which he must have meant those at Louisville, Kentucky. Here his men deserted him, and he had to make his way home to Canada alone, living on wild plants, game, and chance gifts of food from passing Indians. He reached Canada in 1670, with a thrilling story to tell, but the journals and maps in which it was recorded vanished in the eighteenth century—lost by a careless family.

Though the papers in which La Salle told his own story have vanished, there are many descriptions of "the Ohio country" which, though of a later date, give a picture of the unspoiled middle western wilderness he saw, as it was before the white man's blighting hand fell upon it. The beauty of the primitive Ohio impressed all who saw it. Indeed, the French name, La Belle Rivière is supposed to have been merely a translation of the original Indian name, Ohio, though some skeptics have doubted whether any Indian name could be so short, and the word is hard to fit into any of the local dialects. La Salle, who certainly should have known, says that "Ohio" is the Iroquois word and "Olighin-cipou" the Ottawa word, and that both mean "Beautiful River." There is no doubt that "cipou," or "sipi," was a common word for river in several Algonkian dialects.

Such considerations, however, did not dampen the enthusiasm of early visitors. A passing New Englander remarks that though scenery on the Hudson and Connecticut and other rivers often equals anything on the Ohio, "its peculiarity is that it is *all* beautiful. There are no points bare of beauty."

"It has been truly described as beyond competition the most beautiful river in the universe," wrote the English traveler, Thomas Ashe. Thanks to its "meandering course through an immense region of forests," with wooded, vine-hung islands and rich bottom land filled with cane here and there along the banks, the primitive unspoiled Ohio could hardly escape the beauty which even a century of civilization has not been able wholly to eradicate. Far into the nineteenth century, the banks retained much of their primeval charm, because the Ohio's floods discouraged "improvements" close to the shore. They long remained undamaged, save for the raids of steamboat crews, in search of wood fuel. In spring, the redbuds, or Judas trees, gleamed through the bare branches of the forests and were much admired by river travelers. In autumn, the white bark of the sycamores accentuated the colored foliage. Kentucky cardinals with brilliant plumage called to each other across the stream, and Carolina parroquets, red, green, and yellow, flashed among the trees.

The upper stretches were without the growth of cane characteristic of southern rivers. The cane began near the Scioto River, with stalks only about three feet high, their size and abundance increasing as La Salle and his successors went downstream, until near the Mississippi the banks were "covered with an impenetrable growth." Pecan trees also began near the Scioto.

There is still cane along the river, but the cattle were especially fond of its tender young shoots and destroyed a good deal, while the settlers destroyed a great deal more, when they learned that where the cane was thickest the land was best for farming.

"The passage down the river was extremely entertaining, exhibiting at every bend a change of scenery," wrote a traveler in 1803, when white settlement had made little change in the landscape. "Sometimes we were in the vicinity of dark forests, which threw a solemn shade over us as we glided by; sometimes we passed along overhanging banks, decorated with blooming shrubs which timidly bent their light boughs to sweep the passing stream; and sometimes around the shore of an island which tinged the water with a reflected landscape." Many travelers comment on the islands, some of which were several miles long and lay "high out of the waters." Often a buffalo or two swam out to crop the lush island grass, adding a note of life to the picture, and sometimes the scent of wild flowers rolled out from the banks, perceptible to passing boatmen.

There is little comment on the other wild flowers, which must have studded the forest. River travelers kept too far from shore—out of arrow shot—to see them; land travelers had too much else to think about. Near Wheeling, West Virginia, Thaddeus Mason Harris paused in 1805 to note that "In these declivities grow the mountain raspberry (*Rubus montanus floridus*) in great plenty. It is a handsome bush; and the flower, which is of a pale pink colour, and of the size and appearance of that of the sweet-briar, or hedge rose, gives it a very ornamental appearance. We were told that the fruit is large, and exceedingly delicious." He was right, the wild berry being nearly as big and quite as good as the cultivated one.

There was none of the usual forest monotony in the scenery of the wild Ohio River. The most beautiful part of the stream was the "Long Reach," above the mouth of the Muskingum, where the current flows southwest in an almost straight line for sixteen miles. "The river runs a straight course for twenty miles," says Croghan, exaggerating a little, "and makes a delightful prospect; the banks continue high; the country on both sides, level, rich, and well watered."

The forested hills that edged the river added a good deal to the landscape. Sometimes they closed in to make high, steep banks, picturesque with their overhanging trees. Again they swung far back from the stream, leaving room along the shore for "many large, rich, and fine bottoms" or "large, rich, and well watered bottoms, then succeeded by hills pinching close on the river," which stirred Croghan's enthusiasm. There was pretty certain to be game feeding on the luxuriant grasses of the well-watered bottom lands.

Night and moonlight made the Ohio lovelier still. Said Robert Baird, an early nineteenth century traveler who wrote a book on *The Valley of the Mississippi,* "The constant shifting of the scene, the alternation of bright and dark sides of the hills, together with the variation in the appearance of the river—one place reflecting the beautiful beams of the moon, and another enveloped in the deep shadows cast from the lofty and overhanging bluffs—altogether form a scene surpassing in beauty and effect any thing else which I have seen."

In the "spring freshes," caused by melting snow, the river in places rose twenty to forty feet. At that season it ran so swiftly that it was sometimes possible to go from Pittsburgh to the Mississippi in fifteen days, though twenty days was ordinarily regarded as "a good spring passage." Travel was more difficult in dry weather, when the water might be no more than a foot deep on bars and shoals. White men's heavy flatboats or keel boats stuck on these with discouraging frequency; but when La Salle and the Indians were the sole travelers on the Ohio, shoals were no great problems. Twelve inches was water enough for a canoe, which in the worst places could easily be carried to deeper water. White farmers in the early days of settlement reaped their richest harvest from stranded white boatmen, who had to be pulled off with oxen, which Meriwether Lewis once described sardonically as the best sailors on the river. Keel boats could usually expect to make four or five miles an hour, the light Indian canoes being probably somewhat faster, especially with a little help from the paddles. There was always time enough to watch the game along the river, if there was no need to "hunt for the pot."

"The flocks of wild geese and ducks which swarm upon the stream, the vast number of turkies, partridges, and quail we saw upon the shore, and the herds of deer or some other animals of the forest darting through the thickets afforded us constant amusement," says one journal. In the autumn hundreds of squirrels were sometimes found swimming from one shore to another. Meriwether Lewis, on his way down the Ohio to pick up his companion, William Clark, in preparation for the Lewis and Clark expedition, found so many of them in the water that he used his trained Newfoundland to plunge in, catch them, and bring them aboard the boat, where they proved "when fryed a pleasant food."

Boatmen near Marietta found the river "completely overrun with immense quantities of black and grey squirrels." They climbed fearlessly up the oars to rest on the boats, which sometimes had five or six of them aboard at once. Since about a third of the little animals drowned before they reached the other bank, travel was sometimes unpleasant because of "thousands of dead squirrels putrifying on its surface and its shores."

On land, a hunting party could easily bring in several hundred squirrels at once, and kills of one or two thousand are sometimes reported. Kentucky riflemen scorned random shooting at these tiny, lively targets. There was a local Kentucky joke to the effect that a squirrel was indigestible unless shot squarely in the left eye. Some hunters shot squirrels only through the eye and that only when they saw them in the highest treetops. Really distinguished woodsmen like Daniel Boone refused to shoot the little animals at all. They preferred "barking off squirrels," that is, putting a bullet into a branch exactly at their feet. Audubon, for whom Boone gave a demonstration, wrote: "The whip-like report resounded through the woods and along the hills in repeated echoes. Judge of my surprise, when I perceived that the ball had hit the piece of bark immediately beneath the squirrel, and shivered it into splinters, the concussion produced by which had killed the animal and sent it whirling through the air."

The black bears were wary even before the white men came, but, as La Salle found, there were plenty of them. Beaten patches in the grass where they had sprawled, or rotten logs torn to pieces in quest of ants

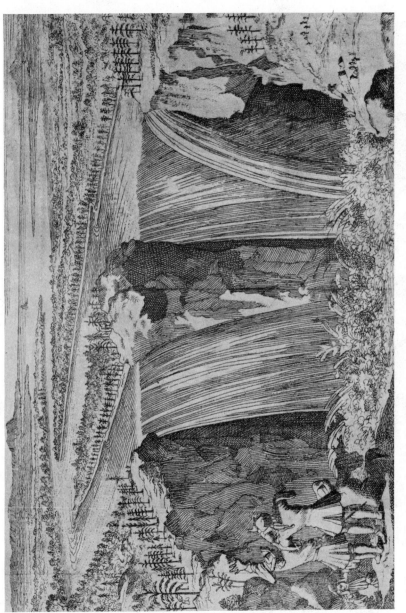

Niagara Falls as sketched by Father Louis Hennepin in 1678. This is the earliest known view of Niagara Falls, and is from *A New Discovery of a Vast Country in America*, by Father Hennepin, published in London in 1699.

COURTESY OF THE NEW-YORK HISTORICAL SOCIETY, NEW YORK CITY

The Cumberland Gap. From *Picturesque America*, 1872.

or grubs, often indicated their presence. Father Jacques Gravier saw fifty in a single autumn day near the mouth of the Ohio and noted that the Ohio River bears were much fatter than those from the Mississippi. A French gourmet expatiates on the flavor of bear cubs which, "when young are agreeable and wholesome food" and "whose flesh is delicate and tender."

The story of La Salle's next venture into the unknown lands of the Middle West is, fortunately, preserved both in his own account and in that of the Récollet priest, Father Louis Hennepin, the missionary who accompanied him. Boastful, vain, and far from truthful, Hennepin was born in Belgium, about 1640, and had early been fascinated by tales of North America, whither he had come five years before he and La Salle set out together late in 1678. Because he went with an advance party some time ahead of La Salle, Father Hennepin is the first white man to leave a description of Niagara Falls, though Champlain had written down what the Indians told him about it.

Hennepin's description is grossly exaggerated—it would, indeed, take a Hennepin to exaggerate even that tremendous spectacle. The Falls, he said, were five hundred feet high—later he made it "six hundred feet and more," though the actual height is only 167 feet. After describing Goat Island, he tells how the "two Torrents" on each side "cast the Waters all of a sudden down into the Gulph by two Great Falls; which Waters are push'd so violently as by their own Weight, and so sustain'd by the swiftness of the motion, that they don't meet the Rock in the least." The space under the falls was "big enough for four Coaches to drive a breast without being wet." The whole spectacle he thought "the most Beautiful, and at the same time most Frightful Cascade in the world."

An official report on La Salle's explorations, dating from 1682, has a detailed report on the Falls, which repeats Hennepin's error as to their height. Here, says the report, the waters of Lake Erie "form a waterfall of unbelievable height, the like of which does not exist on earth. The Niagara river, near this place, is only a quarter of a league wide, but it is very deep and so swift that it drags with it all the animals who try to cross it, without being able to resist its current. It falls from a height of more than 600 feet, and its falls are composed of two sheets of water with an island, 'en talus,' in the middle. Its waters foam and boil in a frightful way. They are continually thundering, and when the wind is from the south they can be heard more than fifteen leagues."

In justice to Hennepin, one must remember the comment of the celebrated geologist, Sir Charles Lyell, who, after his own first view of the Falls was inclined to excuse the missionary's inaccuracies: "It is not wonderful that coming suddenly upon the Falls which no European traveller had ever seen before, he should have believed them to be twice their real height." Actually, Hennepin made them more than three times their real height, but even so he is more nearly accurate than a mid-eighteenth century writer who believed that they were eight hundred feet high!

The Falls, as Hennepin saw them, were very different from the Falls today. Through geologic time, the rushing water has been slowly cutting its way backward up the Gorge. The Niagara River, above the Falls, runs over a thick stratum of hard rock, beneath which is sandstone and shale. There is, therefore, a lip of hard rock projecting at all times, underneath which the softer stone is rapidly cut away. Several times a century—for many, many centuries—there has been a tremendous crash and the projecting upper stratum, after being undercut too far, has collapsed.

Once the great cataract must have tumbled almost directly into Lake Ontario. About the time the Homeric poems were being written, the Horseshoe Falls and the American Falls were one tremendous sweep of water, somewhere in front of Goat Island, which now separates them. A survey by the British Royal Engineers in 1764—which may not have been very accurate—shows the Horseshoe Falls already curving well back from the island, but with a crest which reached the Canadian shore far below Table Rock, now itself vanished.

When Hennepin saw them, almost a century before the survey, the Horseshoe Falls must have been still farther downstream, perhaps four hundred feet below Table Rock, and certainly with a crest straighter than the horseshoe of today. Game, waterfowl, even fish were swept over the falls to be crushed to death below. When, some years after the first exploration, a French garrison was established, the soldiers were delighted to find how well they could live on freshly killed ducks and geese, lying about below the Falls.

A third waterfall burst forth from the Canadian side, near Table Rock, almost at right angles to the Horseshoe Falls. The American Falls, where there is less erosion, looked very much as they do today. When Peter Kalm, the Swedish botanist, saw Niagara in the mid-eighteenth century, this third waterfall had disappeared; but the legend of its existence still remained, for Kalm mentions it.

Successive nineteenth and twentieth century surveys show that the Horseshoe Falls have been consistently retreating two to four feet a year, constantly changing their shape. On the American side, where the flow of water is much less, the change is much slower. In 1790, the Falls were supposed to have receded twenty feet in thirty years, and in 1799 a visitor remarked that "within the memory of the present inhabitants of the country, the falls have receded several yards." The rare blue lobelia, a relative of the cardinal flower, which once blossomed freely all about the Falls, has long been gone.

Having admired the Falls, Hennepin moved on, after various enterprises and adventures, and was soon joined by La Salle, who set to work building a sailing vessel, the *Griffon,* above the Falls. By August, after many troubles, the vessel was under sail and La Salle had returned from a journey to the French settlements. In September he pushed on to Green Bay, in Lake Michigan, traded in furs, and on the eighteenth sent his ship east, while he himself set off with Father Hennepin and others, down Lake Michigan in canoes.

It was a desperate journey. They ran so short of food that for a time there was only a daily handful of dried corn for each man. Some of the men, experimenting with wild fruits, fell ill.

Their luck began to change when they saw crows and eagles clustered around some object on the shore and, paddling hopefully over to investigate, came upon "half of a very fat deer" left by wolves. It was no time for sanitary scruples. The carcass was still edible. They chased away the birds and ate the venison, which by that time must have been very "gamey" indeed.

After this the hunting improved. They lived on "staggs" (which must have been moose or caribou), "wild Goats" (probably does, for though antelope were often called goats they did not exist in this country), "a great many Turkey-Cocks very fat and big," and grapes as large as damson plums. La Salle later remarked that between the Ohio and the Lakes there was "an incredible number of bear, deer, wild goat, and chickens of India [turkeys], against which the wolves wage a bitter war." Buffalo happened, at this particular moment, to be scarce because so many Iroquois war parties had feasted on them while raiding the Illinois Indians; but La Salle himself reports that a little earlier there had been, between the Ohio and Illinois and beyond the Mississippi "more wild cattle than any one can say."

In the dense forest, the grapevines had, as usual, sought the light by climbing to the treetops, from which hung clusters which one seventeenth century writer describes as a foot and a half long. La Salle's hungry Frenchmen, who were thirsty for a little wine, pressed the grapes and made "pretty good Wine," which they "bottled" in hollow gourds and buried in the sand, the resulting fluid—it must have been pretty crude and raw—being "more relishing to us than Flesh."

When they found the footprints of strange Indians, hunting was stopped, for fear the sound of shots might bring on an attack. But one of the men could not resist letting drive at a treed bear, and Fox Indians, hearing the report and discovering the strangers, at once made trouble. It was the kind of thing that worried all commanders in the big woods so long as game remained common. In every column, trying to move stealthily through the forest, there was always some reckless soul who could not resist the perfect shot that was sure to be offered his itchy trigger finger sooner or later. The Kentucky volunteers in the Indian wars just after the Revolution were perhaps the worst of all in this respect, but it was a common failing.

When the Indians found the French alert and ready for them, there was only a slight skirmish and the incident ended in "Dancing, Feasting, and Speeches."

By November, La Salle, Hennepin, and the rest were at the mouth of the St. Joseph's River (which they called the Miami). Still hoping that his ship might have survived, La Salle paused at or near modern St. Joseph's, Michigan, to build a fort.

The magnificent Michigan forests, since devastated by lumbermen, were thick. The flat-topped hill near the river's mouth which La Salle selected, had to be cleared before building could even begin. It took hard work through all of November; and for three weeks, to everyone's disgust, there was nothing to eat except bears, which came down to the banks for the wild grapes. Since the bears were at that season fattening for their winter's sleep, they were, as a later explorer said, "too fat and lushious," and the men soon wearied of their flesh as a steady diet. But bears were easy to get, and La Salle would have no deer hunts till his fort was built.

It is strange that the men objected to bear meat, for most Europeans thought it a great luxury. Being very fond of grapes, the animals would climb the highest trees to get them, the result being meat "excessively rich and finely flavored." Such, at least, was the opinion of Jonathan Carver, an American colonial soldier, who traveled in the West during the middle eighteenth century. Carver says that bear meat was "preferred by the Indians and traders to that of any other animal" and expatiates over the excellence of bear's fat which, he says, is "sweet and wholesome" and "never cloys." La Salle's men felt quite differently about it and were becoming restive when, fortunately, La Salle's one-armed lieutenant, Henri Tonti, arrived on November 20, with two canoeloads of venison. But he also brought the dismal news that the *Griffon,* on which La Salle depended for quick and easy communication with Canada, was lost.

In spite of that, the party started up the chill waters of St. Joseph's River on December 3, looking for the portage that would take them over the watershed, into the Mississippi Basin. It is still easy to paddle past a portage from one wilderness river to another, for a portage is, after all, only a narrow path, winding among thick-set trees and often obscured by underbrush along the shore. La Salle's men missed it entirely, because their Mohican guide, whose quick Indian eyes would have found it soon enough, happened to have gone ashore to hunt.

Realizing that they had lost their way, La Salle landed to hunt for the portage himself and got lost. That, too, is an easy misadventure in the big woods. It was especially easy for La Salle, since the snow was falling and he could not see the sun. After missing his way he ran into a swamp, made a wide swing around it, and pushed ahead through snow and darkness—the very worst thing he could have done. Both he and his men, waiting by the river, fired signal shots, but they were by this time so far apart that neither heard the other.

About two in the morning La Salle saw a fire and, certain that he had at last found his way back to camp, rushed up to it. There was no one beside the little wilderness campfire—only a pile of dry grass; but someone had been lying on it so recently that the impression of a human figure was plain and the grass was still warm. Obviously, the Frenchman had frightened off an Indian hunter, benighted in the wilderness. Parkman's guess that "it was no doubt an Indian, ambushed on the bank, watching to kill some passing enemy" is nonsense. No ambushed Indian ever lighted a fire; nor does a warrior in ambush —alert, armed, and ready—flee from one incautious passing stranger.

La Salle shouted friendly messages in various native languages. Then, when the silent, snow-muffled woods gave back no answer, he built a barricade of bushes so that he would hear anyone approaching, lay down on the warm grass bed himself and went to sleep—so tired that he was willing to risk his scalp.

Rested and clear-headed in the morning, he found his way safely back to camp, bringing with him two 'possums that he had clubbed while they swung by their tails from a limb. That night he and Father Hennepin were nearly burned to death when the dry reed mats of which their wigwam was made took fire.

Their Mohican having come back before La Salle and having found the portage, they were off next morning over a five-mile carry from the upper reaches of St. Joseph's River, across the height of land to the Kankakee and the Mississippi basin. Starting somewhere near South Bend, they must have struck the Kankakee not for from Crumstown, Indiana. It was not very atttractive country to travel through. There were many "marshy Lands, which are so many Quagmires, that one can scarcely walk over them." In the low, flat Indiana and Illinois terrain, the rivers, often blocked by beaver dams and fallen trees, flooded easily, and the country, as a much later traveler observed, was "marshy and pondy in every direction." Through country of the same sort, not far distant, George Rogers Clark and his men were to march during the Revolution, through water up to their armpits, holding rifles and powder horns high over their heads to keep them dry and carrying their drummer boy on their shoulders.

Indians had been hunting along La Salle's route and buffalo horns and bones lay all about. Once the Frenchmen found skin canoes which Indians had improvised to get their buffalo meat across the river.

Blazing their trail and leaving written orders hanging from the trees in the vain hope that the crew of the *Griffon* had survived and would follow them—they had done the same thing at Fort Miami—La Salle, Hennepin, and their party reached the Kankakee River. Near its source, the stream was just deep enough to float bark canoes, but it was soon "as deep and broad as the *Meuse* and *Sambre* joyn'd together"—rivers which Hennepin remembered from his youth in the Low Countries. On the flat terrain, the river twisted and turned. Once they found that, after a whole day of struggle through its windings, they had actually advanced a scant five miles! They had to stick to their canoes, for the country round about was "nothing but Marshes full of Alder-Trees and Rushes," making overland travel hopeless. For more than a hundred miles of river, they could not have found a place dry enough to camp, if the ground had not been partly frozen.

When American surveyors began going over this country in the early nineteenth century, they found it almost unchanged since La Salle's time—"an interminable forest, which is covered with water during the season," or "an endless sameness of marsh, interspersed with a few groves of timber," so that sometimes it was hard to tell where the river really was. In some places a man's weight would "shake the marshes for acres together."

Though there was still a good deal of marshy land of this sort down to about 1870, the present condition of the country through which La Salle traveled, gives no idea of the swamps, ponds, and marshes of those early days. In the last fifty years, most of them have been drained entirely.

When La Salle and his men at last got out of the worst of the marshes, they found only a vast plain, entirely covered with grass. A much later description of the prairies that edged the Illinois River, describes what they would have seen, had they been traveling in spring or summer: Near modern Henry, Illinois, some forty-five miles above Peoria, "for at least 20 miles back from the river was one rich grassy plain, with here and there ridges like waves on the general surface of the ocean, giving that character of what is called 'a rolling prairie' in this country. Not a tree or shrub was visible in all this vast extent, but myriads of bright and variegated flowers were seen mingling with the green grass, as far as the powers of vision could reach. Not a being appeared to dwell on it."

La Salle's men saw this landscape in its most dismal state, for to add to the dreariness of winter, the Indians had been burning over the prairies in their annual buffalo hunts, and in many places there was nothing but a vast expanse of charred black, contrasting with patches of white snow.

More serious than the depressing landscape was the fact that La Salle's provisions were beginning to fail. The unseen Indians had killed or frightened off with their prairie fire most of the game. In sixty miles of travel La Salle's men killed nothing but "a lean Stag, a small wild Goat [a doe?], some few Swans, and two Bustards, which was no sufficient Maintenance for two and thirty men."

The lack of buffalo was puzzling, for they could see horns lying about everywhere. Finally they came upon one "prodigious big wild Bull, lying fast in the Mud of the River." Here was fresh meat, but after they had killed the bull, they had "much ado to get him out of the Mud." In the end, twelve men slung a cable about the huge creature and painfully dragged it to firmer ground. Some months later, when Hennepin and a companion killed a buffalo in the shallows of the Mississippi, they could not move the carcass at all and had to carve off some steaks and leave the rest in the river.

A number of good dinners—even for thirty-odd men—must have followed, for a big buffalo bull represented nearly half a ton of beef. Autumn, when buffalo beef was at its best, was not long past. "The Flesh of these Beasts is very relishing, and full of Juice, especially in Autumn;" says Hennepin, "for having grazed all Summer long in those vast Meadows, where the Herbs are as high as they, they are then very fat."

As they went farther into Illinois, the scenery changed. The burnt plains ended at last. Ascending the low hills which now began to appear along the river, La Salle and his men could see rolling stretches of prairie ahead, dull green even in winter. It is hard to visualize that ancient landscape, now much changed, since with the increase of farming so much of the grassland has been plowed up and now shows bare and brown, instead of green, after the crops are in.

From the Kankakee they passed into the Illinois River, flowing through flat country, which it frequently inundated. Its upper waters were full of beaver, whose silted-up ponds were probably the reason for some of the "terres tremblantes" that made travel difficult. Beyond the marshes which often edged the banks, however, the canoeists saw "nothing but fine fields as far as you could see, broken here and there with groves of trees." The groves were the beginning of what later became known, especially in Michigan, as "oak openings" or "orchards," that is, clusters of oaks standing "near enough for a shady grove, but too distant to make a forest proper."

For many miles, La Salle noted, these prairies came clear to the edge of the river. In other places they were masked by forest, often flooded, edging the river. La Salle came at last—passing modern Ottawa, Illinois, and Buffalo Rock, the latter a favorite place for Indian lodges—to a big village of the Illinois Indians, near the modern town of Utica.

Weary and discouraged men at the paddles looked eagerly ahead. On their left towered a huge cliff—Starved Rock—covered with forest. Along its edge the trees hung out over the clear river below. The river ahead—"as broad as the *Meuse*"—slipped silently among wooded islands. Open, low-lying meadows swept back from the river and on the right, low hills came down toward the village.

On the dry spots in the plain, marshy with the winter floods, they could see about five hundred lodges, each big enough to house several families. These were not conical bark or skin tepees, as most modern Americans suppose, but rounded structures of bent poles, with roofs shaped like a modern Quonset hut and covered with rush mats "so closely sew'd together, that no Wind, Rain, or Snow can go thro' it."

As the Frenchmen drew closer, they had another disappointment. The place was deserted. Each of the lodges should have had five or six fires, shared by families living in chambers on opposite sides of the shelter, but not a single smoke curled from the long narrow vents at the tops of the lodges. The village had been temporarily deserted. Everyone had gone to the buffalo hunts.

What to do? The white men were almost completely out of food. Looking about the empty village, they soon found the pits in which the Illinois, like other plains Indians, stored their corn. Now, robbing a câche is one of the high crimes of the wilderness. However great your own need, anything you take away may leave the legitimate proprietor, who finds his own reserve stores gone, in deadlier peril still. To this day, the Royal Canadian Mounted Police are ready to prosecute any wilderness traveler who violates a câche, though owners are likely to be lenient when danger or hunger offers an excuse. After some hesitation, since there was still no game, La Salle decided, in view of his urgent need, to take thirty or forty bushels of corn, hoping to pay for it later with gifts.

There was much excitement a few days later when, in early January of 1680, they came suddenly upon the Illinois Indians' hunting camp. Fearful of hostility, La Salle swung his canoes into line abreast, so that they "took almost the whole breadth of the River." The Illinois being very swift at that point, his fleet swept downstream at great speed, completely terrifying the Indians, who were carelessly bivouacked on both sides of the stream, so that they could not combine their divided forces quickly.

Though carefully avoiding any signs of hostility, La Salle made no signs of friendship either, lest "the Savages wou'd impute it to our Weakness." The moment the Illinois presented their peace pipe, he produced his own, after which amity reigned. The little matter of the stolen corn was adjusted by a gift of steel axes "and other things." A visiting chief who tried to persuade the Illinois that La Salle was an advance agent of the Iroquois was soon discomfited.

La Salle was already unconsciously preparing himself for his later journey down the Mississippi, a journey which Hennepin—in spite of the lying tales he printed after La Salle's death—never made. As a preliminary, La Salle built Fort Crêvecoeur, a little below Peoria, Illinois, and also constructed a forty-two-foot keelboat from logs sawn by hand on the spot. Since it was certain that the *Griffon* must be lost, La Salle decided that he himself had better return overland to get supplies. Meantime he sent Michel Accau and Antoine Auguel, two of his men, with Father Hennepin, to explore the lower waters of the Illinois. There is no doubt that Accau was the real leader, though the mendacious Hennepin, the only one of the three to leave a written record, represents himself as commander.

"Anybody but me," he writes naïvely, "would have been much frightened at the dangers of such a journey." The dangers were real enough, but there is no reason to suppose that either of his companions was hesitant.

They started down the river at the end of February, 1680. The Illinois broadened and deepened as they descended, flowing, in that flat land, "so softly, that the Current is hardly perceptible, except when it swells." It still made Hennepin think of the Sambre and Meuse, but only of the broad stretch "before Namur." Wooded hills, "with fine Trees," disposed at regular intervals along the banks, were separated by marshy ground, which the autumn and spring rains filled to overflowing. Ascending one of the hills, they looked out over an endless expanse of "vast Meadows, with Forests," spreading out before them in all directions. The ground appeared "blackish" which led the priest to guess that it "would prove fertile." "The Soil," Hennepin noted, "looks as if it had been already manur'd." It was, in fact, the result of centuries of the slow rotting of prairie vegetation, made still more fertile by the "chips" dropped through the ages by millions of buffalo, and fertilized at last with their bones. The constant moisture had favored decomposition. The country was, in fact, one vast compost heap. No wonder it includes today some of the best farm land of the nation.

Somewhere along the way, Accau and Hennepin had picked up "a little Dog," which guarded the canoe at night. They were never attacked, though once Indians chased them in clumsy wood dugouts, which the Frenchmen's light birchbarks easily distanced. They came safely to the Mississippi, were there captured by the Sioux, and after a miserable captivity were rescued by the famous *voyageur*, Daniel Greysolon du Lhut, or du Luth. On his way back to civilization, Hennepin seized the occasion to observe and describe Niagara once again.

Many adventures befell the group left under La Salle's heroic lieutenant, Henri Tonty, in the Illinois country, while La Salle himself was in the French settlements, trying to get fresh support for his ventures; but they add no new information to what is known of the country itself; and La Salle's last adventures in the South came after others had explored much of that country.

XVII

The Wild Middle West

LA SALLE'S SEVENTEENTH CENTURY exploration of the Middle West had been entirely along the rivers. Not until the eighteenth century have we any detailed descriptions of the country as it looked to travelers passing overland through the middle western states and also through the adjoining forests and meadows of Kentucky, which, in spite of their beauty, proved a "dark and bloody ground."

Both French and British eighteenth century exploration of "the Ohio country," which meant most of the Middle West east of the Mississippi, was largely based on Pittsburgh, while Daniel Boone and his comrades moved into Kentucky from Virginia and North Carolina.

It was inevitable that French power, expanding from the St. Lawrence, and British power, expanding from the Atlantic coast, should clash at Pittsburgh, key to the Ohio country. The obscure young major of the Virginia Militia—a certain George Washington—who brought on an armed clash at Fort Necessity and thereby precipitated the Seven Years' War in America, Europe, and India, was merely an accidental agent, precipitating a war that, sooner or later, had to come.

Both French and English had been quick to recognize the strategic value of the great "Y" formed by the three rivers at Pittsburgh, where the clear waters of the Allegheny flowing from the North met the turbid waters of the Monongahela, flowing from the South, and then, as the Ohio River, flowed on into the unknown Southwest until they reached the Mississippi.

So different was the color of the two streams that their waters could be distinguished for a long distance down the Ohio. One early traveler amused himself by steering his canoe to a point exactly between the two currents, so that he could dip up "whitish water on one side, and perfectly green on the other." The same thing was possible on a good many other American rivers, before industry and flood control reduced them to dull uniformity.

The French, coming south from Lake Ontario and Lake Erie to this critical area, recognized its value and its beauty at once. The Jesuit Fathers Dollier de Casson and Galinée, who after leaving La Salle spent the winter of 1669–1670 on the south shore of Lake Erie, probably near Presque Isle, were amazed at lands "with very pretty prairies scattered among them, watered by rivers and brooks full of fish and beaver. There is a quantity of fruit and—what is more important—the country is so full of animals that we saw a hundred roe deer [chevreuils] in a single herd, bands of fifty or sixty other deer, and bears that are fatter and taste better than the most savory pigs in France." During their lonely winter, the priests feasted on apples, plums, grapes, service berries, and a huge store of chestnuts and other nuts, besides the jerked meat of nine deer. They made enough wine, "as good as the wine of Grave," to say mass all winter and could easily have made twenty-five or thirty barrels.

Along the shore of Lake Erie in the rivers' mouths, *"White Bass, a fish resembling herring, but considerably larger"* were so easily taken that after settlements were established they were brought in by the wagonload. "So numerous are they at the waters of the Miami," wrote a nineteenth century American, "that a gig maybe thrown into the water at random, and it will rarely miss killing one." In 1812 a party of three or four men caught half a barrelful in less than an hour—using clubs and stones.

Neither French nor English could fail to note the country's economic value from the moment they left Lake Erie and started down the Allegheny Valley. Said the veteran Major Robert Rogers, hero of Kenneth Roberts' novel, *Northwest Passage*: "The land on the south-side of Lake Erie, from Presque Isle, puts on a very fine appearance; the country level, the timber tall, and of the best sort, such as oak hickerie and locust; and for game, both for plenty and variety, perhaps exceeded by no part of the world." As for the country between Detroit and Sandusky, he had "a good opinion of the soil," which was "timbered principally with white and black oaks, hickerie, locusts, and maple. We found wild apples along the west-end of Lake Erie, some rich savannahs of several miles extent, without a tree, but cloathed with jointed grass [i.e., cane] near six feet high, which rotting there every year, added to the fertility of the soil." From Sandusky to the Muskingum River, Ohio was "level land and good rich country," with "no pine-trees of any sort" but full of "white, black and yellow oak, black and white walnut, 'cypress,' chestnut, and locust." From the Muskingum toward Pittsburgh, chestnut and oak predominated.

The major's enthusiasm was not that of a novice. Robert Rogers knew every inch of the continent between Boston and Detroit, for he had traveled all of it, on horse, afoot, by canoe.

The French, who had known the whole Middle West through La Salle's explorations some seventy years earlier, sent troops down to Pittsburgh and built Fort Duquesne, after which Major Washington appeared—first as a staff officer with an official message from the governor of Virginia, inviting the French to get out, then, on his second trip as the commanding officer at Fort Necessity, from which the French ejected him with scant ceremony.

It is an ironical fact that no one dreamed of the immense value of the oil fields beneath their feet. Occasional wanderers in the wilderness saw crude petroleum—"Seneca oil"—floating on the streams in New York, Ohio, and western Pennsylvania. No one guessed at its innumerable uses, or dreamed that petroleum would one day be a matter of life and death to mighty nations. White men sometimes skimmed the queer stuff off for use as an "infallible specific" for chilblains and rheumatism. It had long been esteemed by the Indians for supposed curative powers—certainly it did nobody any harm. The Senecas, living in western New York, valued their medicinal oil so highly that in selling their lands they expressly reserved the oil spring at Cuba, New York.

The petroleum, says one early traveler, "oozes through fissures of the rocks and coal in the mountains, and is found floating on the surface of the waters of several springs in this part of the country." He noted that it was "very imflammable," and then compared it learnedly with Pliny's bitumen. Beyond that, oil meant nothing. The first white men who came wanted to establish an empire so that they could trade for furs. The later white men wanted farms. That the iridescent scum floating on the streams could be more valuable than either was beyond anyone's imagination.

For years after La Salle, it was impossible for the French to follow up his work. War with the Iroquois was soon renewed and in 1688 French troops had to abandon their fort at Niagara. When, in 1726, the Iroquois at last allowed them to rebuild it, the Ohio country again beckoned. In 1729 De Lery, chief engineer in Canada, led a detachment from Lake Erie to Lake Chautauqua and thence to the Ohio River. Down the Ohio he sailed, mapping as he went, beyond the present site of Cincinnati, to the Miami River.

The next French explorer was Céloron de Bienville, or Blainville, who led a force down the Allegheny and Ohio Rivers, in 1749. Though he kept a journal, Céloron failed to enter a single note describing the country. As he went, however, he buried lead plates with inscriptions claiming the country for France, a few of which have been accidentally found in modern times. A Seneca dug up one of them at once and sent it east to Sir William Johnson as a friendly warning of what the French were doing. The warning was not really needed, for Céloron himself had sent a letter, asserting French claims, to Governor Hamilton, of Pennsylvania, by the hands of English traders whom he drove out of Ohio.

As the East filled up with white men, more and more Indians had been withdrawing to the Ohio country. The Shawnees began to leave the Susquehanna and settle in Ohio where a few of their tribe had always lived. The Delawares, who had long since "drunk up their land" in Pennsylvania, were allowed to depart with an injunction from their Iroquois masters: "We hope you will not drink up this land, too." There seems to have been no objection to the newcomers from other tribes already in the Middle West. The land about Pittsburgh had long been almost empty, and south of the Ohio lay Kentucky, a kind of neutral hunting ground between the Cherokees and the Ohio Indians, without any permanent Indian settlements, the Shawnees having removed their last village, Eskappakithika, late in the eighteenth century. Many of the younger Iroquois had drifted down the Allegheny, liked the country, and settled.

Over all these ruled Tanacharison, the Iroquois viceroy or "half-king," representing the great council of the Six Nations on the Ohio, as Shikellamy represented them at Shamokin on the Susquehanna.

Where there were so many Indians, white traders were sure to go. As early as 1692 or 1693, Cornelissen Arnout Viele, an Albany Dutchman skilled in Indian languages, took a party down the Ohio, greatly to the distress of French officials who soon learned of his exploit, though they never intercepted him. By 1735, one Abraham Wendall was trading along the Allegheny. Other traders quickly followed. It is said that by the middle of the eighteenth century there were three hundred traders in the Ohio country, but these men kept their business secrets as close as possible. They did not want to interest possible rivals in the Indian trade and hence left practically no record of what they found. Enough information drifted East, however, to interest capitalists. The Ohio Company was formed and in 1750 sent the famous and resourceful frontiersman, Christopher Gist, to explore both Ohio and Kentucky.

Gist was no ordinary backwoodsman. Bold, resourceful, fearless and skillful in the big woods as any redskin, he was much better educated than the average Virginia gentleman. In a day when the formal business and official letters of Virginia leaders were marvels of illiteracy, even Gist's rough wilderness diaries were prose models, clear, simple, direct—and properly spelled! Yet he could be ruthless as the roughest backwoodsman upon occasion. It took definite orders from George Washington to keep him from dispatching out-of-hand an Indian who had, he thought, tried to shoot "the Major," while Gist and Major Washington were returning from their trip to warn the French off the Ohio. Acquaintance either with Gist himself or with his son, Nathaniel, probably helped arouse Daniel Boone's interest in Kentucky.

Gist made three western trips, the journals of which have been preserved, between 1750 and 1754, the last recording his famous journey with Washington, to warn off French troops at Fort Duquesne

(Pittsburgh). His first and most ambitious journey in 1750 took him through Pennsylvania, down the river, through Ohio as far west as Piqua and Dayton, then still farther west in Kentucky almost to Louisville, then homeward southwest across Kentucky to westernmost Virginia and south to his home in North Carolina.

Most travelers floated down the Ohio in a canoe or, in later years, in a flatboat or a keelboat. Gist, however, was traveling to "find a large Quantity of good, level Land" for the Ohio Company. There was plenty of good, rich bottom land along the Ohio itself—the early travelers are always talking about it—but Gist wanted to make a thorough survey of the country.

Ohio in those days was wooded, but as Gist moved west toward the prairies beyond the Mississippi, he found the woods becoming less dense. Much of the landscape, even in forested Ohio, was "fine rich level Land, with large Meadows, fine Clover Bottoms & spacious Plains covered with wild Rye: the wood chiefly large Walnuts and Hickories, here and there mixed with Poplars Cherry Trees and Sugar Trees." Like the eastern forests, these were open underfoot. There was practically no underbrush and the trunks were long and straight, their lower branches having died from lack of sunlight and dropped off. Early Ohio settlers found that they could drive about through the forests with sleds and horses.

Eventually these huge forests were cleared by an odd labor-saving device. Settlers would cut each tree half way through over a space of several acres, thereby saving themselves half the work. Then, when the wind was right, they felled a few of the big trees to windward which, as they crashed down, carried the rest with them, sending thousands of tall trees toppling to the ground like so many dominoes. Most of this magnificent timber was simply burned on the spot. The ashes were good for the soil, no one needed lumber, and no one worried over the lost beauty of the forest.

The soil was, in fact, already fertile enough without the ashes. One enterprising traveler proposed gathering them up and starting a potash industry, since the land did not need them. The rapid growth of new trees and plants in prairie soil astonished the first white men who cultivated it. If we can believe an early visitor to the settlements, apples would bear fruit four years from seed (he may have meant "seedlings"), peaches three years from seed were loaded with fruit, locusts two years from seed reached heights of twelve to fifteen feet. This enthusiast even insisted that "in six years a farmer may raise from the seed a forest which will meet every want."

Wild rye grew everywhere in Ohio, westward to the Mississippi, and even beyond. It was almost like the cultivated variety except for a longer beard. Thomas Pownall observes that it "shoots in its spontaneous Vegetations about the Middle of November as the cultivated rye doth." Pines seem to have stopped at the western boundary of Pennsylvania, though there were immense pine forests to the northwest and in the South. The sulphur springs of Pennsylvania gave way to numerous salt licks and springs. Even the bushes around them were sometimes encrusted with salt crystals. Occasionally the streams themselves were salt. The water, when boiled in enormous flat kettles made for the purpose, yielded a fairly good table salt. When first boiled out, the salt had a blue color, giving a bluish sediment to salt creeks and springs. In some streams and ponds even the water was blue—hence the name of the famous Blue Licks in Kentucky, or the Blue River in Indiana, which kept its clear blue color until it emptied into the Ohio.

If, however, the blue crystals were dissolved in pure water and boiled a second time they became "tolerable pure Salt." Earth near the springs was impregnated, creating "licks"—so called because deer and buffalo which craved salt as much as barnyard cattle, came from all the country around to lick eagerly at the saline earth. It was always easy to kill game by lying in wait at any of the licks. In the few wilderness areas now remaining, moose and deer are so eager for salt that it is easy to attract them by spreading it about on the ground—a practice usually forbidden by the game laws because of the slaughter it makes possible.

In some places the buffalo actually ate the salt earth. At the famous Blue Licks the earth had been eaten away to such a depth that the huge bodies of the buffalo were completely concealed. Sometimes the great trenches ran side by side with only a thin wall of earth dividing them. Michael Stoner, the famous Pennsylvania Dutch frontiersman of Kentucky, was nearly killed by attempting a prank in one of these excavations. Traveling past the Blue Licks with Daniel Boone, he saw a buffalo eagerly licking the earth of one such trench. The two woodsmen were in no need of meat but Stoner thought it would be amusing to scare the animal. He crept down the parallel trench, which earlier buffalo had dug in their search for salt, until he was opposite his own buffalo, whose attention was wholly taken up with the salt. Then rising suddenly, he thrust his cap across the thin dividing wall almost into the animal's face. Instead of running, the great brute charged straight into the thin earth wall. As the huge horns, head, and shoulders burst through the earth, almost on top of him, Stoner ran for his life, wildly yelling to Boone in Pennsylvania Dutch-English: "Schoot her, Gaptain! Schoot her, Gaptain!" Stoner was still running when the buffalo gave up the chase, while Boone, seeing that his companion was in no real danger, rolled upon the ground with laughter.

There were relatively few buffalo in the heavily wooded country north of the Ohio, for the salt licks and the heavy growth of cane, rushes, and "wild peas" attracted the animals to Kentucky. A herd of twenty is mentioned as remarkable, and an English visitor was very much excited at seeing "more than a hundred together"—which would have amused a Sioux or Comanche. There were rather larger herds on the lower Ohio, and buffalo roamed Kentucky in herds of several hundred at a time, though never in the huge masses of the western plains where far into the nineteenth century one might see a hundred thousand or more at a time.

Except when an individual animal was wounded or a whole herd was frightened and stampeded, these small herds were seldom dangerous. Daniel Boone and his friends on one occasion amused themselves by chasing a Kentucky herd across a river, simply for the fun of counting them. This kind of thing was all very well if you knew which way the herd was going to head, but it was almost certain death to get in the way of a stampede. The quick-witted Boone once saved himself in such a predicament by shooting one animal and crouching behind the huge carcass while the others thundered past it.

White hunters soon exterminated buffalo and elk. They were all gone, east of the Mississippi by the second quarter of the nineteenth century, or earlier; but the deer, as usual, increased as hunters kept down beasts of prey, and as settlers opened up the forests to provide more grazing lands. Just before 1840, there was a brisk trade in deer hides and venison hams, the latter worth seventy-five cents to $1.50 a pair. Wolves remained a pest for a long time and often frightened farm wives by prowling about in broad daylight, always seeming to choose the hour when the farmer was in the fields, and there was no danger from his rifle. "Partridges," which seem to have been Bob-White quail, could be netted in winter by the hundreds, long after settlement began. The clearing of the forests probably benefited them as much as it did the deer.

Where the country was open, prairie chickens ran in flocks of several hundred at a time and had a habit of lighting, when disturbed, on the nearest tree or fence rail, allowing hunters to approach to within fifteen or twenty paces. Local hunters shot them through the head with their singleshot rifles but could kill only one bird at a time. A man with a shotgun could kill a hundred a day. An English visitor thought them very much like Scotch grouse and "delicious eating."

One other game bird persisted until it was completely wiped out by ruthless commercial hunting and the gradual diminution of the forests. Over the middle western forests beat the multitudinous wings of enormous flocks of passenger pigeons, which remained as large as ever in the Ohio country until the beginning of the nineteenth century and in Michigan and Wisconsin almost to its close. In 1803 a pigeon roost near Marietta, Ohio, was supposed to cover a thousand acres, and another was even larger. The pigeons wiped out all life in areas like this. "The destruction of timber and brush on such large tracts of land by these small animals is almost incredible," wrote a settler near there. "How many millions of them must have assembled to effect it." One gets an idea how many from a minor agricultural tragedy in Illinois, where an unexpected flock of pigeons came down in the local forest, devouring all the "mast" (beechnuts, acorns, chestnuts) on which the settlers had relied to feed their hogs. As a result "numbers of hogs starved to death."

Long stretches of the Ohio woodland were fairly open. The famous trader, George Croghan, one of Gist's contemporaries, often enters in the journals of his overland trips, "pretty clear Woods," or "clear Woods

& good road." Elsewhere there were patches of briars and brambles, through which travelers struggled as best they could, their leather clothing affording some protection. Many of the middle western Indians, as La Salle had already found, following the custom of the plains Indians, burned off the country occasionally to keep it open enough for game. Otherwise the eastern forests would have gone on moving ever farther to the west until they covered the country, without a break, as far as the Mississippi.

Early white settlers in Michigan, adopting the Indian custom, sometimes burned the meadows to make the grass "tender." When they got out of hand, prairie fires were a terrible danger. "These fires," wrote an early eastern visitor to Michigan, "travelling far over the country, seize upon the large prairies, and consuming every tree in the woods, except the hardiest, cause the often-mentioned 'oak openings,' characteristic of Michigan scenery. It is a beautiful sight to see the fire shooting in every direction over these broad expanses of land, which are kindled at a variety of points. The flame at one moment curls along the ground, and seems to lick up its fuel from below, while at the next it tumbles over like the breakers of the sea upon the dried grass, and sweeps it in a wave of fire from the ground."

A traveler in Illinois describes riding along a roadside near Peoria with a "wall of fire as high as our horses' ears" not far away. "The prairie presented exactly the appearance of a broad burning pool," and as the fire rolled past "like the waves of the sea itself, when they break upon the shore, a thousand forked tongues of flame would project themselves far beyond the broken mass, and greedily lick up the dry aliment that lay before them."

"It was the most glorious and most awful sight I ever beheld," wrote Elias Pym Fordham, an English settler in Indiana. "A thousand acres of Prairie were in flames at once;—the sun was obscured, and the day was dark before the night came. The moon rose, and looked dim and red through the smoke, and the stars were hidden entirely. Yet it was still light upon the earth, which appeared covered with fire. The flames reached the forests, and rushed like torrents through. Some of the trees fell immediately, others stood like pillars of fire, casting forth sparkles of light. Their branches are strewed in smoking ruins around them." That night five large fires were blazing, some of them miles away but still visible.

The glow could sometimes be seen for forty miles and the advancing prairie fire might be preceded by a shower of "flakes and cinders" for about the same distance. In the autumn, when grass and woods were dry, there was usually a fire blazing somewhere on each bank of the Mississippi, until rain, damp ground, or a broad stream extinguished it.

It was perhaps one of these fires that touched off an exposed vein of coal on the Muskingum River, in Ohio. The coal burned for a full year. In Illinois a prairie fire kindled a stump which set off the coal bed above which it stood. This burned for several months, until falling earth put it out. But these fires were trivial compared with those in the lignite beds in the Canadian Far North, which the explorer, Alexander Mackenzie, saw burning in 1789 and which were still burning in the twentieth century.

The forest fires, however terrible, had one advantage. They decreased the density of the forests and thus encouraged the deer, so that the Indians were likely to kindle fires and let them run whenever they wanted more deer—which, as one warrior explained, were their cattle. As a result, the animals were everywhere. Christopher Gist, exploring the Middle West, notes casually: "Being in Want of Provisions, I went out and killed a Deer." It was as simple as telephoning the butcher. Hunters rarely took anything but the haunches, the choicest meat.

Other staples of aboriginal diet were almost as easily secured. Bear and wild turkeys haunted the Scioto Valley, and where the rather sluggish stream overflowed its level banks, often to a width of two or three miles, the silt made "prodigious rich" bottoms. In these grew "vast fields of rice, which Nature here produces spontaneously."

Toward Lake Erie, there was "fine Land, wide extended Meadows, lofty Timber," with more wild rice in the marshes. The low, wet land exactly suited the beaver, of which a trapper could take twenty or thirty in a single night. The trees were mostly oak, mulberry, walnut, chestnut, and poplar. The present site of Cleveland consisted of "fine uplands, extensive meadows, oake, and mulberry trees fit for ship-building, and walnut, chestnut, and poplar trees suitable for domestic services." Near the mouth of the Cuyahoga were "the celebrated rocks which project over the Lake. They are several miles in length, and rise forty or fifty feet perpendicular out of the water. Some parts of them consist of several strata of different colours, lying in a horizontal direction, and so exactly parallel that they resemble the work of art." As late as 1835, the mouth of the Cuyahoga was still unspoiled by settlement. The view was "a very pretty prospect of the Cuyahoga winding through a piece of rich meadow-land below us [now the city of Cleveland], and affording, as the high grounds recede at its entrance into the lake, a striking view of Erie in the distance."

Ohio forests were much like those of Pennsylvania, except for the scarcity of pine and hemlock. There was no white pine below Pittsburgh and no yellow pitch pine below Louisville. Indeed, Major Robert Rogers, who traveled across Ohio through "level land and a good country," observed "no pine-trees of any sort," but a good growth of various oaks, black and "white" walnut, "cyprus," locust, and chestnut. The trees between the Muskingum and Pittsburgh were mainly oak and chestnut.

Most of the trees in these virgin forests were much larger than any ordinarily seen today. They had grown for centuries, undisturbed— just how many centuries we rarely know, for no one thought to count their rings when the white man's axe and saw brought them crashing down at last. But a few ring-counts have been recorded. The annual rings of two oaks cut down near Muncy, Pennsylvania, about 1833, showed that the trees were 460 and 390 years old. They had both been well grown when Columbus landed on Santo Domingo; and, as this pair were selected quite at random, there must have been others even older. William Penn's "Treaty Elm" in Philadelphia, which fell in 1810, had 283 rings. It had been 187 years old when Penn treated with the redskins in its shade; it had begun to grow in the year when Cabeza de Vaca sailed. Even these trees were not old by far western standards. So conservative a botanist as Asa Gray felt sure that some of the sequoias in the Rockies had begun their growth before the birth of Christ.

In the Ohio country, where interested travelers took the trouble to measure the trees, walnuts and sycamores grew six or seven feet in diameter. As far west as Chillicothe, white oaks, "the glory of the upland forests," grew stands so thick that the trunks, pushing up toward the light, might rise eighty feet without a branch. One oak measured by a curious Englishman was six feet in diameter at its base and three feet in diameter at a height of seventy-five feet. Near Greenfield, Ohio, a traveler saw "thousands, I think, of these magnificent trees within view of the road for miles, measuring fourteen or fifteen feet in circumference; their straight stems rising, without a branch, to the height of seventy or eighty feet, not tapering and slender, but surmounted by full luxuriant heads." Most of the eastern forests were like that in the beginning. Until about 1790 trees two to five feet in diameter were common and only as trees passed six feet or reached eight did they attract attention. Even in the twentieth century New York City still had one tulip tree ten feet through at the base.

The cottonwoods, or sycamores, which grew close to the river banks, were more frequently swept away by floods than other trees, and so produced most of the "planters," "snags," and "sawyers" which were the plague of white river men, though much less dangerous to the light Indian canoes. Large sycamores invariably had hollow trunks, some so large that farmers cut them down carefully and used them as pig-sties and well-houses. Smaller sycamores furnished grain-bins and casks. A very big sycamore could shelter a fairly large number of men—one traveler says twenty or thirty. Along the Mississippi and for some distance up the Ohio, the cottonwoods were big enough to make "pirogues" (dugout canoes) sixty or seventy feet long and sometimes four feet across, two of which—placed side by side to give stability—would carry ten or fifteen tons. Daniel Boone made a sixty-foot dugout with a burden of five tons out of a single tulip poplar, the stump of which was still being pointed out in 1851. Incredible as this seems, a specimen of such a dugout is still preserved in St. Louis.

A hundred years before Daniel Boone, one white man had crossed Kentucky from the Ohio to Tennessee and had lived to tell the tale—though he reported his adventures without troubling to describe the wonderfully beautiful primitive land through which he traveled. This was Gabriel Arthur, a servant—apparently a bond servant—of Colonel Abraham Wood, a planter living at what is now Petersburg, Virginia.

In 1671, two Virginian adventurers of whom little is known, Thomas Batts and Robert Fallam, had ventured over the Appalachian divide into the Kanawha River Valley, in West Virginia. Interested by the possibilities their story suggested, Colonel Wood in 1673 sent out a party of his own, of whom young Arthur was one. Captured by the Cherokees, he escaped torture, was accepted as a friend, and presently joined his captors in a war party going against the Shawnees along the Ohio. Captured again, this time by the Shawnees, he persuaded them to release him by explaining to the tribe, who "had not any manner of iron instrument," that he knew where to buy hunting knives like his own, for nothing but a few beaver skins. Delighted by such a prospect, the naïve Shawnee warriors sped him on his way back across Kentucky to Tennessee, thence northward to Virginia, where he arrived June 18, 1674—and stayed.

Soon other adventurers were crossing the mountains beyond which mystery lay. Governor Alexander Spotswood, of Virginia, on the most famous of his explorations, led a group of gentlemen into the Shenandoah Valley in 1716. Dr. Thomas Walker, the Fredericksburg surgeon, explored this "Valley of Virginia" again in 1748, and in 1750 passed through the Cumberland Gap into Kentucky itself. French explorers, coming down the Ohio, are supposed to have gone south into Kentucky as far as Big Bone Lick as early as 1739, though otherwise they traveled mainly along the line of the river. One man, of whom almost nothing else is known, James McBride, went down the Ohio to the Kentucky River's mouth in 1754 and there "marked a tree, with the first letters of his name, and the date," which were still visible thirty years after.

Not until the late 1760's did the various parties of "Long Hunters" and the Boone brothers, Daniel and Squire, begin those journeys into the "dark and bloody ground," which soon led to the first permanent white settlements. The white trader, John Finley, or Findlay, who is known to have been in Kentucky as early as 1767, was the man who stirred Daniel Boone's interest in the land with which his name is forever associated. Almost nothing is known about Finley, save that he traded along the Ohio and Kentucky rivers, journeyed as far as the Falls of the Ohio at Louisville, and returning, enthralled Boone with his tales of the wonders of Kaintuck.

The Long Hunters were so called because of the long periods they spent in the unknown country beyond the Cumberland Gap. Some of them are said to have remained in the wilderness two years at a time, returning at length with loads of deerskins and furs, or at other times coming back disconsolate and empty-handed, having been robbed by indignant Indians, who regarded them as mere trespassers and thieves, stealing the wilderness wares that rightly belonged to the red men. Altogether, about eighty Long Hunters are supposed to have gone beyond the Alleghenies into southern Kentucky and northern Tennessee between 1769 and 1774.

Kentucky at that time was an almost empty country, claimed by both Cherokees and Shawnees, but settled by neither, since it was used mainly as a hunting ground. Finley, who had thus far traveled by river, wanted to go overland to this wonderful region, a journey for which he would need experienced woodsmen as companions. With Daniel and Squire Boone, and their brother-in-law, John Stuart— as stout a trio as could have been found—and with three "camp-keepers," who seem to have been mere employees, he set off in the spring of 1769. Passing through the Cumberland Gap, they had by early June established a permanent base camp on what is still called Station Camp Creek—the "station camp" being a permanent base, from which the hunters could work through the wilderness in all directions, while the camp-keepers cared for their skins and furs.

Before long, Daniel Boone was off on one of those wilderness rambles that were to him the breath of life. When he reached Big Hill, be-tween the Rockcastle and Kentucky rivers, he climbed it and from its summit looked westward over the rolling, generally level, fertile country, filled with grasslands and forest, that he had come to find.

They had not hunted long before there was Indian trouble. Then Stuart disappeared—Boone found his skeleton, identified by a powder horn lying near it, with his initials, five years later in the trunk of a hollow sycamore. The skeleton's broken left arm, still marked with the discoloration of a lead bullet, showed how he had met his end. The rest of the party either gave up or went home for supplies. By

1770, Daniel Boone was all alone in Kentucky, rejoicing in the "elbow-room" he loved all his life, and waiting for his brother Squire to return from the settlements with fresh supplies. Rapturously, he wandered through this beautiful, primitive land, wandered so widely that when a few years later the time came for white settlement, there was no living being, white or red, who knew it better.

Beautiful as both sides of the Ohio River were, the virgin wilderness of Kentucky, as Boone found it, was something special. One early arrival speaks of "the pleasing and rapturous appearance of the plains of Kentucky. A new sky and strange new earth seemed to be presented to our view." "The face of the country," said another, was "delightful beyond conception."

Most of a state that is still beautiful was then forested, but there were also many open spaces like "the Barrens" (which were not barren at all), or "the Great Meadow" covered with clover, where in the shade of a great elm "surrounded by a turf of fine white clover, forming a green to its very stock to which there is scarcely anything to be likened," Daniel Boone and his associates established Boonesborough, in 1775.

"The country, in some parts, is nearly level," wrote John Filson, Boone's biographer, "in others not so much so; in others again hilly, but moderately, and in such places there is most water. The levels are not like a carpet, but interspersed with small risings, and declivities, which form a beautiful prospect. A great part of the soil is amazingly fertile." Kentucky looked much more level in early days, when it was clothed in bluegrass, cane, and forest than it does today, when most of this has been cut away to reveal its rolling contours.

In and around what is today Barren County lay "the Barrens," so called because the land was open prairie, without forest, without sign that forest had ever been there. It was carpeted with grasses, wild rye, wild oats, and flowers. Here buffalo and elk grazed, and their bones, horns, and skulls lay bleaching all about. There was so much game in Kentucky and Tennessee that one hunter counted a thousand animals near a single salt lick. Another found a lick so crowded with animals that he was afraid to dismount, and when he did shoot two deer, the stampeding game trampled the carcasses so badly that he could not skin them.

Felix Walker, obscure member of a group who went out in 1774, noted: "So rich a soil we had never seen before; covered with clover in full bloom, the woods were abounding with wild game—turkeys so numerous that it might be said they appeared but one flock, universally scattered in the woods." It was, in short, like all the rest of the country along the Ohio River, only more beautiful.

The middle western prairies were, as the veteran frontier parson, the Reverend Timothy Flint, remarked, "diminutive, though fertile copies of the more western ones." They might be completely level for several miles at a stretch, with no vegetation except coarse grass and cane, which grew "often higher than a man's head." "The whole country is prairies; you meet only some clumps of wood," wrote a priest traveling on the Mississippi in 1699. The reverend gentleman had a good deal of trouble because the prairie grass grew so tall that a boy lost himself in it; and the party of missionaries and explorers had to hunt for several days before they could find him. Someone thought of burning off the grass as the Indians did but there was so much of it that they were afraid of roasting the lad alive before they discovered him.

When wild flowers were in bloom, prairies east of the Mississippi presented a picture now largely lost in farm lands. As late as 1832, however, they looked much as they had looked in prehistoric time. "From May to October, they are covered with tall grass and flower-producing weeds," wrote Robert Baird, the author of a little book on the Mississippi. "In June and July, these prairies seem like an ocean of flowers, of various hues, and waving to the breezes which sweep over them. The heliotrope or sunflower, and others present a striking and delightful appearance."

Many of these stretches were probably due to the "exciccation," or drying-up, of old lake bottoms, the result being a rich black soil, "which at once absorbs the rain that falls upon it, so as never to be muddy." On the whole, wrote a settler, "the prairie is fine, dry, light land, and rolling."

In Illinois, especially between the Great and Little Wabash, the country was "intersected with a vast number of creeks and streams, and interspersed with prairies of natural meadows, containing from 1,000 to 100,000 acres. They are very irregular in figure, and are dotted and clumped with trees, like English parks. Some of the smallest are low, flat, and swampy, but the greatest part are high, dry, and rolling." The approach to Peoria, Illinois, was "through alternate prairies and richly wooded bottoms, that fringe the lake with vegetation of stupendous growth, and give glimpses of its sparkling waters through festoons of vines." The river expanded gradually to a width of two or three miles as it approached the lake and the current became barely perceptible. The "heavy bottoms, densely timbered" remained untouched far into the last century, being so moist, swampy, "unwholesome and feverish" that there was little temptation to clear them. "It is a beautiful spot to look upon, in its primitive and unbroken wildness," wrote a traveler a century and a half after La Salle, as he gazed upon an almost identical landscape, "but the idea of disease and death lurking in every ripple and concealed beneath every leaf, drove from my mind all idea of beauty."

Country like this, of course flooded easily as did all the lower Mississippi. Around the village of Chicago, to the north, there was nothing for many miles save "a dead level of prairie," and this was inundated nearly every spring.

The first white comers were amazed by the size and number of the fish, a fact which suggests that as early as the Revolution the eastern streams had been partly "fished out." Harris, an early nineteenth century traveler, mentions black catfish ranging from six to 110 pounds; yellow catfish from six to fifty pounds; pike of from eight to thirty-five pounds.

Most of these fish stories come from the upper part of the Ohio River, but there is no doubt that the fishing was equally good all the way to the Mississippi. The fish were not really so miraculous as Easterners thought. There were far bigger ones farther west, in the Mississippi and the Great Lakes. Early fishermen, for example, were impressed by a mere sixty-pound catfish, not guessing at the size of the huge Mississippi River "cats," who seem to have sent only their smaller relatives up the Ohio as far as Pittsburgh.

The Chippeway Indians in the vicinity of Sault Ste. Marie lived entirely on fish. The illustration is from a pencil sketch by George Catlin and dates from 1832–1839.

The earliest known view of Chicago, depicting the area sometime between 1816 and 1820. Fort Dearborn is shown to the left of the Chicago River and the house of John Kinzie, often called the "Father of Chicago," is at the right.

The fish in Lake Erie, and the Youghiogheny, Allegheny, Monong-ahela, and Ohio rivers were both big enough and numerous enough to startle Easterners, who by this time had entirely forgotten the magnificent hunting and fishing that had once existed in the sea-board states—by this time thickly settled. A fisherman of 1823 com-plains bitterly that he took thirty barrels of fish in the Allegheny in a single cast of the net, but unfortunately the net broke and he got only ten barrels!

There are many records of big fish that did not always get away. General Harmar, that doughty if not always successful Indian fighter, mentions twenty-one pound pike in exultant tones which show clearly that the fish he had been used to in the East were much smaller. The sturgeon were not as big as the biggest Captain John Smith had seen in Virginia, but they did go up to four and five feet, weighing fifty to sixty pounds—though they were such odd-looking creatures that fastidious Easterners, unacquainted with their flavor, refused to eat them. No one caviled at the perch, which were common enough at eight pounds, not uncommon at twenty, and ran up nearly to thirty. Even Colonel John May, a fussbudget of a Boston businessman, who re-fused to touch sturgeon—today a luxury—admitted that the western perch were better than haddock. He unbent to the point of enthusiasm over a "lobster and oyster" dinner. As neither lobsters nor oysters are found inland, and as there was no way of transporting them in those days, it is clear the Bostonian colonel was eating—and enjoying—river mussels of some kind and the big river crayfish, which reached six inches in length—"almost like our lobsters in Boston."

Colonel May was much startled by "a terrible fish, if such it may be called, named an alligator. It was about eighteen inches long; as big as a man's wrist; with large flat head, something like a bull-frog. He had four legs of the bigness of a gray squirrel's, and a tail five inches long, near two inches wide; and was of a sickly ash-color, and as spiteful as the devil."

The colonel was getting his first glimpse of one of the two species of giant salamanders, still common in eastern American streams, usu-ally known as "mud-puppies" or "water dogs" (*Necturus maculosus*) and "hell-benders" (*Cryptobranchus alleganiensis*). They swarmed in the rivers near Pittsburgh. Indeed, though these large salamanders are rarely seen except by interested zoologists and disgusted fishermen, there are still enough of them about to be a nuisance to water companies; but as they are quiet creatures, protectively colored, that stick close to the beds of streams, most people never guess that they exist. Every now and then, especially in low water, one takes a fisherman's bait and the emergence of the squirming, thrashing, strange-looking creatures with four unexpected legs, is quite as sensational as Colonel May's description suggests. Though the animals are quite harmless and are even eaten by certain bold individuals, their appearance is so startling that most modern fishermen, as terrified as Colonel May, simply cut their lines to get rid of them.

XVIII

Father of Waters

ALTHOUGH IT IS the largest river in North America and second largest in the world, exceeded only by the Nile in length and by the Amazon in volume, and though it was one of the first American rivers seen by white men, the Mississippi was one of the last to be explored. Of all the great American rivers, only the Columbia—lying in the far Northwest, completely out of the path of early wanderers—was explored later than the Father of Waters.

Who the early explorer was that first sighted the Mississippi delta, we do not know; but it is certain that not long after Columbus, some curious white man had been collecting information about its geography. In 1513, an astonishingly early date, the Mississippi delta is represented, with fair accuracy, in a new edition of the ancient geography of the Greco-Egyptian astronomer, Claudius Ptolemaeus. It has been suspected that this information was, in some mysterious way, collected by Columbus himself, and the map is traditionally called "the Admiral's Map." By 1520, only seven years later, Cortez is including even more detail in a map sent to the Emperor Charles V.

Most of this cartography is probably based on little more than conversations with Indians and intelligent guesses as to the lie of the land; but the delta itself is traced so accurately that it is reasonably certain this part of the old map is based on somebody's first-hand observation.

However that may be, it was not long before the Spaniards were beginning to explore the north coast of the Gulf of Mexico. In 1518, Francisco de Garay, governor of Jamaica, then a Spanish possession, sailed along part of it and may have seen the great river's mouth. In 1519, Garay sent out the sea captain, Alonso de Piñeda, to seek any possible waterway from the Gulf of Mexico to the Pacific. Running up the Florida coast, Piñeda sailed on west to a river, described as "very large and carrying much water"—which may not have been the Mississippi, but certainly sounds like it. Up this stream he sailed for about twenty miles, passing "forty towns on either side" and "admiring very much the land." His pilots made a map which, if it could now be found, would probably prove definitely that he was in the Mississippi. As it is, no one is quite sure whether Piñeda may not, perhaps, have been in the Mobile.

Cabeza de Vaca also, though he never explored the great river, certainly knew that it existed, since he had sailed past the delta before he was shipwrecked. Very likely it was from him that De Soto learned about it. Certainly De Soto and all his men knew just about what they were going to find when they came out of the woods to the river bank near Memphis. None of the various writers who describe De Soto's adventures suggest that anyone felt the least surprise when they at last reached the Mississippi, except that its immense width did startle them, as it was bound to startle any European. Indeed, long before reaching the Mississippi, De Soto had ordered a lieutenant to return to Havana and meet him six months later on the delta, which, as things turned out, the dauntless Spaniard never lived to see.

The survivors of De Soto's expedition, who sailed down the Father of Waters for several hundred miles on their way to Mexico after their leader's death, were the first white men who had seen more of the river's course than the first few miles immediately above the delta.

After that, there was no more Spanish exploration of the Mississippi Valley for a long time, though a few missionaries may have reached it overland from New Mexico; and there is a vague story that a Portuguese sea captain, Vincent Gonzales, sailed up a large river—otherwise unidentified—between Apalache and Tampico.

Meantime, far to the north, French explorers penetrating inland from the St. Lawrence, began to hear tales of a Great (Missi) River (Sipi) that lay somewhere or other—Indians were always a little vague about this kind of thing—ahead of them. It is even possible that

Jean Nicolet, a veteran French agent who already had been in the woods and among the Indians for about twenty years, actually reached the upper waters of the Mississippi as early as 1639. All that is really known is that he went from Lake Michigan to Green Bay, thence up the Fox River and over the portage at its headwaters. This would have brought him to the Wisconsin River—he was, in other words, following the usual route to the Mississippi, and was actually on one of its tributaries. Probably he stopped on the Wisconsin and never went far enough to reach the main stream itself. Nothing else is known save a priest's casual remark that had Nicolet "sailed three days more on a great river" he would have "found the sea." That, of course, was impossible, but the missionary may have heard Indians trying to say that had Nicolet traveled farther down the Wisconsin he would have reached "the great water," that is the Mississippi.

In 1641, two Jesuit fathers heard stories about a strange tribe, the Sioux Indians, who dwelt on a great river; but as the perpetual war between the French and Iroquois broke out again, they could not visit them. The two Frenchmen (probably Radisson and Groseilliers) who wintered near Lake Superior in 1658, heard more about the Sioux and "a beautiful river, large, broad, and deep, which would bear comparison, they say, with our St. Lawrence." Missionaries in New York State also began to hear tales of "a beautiful river which leads to a great lake as they called the sea, where they traded with Europeans, who pray to God as we do, and have rosaries and bells to call men to prayers." The great river was probably the Ohio and Mississippi, which many Indians thought of as a single stream, the upper Mississippi being a mere tributary.

Father Allouez, a noted Jesuit, who for the first time records the name "Messipi," also heard that this great river seemed to enter "into the sea by Virginia." In 1669 Allouez himself, following in Nicolet's footsteps, went up the Fox River, over the watershed and down to the Wisconsin, "a beautiful river running southwest." Like Nicolet, he too was now on tributary waters which he knew led "to the great river named Messi-sipi, which is only six days sail from here."

Presently Father Dablon, Superior-General of the Jesuit missions in Canada was writing: "Some Indians assure us that this river is so beautiful that more than three hundred leagues from its mouth, it is larger than that which flows by Quebec, as they make it more than a league wide. They say, moreover, that all this vast extent of country is nothing but prairies, without trees and woods, which obliges the inhabitants of those parts to use turf and sun-dried dung for fuel, till you come about twenty leagues from the sea. Here the forests begin to appear again." Indians who had made the journey described how, far to the south, they had seen "men like the French, who were splitting trees with long knives, some of whom had their house on the water." In other words, they had seen Spaniards cutting trees into planks with saws, and had seen ships anchored offshore.

French officialdom at last began to take notice. Every new fact about the mighty stream made it sound like the long-sought way to the Pacific. Certainly it was very far to the west and as it flowed south, it might well flow into the South Sea. It was high time to undertake official exploration. The government, about 1672, proposed to send Louis Jolliet "to discover the south sea," and to explore "the great river Mississippi, which is believed to empty in the California sea."

In Jolliet, they had found an almost ideal man for their purpose. Born at Beauport, near Quebec, in 1645, he had been educated in the Jesuit College at Quebec, had received minor orders, and had at one time intended to become a member of the Society of Jesus. Giving up his studies for the priesthood, he had visited France, returned to Canada, and plunged into the wilderness.

Father Dablon, Jesuit Superior in Canada, under whom Jolliet had studied, wrote that he was "endowed with every quality that could be desired in such an enterprise. He possessed experience and a knowledge of the languages of the Ottawa country, where he had spent several years; he had the tact and prudence so necessary for the success of a voyage equally dangerous and difficult; and, lastly, he had courage to fear nothing where all is to be feared."

As usual in expeditions of this sort, both French and Spanish, a priest was sent along to do missionary work—in this case, the famous Father Jacques Marquette.

The daring little band was under Jolliet's command, while Father Marquette was attached to the expedition for religious purposes only.

Because Jolliet's map and papers were destroyed while those of Père Marquette were preserved, the story of the two men's exploration is usually told from Marquette's point of view rather than Jolliet's. Nothing, one may be sure, would have distressed the devout and unworldly priest more than this.

A better companion for the dangerous task, it would have been hard to find. Père Marquette had, of course, passed through the usual rigorous intellectual training which the Society of Jesus has always required of its priests. He spoke six Indian languages fluently and had already had long experience in the wilderness. Moreover, he was a man of singular sweetness and gentleness, utterly indifferent to worldly matters, equally incapable of fear, jealousy, or personal ambition, with a temper by nature so placid that the worst hardships of the wilderness left it wholly undisturbed.

With five companions in two birchbark canoes, Jolliet and Marquette started from Mackinac Island, May 17, 1673. Determined that "if our enterprise was hazardous, it should not be foolhardy," they had been at pains to learn in advance everything that the Indians of the Great Lakes could tell them about the route overland to the Mississippi, the course of the river itself, and the tribes living on its banks. Like Nicolet and Allouez, they followed the usual Indian route, from Green Bay on Lake Michigan, up the Fox River, over the low watershed at its source, and down the Wisconsin into the Mississippi itself.

At Green Bay, they turned into the Fox River with a gentle current —a matter of no small importance to canoemen pushing upstream— and full of migrating waterfowl, attracted by the abundant wild rice. They were traveling in wild rice country. In modern times the growth of this staple grocery of the wilderness is so restricted and the demand for it so great that it is all gathered long before winter sets in. But in these early days there was so much of it that in parts of the Fox River a single patch might cover a space five miles by two, so thick that sometimes passage for a canoe had to be chopped through it. Often, in spite of its value as a food supply, the luxuriant growth became a mere nuisance.

Neither the Indians nor the waterfowl could eat enough to exhaust the endless grain supply, for one small lake could produce enough to feed two thousand people. Jolliet and Marquette found the tall stalks swaying above the water, "still full of grain, though it was now late spring and the new growth was ready to begin."

Father Marquette described the "wild oats" as "a kind of grass which grows spontaneously in little rivers with slimy bottoms, and in marshy places; they are very like the wild oats that grow up among our wheat. The ears are on stalks knotted at intervals; they rise above the water about the month of June, and keep rising till they float about two feet above it. The grain is not thicker than our oats, but is as long again, so that the meal is much more abundant."

Wilderness ways change slowly. The exploring priest describes, in 1673, exactly the way in which to this very day the Ojibway Indians of Minnesota and Ontario still gather their wild rice harvest: "In the month of September, which is the proper time for this harvest, they go in canoes across these fields of wild oats, and shake the ears on their right and left into the canoe as they advance; the grain falls easily if it is ripe, and in a little while their provision is made." The Indians then trod out the grain with moccasined feet, winnowed away the chaff, and dried the rice over a fire, after which they pounded it into meal— a practice horrifying to the modern epicure, who now pays large prices for it at a "fancy" grocery and boils it whole, as the perfect accompaniment to fowl or game.

The worthy father also paused to investigate a marvellous herb whose root, "very hot," with "the taste of powder when crushed between the teeth," was supposed to be a specific against snake bite—as it probably was in Canada, where poisonous serpents are practically non-existent. Snakes were said to flee the presence of anyone rubbed with this wonderful plant, and some ambitious annotator has added the information that "if two or three drops are put into a snake's mouth, it immediately dies." One wonders if anyone was ever foolish enough to pry open the mouth of a rattler or a copperhead, to try it!

Before leaving the Fox River, they made a short halt at a village of the Maskouten, or "Fire Indians." The view from the village, Père Marquette noted, "is beautiful and very picturesque, for from the eminence on which it is perched, the eye discovers on every side prairies spreading away beyond its reach, interspersed with thickets or groves of lofty trees."

Beyond this agreeable campsite, Jolliet and Marquette reached the flat, swampy watershed—a "drowned prairie," La Salle later called it—between the Fox and Wisconsin rivers, too late for the spring floods and therefore had to portage. A little earlier, they might have had the unique experience of paddling over a watershed; for here, when the streams were highest, there was a queer temporary lake, whose waters covered the divide and flowed in two directions, part going down the Fox, into the Great Lakes, and part down the Wisconsin, into the Mississippi. Jolliet and Marquette found the high water gone, but the ground still so wet that their portage was "cut up by marshes and little lakes."

They did not, however, find this portage in such bad condition as did Pierre Le Sueur, a former Jesuit donné, or lay assistant, who had become an active trader much interested in mining possibilities and who in September, 1700, found half of it "un pays tremblant"—one of those dreadful muskegs, where the traveler leaps from one sinking hummock to another, trying never to stay on any one quite long enough to be overwhelmed by mud and water.

Parts of Michigan and Wisconsin were then much more broken up by small lakes, ponds and marshes than they are today, after much artificial drainage. In this they resembled Ohio, Indiana, and Illinois.

In winter, as La Salle discovered a few years later, this could be rather a grim landscape. An early nineteenth century traveler describes how his way "led through oak openings of rolling land, called 'the Short Hills,' which I can best assimilate to a collection of enormous graves—the tombs of households, if you choose—thrown confusedly together upon a perfectly level surface; where a patch of wild meadowland, a cranberry marsh, or a bog that looked like the desolated bed of a lake, and frequently, indeed, the shallow lake itself, filled up the intervals. The huge oaks that crowned the summits of these formal mounds were the only objects that relieved the dreariness of the landscape." One might, in winter, travel thus for miles without seeing more than a raven, the deer and moose having "yarded up," the bears having hibernated, and most birds having fled southward. At other times even the winter woods might be rather lively, large flocks of snowbirds twittering among the burr-oaks, jays screaming here and there, and "packs of grouse," sometimes taking wing in the openings—probably hens and their grown broods which had not yet separated.

In spring, the season which Jolliet and Marquette wisely chose for the start of their dangerous journey, luxuriance burst out again.

A portage of only a mile and a half brought them over to the upper waters of the Wisconsin River, "very broad, with a sandy bottom, forming many shallows"—the kind of water to which the light Indian birchbark is perfectly adapted. The stream was full of "vine-clad islets" (Marquette, like all the other French explorers, however intent he might be on holy things, had already noted that "good wine could be made"), while around them lay open prairies, hills, and woodland, with practically no small game, but with "deer and moose in considerable numbers" along the stream.

The game animals were staying close to the river, as they love to do in hot weather. Even today, in the wilder Canadian woodlands, you sometimes have to stop your canoe to chase the moose away. Deer are more timorous creatures, likely to bolt at the first sight of man. But a moose, comfortable among the lily pads of a wilderness stream, is often quite fearless and reluctant to move at all. When he does at length throw back his mighty antlers and lift his great nostrils haughtily in the air, he gives the abashed intruder the impression of a proud proprietor, disturbed without warrant on his own land, but too well-bred a gentleman to make a fuss about it.

After something more than a hundred miles of easy paddling down the Wisconsin amid delightful scenery, with food to be had for the killing whenever they wanted it, Jolliet and Marquette turned into the clear, limpid main current of the upper Mississippi on June 17. The Mississippi at the mouth of the Wisconsin was, then as now, relatively small, compared to the tremendous river into which it is transformed after the Missouri and Ohio have poured in their floods. Nevertheless, the Frenchmen were delighted and impressed when, on sounding, they found a depth of ten fathoms, or sixty feet. This must have been in one of the narrow places where the whole Mississippi current is compressed into a little more than two hundred yards.

Elsewhere they found a width of about two miles, with "very high mountains" on the right (west) bank and "fine lands" on the left, with many islands. Nowhere was there any sign of humanity.

The banks of the upper and middle Mississippi were edged with sycamore, white and black oak, white and black ash, elm, gumtree, hickory, black walnut, and dogwood, the latter much larger than that of the northern states, though the trees thinned out and even disappeared in many places as one went downstream.

As they floated down the wild, silent stream, between the empty lands of Iowa and Illinois, they noted how the woodlands of the upper river were changing to prairie country, though they could not guess at the incredible richness of the future farm lands through which they were passing. A much later settler remarked of the soil around "Kekalamazoo," in Michigan, that it was "so fat that it will grease your fingers"; and as they left Michigan and Wisconsin behind, Jolliet and Marquette were coming into country more fertile still. Iowa, past which they paddled, is credited with one fourth of the Class A farm land in the whole United States. Only in a few favored areas of Europe, is there anything to match it.

"There is now almost no wood or mountain, the islands are more beautiful and covered with finer trees," noted Père Marquette. There were still deer and moose, but as yet no buffalo, along the banks, together with waterfowl—also "bustards" (probably wild geese) and "wingless swans, for they shed their plumes in this country." Their failure to find buffalo was probably accidental, for another priest going downstream in 1699 remarks that "from Chikagou to the Akanseas [Arkansas River] in the Misissipi, the bison and cows are so numerous that you cannot lack provisions if you have powder and ball." This party found bear and deer numerous and so fearless that they killed several with swords!

The travelers had seen no fish in the Wisconsin River, probably because they spent no time trying to catch them; but they soon noticed the "monstrous fish" of the Mississippi, which could not be ignored even when no one wanted to catch them. One of these, according to Marquette, "struck so violently against our canoes that I took it for a large tree about to knock us to pieces."

Most modern writers assume that this was one of the huge Mississippi catfish; but it may quite as easily have been a sturgeon, drowsing
in the sun near the surface until startled by the passing canoes when,
naturally, it bolted—a hundred pounds or so of muscle—for the safety
of deep water.

If the immense creature really was a Mississippi catfish, it is just as
well that it got away, for it took French explorers some time to realize
how formidably the American catfish was armed. Iberville, who a few
years later explored the lower reaches of the great river, remarks that
in it swam "fishes that have a sting." One of his sailors was so badly
hurt by catfish spines that the loss of his leg was feared and he was
not able to stand for two months—no doubt mainly because the
wound became infected.

Jolliet and Marquette met with less painful ichthyological surprises.
Casting their nets, the French newcomers took sturgeon and spadefish, the latter "a very extraordinary kind of fish; it resembles a trout
with this difference, that it has a larger mouth, but smaller eyes and
snout. Near the latter is a large bone, like a woman's busk, three
fingers wide, and a cubit long; the end as circular and as wide as the
hand. In leaping out of the water the weight of this often throws it
back." This was "le spatule" of the later French voyagers and *Polyodon
spatula* of Linnaeus and modern ichthyologists, which both De Soto
and Radisson had already seen. It is a rare creature today, but with
its bony shovel nose is still startling as ever to the twentieth century
fishermen who occasionally take one or two.

"A woman's busk" was the flat bone used by ladies of the time
for stays; and persons who think such a comparison unlikely to occur
to the saintly Marquette have tried to persuade themselves that this
passage must be an excerpt from Jolliet's lost journals.

Once the voyagers saw "a monster with the head of a tiger, a pointed
snout like a wild-cat's, a beard and ears erect, a grayish head and neck
all black"—obviously either a lynx or a melanic form of the ordinary
American cougar, or mountain lion, which, so long as the deer supply
held out, ranged all of the United States. It is true that the cougar
has no beard but it has the stiff bristling whiskers common to all cats.
Does not Shakespeare say "bearded like the pard"?

Indians hunting buffalo, a painting by Charles Wimar, 1861.

U. S. FOREST SERVICE

Indian paintings on a cliff at North Hegman Lake, Superior National Forest.

Farther down the Mississippi, near Natchez, what must have been the same animal was called a "spotted tiger." Even in 1810, a traveler says, "Although not numerous, yet of late years they are frequently met with."

Near modern Rock Island, Jolliet and Marquette noticed that moose and deer began to grow less frequent, while they saw more and more buffalo ("pisikous, or wild cattle") and more wild turkeys.

For one stretch of 280 miles, Jolliet and Marquette saw game every fifteen minutes.

On their left they passed the mouth of the wild Rock River, running through high, undulating land, rather sparsely wooded, named for the rocks over which its current tumbled, and with water so clear that idlers on the banks could see "the minutest object that lies upon its bottom, including pike and catfish up to 150 pounds, redhorse and perch that ranged between three feet and ten." The springs which fed it were so cold that it hurt to dip the hands in them for more than half a minute.

They had to take considerable risks in hunting buffalo on foot. "When attacked," wrote Père Marquette, "they take a man with their horns, if they can, lift him up, and then dash him on the ground, trample on him, and kill him. When you fire at them from a distance with gun or bow, you must throw yourself on the ground as soon as you fire, and hide in the grass; for, if they perceive the one who fired, they rush on him and attack." There were no horses in this part of the plains country yet and hunting buffalo on foot, with bow and arrow or clumsy muzzle-loading firearms, was very different from hunting on trained ponies with powerful rifles. A herd of four hundred seemed remarkably large to these early travelers, who had no idea how huge the western buffalo herds could be. This small herd created an amusing sensation when it was reported at Quebec, and its supposedly huge size was relayed to the royal government in Paris again and again. La Salle was equally naïve in reporting buffalo along the Illinois and Wabash, "in prodigious quantities," in numbers "greater than can be believed."

Thus far, Jolliet and Marquette had seen no Indians nor even Indian sign. Now, on the west bank, probably nearly opposite Quincy,

Illinois, they saw "footprints of men by the water-side, and a beaten path entering a beautiful prairie." Clearly there was a village somewhere inland. Leaving their men in safety in the canoes, Jolliet and Marquette themselves set out to hunt for it—a risky business since strangers, however peaceful in their intentions, were likely to be killed out of hand. By good luck they reached the first village undiscovered and approached so near that they could hear the Indians talking. Farther on they could see two other villages.

To prove their friendly attitude, they now shouted with all their might, and then stood where they were in full view—no enemy does that. Indians came rushing from the lodges. The explorers must have held their breath, for the next few minutes meant life or death. Then four old men slowly approached bearing peace-pipes. The danger was over. These were Illinois Indians, whose Algonkian dialect resembled other Algonkian languages known to Father Marquette closely enough so that he could make himself understood. As they seemed perfectly friendly, Jolliet and Marquette remained with them for a few days and then "about the end of June, at three o'clock in the afternoon," started down the river again.

They now had open prairies on their right, and precipitous rocky shores on the east bank, with forests growing on them. These woodlands were immensely picturesque. A wandering German artist describes them in the mid-nineteenth century—still much as Jolliet and Marquette had seen them—vine-hung oaks, elms, poplars, nut trees, locusts, maples, and persimmons: "What distinguishes these native forests from others is the rank growth of creepers and climbing plants and the dead trees. . . .

"As soon as the foliage is in full leaf, the mighty trunks themselves are hidden from view by rank luxuriance of creepers and twining plants.

"Interlacing with one another and intertwining about the trees these vines made a sylvan decoration the richest as well as the most graceful that one can imagine. The festoons sway with the gentlest breeze and loosen themselves from the support of the twigs. Sometimes, under a gust of wind, garlands as thick as a man's arm are detached and hang suspended from the boughs to the ground like the rope of a sail."

As the Frenchmen approached steep cliffs on the east bank, near Alton, Illinois, they "saw two monsters painted on one of these rocks, which startled us at first, and on which the boldest Indian dare not gaze long. They are as large as a calf, with horns on the head like a deer, a fearful look, red eyes, bearded like a tiger, the face somewhat like a man's, the body covered with scales, and the tail so long that it twice makes the turn of the body, passing over the head and down between the legs, and ending at last in a fish's tail. Green, red, and a kind of black, are the colors employed. On the whole, these two monsters are so well painted, that we could not believe any Indian to have been the designer, as good painters in France would find it hard to do as well; besides this, they are so high upon the rock that it is hard to get conveniently at them to paint them."

These were simply Indian rock paintings of a not unusual sort, though of more than usual size. The larger figure was about eight feet long and five feet high, while the other figure—which, by the seventeenth century had been reduced to a mere head—had probably at one time been of about the same dimensions. They commemorated the slaying, by the hero Wassatogo and his warriors, of an enormous mythological animal, half-beast, half-bird, which lived on human flesh —a legend which may have some remote kind of basis in fact, since a cave filled several feet deep with human bones was discovered far up the cliff in the latter nineteenth century.

This creature was called the Piasaw, or "man-destroying bird." It was brilliantly colored and so strong that it could carry a buffalo or a horse (this must have been a very late addition to the myth).

Whatever the reason for their being painted on the cliff, these figures were "medicine" of some kind, as are the much smaller rock paintings which still survive along the border lakes between Superior and Rainy Lake and in the Ontario forests to the north—before which I have myself seen fresh offerings lying as late as 1926.

Marquette and Jolliet had, as a matter of fact, seen only one of the numerous Indian rock paintings and rock carvings of the neighborhood. There were two sets of rock paintings not many miles away, up the neighboring Illinois river, and along the Mississippi several groups of rock carvings, especially carved prints of naked feet, which the Indians of Illinois and Missouri made very frequently. All these the explorers passed without seeing, or at least without mentioning them.

Marquette made a rough sketch, giving "pretty nearly the figure of these monsters," but his drawing has long since vanished. The historian Parkman possessed a modern copy of an old map, on which appeared a sketch of the rock paintings. This, he thought, might be a copy of Marquette's original; and on one occasion he himself made for a friend another copy—which was at best a copy of a copy of a copy of Marquette's original. Parkman's copy is now at Harvard.

The paintings interested a good many subsequent voyagers on the Mississippi, the next visitor being La Salle's assistant, Henri Joutel, who on September 2, 1687 "arriv'd at the Place where the Figure is of the pretended Monster spoken of by Father *Marquet*. That Monster consists of two scurvy Figures drawn in red, on the flat side of a Rock, about ten or twelve Foot high, which wants very much of the extraordinary Height that Relation mentions."

Father Anastase Douay, another missionary passing later, was contemptuous of the stories told of these paintings by Marquette and Jolliet: "It is said that they saw painted monsters that the boldest man would have difficulty to look at, and that there was something supernatural about them. This frightful monster is a horse painted on a rock with matachia [an Indian pigment], and some other wild beasts made by the Indians. It is said that they cannot be reached, and yet I touched them all without difficulty." Probably he passed during high water, which made it easier to scramble up the cliff; for there is no doubt that the figures were some distance above ordinary river levels. Douay's Indians, in spite of the priest's efforts to dissuade them, left offerings of tobacco "to appease the manitou"—exactly the practice that persisted in Ontario into the twentieth century.

In 1699, came a young priest from Quebec, a rather unusual missionary, as he seems not to have been a member of any order—though that made no difference to the Indians, who impartially murdered him a few years later. Traveling down the Mississippi with a group of other priests the Reverend F. J. Buisson de St. Cosme saw the monsters, for which he thought the Indians had "some veneration."

He describes the paintings as "almost effaced," but he was wrong about that. They were still clearly visible for the next century and a half, though somewhat scuffed up by bullet marks toward the end. St. Cosme was probably misled by the odd effect which a wet atmosphere had on the figures, perhaps because the rocky background changed color a little as it absorbed moisture. Old American settlers, who remembered the pictures about the middle of the nineteenth century, agreed that dampness brought out the paintings clearly, whereas very dry weather obscured them. Of the larger figure, one old man remarked: "Sometimes you could see its wings and sometimes you couldn't." This accounts for the discrepancies in some of the early descriptions. St. Cosme passed in December, when the air was probably cold and dry.

Though the Indians had left offerings to the monsters in the seventeenth century, they began firing at them with arrows and later with rifles in the eighteenth. The first mention of this is by a certain A. D. Jones, who visited the spot, examined the figures, and found "ten thousand bullet marks on the cliff."

At about the same time the artist, Henry Lewis, was floating up and down the Mississippi, making the sketches which he later combined in a "Panorama of the Mississippi." This was a single painting, so long that it had to be mounted on rollers and displayed section by section, showing mile after mile of the great river. It was the sort of "art" popular both in Europe and America until some time after the Civil War. If it had survived, this would give us an almost exact representation of the landscapes seen by Marquette and Jolliet, plus a few such extraneous features as steamboats and scattered cabins; for, in spite of settlement, the general appearance of the river had changed very slowly. Lewis, however, took his panorama to Germany where it eventually disappeared.

Luckily, he also used his pictures to provide colored illustrations for an elaborate work called *Das Illustrierte Mississippi-Thal,* published in Düsseldorf, which appeared in English in 1841. Lewis both drew and described the Piasaw monsters, which were still plainly visible, forty or fifty feet above the river on a craggy mass of bluish grey rock, rising about one hundred feet, with a single smooth face. On this, according to the text accompanying the pictures, was "emblazoned a hybridous animal, having a head resembling that of a fox, from which protrude large horns or antlers; its back is supplied with wings, and it has a long curling tail, and four feet, or rather, four huge claws. The sketch of the figure is very rough and evidently executed by no master hand."

The lasting quality of the mysterious red pigment is characteristic of similar cliff paintings in Ontario, which are usually placed on a cliff with enough overhang to give a little protection against the weather. How long those in Ontario have been there, no one really knows, but they have changed little since white men saw them about 1910. Even then they were regarded as very old by the local Ojibways—a manifest truth, since "oldest Injun say so." They are strange things to find in the wilderness today—touching relics of an ancient, vanishing faith, and a little eerie. I have left offerings before them myself.

One William Dennis, otherwise unknown, made a lively pen and ink sketch April 3, 1825, later preserved "in the old Gilham family of Madison county," the original of which survived long enough to be reproduced by the Bureau of American Ethnology.

The portion of the cliff on which the pictures were displayed was eventually quarried away by convicts of the Illinois state penitentiary. Local enthusiasts later proposed repainting the monsters on what the convicts left of the cliff, but the plan was in the end given up—which was probably just as well. When Francis Parkman passed the spot in 1867, he noted with disgust that the remaining rock walls were adorned with an advertisement for "Plantation Bitters."

Jolliet and Marquette, fortunately, could not even guess at the ultimate degradation which "outdoor advertising" would some day bring to the still unspoiled beauty of the American landscape. Chatting about the monstrous figures, as they went "sailing gently down a beautiful, still, clear water," they had not long passed the cliff of the Piasaw Bird, when they found the country beginning to change abruptly. As far as the vicinity of St. Louis, they had had high cliffs on the eastern bank with prairies and "bottom" land on the west bank. Now this was reversed. Limestone bluffs, carved by the weather into picturesque

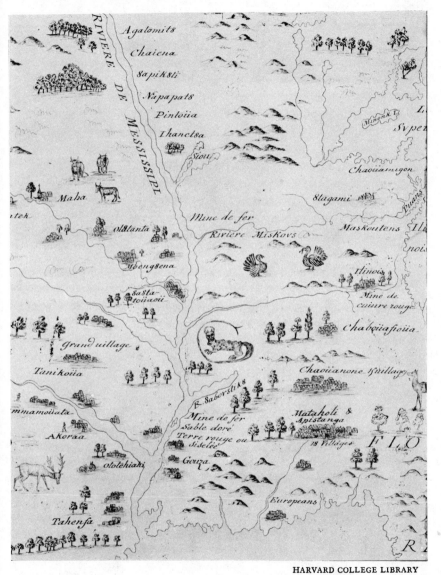

Parkman's copy of an early map of the upper Mississippi, showing the Indian cliff painting of the Piasaw monster.

Curtain Falls, on the International Boundary Canoe Route, Superior National Forest, Minnesota.

Virgin red and white pine along the shores of Boulder Bay, Boulder River and Lac la Croix, Superior National Forest, Minnesota.

Primitive Forest of white pine type near Elk Butte, Idaho.

Here the American landscape remains as it was before the pollution of the white man.

Scene in Lolo National Forest, Selway Wilderness area, Idaho.

Minnetaree village of earth-covered lodges on the Knife River, painted by George Catlin in 1848. Photo from the Smithsonian Institution.

forms, began to approach the Mississippi on the west and bottom land appeared on the eastern shore.

They now began to pass the fertile land later to be known as the "American Bottom," or "Tiwappaty Bottom"—a band of marshy, alluvial plain extending along the east bank of the Mississippi from Alton to the mouth of the Ohio. This beautiful, though monotonous, landscape was from one to eight miles wide, "an unbroken wild of timber," most of the way. Its "continuous waste of forest, with its trees kissing the very wave," masked the high bluffs behind it with a thick screen of leaves.

Many of these trees were cypresses, which began at the Ohio's mouth and grew all the way to the Gulf. "This tree," wrote a later observer, "raises a straight column from a cone-like buttress, to the height of sixty or eighty feet, and then throws out a number of horizontal branches, which interlacing those of others around, form an elevated umbrageous canopy." One observer, perhaps exaggerating, says that these trees of the primitive forest rose "one hundred feet without a limb." Sometimes the trees grew only four or five feet apart, the characteristic cypress "knees" spreading out around the trunk till it was hard to walk, especially as one could not see ahead in grass four or five feet high. "Roaring" of bullfrogs, playful squirrels, the brilliant color of tanagers and jays flitting in the branches did not quite offset the effect of the dark branches far overhead, which cut off the sun almost completely.

"Nothing is so solemn and lugubrious as a cypress grove," said a French visitor. "The darkness, the impressive silence, the profound solitude, the dangers of every step inspire the mind with religious thoughts. The depth of a cypress grove is a real poem."

Cypress grew thickly along the Mississippi until the early nineteenth century, though by that time the lumberman's axe was busy, and thousands of cypress trunks were being floated downstream to New Orleans.

Elsewhere lay the "prairie tremblante," swampy ground with a thin crust over which hunters could venture "only by going very fast and at the same time with much caution, always putting one's foot on the roots of trees and tufts of reed." Even with these precautions, the "ground" sank perceptibly at every step. It became customary to carry the rifle horizontally, so that it provided something to grip when the crust opened under one's feet to the slimy depths below.

Beautiful though it was, there was a little too much of this sort of scenery. One traveler called it simply "dull, level bottom." This was especially true where the land was simply a vast bed of rushes, growing eight feet high and standing so thick it was hard for a man to force his way through. Probably a good many of these "rushes" were the usual cane, which grew to about this height at the Ohio's mouth, while farther downstream it grew "twenty, thirty, and forty feet high in the woods, especially from the Akansea [Arkansas River]." Though Gray's *Manual,* the botanist's Bible, cautiously admits only a height of thirty feet for cane, Major Amos Stoddard also observed stalks forty feet high. Occasional streams meandered through the Bottom, making a number of lakes, "with fine high banks," which teemed with fish and in autumn were clamorous with waterfowl.

Though Father Marquette does not mention them, wild horses later roamed the American Bottom, probably attracted by the rushes, which settlers found to be useful winter fattening for their cattle. They were "sometimes seen" on the west bank about 1810.

We owe most of our descriptions of the Bottom to later travelers, who, even in the early nineteenth century, must still have seen it in almost the virgin state which Jolliet and Marquette beheld; for the country was by that time so malarial that few settlers entered it. Even the Trappist monks who, about 1805, established themselves on a Cahokia hillock, created in primitive times by the mound builders, were soon killed off by malaria, though their site was for many years known as "Monks' Mound."

Jolliet and Marquette seem to have been quite unaware that they were passing between the great prehistoric mounds of the middle western states and Missouri. From the river and through the forest they could not see many of them and would probably not have been greatly interested anyhow. Incoming American settlers traveling by land noticed them at once, and many farmers found those mounds with flat tops convenient sites for homes and farm buildings, well above

the malarial lowlands which they feared. The mound builders themselves—who seem to have been merely the ancestors of the local Indians
—had probably been gone for some centuries, though mounds were still
being built and used farther south when the Spaniards arrived.

The bluffs that here approached the Mississippi on the western side
rose to a height of one hundred feet, in those days carrying a fringe of
tall trees on their summits which made them seem still more lofty.
The branches were full of buzzards' nests, from which the great birds
wheeled out in wide circles to inspect passing craft. The rock crevices
were filled with wild flowers—three species of phlox, fireweed, trades-
cantia, and the exquisite white and yellow moccasin plants, among the
most beautiful of North American orchids, which are rarities today.
Occasional breaks in the wall of rock and forest gave enticing glimpses
of rich prairies lying farther back.

Just as this change in the landscape was beginning they heard, near
modern St. Louis, a disturbance in the waters ahead like "the noise
of a rapid into which we were about to fall." It was the violent entrance of the flooded Missouri, "the Big Muddy," or "Pekitanoui," into
the Mississippi, which from that point down is never clear again. They
had arrived at the Missouri's mouth at the time of the July floods, when
the melting snows of the Rockies at last make their full force felt
hundreds of miles away.

"I have seen nothing more frightful," wrote Father Marquette; "a
mass of large trees, entire, with branches, real floating islands came
rushing down the mouth of the river Pekitanoui, so impetuously,
that we could not, without great danger, expose ourselves to pass
across. The agitation was so great that the water was all muddy and
could not get clear." La Salle, passing a few years later, remarks that
the Mississippi was perfectly clear above that point, but below it so
full of mud as to be nearly undrinkable.

Father St. Cosme, passing in December, 1699, when the Rocky
Mountain floods were still locked up in ice and snow, noted no specially violent current where the Missouri joins the main stream; but
even in mid-winter, the big tributary was "so muddy that it spoils
the waters of the Micissipi, which down to this river are very clear."

Though they shared the same channel, the two rivers did not really mingle their waters for a great distance below the junction, the muddy Missouri waters along the west bank being clearly distinguishable from the clear waters of the upper Mississippi. "Side by side they flow on in their individual independence," wrote a nineteenth-century river-traveler, "each seeming unwilling to assimilate with the other, and striving to oust each other from the course—the clear waters of the Mississippi slightly tinged with green, glancing from their bright surface the rainbow sparkles of sunlight, more brilliant than any gems; and the Missouri, dull, stern, opaque, beautiful but in its wild grandeur." The difference is probably less noticeable nowadays, when the upper Mississippi, with its banks cleared of forests, is also somewhat silty. In 1801, water could be "drunk clear on one side, and muddy on the other," for sixty miles downstream.

Snags and floating timber are still a river problem but in the early days, long before the beneficent labors of Army Engineers in charge of rivers and harbors, they were far worse than modern Americans can imagine. The Mississippi from St. Louis down has two periods of flood—the first, or "Mississippi rise," in March and April, caused by melting snows along the river's own headwaters; then the "Missouri rise" at the end of June or early July caused by floods in mountains, where the ice breaks in April and May to rush the long way to St. Louis.

Bit by bit the waters ate at the tall clay bluffs which form the Missouri's banks, sometimes undermining a tree for years until at last it fell and was carried down the stream. The roots, weighted with sand, would sink while slowly the river nibbled away at leaves, branches and limbs. Sometimes the tree would be wholly buried in sand, to bob up again at a fatal moment for river mariners. The result was "snags," which lay completely under water, only to be discerned by the skilled eye of a river pilot, or "sawyers," which bobbed up and down in the current. When the first steamboats came to St. Louis in 1819 and after, they often had to be built with "snag chambers" forward, like the bulkhead-compartments of modern ocean-going liners, so that if a snag ripped the bow off, the steamboat would still float.

From the Missouri, Jolliet and Marquette floated peacefully downstream to the mouth of the "Ouaboukigou," or Wabash, by which they meant the Ohio. What is today called the Wabash does not, to be sure, flow directly into the Mississippi; but some Indians and many of the early French regarded the Wabash and the lower Ohio as a single river, just as others regarded the Monongahela and the Ohio.

Where the clear water of the primitive, unsullied Ohio flowed into the Mississippi, there was again, for some distance, a perceptible difference in their waters, for the muddy Missouri waters had by this point made the whole Mississippi turbid. "Where the waters of the Mississippi and Ohio mingle," said a much later traveler, "they look like putting dirty soapsuds and pure water together."

Though the Frenchmen seem to have had no hesitation about drinking the muddy Mississippi water, later voyagers were squeamish until they found that "the Mississippi water was very good water, when filtered." Generations of St. Louisans in after years drew off the muddy water and let it settle before they drank it. Eventually white men got the queer idea that the muddy Missouri water was good for them, better than clear spring water. It was said to be purgative and also a cure for "dispepsy." They valued it particularly when the water was very high and charged with a great deal of sand brought down from the upper waters, instead of mud, making it thick and white. This settled easily when the water was allowed to stand, especially if a little cornmeal was added, and it then became "comparatively clean, appearing as if it was slightly tinged with milk." The sciences of bacteriology and river control have changed all that, too.

The mouth of the Ohio swarmed with passenger pigeons and waterfowl. One traveler found here in 1810 a willow grove, forty acres in extent, so filled with roosting and nesting pigeons that it "had not only all the branches broken off, but likewise many of the middling sized saplings were bent to the ground, while the surface was literally coated over with dung and feathers." Wild geese and wild ducks were so tame that they would not take to the water, unless driven in. In two hours he killed fifteen. Wild turkeys, drinking by the river, were not in the least disturbed by a hunter only thirty yards away. Taking advantage of this fearlessness, early settlers often caught wild goslings and broods of wild turkey chicks, which they had no trouble in domesticating.

Presently the Frenchmen began to meet Indians who dressed and acted more or less like Iroquois. Though Father Marquette's journal does not identify them, it is clear that they were Tuscaroras, friends and close relatives of the Five Nations of New York who, about 150 years later, were to move to New York, join their kinsmen, and change the Five Nations into the Six Nations. Their speech, the New York Iroquois sometimes complained, had a pronounced Southern accent; but Père Marquette, no linguistic purist, was content that his knowledge of other Iroquois dialects enabled him to make it out.

These Indians were already in touch with white men. Spaniards? Or the heretic English in Virginia? They had firearms, carried their powder in glass bottles, and had other goods which they said they bought "of Europeans on the eastern side." Père Marquette noted with sorrow that he did not "see any one who seemed to have received any instruction in the faith."

Floating on down the river between Arkansas and Mississippi, they began to find both sides of the river lined with high cottonwood, elm, and "white wood" (tulip poplar), but since they could still hear buffalo bellowing, they assumed that there must be prairies behind the screen of trees. The cottonwood would one day be a favorite fuel for passing steamboats, pausing to "wood up" along the bank. They saw "quails" and killed "a little parrot with half the head red, the rest, with the neck, yellow, and the body green." This was a Carolina parroquet, a species then common, flying in flocks of about a dozen, though much larger flocks are described along the Missouri.

The beautiful Kentucky cardinal was also common along the lower Mississippi and throughout the South. The first explorers did a brisk trade in its feathers, which became popular among European milliners. Fortunately, this was a passing fad, which died out before the cardinal shared the fate of the egret, whose mating plumage was so beautiful that the whole species was nearly exterminated to provide nineteenth century belles with hats. Both species are now increasing and the cardinal, in the last thirty years, has begun to spread far north of the Mason-Dixon line.

Indians, at first hostile then friendly, told Marquette and Jolliet of a "great village called Akamsea"—generally supposed to be the same word as modern "Arkansas"—which was probably not far from the village of Guachoya where De Soto had died one hundred and thirty years earlier. The Akamsea Indians were "very courteous and liberal of what they have," but they hadn't very much in spite of the richness of the country. They dared not hunt buffalo for fear of powerful enemies—precisely the situation in which Lewis and Clark found the Shoshones a century and a half later—but they did have plenty of corn, of which in that luxuriant climate they could grow three "cropps" a year. Marquette saw "some ripe; more just sprouting, and more just in the ear." The learned father, linguist though he was, thought their language "extremely difficult, and with all my efforts, I could not succeed in pronouncing some words."

Unknown to Père Marquette, America had at that time at least thirty-five distinct linguistic families, not nearly so closely related as, let us say, English and Russian; but completely separate and without cognates of any kind, differing as completely as the Indo-European and the Semitic languages. One authority thought he found thirty in Oregon alone. It is curious that the Indians, closely related racially, as they undoubtedly were, should differ so widely in speech. But it is true that languages without a written literature change very rapidly; the isolation of distant tribes helped linguistic change; and it is probable that war and hardship, wiping out a whole generation rather frequently, speeded up the changes that go on, even in our own time, between the speech of one generation and another.

Père Marquette, skilled mainly in languages of the Algonkian and Iroquoian groups, was now encountering a new linguistic group (probably Caddoan), entirely unlike anything he had heard before. His earlier meeting with the Iroquoian Tuscaroras (if that is what they were) had been merely a bit of luck, which probaby gave him a little too much confidence in his ability to chat with Indians.

Jolliet and Marquette now took counsel together. From what the Indians told them, they knew they were approaching the Gulf coast, which was Spanish territory. They had, after all, accomplished their main purpose—to explore the Mississippi and locate its mouth. Plainly, the river emptied into the Gulf and not, as they had hoped, into the Pacific; nor, as they had feared, into Virginia waters. They also knew the jealousy of the Spaniards toward white intruders. "We risked losing the fruit of this voyage, of which we could give no information, if we should throw ourselves into the hands of the Spaniards, who would undoubtedly, at least, hold us as prisoners." There was also the chance that the Indians farther down the river, under Spanish influence, would prove hostile.

The two decided to return and, on July 17, turned back up the river, "which gave us great trouble to stem its currents." No wonder, for they were traveling in flood time and the river was probably flowing five or six miles an hour. Near Alton, Illinois, they turned off into the Illinois river, noting that they had hitherto "seen nothing like this river for the fertility of the land, its prairies, woods, wild cattle, stag, deer, wildcats, bustards [wild geese], swans, ducks, parrots [the Carolina parroquet again], and even beaver; its many little lakes and rivers." Carrying their canoes overland, they reached Lake Michigan and in September turned again into Green Bay, which they had left in June.

The entire course of the Mississippi, except the stretch above the Wisconsin's mouth, had now been traversed by white men. De Soto's men had traveled from Arkansas to the mouth. Marquette and Jolliet had traveled from the Wisconsin to Arkansas. La Salle would soon explore the lower Mississippi again, and would be murdered there; others were busy men of affairs who had no time to comment on the landscape.

Jolliet struck off at once for Quebec, carrying his journals and a map. In his eagerness to report, he tried to shoot the last rapid instead of portaging around it. His canoe overturned, all his records were lost, and he himself was saved only after he had been in the waters of the St. Lawrence four hours. He seems, however, to have left copies with Père Marquette and he immediately set down from memory the story of his voyage, though with the passage of time, these documents also have vanished.

The hardships of the voyage had been too much for Père Marquette, whose body was a good deal weaker than his determination. He started back on a mission to the Illinois Indians in November, 1674, was dangerously ill on the voyage but recovered, reached the Illinois town, preached to the Indians, and then started back for Lake Michigan once more. As they passed "the mouth of a river, with an eminence on the bank which he thought suited for his burial," he knew his hour had come, and the party went ashore.

The valiant priest confessed the men with him, promised not to forget them in heaven, wrote out a list of his own faults to be sent to his religious superior, and then told his companions to get a little rest, promising to call them when he knew he was dying. After two or three hours they heard him call and approached his bed, holding the crucifix before him. He died with his eyes fixed, not on the crucifix but just above it, smiling happily as if the last things those old dying eyes beheld on earth were not earthly at all, as if he saw some ineffable vision opening to him alone, above the great sign of his faith.

XIX

Beyond the Mississippi

As soon as the eager French had gained some knowledge of the Mississippi and had located the mouths of its great western tributaries, they realized that these rivers, flowing in from the mysterious West, must open a way through unknown lands to the Far Pacific. La Salle, evidently relying on Indians' tales, was convinced by 1681 that the Missouri was "navigable all the way for more than 1200 miles westward," and that the country between it and the Mississippi was "open and like one vast plain."

As early as 1719, when the idea of a Northwest Passage by sea began to seem an idle dream, the French explorer, Bénard La Harpe suggested that it must be possible to go up the Missouri or "Alkansas" rivers and then overland to "California"—which then meant most of the West Coast—to some natural harbor, from which trade with Asia and South America would be easy. Rivers flowing into the Pacific, beyond the mountains, he felt sure must certainly exist, though as yet no one had found any really big ones. It was the first adumbration of the great idea which almost a hundred years later induced Thomas Jefferson to send the Lewis and Clark expedition up the Missouri and down the Columbia.

The discovery of the Rocky Mountains soon showed the too sanguine Frenchmen that this was not going to be quite so easy as had been expected; but it was a long time before anyone guessed just how big "the Shining Mountains" really were and how hard it was going to be to get across them.

Nevertheless, as French colonization moved slowly along the Mississippi during the very early eighteenth century, passing voyageurs began to look, with longer and longer thoughts, up mysterious rivers, opening off to the west and offering roads to unknown lands, strange tribes, new scenes, unguessed wealth, treasure perhaps equalling that of Cortez, mines such as no man knew, honor, glory, riches, and ever the bright face of danger and the constant beckoning of far adventure.

Three great valleys began to seem the most promising as the Frenchmen, traveling up and down the Mississippi, began to know it better. About two hundred miles above the Mississippi's mouth—depending from what point you measure, for in this part of the world rivers decline to stay in one place very long—was the Red River, named from the mud that colored its water. Nearly the same distance upstream from this, was the Arkansas, variously know as the Alkansas and the Acamsea. (None of the early travelers ever understood Indian vocables in quite the same way. After all, they met various bands with variant pronunciations.)

Almost double that distance farther north, was the Missouri, whose boiling, muddy torrent, pouring into the Mississippi, no traveler could overlook—he was certain to find his canoe either snagged or overset if he did. There were other streams, too, flowing in from the west, but these were smaller. Neither they nor the innumerable sluggish bayous, full of fish, snakes, and alligators, and overhung by the thick tunnel of overarching trees with drooping Spanish moss, seemed promising.

French attempts to reach the Far West began early. Jolliet himself had realized, on his return journey, that, though the Mississippi itself offered no route to the Pacific, its great tributaries probably did. By 1686, La Salle's faithful lieutenant, Henri Tonti, coming down from Canada had established a little log fort some distance up the Arkansas River. Unknown Canadians—who, alas! left no description of what they saw—were soon searching the strange new western country beyond the Mississippi. As early as 1706, two of them were "running from village to village in the Missouri," far enough west to encounter Spaniards coming overland from Mexico and resentful at finding their

French rivals already on the plains. By 1708, other unidentified voyageurs had gone nine hundred or even perhaps 1,200 miles up the Missouri "from the sea." Even though much of their journey was on the Mississippi itself, it certainly took them far to the northwest along its still mysterious tributary.

In 1713 a slightly too clever Spanish priest, Fray Francisco Hidalgo, was yearning to get back to his earlier missionary work among the Tejas Indians. But the government of New Spain was indifferent. No explorers or missionaries were being sent to Texas. Fray Francisco, struck with a much too bright idea, decided to stir things up a bit. From Mexico he wrote secretly to the French governor of Louisiana, hinting that French traders would find a warm welcome beyond the Rio Grande. Eagerly snatching at the bait, His incautious Excellency dispatched Louis Juchereau de St. Denis, with a few Canadians, up the Red River in 1714. He went as far as an abandoned Spanish post, about 150 miles (67 leagues) below Natchitoches. Returning to the Natchez Indian villages on the Mississippi, long enough to send a report to the governor, he started back up the Red River. This time he pushed on past Natchitoches to the country of the Assinais Indians. Then taking some Indians with him, he struck off across Texas to the Spanish post and mission of San Juan Bautista on the Rio Grande.

St. Denis was a Frenchman and he had a way with him. The Spanish commander, a certain Captain Raimond, had a niece. In no time at all, St. Denis had persuaded the señorita to marry him; and to his proposal there seems to have been no objection from her uncle. Eligible *partis* were rare along the Rio Grande in those days and a French nobleman was a fine match. Sent on to Mexico City, St. Denis made friends with the governor and eventually guided a party of Spaniards back to the Indian country, married his fiancée, and returned to Mobile.

When St. Denis made the journey again in 1717, his wife's uncle felt regrettably compelled to clap him into jail as an unauthorized traveler. Taken to Mexico City, he was jailed again, but stone walls did not a prison make for that blithe spirit. St. Denis talked his way out of prison, and by February, 1719, was safely back at the French post of Natchitoches, where for several years he was in command.

The description of the territory that St. Denis and his men crossed shows that Texas was still very much as it had been in the days of Cabeza de Vaca. Moving two or three hundred miles inland, parallel to the coast across the Sabine, Trinity, and Brazos rivers, the Frenchmen found enough buffalo and other game to live on. The country itself was very much like modern Texas—prairie, alternating oak and pine forest, with some mesquite. Sometimes the woods were so thick they had trouble getting their horses through. At other times the Texas woods were open enough for easy travel.

St. Denis appears to have followed a route far enough south to escape the long narrow belt of tangled woodland known in later times as the "Cross Timbers." This ran from somewhere near the Red Fork of the Arkansas across the Red River, near the False Wachita, past the sources of the Trinity River, until it ended somewhere near the Brazos or the Colorado of Texas. It does not seem ever to have reached the Pecos River. This was "a continuous brushy strip," five to thirty miles wide, with oak, hickory, elm, and "shin-oak," a dwarf tree, beneath which the undergrowth was at places "so matted with grapevines, green-briars, etc., as to form almost impenetrable 'roughs.'"

For a long time it was an almost impenetrable barrier between the interior prairies and the Great Plains, and it was so well known to the later white settlers that it was often used as a kind of datum line, like the Greenwich meridian, from which to measure distances.

As Fray Hidalgo had foreseen, the arrival of St. Denis and his Frenchmen had much disturbed the administration in Mexico City, which now felt itself forced to do something drastic to forestall further French intrusion. By 1716 the Spaniards had new missions almost on the modern border of Louisiana, though no one seems to know whether the adroit Fray Francisco got back to his mission, as he desired.

Three French expeditions opposed the Spanish in 1719. The first was a mere squad from Natchitoches, who captured one outlying Spanish mission and scared the missionaries out of another. The second group, a band of French traders led by Clause (or Claude) du Tisné, went up the Arkansas, explored its northwest branch, reported prairies and promising forests, and discovered that the Spaniards had already filtered into the country. A third group, more traders, led by

Bénard de la Harpe, explored the middle course of the Red River, then went north to the Canadian and Arkansas valleys.

The lower reaches of the Red River were by this time well known to the French, who already had one small fort at Natchitoches. French missionaries were already at work and there were a very few scattered French settlers. Flowing as it did through a lowland of less than a hundred feet elevation, the lower Red River was sluggish, except at the occasional rapids; but navigation with pirogues was difficult because it was divided into two main channels, which were in turn broken up into innumerable small channels, among which it was not always possible to find the right one. In many places it opened into lakes. Some of the smaller channels were so covered with overarching mossy trees and other vegetation that you could hardly see the light. There are still places like that in Louisiana bayous. Snakes hanging from the branches and alligators swarming in the water added to the traveler's troubles. Occasionally he had to drag his canoe through more mud than water, and near Natchitoches navigation ceased altogether.

This was due to the "Red River Raft," an extraordinary tangle of old logs, trees, silt, leaves, and green vegetation, which permanently blocked the river for at least thirty and perhaps a hundred miles. A French report of about 1721 says the river is blocked for about ten leagues by this "embarras," but there is no doubt that in later years the raft was two or three times that length. In 1805, the Raft was "Near 50 Miles by the course of the River," its lower end being at a village called Campti, fifteen miles above Natchitoches. It was not at that time a continuous mass of timber, but blocked the stream at its innumerable bends, leaving some clear stretches of open water between them.

Underneath this crazy mass of logs, sod, and branches, gurgled the sluggish river. Above the Raft, enough soil had settled so that full-sized trees grew on it, and one could pass from bank to bank without difficulty. At some points, horsemen are said to have ridden clear across the Red River without even guessing that there was water beneath them.

The moisture made this floating "land" extremely fertile, producing a minor jungle of intertwining vegetation that locked its tangle ever more closely together year by year. Even in the nineteenth century, this part of the Red River "had more the appearance of a forest than of a river," and it is just possible that La Harpe, working his way around it, through little bayous along its edges, took it for dry land.

The Red River Raft has been compared to a great serpent, always crawling upstream and forcing the river into new lateral channels. Each year the river swept new debris against its upper end. Each year the raft lost a few logs and trees downstream. Each year, therefore, it moved a little farther up the choking river.

In prehistoric times—prehistoric, that is, by American standards, perhaps as late as 1400—the Raft is supposed to have formed for the first time near the entrance of the Red River into the Mississippi. The earliest white men found it as far north as Natchitoches, and by 1833 the gently heaving mass had—almost like a living creature—wriggled and writhed its wooden but sinuous way four hundred miles from the river's mouth. In 1828 the *Arkansas Gazette* complained: "the raft is not standing still, but it is gradually progressing upwards, like a destroying angel, spreading desolation" for as the Raft moved up the stream, it sent the water flowing out over the land around it.

By that time the new United States Government had begun to pay some attention to the problem. The Raft, forcing the river from its bed over the adjoining land, was making too much trouble for settlers and it completely blocked steamboat navigation, which was now beginning to assume importance in western commerce. The War Department ordered a survey in 1824, the Arkansas Legislature petitioned Congress for removal of the Raft in 1825, and by 1833 Captain Henry W. Shreve, of the Engineers, had cleared a channel through the tangle for seventy-one miles, which he thought was about half way. By 1838 he had cleared a channel all the way, but it closed again that same year. It was not opened again until 1873 and the obstinate Red River Raft was not wholly conquered until 1880, after approximately five hundred years of obstruction. It had probably existed ever since the Red River, abandoning its direct course into the Gulf of Mexico at Atchafalaya Bay, began flowing into the Mississippi.

There were similar obstructions in some other rivers in the flat delta country. The Chafalia outlet of the Mississippi was "completely obstructed by logs and other materials," at several points. Twenty miles of its course contained ten or twelve rafts with a total length of about nine miles, over some of which the traveler could pass at all seasons, as the "floating bridge" rose and fell with the water, but always stayed in place. Willows, some of them ten inches in diameter, covered these curious natural structures. Iberville, exploring for Louis XIV, sometimes found his way so badly blocked with wooden obstacles that he had to portage around them. One tributary was blocked for six miles and in a bayou the mass of timber was thirty feet thick.

So many snags reached the bare, grassy, treeless mouth of the Mississippi itself, that they made a bristling line several miles long—adorned with solemn, perching pelicans and snowy egrets—which led the Spaniards at one time to call the Mississippi the "River of the Palisades." These were so formidable an obstacle that Iberville, an experienced naval officer reported that the wood had turned to stone. He describes the river mouth as "barred by rocks of petrified wood, changed into black stone," a report which was scientifically all wrong, but at least gives an idea what the obstacle was like. Nearly as bad were submerged islands completely covered with dead trees or tangled masses of timber on the upstream ends. The latter, sometimes solid for a quarter mile, were later known to American rivermen as "floating islands" or "wooden islands."

La Harpe apparently coaxed his pirogues around the Red River Raft as best he could. He mentions merely "beaucoup d'embarras de bois," and "des prairies inondées," so wet there was no place to camp, through which he had to drag his canoes. It sounds as if he used the side channels into which the Raft forced some of the Red River's waters. Eventually he took a tributary stream leading north and reached a point somewhere near the watershed of the Canadian River, which he may have crossed. At any rate, he reached some point in eastern Oklahoma, the country of the "Nassonites." He found "les prairies des plus belles et des plus fertiles," with fine black earth in which grew cypress, cedar, oak, willow, ash, "plaqueminiers," with a fruit like medlars (probably persimmons), mulberries, plums, and the eternal North American grapevines, from which his men made six barrels of wine. Game included buffalo, bear, antelope, hares, rabbits, snipe, and wild turkeys.

All of this again stirred up the Spaniards, especially as La Harpe sent letters overland to their outlying posts—ostensibly friendly but showing all too clearly that the French were moving into the Red River and Arkansas River country. The Mexicans promptly sent out the Marquis de Aguayo, who re-established Spanish posts and missions in Texas, thus blocking both the French and the devil in that direction.

To see what people like La Harpe and Du Tisné were doing farther north, the Spanish governor, in June of 1720, sent out another expedition, under Don Pedro Villasur. (His signatures, by the way, show that he spelled it with an "s," not the "z" which some modern historians have favored.) With him went a force of 110 men—about forty professional soldiers, some sixty friendly Pueblos, and a few servants and "citizens." Don Pedro marched and marched—from Santa Fé through Taos and La Jicarilla to the Arkansas River, then to the Pawnee country on the upper Platte River and into the middle of Nebraska, covering part of the route which the Mallets took later. He might have returned with an interesting description of primitive North America, had he not been attacked by Indians, presumably Pawnees, who wiped his expedition out so thoroughly that only thirteen white men got home alive.

It was a bad blow to Spanish prestige among the Indian tribes. The French following up the advantage eagerly, at once sent Étienne Venyard de Bourgmont (or Bourgmond) through Missouri and into Kansas to promote trade. Bourgmont was a frontier veteran who, after making Detroit too hot to hold him, had found it wise to spend the last fifteen years or so up the Missouri among the Indians, where he acquired the added advantage of an Indian wife.

Pausing to build Fort Orleans somewhere in western Missouri, probably not very far from Kansas City, De Bourgmont went up the Kansas River to the Padoucah tribes, with whom the French were especially eager to form an alliance. Fortunately for the Spanish, eastern Indians began to fight the French about this time and De Bourgmont's promising beginning could not be followed up. A memoir of September, 1723, written before he started, shows that already the French were well informed about the Missouri, its tributaries, mineral prospects, and Indians as far up as the Arikara settlements.

From Fort Orleans, De Bourgmont started off with exploring parties in the early summer of 1724. A junior officer took a detachment by water to the Kansas and Padoucah Indians in late June. Early in July, De Bourgmont himself followed overland with eight white men, about a hundred Missouri Indians, and sixty-four Osages. He went up the Missouri to the mouth of the Kansas and some distance beyond, then struck south across country to the Kansas again, up which he went till he reached the Padoucah villages on its upper waters.

None of these explorations produced much description of the country, except for a few notes on minerals and occasional, distressingly brief descriptive touches, mostly by De Bourgmont. These show Kansas prairies still lying vast and empty, very much as Coronado had found them—"great single stretches of prairies, hillocks, depressions, with many stones, big and little." The rivers were lined with trees and there were scattered groves here and there across the prairie. The French saw some slate, or what appeared to be so, and also reddish marbly stones, thrusting two or three feet—occasionally six—through the thick prairie soil.

Though these Frenchmen never struck the really big buffalo herds, the travelers were agreeably amazed by the numbers they saw. In one day De Bourgmont passed thirty herds, each of four to five hundred animals. Rejoicing in the abundance of meat, they lived "à discrétion" on buffalo tongue, apparently without discovering the delicacy of the meat in the hump, and wasting the rest of the carcasses.

They often found "cerfs" and "bîches," which may have been deer or wapiti, sometimes in herds of two hundred at a time. There were also numerous antelopes (chevreuils). Though wild turkeys stayed close along the streams, there were great numbers of them there.

Next, between 1739 and 1742, the brothers Paul and Pierre Mallet, with a party of eight Canadians—the first recorded Santa Fé traders—went up the Missouri as far as the mouth of the Platte and then overland to Santa Fé. Returning in 1740, they had explored most of the Canadian River from the Rockies to its mouth, reporting to a some-

Indians on the move over the plains. From a water color in *Migration of the Pawnees*, by Alfred Jacob Miller.

Mount Olympus (elevation 7,915 feet) and the White Glacier in Olympic National Park, Washington.

The scenery in many of our national parks appears as unspoiled today as it appeared to the first parties of white explorers.

A view of the Yosemite National Park, California, showing El Capitan (left) rising 3,604 feet above the valley floor.

Yellowstone Canyon and the Lower Falls, where the Yellowstone River plunges 308 feet.

Canyon de Chelly National Monument, Arizona.

Buffalo Crossing the Yellowstone, painted by Charles Wimar, 1859.

what astonished French governor in New Orleans. They were immediately sent back to guide an official French party under Fabry de Bruyère, which explored along both the Arkansas and Canadian rivers well into Oklahoma before Bruyère gave up the effort to reach Santa Fé and turned back in 1742.

The original journey of the Mallet brothers was a sadly illegal undertaking. Spanish law strictly forbade foreign traders to enter Spanish territory; but His Excellency, the Viceroy of Mexico, was a long way from Santa Fé, and no one knew exactly what the Spanish domains were, anyhow. The boundaries were certainly somewhere far off in territory actually occupied by Indians, and the government in Mexico City had no way of knowing who was there. When the Mallet party reached Santa Fé, they found to their delight that the Spanish frontiersmen—like a good many other people—were far more interested in purchasing the goods they needed and in selling their own goods, than they were in strict obedience to the letter of a far-off law.

Mallet's route can be pretty well made out from the scant official notices of their journey, but unfortunately any description of the country as they saw it has to be filled in from notes by less hurried travelers of later years, though at a time when the country had still changed very little. From the Missouri River they went part way up the Platte (which they named "La Platte"), then successively across the Smoky Hill River, up the Arkansas and thence to Santa Fé. They had thus crossed the states of Nebraska, Colorado, and New Mexico.

Along the Platte they must have seen—in the words of an American dragoon who passed through the unchanging plains with a detachment in 1835—"an unbounded prairie, a broad river, with innumerable herds of buffalo grazing upon its banks, and occasionally a solitary tree standing in bold relief." Some parts of the river were "skirted with only a few small willows." One traveler thought that from Kansas to the Rockies there was, "not the arrangement of a tree to a hundred miles."

Though the country was all "open prairie, entirely destitute of trees," the landscape was full of life—"immense droves of elk, buffaloes, and white [grizzly] bears, which haunt the buffaloe range to prey upon those noble animals." The Platte was full of beaver then; but, as it was easily reached when Americans began to go up the Missouri, the country was pretty well trapped out by the early nineteenth century.

Southward was more prairie, more immense buffalo herds, deer, a gradual increase in timber, and great quantities of wild fruit in season. The wild strawberries which had delighted the first discoverers of New England and Coronado's men in Kansas were even thicker in some of this prairie country. In Iowa in 1834, Lieutenant Colonel S. W. Kearny's command rode through mile after mile of prairie "reddening with strawberries," which must have extended for some distance to the south.

As the Mallets moved over the divide btween the Platte and the Arkansas, near the headwaters of the Kansas, the country became mountainous. The "dragoon journalist" long afterward described the Colorado mountains as the Mallets must have seen them—weathered and wind-carved "in the form of an immense fortification with turrets and rock-crowned battlements, and pine trees along the covered line relieved against a clear blue sky." The passes "appeared to be guarded by large terraced watch-towers."

Approaching the timbered country, the Mallet party must have seen the same landscape that the dragoon describes: "an unbroken barren as far as the eye can reach faintly on the extreme edge may be discerned the river timber which resembles the first faint glad sight of land at sea." Buffalo here were in herds of two or three thousand, more than De Bourgmont saw; and by 1834 herds of wild horses had become common. Colonel Dodge and his First Dragoons found the Pawnee-Pict country near the Red River full of these mustangs, together with bear, deer, and buffalo. The de Bourgmont and Mallet parties do not mention wild horses, though a few precious domesticated animals were treasured by their Indian owners.

Once the first horses had broken loose from Indian raiding bands or New Mexican ranches, however, and begun to shift for themselves on the plains, their numbers increased with immense rapidity. Chance had brought the wild mustangs to an almost ideal country, with endless Elysian fields in which to pasture, where they could easily outrun their only enemies, the wolves, cougars, and grizzlies. The plains in those days were a kind of equine heaven. Never before or since have so many horses lived a life so wild, so safe, so comfortable, and so free.

Near the Red River, and probably elsewhere, the prairie was "scattered for miles in extent with small honey locust trees." These were full of "honey beans," the usual locust seed pod, which the cavalry horses much appreciated, and which were probably just as appetizing to wild horses and buffalo.

Leaving behind one of their number, who had fallen in love with a New Mexican girl and married her, the other seven of the Mallet party started back for French territory, going overland to the Canadian River (which seems to have been named for them), down which they traveled to the Mississippi, and so to New Orleans. They had thus passed through three more future states—Oklahoma, Arkansas, and Louisiana, the latter already partly settled.

The Canadian River country was unlike that through which they had journeyed westward. The American dragoon marching through in 1834, before white settlement had begun and when the country was just as the Mallets had found it, says: "At times we found ourselves in the middle of a large Prarie the surface unobstructed as far as the eye could reach, at others winding our way through rich woodlands over craggs and thro dells delightfully Romantick." At other times, says the dragoon, "we rode through several thickets composed of nettles & briers so thickly matted together—as almost to forbid a passage— our horses were so torn by them that the blood literally streamed down their legs and breasts."

Though the country was rough and dangerous, the Mallet party do not seem to have had much real difficulty, beyond losing several pack horses and the valuable trading goods they carried in crossing a swift river on their westward journey. The First Dragoons, however, made heavy going of it. When Colonel Dodge and his detachment finally reached the Pawnee-Pict country in 1834, only 190 men out of five hundred were still fit for duty. One disgusted soldier thought the Missouri-Arkansas area chiefly "remarkable for insects such as snakes, Ticks, & Cattipillars." De Bourgmont's men had suffered terribly from fever, which sounds as if from somewhere the malarial parasite had by this time entered North America.

XX

Up the Missouri

THE IMMENSE AREA drained by the Missouri River came last in the exploration of the Mississippi Valley. It was left for the new and youthful United States of America to send out Lewis and Clark, who covered the entire length of the Missouri for the first time; and then fulfilled the dreams of their predecessors by pushing westward across the Rockies, to the Pacific coast.

The French had been interested in learning more about the Missouri for a long time. As early as 1720, a Jesuit, instructed to examine future routes to the Pacific, had suggested two possibilities: One was to establish a series of trading posts among the Sioux, as bases for the overland journey. The other was to ascend the Missouri and then go on, by routes which at that time could only be guessed at, to the Pacific coast. The first scheme was plainly impossible—the worthy father just didn't know what Sioux Indians were like, though the French soon found out. The Missouri route, on the other hand, was promising.

Though De Bourgmont and one or two unknown adventurers had gone some distance up the Missouri in the first quarter of the eighteenth century, the trader, Jacques d'Eglise, is the first who left even a meagre record of what he saw there. From 1790 to 1792 d'Eglise was living among the Missouri Indians, mainly because trading along streams already known was forbidden, and he had to press into the unknown West to trade at all. Louisiana officialdom—by this time Spanish, since France had transferred her Louisiana territories to the Crown of Spain—cross-examined him carefully on his return; but

Eglise had more courage than brains: His reports were too meagre to be of much help.

As the turn of the century approached, the rhythm of exploration quickened. Eglise was soon followed by another trader, Jean Baptiste Trudeau, who in 1794–1795 went as far as the Arikara villages, near the boundary between North and South Dakota. In 1795, a certain Lecuyer, of whom little is known, led an expedition as far as Ponca Indian country, where he failed ingloriously. James Mackay, a Scot in Spanish employ, set out for the Pacific the same year, but turned back when he reached Nebraska. He was followed by John Evans, who brought home a map of the river as far as the Mandan country, which Vérendrye, coming overland, had visited long before. And as early as 1790 the American War Department secretly attempted to send a disguised officer, Lieutenant John Armstrong, a Revolutionary veteran who had joined the Regulars, to explore the "Missouri, up to its source and all its southern branches." This was so very secret that even Thomas Jefferson, the great advocate of western exploration, was never allowed to know anything about it. Armstrong and his party were to be "habited like Indians in all respects," to conceal the illicit presence of American troops in Spanish territory; but it turned out to be a quite impossible mission. Armstrong, who in the end started out alone, got no farther than St. Louis and Ste. Geneviève.

In 1802, the daring trader, James Purcel, or Pursley, worked his way upstream, fought the Kansas Indians along the Osage River, then made his way to the headwaters of the Arkansas, where he was still living in 1804.

None of these men brought back much description of the landscapes that they saw. The first traveler to leave anything of the sort was François Marie Perrin du Lac, a traveling Frenchman, who went up the Missouri in 1802, the same year as Purcel. Preceding the Lewis and Clark expedition by more than a year, Perrin du Lac had his *Voyage dans les deux Louisianes* in print a year before the American expedition returned to St. Louis. But his entire journey occupied only three months, and he turned back near the White River, about one third of the way across South Dakota. One other French trader, Régis Loisel, ascended the Missouri for a considerable distance just before Lewis and

Clark, who met him returning as they were toiling upstream; and during most of this time, Canadians must have been coming overland into the Dakotas.

We do not really know much about other white men, who went to live in the wild Missouri country a little before this time. Some—like Pierre Antoine Tabeau, David Harmon, Joseph Gravelines (whom Lewis and Clark thought "an honest discrete man"), and David Thompson—were men of character and ability. Many of them loathed the hardship, loneliness, danger, and endless days without any companionship save treacherous, greedy, and filthy Indians. They stuck it out, because it was the only way they knew to make a living, or because, like Thompson, they were fascinated by exploration.

Others, from the middle of the eighteenth century onward, were vagrants, fugitives, ne'er-do-weels, and squawmen. Indian vices did not trouble these fellows, who enjoyed them thoroughly and shared them heartily. Life might be risky on the plains, but it was easy and, for them, agreeable. There were always shelter, food, and clothing. There were no police. Squaws were complaisant and often attractive— at least, they looked attractive a thousand miles from civilization. True, they were rarely clean; but neither were these white husbands. You could have as many "wives" as you wanted. You could get rid of them easily. You could also beat them if you wanted to. Family cares—indeed, the cares of two or three families—were not in the least burdensome.

There is no record of these obscure squawmen except as they are casually mentioned by traders and explorers, who found their knowledge of Indian languages, life, and ways very useful. But there were a good many such characters, described by one uncharitable trader as "a set of worthless scoundrels, who are generally accustomed to visit those parts." There was the unsaintly old rogue with the pious name, Toussaint Charbonneau, who added a new squaw to his harem every time he got the chance, including the great-hearted Sacagawea, who took her newborn papoose with the Lewis and Clark expedition to the Pacific Coast, through all the hardships of the journey, and brought her baby back, not only alive but healthy. It was Charbonneau who, in his unsanctified old age, invented an unholy scheme for procuring

red prostitutes near the Rockies and bringing them East, for the enter-
tainment of visiting traders. About the only good things you can say
about Charbonneau are that he did know some native languages and
that he was an extraordinarily fine cook.

There was the squawman, René Jussome, feelingly characterized by
an unappreciative associate as an "old sneaking cheat."

Or there were men of undoubted ability and courage, however
drunken, brutal, and riotous upon occasion, like old Pierre Dorion,
and his son,—skilled and sturdy frontiersmen, who spent long, arduous,
and risky lives among the Sioux. There was really nothing to be said
against Dorion except that he occasionally took a club to his wife;
and after all, the lady could—and frequently did—retaliate by running
off and living in the woods.

Good or bad, all these men lived minor epics—or at least first-class
dime novels—but they are lost epics now. Most of the central figures
could not even read and write.

The first real account of the country comes from the Canadian trader,
Pierre Antoine Tabeau, who went up the Missouri in 1802 with Régis
Loisel and remained among the Indians for several years. He was already there to greet Lewis and Clark, who knew all about him and
were looking for him, when they reached the Arikara villages near the
northern boundary of South Dakota.

Tabeau's predecessors seem to have been too tired most of the time
to keep any records. Tabeau fortunately, was a highly literate individual, who—alone among the Arikaras, whom he privately despised—
found time hanging heavy on his hands, and so kept a copious journal,
which has survived in three copies: one in the Library of Congress;
another in the Coe Collection at Yale; while a third, formerly in the
Arch-Episcopal Library at Montreal, was some years ago lent to an
unknown investigator who kept it and disappeared.

But, however informative Tabeau may be, it remained for Lewis and
Clark to make the first really complete report of the Missouri country.
Since their expedition was strong enough to have no great fear of
Indians, they could go where they pleased. Clark was an experienced
map-maker, who had already been trained as a Regular Army intel-
ligence officer under Wayne. He was also skillful enough with pen

and pencil to make sketches of birds and plants, though landscapes seem to have been beyond his artistic power. Lewis had been given special scientific training for the expedition. Both officers and several of the enlisted personnel kept diaries. All of this was supplemented within the next thirty or forty years by a series of travelers and artists in search of adventure, who often lived for months at a time in trading posts on the extreme frontier. Through their writings, drawings, and paintings, we really know more about the earliest days on the Missouri than we know about any other part of the ever-advancing first frontier.

When Lewis and Clark started up the Missouri in May of 1804, pioneer days in the new American territory of Louisiana were approaching their end. St. Louis was a flourishing little town. Daniel Boone and others had brought in numerous American settlers some years before the United States acquired Louisiana. The French habitants had long been established. Settlement now stretched up the river to St. Charles, Femme Osage, and beyond. Northwest to a point beyond Bismarck, North Dakota, a few adventurous whites had penetrated.

From the Pacific coast eastward, one or two inquisitive sailors had taken small boats up the Columbia River for about a hundred miles. On the Canadian side of the boundary, Alexander Mackenzie had crossed the continent in 1793; and one or two Hudson Bay men had made some ill-recorded ventures near the Rockies. Spanish settlements in California had by this time reached a respectable age.

But between the thin fringe of half-explored or partly settled territory on the Pacific and the frontier advancing from the Mississippi was a wide unknown—represented on all maps then and for years afterward, as a great white space. Through this Lewis and Clark made their way. Past lands that later would be Missouri and Kansas, Iowa and Nebraska, North and South Dakota, they waded, splashed, paddled, poled, "cordelled," and cursed their way, until, in Montana, they left the plains behind them and approached the Rockies. They had thus crossed the various terrain compartments known to geographers as the Mississippi flood plains, the high plains, and the Missouri Plateau—which is not in Missouri at all, but in Montana and the Dakotas. Almost imperceptibly, the land had risen under them, so that when they left their boats at last they were only a short distance

Bluffs of the upper Missouri. Painted by Karl Bodmer. From *Travels in the Interior of North America* (1832-34) by Maximilian Alexander Philipp, Prinz von Wied-Neuwied.

The Great Falls of the Missouri. From *Pencil Sketches of Montana*, by A. E. Mathews, 1868.

from the Continental Divide, though they had to climb much higher before they could find a pass that would take them through the Rockies.

The thousands of miles of unknown, untouched, unspoiled, primitive country through which they passed, lay as it had lain for ages, varied as it was wild, changing as they struggled slowly up the Missouri toward the Rockies. Though the lower Missouri and its tributaries flowed through prairie country, there was a good deal of timber along their banks. Cottonwood, cedar, ash, hickory, oak, walnut, willow grew along the lower Missouri.

Often the scenery had romantic beauty. Even after the white man had come, the Petite Osage plain in Saline County, Missouri, remained "one of the most romantic and beautiful places in the State. The traveler approaches the plain over a very high point of adjoining prairie; suddenly the eye catches a distant view of the Missouri on the right, and a growth of lofty timber adjoining it about two miles wide. In front is a perfectly level, rich and beautiful plain of great extent, and diversified by small groves of distant timber, over which is a pictorial view of nearly twenty miles. On the left, it is bounded by a branch of the La Mine River which is handsomely skirted with timber."

Farther up the Missouri, many kinds of trees disappeared until there was little left but willow and dwarf cottonwood. Then, in the foothills, the characteristic Rocky Mountain forest began to appear. From about Sioux City, Iowa, onward, the trees grew smaller and smaller, though the landscape remained beautiful.

"The scenery now undergoes an entire change," wrote a voyager who passed in 1811, seven years after Lewis and Clark. "Forests are seen no more; the wooded portions of the river are composed of small cottonwood trees, whose slender and delicate growth have a much more beautiful appearance than the huge giants on the lower part of the river. The uplands look like old fields, and the bottoms are rich meadows."

Ash trees ceased almost entirely at the willow-covered mouth of Platte River, a matter of some importance for boatmen who needed new poles, oars, masts, or axe helves. At Great Falls, Montana, Lewis and Clark found nothing but cottonwood and willow—woods so soft that one man whittled out and broke thirteen new axe helves in a single day.

Many of the western rivers were almost entirely without woodland, even along the banks. The Indians kept the Platte country burned right down to the river's edge, so that there was no wood at all except on the islands. Campers had to wade or swim for their firewood. The Kansas also was "almost devoid of wood." But enough grew elsewhere to keep the Missouri full of snags and floating timber.

Thus the Lewis and Clark's chief difficulties at first were snags, collapsing banks, and "embarras." Snags were a Missouri River speciality. Many of the worst ones in the Mississippi itself had dragged hundreds of miles along the Missouri River bottom and then bumped their way slowly down the ooze at the bottom of the main stream.

For hundreds of miles the Missouri flowed between huge bluffs, at first of stone, then almost wholly of thick clay. When the mighty stream was in flood it gnawed beneath the bluffs, dragging down impartially single trees or whole woodlands at once. After settlement began, entire riverside farms sometimes vanished, an acre at a time falling in a single splash, to become merely floating mud, on its way to the Mississippi Delta.

Dragged along the bottom, banged by floating timber, scoured by sand, the water-logged tree trunks soon imbedded their heavy roots in the bottom while the jagged stumps of limbs thrust up through the water or lurked just under its surface ready to impale any river boat that happened to strike them. One of these could hold up a forty- or fifty-ton vessel.

Sometimes they swayed up and down at intervals of several minutes, rising suddenly under the bow of a boat where an instant before the smooth surface had seemed perfectly safe. General Hugh L. Scott, one of the last old soldiers of the plains, has left a vivid description of how "one of those dancing sawyers came around the bend, made when a cottonwood-tree is undermined. It comes down with the current, root first, until it strikes a bank; then, top first, the branches broken and sharp, it dances up and down with the waves like a *chevaux de frise,* ready to rip up any one who gets in front of it."

And rip them up it very frequently did. The sharp stubs would rise in the water with enough violence to smash through the bottom of any river craft. Voyagers soon learned to load their pirogues heavily at the stern and lightly at the bow, so that they could ride up on the snags easily, without too much damage. Clark had to stop the entire expedition when it had barely started, to reload each boat in this way.

Weary Missouri boatmen, going into camp for the night were sometimes appalled to find the ground giving way beneath them, while the big trees that edged the banks crashed down around them. This happened with alarming speed. "The sand began to dissolve, and every instant to diminish like the melting of snow," one early traveler noted, as he scrambled for safety. The sandbank under a Lewis and Clark camp crumbled at half past one in the morning, while everyone but the guard was sound asleep. Wakened by the sentry, they jumped for the boats, loaded them, and got away just as the bank under which their boats had been moored caved in completely, "which would Certainly have Sunk both Perogues." A trader who was already far up the Missouri as the expedition was starting, saved himself because the bank on which he was preparing to camp, "only partly and gradually crumbling away," gave him time to load his boat and escape—suffering nothing worse than damage to fifty pounds of gunpowder, which got wet. (Lewis and Clark, experienced Army men, were careful to carry their powder in sealed lead kegs, which protected the powder while sealed and could be melted down to make bullets when empty.)

Other "voyagers who had camped in a high, wooded cover," says Tabeau, "not realizing that underneath it was being undermined by the current, believed that they were quite safe at the very moment that the banks crumbled, sweeping away in their fall the trees which engulfed the cargo and the boat." Whether these luckless wights ever got home alive, Tabeau does not say. Occasionally the high earth banks collapsed on top of canoes passing under them.

The lower Missouri was edged by really big trees. The cottonwoods were several feet through, with trunks rising seventy or eighty feet before the branches began. Sometimes, as one of these giants fell, its roots remained embedded in the banks. It then became a kind of dam, catching all the debris that the river constantly swept down, floating logs, sticks, moving snags, and dead buffalo, whose carcasses sometimes floated as far as St. Louis. One party upstream counted thirty or forty of them daily.

The "embarras" was a reproduction, on a small scale, of the Red River Raft. The Missouri's current was too swift to allow anything like the miles of tangled timber in the Raft to accumulate, but the average embarras was bad enough, in spite of that. An experienced riverman once defined it as "an accumulation of trunks, roots, branches and entire trees swept away by the great rises of waters, which are caught up first near the banks and are in a short time covered with mud and sand, which finally stops them altogether. The first ones serve as a stay for others, which serve in turn for those which follow, and all by being entwined and gathered together become a solid mass and form an immovable bridge, all bristling with branches and stumps, which extends far out into the water. The water, incapable of breaking this dyke, escapes from it with extreme rapidity and is often impassable with the oar and impracticable for towing."

When the swift current rushing past the end of an embarras made it impossible to go around it, the boatmen had to cut a way through, trying to hold their craft steady in the current, chopping from its wobbly deck or climbing out on the unsteady mass of wood to swing an axe, while an occasional tree crashed down across the deck and everybody dodged. Often this had to be done in heat which compelled the crews to work half naked, while Missouri mosquitoes bit till the men were "covered with blood and swellings."

Other insects were even worse. Horseflies, gadflies, generally known as "green-heads," tormented men and horses alike. The story that they actually killed horses cannot be proved, but certainly many a poor nag reached camp dripping blood, and horses sometimes simply bolted, uncontrollable from pain. Travelers and their mounts often had to take refuge among encircling fires, or moved only at night, when the the flies were gone. Amid such troubles, nobody noticed another insect plague, the Rocky Mountain locust, though it had been working busily on the prairie vegetation for centuries. Only after agriculture began, did this bane of modern farmers become a menace. It was first reported from Fort Osage in 1820 and 1821, when the grasshoppers were "covering the whole country and eating it up."

One useful insect, the honey-bee, was just beginning to come into the country, advancing perhaps at about ten miles a year. There had been none west of the Mississippi until 1797, but by 1809 "bee trees," often with eight or ten gallons of honey in each, were found six hundred miles up the Missouri, the swarms' advances being assisted by the masses of prairie flowers and innumerable hollow cottonwoods. Collecting "wild" honey soon became a regular trade, but as the western Indians—who originally had had nothing sweeter than cornstalks—soon acquired a taste for it, the bee-hunters were frequently robbed.

The Lewis and Clark expedition, as it set out up the Missouri in May, 1804, was passing through some of the richest and most beautiful plains country in the world, which the Louisiana purchase had only a few months before added to the United States, but most of which no white man had ever seen. Settlement had already made some kinds of game scarce along the lower Missouri. There were by this time no buffalo there and the really big herds roamed inland, far up the river, in the Dakotas and Montana. Nor would the expedition encounter that terror of the plains, the grizzly bear, about which white men still knew practically nothing, until they had passed the Mandan villages just above modern Bismarck, North Dakota.

Not all the wild life had been driven away from the Missouri's lower reaches, however. The sandhill cranes, now almost gone, haunted both Mississippi and Missouri, sometimes flying so high that they could not be seen, though the harsh, grating cries of the invisible birds were loud enough to be audible even then. Pelicans flapped heavily about; a single island might lodge hundreds of them.

More beautiful were the brilliant flocks of Carolina parroquets, about the size of a dove, bright green and red in color with yellow or orange markings on the head. In the East, the birds were usually found in small flocks but here they flew in larger groups, which whirled only a few feet from travelers, "the splendid green and red of their plumage glancing in the sunshine." Settling in the brilliant winter sunlight on a bare white sycamore, their green feathers gleamed while "the many yellow heads looked like so many candles." One early settler wrote: "The sight always reminded me vividly of a kind of Christmas tree."

At first they were entirely fearless, whirling and circling in flocks within a few feet of travelers. When the flock was fired into, the survivors merely curved their necks to look down at the wounded birds flapping on the ground. The parroquets were beginning to vanish by the middle of the century, partly because settlers killed them off to protect orchard fruit. There was no other motive for hunting them, as their flesh was dark and unsavory, though fishermen found it good bait.

Wild geese and ducks were common all along the river, and in the nesting season their eggs and those of the pelicans "were found every moment on sand bars." Wild turkeys seem to have been confined to the lower Missouri, where there were a good many at this time, though later travelers found them beginning to spread upstream.

Turkeys were very tame along tributary streams like the Osage, where there were "beautiful forests full of stags and wild turkeys." The birds merely looked down from the treetops at canoes, passing down the stream near "cliffs rising high above it, with pine trees and red cedars growing in the cracks. The bald eagles soared above their tops; at the foot of these abrupt shores, pink and white mallows were reflected in the smooth mirror of the Osage River, beautifully shaded by wild vines."

There were never very many beaver on the lower Missouri. Even Daniel Boone took only sixty during a "spring hunt." Deer remained common for a long time—some early settlers even had tame ones wandering about the barnyard—but they were scarce for a long way above the Nodawa River, the bare Nebraska plains being too open. Thickets here offered little concealment and even the rushes along the river began to disappear. Deer of several species—some with fat four inches thick—became common again higher up the river. Alexander Henry tells how he heard them "whistling in every direction." "We kill whatever we wish," say the Lewis and Clark *Journals,* exulting in "fine veal and fat beef," varied with "venison and beaver tales when we wish them." The large, muscular tail of the beaver was a delicacy especially esteemed by Captain Lewis, and later by the Mountain Men, though some fussy gourmets professed to find the flavor a little too fishy. That was probably imagination for a beaver lives on bark, not fish. Major General Hugh L. Scott, a veteran of the last Indian days on the Great Plains, thought beaver tasted "like tender cold roast pork."

Almost from the start of their journey, Lewis and Clark's men could see "immense herds of Deer" on the banks; and though the expedition ate "4 deer, an Elk and a deer, or one buffaloe" every day, there was never any trouble getting fresh meat of some kind until they began to cross the Rockies.

Prairie pastures were endless and lush for the first few hundred miles upstream. In Missouri River bottoms, the grasses sometimes reached as high as the head of a man on horseback and were so thick that even a horse could hardly push through them. Growing four or five feet high, matted together and tangled with vines, these edged the Missouri for several hundred miles, "so thick and tall, that it was both painful and difficult to walk along, even at a very slow pace."

When the rushes dried out, they were kindling for prairie fires, from which a man on foot had no hope of escaping alive, unless he could get out on the river itself. There were not many rushes along the Platte River, but the prairie grass burned nearly as savagely. Lewis and Clark just missed being caught by a prairie fire on the Missouri, which swept past their camp "with great rapitidity and looked Tremendious," burning two Indians and injuring others. One little Indian boy was saved only because his mother threw a "green" buffalo hide over him with the moist skin side uppermost—a device which the novelist Cooper later took over.

When a buffalo herd was caught in the flames many were always burned to death. There are pathetic stories of scores of huge beasts staggering about on the ashen prairies, blinded, their hair singed off, their bodies scorched, slowly dying of hideous burns.

Sometimes in the autumn, immense numbers of migrating squirrels crowded into the Missouri River, just as they did in some rivers of the East. Nothing stopped them. An early settler tells how "in dense columns they pursued a beeline to their destination and allowed themselves to be deflected from their course by absolutely nothing, not even a great river as wide as the Missouri." Thousands of them died, especially if the column landed in marshy ground, where they were pressed into the mud, until at length their bodies made a bridge for those pressing on behind. Destructive to crops, these mass migrations were a menace to early farmers. When one big hunt had killed four thousand, the riflemen, weary of counting, measured the rest of their kill by the bushel. A Christmas hunt, in which thirty hunters participated, in 1832 bagged 1,200.

The animal life of the plains changed as the little band crossed the southern border of South Dakota. Lewis and Clark's pot-hunters, who ranged along the banks while the others struggled with the boats, seem to have killed their first buffalo—a day's supply of meat for the entire expedition—in Union County, South Dakota, in the extreme southeastern corner of the state. A party led by the great fur trader, Manuel Lisa, in 1811, saw their first buffalo only a little farther upstream, somewhere near the present city of Vermillion.

The buffalo herds increased in size as Lewis and Clark ascended the river, growing to numbers which, however incredible they seem, are well attested by many observers. Having no idea as yet how big a herd could be, Lewis and Clark's men were at first naïvely surprised at what they thought "great numbers." These first "gangues" must have been in fact rather small, for a day or two later they were still more surprised by seeing a mere five hundred buffalo at once—a herd not much bigger than Father Marquette had seen on the Mississippi's banks about a hundred years earlier. In the real buffalo country, a single herd might extend for twenty-five miles, and Colonel Henry Dodge, veteran plains cavalryman, tells of riding all day without reaching the end of such a mass. General Hugh L. Scott, as a young lieutenant, once sat with Benteen, the hero of the Custer massacre, on a high mountain peak giving a view of twenty miles in all directions. The experienced Benteen assured him that there were three hundred thousand buffalo to be seen below them "in one view." Veteran hunters of earlier days declared that when the weather was right, they could detect a big buffalo herd out of sight over the horizon, simply by the cloud of vapor which rose as the animals breathed.

In the mating season, bulls were engaged in combat, amid deafening bellows, all over the plains. "The males were fighting in every direction, with a fury which I have never seen paralleled, each having singled out his antagonist," wrote the English botanist Bradbury. "We judged that the number must have amounted to some thousands, and

A buffalo herd, as painted by George Catlin.

Herds of bison and elk on the upper Missouri, painted by Karl Bodmer. From *Travels in the Interior of North America* (1832-34) by Maximilian Alexander Philipp, Prinz von Wied-Neuwied.

View of the Stone Walls on the upper Missouri, from a painting by Bodmer. From *Travels in the Interior of North America.*

The Yellowstone River. From *Picturesque America*, 1872.

that there were many hundreds of these battles going on at the same time." Even a shot produced no effect on the gladiators, and "the noise occasioned by the trampling and bellowing was far beyond description." You could, in fact, hear the "dull hollow sound" five or six miles away. No wonder Clark once complained it disturbed his sleep.

Lewis described a similar scene near Great Falls, Montana: "it is now the season at which the buffaloe begin to coppelate and the bulls keep a tremendous roaring we could hear them for many miles and there are such numbers of them that there is one continual roar. our horses had not been acquainted with the buffaloe they appeared much allarmed at their appearance and bellowing. when I arrived in sight of the white-bear Islands the missouri bottoms on both sides of the river were crouded with buffaloe I sincerely beleif that there were not less than 10 thousand buffaloe within a circle of 2 miles arround that place."

Hunting, among so many animals, was so easy that most of the kill was usually wasted. Hunters took the choicest parts of the buffalo and left the rest to rot. The "fleeces" on each side of the spine, weighing perhaps a hundred pounds each, were frequently all that any one could use. These included the "hump," where the best meat was found. Sometimes the hump alone was taken, together with the tongue, an especial delicacy. The marrow bones were also much valued, both because the marrow was delicious and because the big bones could be strapped to a saddle and carried for emergency meals.

It was always simple to deliver the meat to the rest of the party traveling along the river. The hunter merely hooked it over the branch of an easily visible tree on the bank, high enough to be out of reach of the hungry gray and white wolves, a dozen of which were sometimes in sight at once, slinking on the heels of the buffalo herds. The boats, coming upstream, took it aboard as they passed, improved by this short period of hanging.

Though buffalo hunting was easy it was not very safe. Buffalo usually ran a short distance when shot, even if the wound was mortal, and might turn on the hunter. This was dangerous, especially to a man on foot or a man whose horse had thrown him. One hunter got into trouble because he caught a buffalo bull by the tail and then did not dare let him go, for fear of being trampled. Dragged over the prairie so close to the bull that his companion was afraid to shoot, he finally worked his knife out of its sheath and hamstrung the buffalo with his free hand.

As the great herds appeared, Lewis and Clark also began to see other animals typical of the new faunal region they were entering. The first prairie dog town, a small one of only four acres, created much excitement, though it was not really so remarkable as it seemed, for some prairie dog towns covered a hundred acres. Eager to have a specimen to send back to President Jefferson, sponsor of the expedition, Lewis and Clark turned out their entire force, collected all their utensils, and poured four barrels of river water down one of the holes, the result of all this turmoil being the eventual emergence of one half-strangled little animal, which they caged and sent home as a gift to the President of the United States, when a boat went downriver the following spring.

The Americans now saw for the first time the brilliant black and white western magpie, unknown in the East, which they thought "a butifull thing." They captured four, tended them in cages all winter, and sent them also back to Mr. Jefferson, who was fond of birds and habitually kept a tame mockingbird hopping about the White House.

On prairie land so smooth and grassy that it looked "like a bowling green," they now could often watch buffalo, deer, elk, antelope, bear, turkeys, ducks, and wild pigeons, all feeding at once, especially where the small oak trees provided plenty of acorn mast.

Again, there would be only "immence herds of Buffaloe, deer Elk and Antelope which we saw in every direction feeding on the hills and plains." The expedition was now encountering fairly big western buffalo herds. Three thousand at a single glance made previous "gangues" seem small.

Though the lumbering buffalo were not hard to kill, the antelope, which they called "goats," were another matter. If caught swimming, they could be killed with sticks; but on land it was very difficult to get near enough for a shot with the short range rifles of the period, since they were "extreamly shye and watchfull." Quick-eyed, with a keen sense of smell, they usually lay down to rest on the highest fold of the rolling prairie, so that they could see an approaching enemy for some distance. Then they were off, in an instant, at a gait so swift that "it appeared reather the rappid flight of birds than the motion of quadrupeds." It was some time before the white men learned the Mandan trick of building a funnel-shaped corral and driving the fleet-footed creatures through it and into a pen, where they were helpless. The Mandans could capture one hundred antelope in two days by this simple device, which was exactly the same as that Champlain had found the Hurons using to hunt deer, two hundred years before.

The men of the expedition did not care much for antelope meat if they could get fresh elk, deer, or buffalo. There never was much meat on an antelope, at best; and, if the animal had been feeding on sage-brush, what food it did provide was not very palatable.

At the Mandan villages beyond Bismarck, North Dakota, they went into camp for the winter, carefully fortified and guarded night and day by an alert sentinel, so that, in spite of threats from the Sioux, they were never attacked.

The expedition really plunged into the unknown when they left the Mandans in the spring of 1805. Beaver began to appear more frequently as they approached the Rockies, such fine ones that Lewis, examining some pelts taken by three French trappers, thought them "by far the best I have ever seen." Little hunted, the animals were bold enough here to show themselves by daylight, so that they could be shot instead of trapped.

"Coal"—actually lignite—could sometimes be seen along the river. One bed was on fire, burning with "a strong sulphurious smell" and travelers continued to find others burning for years to come. Some veins, perhaps including this one, were still burning in the twentieth century. Alkali (mostly sulphate of soda) appeared in white patches on hills, river banks and sandbars. The river dissolved enough of it to make the water unpleasant to drink and purgative in its effects. Lewis was on one occasion poisoned by the water. Near the Platte River's mouth, the water standing on the prairie in little pools was "so bitter and pungent that it seems to penetrate into the tongue, and almost to produce decortication of the mouth." Occasionally lumps of light stone, which the explorers described as pumice, came floating downstream. Indians found it very convenient for smoothing raw hides.

They were now getting into grizzly bear country. No white man, at that time, knew much about grizzly bears. The Vérendryes do not mention them. Henry Kelsey, veteran of the Hudson's Bay Company (who, as a boy, had known Radisson) had in the summer of 1691 encountered "a Bear wch is Bigger than any white Bear and is Neither White nor Black But silver hair'd like our English Rabbit." Kelsey is said to have killed two of these animals, which were certainly grizzlies.

Another Canadian, Edward Umfreville, had heard some tall tales about the "grizzle bear" in 1790 and Alexander Mackenzie, the Canadian explorer, had seen tracks in 1795, noting that the Indians showed "great apprehension of this kind of bear, which is called the grisly bear." But neither Umfreville nor Mackenzie saw the animals themselves.

All winter long, Lewis and Clark's Americans had been listening skeptically to Indian accounts of grizzly bears. They could kill a grizzly, sometimes, the Mandans said; more often the grizzlies killed them. A grizzly hunt was as dangerous as war. A necklace of the great claws was one of the highest distinctions a warrior could achieve. The Americans were not much impressed. No doubt grizzlies were hard for Indians to kill with lances, bows, arrows, and inferior rifles. It would be different when the bears faced the U.S. Army rifles of the Corps of Discovery.

They had not gone very far beyond the Mandan villages when they began to see bear tracks along the river, especially where there were dead buffalo. The footprints were larger than any of these experienced hunters had ever seen. They measured one. It was eleven inches long and seven and a half inches across. (Later explorers mention grizzly tracks fourteen inches long; but these, being in snow, may have been enlarged by melting.) Though tracks now appeared constantly, the bears themselves never showed up. The huge but invisible creatures seemed timid. Lewis himself noted in his journal that they must be "extreemly wary and shy," and the whole expedition was valorously "anxious to meet with some of these bears."

They got their wish, soon enough. Within a few days, Lewis himself, accompanied by one soldier, ran into two grizzlies; and, being overconfident, both fired at once, thus leaving themselves helpless with both rifles empty. If the bears had attacked together, both men would have been mauled to death then and there. Luckily, one of the animals fled, the other charged. Lewis ran for his life some seventy or eighty yards. Then, being badly wounded, the bear let him get away and began a series of rushes. All this was extremely dangerous, for up to a hundred yards a grizzly, big as he is, can move as fast as a horse. The two hunters skipped frantically about over the prairie, trying to keep safely away from the bear till they could pour some powder into their rifles and ram home their bullets. They finally managed to reload, fired again, and killed the beast—after which they made the humiliating discovery that this was nothing but a half-grown cub.

In spite of this experience, the whole party still remained overconfident as to their ability to deal with grizzlies: "in the hands of skillful riflemen they are by no means as formidable or dangerous as they have been represented." The next grizzly was caught on a sandbar, so that everybody could blaze away at it from the canoes in perfect safety. Nevertheless, they had to put ten bullets into the animal before they killed it—a fact on which the expedition meditated seriously while boiling the creature down to make "bear oil," apparently ignoring the quarter ton of meat.

Although grizzlies could be eaten, they were not so palatable as the black bear, tasting very much like "coarse pork." The oil, however, was valuable in cookery—"better than lard for any culinary purpose"—and when properly treated would "keep good and sweet at any season." "Bear fat," much of which must have come from grizzlies, soon came to be preferred to butter or lard in New Orleans, and hunters learned to boil it "upon sweet-bay leaves," which improved its keeping qualities. One big bear at the right season might provide thirty gallons of oil, fifteen or twenty gallons were common.

The trouble was that grizzlies were almost unkillable or, as Lewis put it, "hard to die." The muzzle-loading rifles of the early nineteenth century did not have the velocity, and hence the shocking-power, of modern express rifles. Even a shot into the heart did not stop the brutes, which sometimes ran a quarter of a mile with a bullet there. The one really vital spot, the brain, was protected by a thick covering of flesh and a thick frontal bone. Only twice did the Lewis and Clark expedition ever bring down a grizzly at a single shot. Drouillard, a professional woodsman and hunter specially selected for his skill, did it once and Clark, an expert infantryman, later duplicated his feat.

As the habits of the bear became better known, a few fearless hunters, with confidence in themselves and their weapons, made a habit of walking up and ending matters with a shot at close range. Zenas Leonard, a Pennsylvania trapper, tells of one hunter who got so close that he could thrust the muzzle of his long rifle between the snarling open jaws and huge fangs and drive a one-ounce bullet through the roof of the mouth and into the brain. At least one other hunter habitually approached the bear, confident that it would always stand upon its hind legs before attacking. He was thus able to get very close, firing only when the huge creature unconsciously gave the signal by rising. Still another reckless fellow, who had an injured left arm, made a practice of sitting down so that he could rest his rifle on the bad arm, letting the bear approach, and ending matters with a single shot—it had to be unerring and it always was—in the right place at the right moment.

Few hunters cared for these daredevil methods. However perfect the marksmanship, flintlock rifles occasionally misfired, the hunter might slip at the last moment, or the bear might do something entirely out of character. Any one of these events meant certain death.

It may be true, as some zoologists insist, that grizzlies would not have attacked unless wounded or frightened, but nobody ever waited to find out. Somebody always shot at them, and then there was trouble. Trappers on the Smoky Hill River, a tributary of the Kansas, killed "eight that made an attack on us" in a single day. Twenty men stood guard the following night; and it was well they did so, for two more bears tried to enter their camp in the darkness. Another hunter was rushed by three very young grizzly cubs, no bigger than raccoons, which "deeply bit and scratched" his legs. Perhaps they were merely playful, but that was no comfort to their victim. No wise man ever went near a bear cub. Even the young of the inoffensive black bear of the East were sometimes a danger. Being entirely fearless themselves, they would gambol up to any one passing in the woods, where-upon the mother took alarm and attacked.

Since a grizzly cannot ordinarily climb a tree with his blunt claws, imperilled hunters scrambled up the biggest one they could find. But trees were scarce in much of the grizzly country, and if they happened to have sloping trunks the bears sometimes followed, in spite of their blunt claws. Two plainsmen attacked in 1821 managed to get up one of these sloping trees, only because their mongrel bitch delayed the bear after a rifle missed fire. While the huge brute crawled up after them, one hunter coolly "sharpened" his flint and fired point-blank, while the bear gripped his companion's head in its jaws. The injured man said as he was rescued: "I am killed that I Heard my Skull brake —but We Weare Willing to beleve He Was mistaken—as He Spoke Chearfully on the Subgect till In the after noon of the second day When he began to be Restless and Some What delereous—and on examening a Hole in the upper part of His Wright temple Which We beleved only Skin deep We found the Brains Workeing out—We then Soposed that He did Heare His scull brake." He died on the third day.

No tragedy of this sort befell the Lewis and Clark party, but they had many narrow escapes. Lewis, by nature a solitary who loved wild nature, was with one companion the first to reach the Great Falls. He has left a classic description. As they approached, the country became "more roling than that we had passed," so that from the higher ground they "overlooked a most beatifull and level plain of great extent or at least 50 or sixty; in this there were infinitely more buffaloe than I had ever witnessed at a view."

Sending several men out to kill some beef, he pushed on until his ears were "saluted with the agreeable sound of a fall of water," and presently he could see "the spray arrise above the plain like a collum of smoke," now reaching high in the air, now disappearing entirely as the wind changed. Hurrying down the little hill on which he stood, he beheld the "sublimely grand specticle" of the Falls of the Missouri, which is still impressive enough even though a power dam has some-what tamed its primitive grandeur. Lewis climbed out till he reached "some rocks about 20 feet high opposite the center of the falls" and "prarallel to it," about a hundred and fifty yards downstream.

This was the kind of thing the explorer thoroughly enjoyed and he "wished for the pencil of Salvator Rosa or the pen of Thompson, that I might be enabled to give the enlightened world some just idea of this truly magnificent and sublimely grand object, which has from the commencement of time been concealed from the view of civilized man."

The Missouri at this point was about three hundred yards wide. For about a third of this distance, "a smoth even sheet of water" dropped a sheer eighty feet. The rest of the Falls were a still more thrilling sight—"the grandest sight I ever beheld," wrote Lewis. Here the river fell from about the same height but, says Lewis, a mass of projecting rocks "receives the water in it's passage down and brakes it into a perfect white foam. which assumes a thousand forms in a moment sometimes flying up in jets of sparkling foam to the height of fifteen or twenty feet and are scarcely formed before large roling bodies of the same beaten and foaming water is thrown over and conceals them." Later, in a marginal note, he decided that maybe "a Titian" might have done as well with the Falls as Salvator Rosa or James Thomson. The enlisted man with him, not in the least enraptured, reflected that there are always fish below falls and presently produced a large number of trout, sixteen to twenty-three inches in length, for supper.

In spite of the immense food supplies that game provided in country where "two good hunters could conveniently provide a regiment with provisions," there were no Indians. In five months of travel over the vast stretch from near Bismarck, North Dakota, to the foothills of the Rockies, the expedition did not see a single human being. There was not even much "Indian sign." A moccasin, a football, some old lodge poles, and a few similar traces were all they found to show they were not the sole representatives of mankind who had ever passed that way.

At last, as they approached the western edge of Montana, they began to see great smokes on the prairie. These, though they did not know it, were the signals of a Shoshone band, calling in their few scattered hunters from the buffalo plains. They found the spot where an Indian had silently watched their camp from a hillock and as silently departed.

Animal life on the plains began to change. They were amazed at "a large herd of the Bighorned anamals"—Rocky Mountain goats—which they saw moving easily about on almost perpendicular rocky cliffs. Lewis wrote: "on the fase of this clift they walked about and bounded from rock to rock with apparent unconcern where it appared to me that no quadruped could have stood, and from which had they made one false step the[y] must have been precipitated at least a 500 feet." They continued to see the Bighorn until in the higher uplands of western Montana they passed out of its range. Since these climbed too high for hunters to reach conveniently, they killed few of them; but later travelers, who killed a good many, found their flesh rather better than ordinary mutton.

In mid-summer the wild geese, "swans," "duckanmallard" (a queer old name for the mallard), and other waterfowl had not recovered from their spring moult. As their wing feathers were not fully grown, they could not fly. With them were partly grown young, which could not fly either. Mere swimming and diving were no defense against the hungry men of the expedition, who seized the chance to feast on roast fowl, including a good many caught and brought in by Lewis's big Newfoundland dog, who had already distinguished himself by catching Ohio River squirrels while swimming.

They were by this time in some of the finest beaver country in North America, where those fearless trappers, the Mountain Men, were later to reap an enormous harvest of pelts. Clark, glancing into side streams as he passed, reported "beaver dams succeeding each other in close order, and extending as far up those streams as he could discover them." In some places there were so many beaver ponds that one could hardly flounder through them all. Some of the dams were five feet high and the resulting ponds overflowed five acres. The beaver and otter were in all these tributaries and filled the mountain streams that lay ahead—as the ruthless fur companies were soon to discover.

All around them, various wild berry bushes were coming into fruit. Even here, North America was a land of small fruits, upon which the records of practically all early visitors have expatiated. The bears ate all impartially, but do not seem to have cared for the wild onions, of which Lewis gathered half a bushel, pronouncing them "white crisp and well flavored." The trees along the river were now mainly willows and cottonwoods, not always enough for firewood; and under them grew roses, honeysuckles, sumac, thorntrees, and sage. "High plains" replaced the low flat river bottoms between the stream and the mountains, now only eight to twelve miles apart—the more distant with snow-capped summits.

Presently the river took them into the "Gates of the Mountains," "the most remarkable clifts that we have yet seen," which are still called by the name the explorers gave them and which are still one of the most magnificent bits of scenery in North America, though temporarily marred by forest fires. Rising to a height of 1,200 feet, sheer from the water's edge, the perpendicular cliffs with their projecting rocks seemed ready to crash down on the boats. The whole river, compressed here to a mere 150 yards, was deep and swift. The men were just able to coax the boats through, which was fortunate, since the water was too deep for poles and for three miles there was only one small spot where a man could get foothold ashore to use the tow-rope or "cordelle." The black granite of the lower rocks changed to a lighter brown and yellow at the crests. "Every object here," wrote the melancholy Lewis, "wears a dark and gloomy aspect."

Beyond this, the Missouri broke into its "Three Forks," to which Lewis and Clark gave the names they still bear—the Madison, Gallatin, and Jefferson rivers. Though the expedition was now in the very heart of the Montana gold-mining country, no one noticed the shining specks that lay in the clear, cold water under their keels. They were too intent on pushing forward. The stream was getting swifter, narrower, colder. The Great Continental Divide lay just ahead. The early Montana winter was coming. They must push on swiftly.

The expedition was now in great danger, not from Indians but from the absence of Indians. The white men could not go much farther with their boats. It was too late in the season to turn back—the river would soon be frozen behind them. Game here was scarce. It would be almost impossible to get food if the little band now tried to "fort up" for the winter, as they had done successfully the year before amid the plenty of Dakota prairies.

Though it was only September, the weather was already getting chill, and in a few more weeks heavy snowstorms would block the

The Gates of the Mountains. From *Pencil Sketches of Montana*, by A. E. Mathews.

Helena, Montana, circa 1865. From *Pencil Sketches of Montana*, by A. E. Mathews.

Rocky Mountain passes. The only hope was to carry out their original plan—however impossible it began to seem—of getting horses from friendly Indians and making a dash for it across the Rockies before the early mountain winter set in.

The rest is familiar history. At the last moment Lewis made contact with a Shoshone band which—by what seems at first thought an impossible and miraculous coincidence—had as chief, Ca-me-âh-wait, the brother of the squaw Sacagawea. Though all the journals at this point read like a "recognition scene" in Greek tragedy, the coincidence was not so great as it seemed. Sacagawea—originally captured along the river and dragged off to the Minnetaree country and her forced marriage to old Charbonneau—had come from this country. She had been recognizing bits of familiar scenery for some time. The river literally "canalized" the advance of the expedition. Naturally, it led them straight into the heart of Sacagawea's native country, where, just as naturally, they met her kin.

The Shoshones were at this time a miserable, half-starved tribe. Their tribal enemies, the savage Blackfeet, in touch with traders to the East, were well supplied with firearms, which made them masters of the buffalo plains, while the Shoshones, living on the roof of North America, were cut off both from the eastern traders and from the traders now appearing at the mouth of the Columbia. They could, with much hardship, reach Spaniards far to the south, but the Spaniards stubbornly refused to sell them arms.

When the American expedition arrived, there were only four rifles in the entire band; and with bows and arrows it was almost impossible to kill the scarce and wary game. It took forty or fifty hunters half a day to kill two or three antelope, a negligible meat supply. When Lewis shot a deer, it was a tribal sensation, for the Shoshones had been living mainly on roots and cakes made of dried berries. Their fishing equipment was so bad that it was almost impossible to catch the trout that swarmed in the mountain streams; yet the white men, with a "bush drag"—that is, an improvised net woven of willow withes for lack of cord—took 528 "very good fish, most of them large trout" in two hours.

On the neighboring plains were tons of meat, to be had for the killing;

but the Shoshones scarcely dared visit the buffalo country, lest they be attacked by the powerful and hostile Blackfeet, who had firearms against which they could not defend themselves. At most, they ventured hastily out among the buffalo herds, killed what they could, then scurried back to their inaccessible Rocky Mountain heights, where there was safety.

When they learned from these white strangers that traders would soon be following, with supplies of arms and ammunition, they were overjoyed. The days of starvation and Blackfoot tyranny would soon be over. They would be able to defend themselves. They would hunt buffalo freely. They would eat meat. Small wonder that they supplied horses for the travelers who brought such news.

Over the Continental Divide, through the Lemhi Pass, they went, through the Bitterroot Mountains, down the Bitterroot River almost to Missoula, Montana, then up and over the terrible Lolo Trail. Horses slipped and fell. Snow turned to rain and sleet. Animals almost disappeared and even the few goats, deer, beaver, ducks, and pheasants that they saw were hard to shoot.

Up the Lolo Trail they climbed, through "high mountain countrey," covered with eight different kinds of pine, spruce, tamarack, and fir trees, many of which had fallen either from wind or fire. The side of one mountain had been burned off completely. The footing was desperate. Horses fell repeatedly. One rolled a full hundred yards. Animal life at such heights was scarce, and though they saw a few deer they killed few or none and had to eat one after another of their precious pack animals. Rocks, endless fallen timber, cold gradually "dampened the sperits of the party."

Knowing that nothing is quite so good for morale as food, Clark hurried forward with a small hunting party, hoping to send back some meat. He failed, but suddenly, "from the top of a high part of the Mountain" (probably the modern Rocky Ridge) he found himself looking down into the Clearwater Valley in Idaho, "an emence Plain and *leavel* Countrey." He camped that night without anything at all to eat, but had his reward next day as he came into the beautiful wooded valley of the Clearwater, with its thick forests, majestic hills, open valley plains, and the river itself, running so swiftly, for all its smoothness, that it makes a curious hissing sound as it flows.

Lewis' men, following after him, were eating a mixture of pheasant, wolf meat, horse meat, and crawfish gathered up in a brook. Lewis describes this as "one more hearty meal, not knowing where the next was to be found." Clark's hunters ahead, failed again, but Clark had in the meantime bought from the Indians dried fish and roots, with which he sent a man hurrying back along the trail to meet his partner.

There was a long halt to recover from the mountain crossing. Some of the men were so exhausted that they could not quite finish the march and lay by the road, till horses could be sent back for them. Lewis himself was barely able to ride a gentle horse. Game was still scarce and the Indian diet of roots and dried salmon made everybody ill.

But they had explored the entire length of the Missouri—something no man, white or Indian, had ever done—and they had crossed the Rockies. The rest of their adventure is part of the story of the Columbia River and the Pacific coast. There was a pause to recuperate. Then, enthusiastically they started off down the Clearwater to make some more history.

XXI

"The Coast"

IF YOU DISCOUNT the wild and unverified tale of early Chinese explorations of the Pacific coast—which, if they ever took place, certainly led to nothing—the first explorer, except for Indian migrants, who may have set foot on the Pacific coast was probably Hernando de Alarcón. There is a story that a Chinese explorer visited the California coast, near Monterey, about the time Hannibal was attacking Rome (217 B.C.) —and seized the occasion for tactfully praising the California climate. And there is also the story that another Chinese expedition was somewhere on the coast about the fifth century A.D. But these are dubious stories of the exploits of shadowy figures in ancient Oriental annals, obscure, unconfirmed, beyond verification, and probably misunderstood.

There is no doubt about Alarcón. He was the hopeful Spanish naval commander who tried to support Coronado's expedition overland to Kansas—by sailing up the Gulf of California and into the mouth of the Colorado River! There are plenty of sound documents for Alarcón. He did sail past the southeastern corner of the modern state of California. He certainly saw California soil, and quite likely he landed on it. Unfortunately, though Alarcón says he went ashore, he never says specifically on which side of the Colorado he went ashore. But whether he merely looked at the land that would some day be California or whether he and his men actually set foot on it, does not matter very much. His journey led to nothing, so far as California is concerned and he gives no description of what he found, if he found anything. At best, he merely touched on a corner of the state.

He was not even the first to see California, for on September 28, 1539, Francisco de Ulloa, another sailor from Mexico, had looked across from the Gulf of California and, far distant, had seen "many summits of mountains, the bases of which we could not see for the earth's curvatures." Those distant, shimmering mountaintops were certainly in what the Spaniards soon would call Alta California, the modern state.

The first real exploration, about which anybody can be sure, was by a Portuguese sea captain in the Spanish service, Juan Rodriguez Cabrillo, sent out by the Mexican government in 1542. With two small ships, a priest, such sailors as would join the risky enterprise, eight months' supply of food, and Indian interpreters, he sailed on June 27.

Of Cabrillo himself nothing is known, save that he had been both sailor and soldier for the Spanish king, a conquistador in Mexico, was possibly an expert with the crossbow, and was regarded by his superiors as "a good man and well versed in navigation"—as, indeed, his exploits proved.

Cabrillo sailed up the coast of Lower California, passing the place where the southern boundary of the United States would one day be, and reached San Diego at the end of September, 1542. Probably he arrived on September 29, for he piously named the new harbor for San Miguel, whose day it is. From San Diego, he went to Santa Catalina and then to San Pedro Bay, which must have been thickly populated by Indians, since he named it Bahia de los Fumos, because of the smoke of many campfires. Crossing Santa Monica Bay and passing Point Dume, he found another Indian town, which he called Pueblo de las Canoas, probably near Point Mugu, and anchored near a beautiful valley, observed "high, very broken sierras," and learned from the Indians of a river which did not reach the sea. Probably this was the Santa Clara, which is believed at that time simply to have ended in a bog.

Thence he went on up the coast to a point somewhere near Dos Pueblos Canyon, passing level country "with many savannahs and groves of trees," and met what must have been the Chumash Indians, friendly, dressed only in skins, and having "many towns and much food." In their lank black hair, he noted, they wore "many daggers made of flint, bone, and wood"—of which modern archeologists have since dug up a great many. Though these Indians did not themselves eat corn, they told the Spaniards that there were many cornfields inland, and Cabrillo was surprised to find them living in large houses with gable roofs, a custom by no means usual along the coast.

Apparently Cabrillo went as far north as 45°, along the Oregon coast. Like all later coastal explorers for two hundred years, these failed to see San Francisco Bay but, perhaps on the return journey, they did discover (or rediscover) Monterey. For two days in November, 1540, Cabrillo sailed about the Bay looking for a harbor, but was afraid to go ashore because of the surf. The land, he could see from his quarterdeck, was full of pines, which came down to the shore.

About this time, Cabrillo was injured in a fall, from the effects of which he died, January 3, 1543, and his pilot, Bartolomé Ferrer, or Ferrelo, taking over the command, resolutely turned back north again and sailing to what may have been the Oregon coast, found evidence that a large river was somewhere near, which may have been the Columbia; certainly did not find the Columbia itself; and finally brought his ships safely home to Mexico. Though he had little chance to write topographical descriptions, Ferrer was much impressed by what seems to have been the stretch of California coast between Point Carmel and Cape St. Martin: "the land is very high. There are mountains which seem to reach the heavens, and the sea beats on them; sailing along close to land, it appears as though they would fall on the ships. They are covered with snow to the summits"—apparently the northern part of the Santa Lucia Range.

There was not much in Ferrer's report to inspire the Mexican government with further immediate interest in the Pacific coast. Plainly there was nothing in those wild parts remotely resembling the Aztec or Inca empires, and the gold-hungry Spaniards never guessed that they had been sailing past one of the great gold fields of all time. Not until 1570 did they again concern themselves with Alta California. Even then they did no exploring but merely listened with alarm to the wild rumor that the English heretics had found the long-sought Northwest Passage, or Strait of Anian, and were raiding from the North, looting Mexico and Peru.

There is no evidence that anyone else visited California and Oregon

—certainly no one else left a record—until, in 1579, Francis Drake (not yet a knight) came sailing north through the Pacific. He had left Plymouth in 1577, crossed the Atlantic, passed through the Straits of Magellan "with its hell-darke nights and the mercyles fury of tempestuous storms," and then had sailed north along the South American and Mexican coasts, raiding as he went. His arrival was a painful surprise to the Spaniards, who, supposing themselves completely secure in a Pacific that was all their own, had taken no defensive precautions whatever. Off Peru, the astounded crew of an unarmed treasure galleon watched with disgust while Drake transferred to his own holds jewels and precious stones, thirteen or fourteen chests full of coin, eighty pounds of gold, and twenty-six tons of silver. (In the end, he brought home to England plunder worth $4,000,000.)

After Drake had stripped the galleon, he realized there was no use trying to capture any more treasure. With his little ships loaded to the gunwales, he turned northward to carry out—or at least to make decorous pretense of carrying out—one of his two assigned missions, a search for the non-existent Strait of Anian. It is perfectly plain that he was not much interested in the Strait of Anian and rather doubted its existence. Still, he had been told to look for it, and he had to have something to report.

In pursuit of orders, Drake sailed north to at least 48° if his navigation is correct,—that is, nearly to the present American-Canadian border, and on June 5, 1579, was driven by heavy weather into what may have been Chetko Bay, Oregon, almost exactly at 42°. Thence, through "thick stinking Fogs, which nothing but the Wind could remove," he drove south to 38°, just north of San Francisco. "They found the Land low and plain, with some few Hills covered with snow," and then "neither for 14 Days could they see the Sun for the Fogginess of the Air." Where they could see the coast at all, it appeared "to bee but low and reasonable plaine; every hill (whereof we saw many, but none verie high), though it were in June, and the sunne in his neerest approach unto them, being covered with snow."

If Drake had run on down the coast, he would have found the Golden Gate and San Francisco Bay; but just around Point Reyes, he spied white cliffs like those of Dover and a conveniently hard beach for heaving his vessel down and repairing her bottom.

As the *Golden Hind*'s bottom needed cleaning and repair, he careened her. While the ship's carpenters were at work, the Englishmen went a little way inland, though not far enough to discover San Francisco Bay, only about thirty miles to the south. What they recorded is very little use in finding what primitive, sixteenth century California was like. The English were more puzzled than pleased to find "the whole Countrey to bee a warren of a strange kinde of Connies." These were the California gophers, or ground squirrels, which swarmed all over the state until, in modern times, their inconveniently large numbers were reduced by poisoning. Drake's men also noted deer, but paid surprisingly little attention to the sea otters which, clad in priceless fur, disported themselves in large herds about the coast.

Because the "white banckes and cliffes, which lie toward the sea" reminded the homesick mariners of the white cliffs of Dover, they named the country New Albion, though at first the California coast did not make a very good impression. "How vnhandsome and deformed appeared the face of the earth itself!" says the author of *The World Encompass'd,* "shewing trees without leaues, and the ground without greenness in those moneths of June and July." In other words, they had arrived in the middle of a dry summer, when the brown California landscape was as different as possible from the moist green English countryside. But when Drake's men went a little way back from the coast, they changed their minds: "The inland we found to be farre different from the shoare, a goodly country, and fruitful soyle, stored with many blessings fit for the use of man."

Before he departed, Drake took formal possession of the country in the name of Queen Elizabeth. He "set up a monument of our being there, as also of her Maiesties right and title to the same, namely a plate, nailed upon a faire great poste, whereupon was ingraven her Maiesties name, the day and yeere of our arrivall there, with the free giving up of the province and people into her Maiesties hands, together with her highnesse picture and armes, in a peece of six pence of current English money under the plate."

Having inserted the sixpence—which somebody for some reason, had carried half way around the globe—Drake bore away for the Farallones Islands, where he laid in a supply of seal meat and sea birds, and thence to the Orient. He had missed San Francisco and the Golden Gate on his northward journey, and his course for the Farallones was just far enough offshore so that he now missed them for a second time. Tradition among the Indians has it that he left some pigs ashore, which multiplied rapidly and greatly astonished subsequent Spanish explorers.

Indians were soon pounding at his plate with stone axes; and there is not much doubt that the sixpence was soon picked out for the adornment of some warrior. The post rotted away and the brass plate fell to the ground. Then, one day in 1923, a San Francisco banker went fishing on the Laguna River, near Drake's Bay. While the banker fished, his chauffeur, idling about, found a dull, flat and dirty piece of metal, five by eight inches and about an eighth of an inch thick. It seemed to have lettering and the chauffeur, having nothing else to do, was curious enough to wash it off. But as he still could not read it and as his employer was not in the least interested, he tossed it in the car and left it. Finally, tired of carrying it about, he threw it down by the roadside between San Quentin and Kentfield. Here someone else must have found it, carried it a while, then thrown it away again; for when next found, the plate was some distance away.

In 1926, a resident of Oakland, picnicking near the head of San Quentin Bay, found Drake's brass plate once again; decided it was just the thing to use in repairing his automobile; put it away. Some months later, getting the plate out for use, he became curious as he noted markings on it. By great good luck, he showed it to a pupil of Professor H. E. Bolton, of the University of California, who had long been adjuring students to keep a sharp eye out for Drake's plate, which he had long hoped would sooner or later turn up.

The question now was authenticity, American historians having learned from experience, mostly sad, not to take "finds" of this sort at their face value. Practical jokers have for years been sowing North America with forged inscriptions, both on stone and metal. Since the plate, if genuine, would be one of the principal treasures of the University of California, it was finally decided that the tests had better be made in laboratories as far removed from its own as possible; and the brass was submitted to Dr. Colin G. Fink, a Columbia University electro-chemist.

Under tests of every conceivable sort, the plate "stood up" successfully. Its three-century patina was natural, just such as might, chemically speaking, have been expected from the soil in which it was found—which also was tested. Metallurgical tests showed that the metal was an Elizabethan, not a modern, alloy, containing more magnesium than modern brass. It had been hammered in the ancient way, not rolled as in a modern foundry. A fragment of plant tissue, caught in a crevice, had been there long enough to be mineralized. A 1564 sixpence, inserted in the hole, fitted.

Only certain indentations, made after the letters had been cut, were puzzling. Then someone had an idea. From an accommodating archeologist, the technicians borrowed a prehistoric stone axe, whacked a similar plate of brass—and got the same sort of markings. After that, there was no more question. This was Drake's plate and as such is proudly exhibited today in the library at Berkeley.

One extraordinary aspect of the report of Drake's visit is the description of "extreame & nipping cold" off the California coast in June and July, cold so bitter that it took six sailors to do the work of three. There are further harrowing descriptions of winds, "which brought with them such extremity and violence, when they came, that there was no dealing or resisting against them." This cannot possibly be true. It is conjectured that deliberate falsehoods were inserted in the story to satisfy Drake's backers in London, who had ordered him to search for the Strait of Anian. Judging correctly that the Strait of Anian did not exist, Drake wasted no time hunting for it. Eager to go ahead with his other mission, opening trade with the East Indies, he sailed westward across the Pacific and saw the western rim of North America no more.

The presence of the English raider in the Pacific startled the Spaniards, and when the Spanish ambassador in London began to report that Drake contemplated a second voyage, there was a sudden outbreak of interest in California. At about this time, that is, in 1584, came a new report on California from Francisco de Gali, who was the Spanish naval officer who happened to command the Manila galleon, which annually brought porcelain and silk east to Mexico. Taking a more northerly course than usual, Gali came south along the coast from near Cape Mendocino (about 39° 45′) observing "a very high and fair land with many trees, wholly without snow," but with a great many "lobos marinos," or seals. Gali had a high reputation. The archbishop who was also viceroy, Pedro de Maya, said that "in regard to cosmography and the art of navigation he could compete with the most select minds of Spain." His report therefore stirred up still more interest. He was asked to advise on a permanent settlement in California as a kind of way station for the annual galleon; but a new viceroy proved indifferent, and the matter dropped.

When in 1587, another English raider, Thomas Cavendish, showed up in the supposedly secure Pacific, capturing the galleon, *Santa Ana,* from which he made a rich haul of silks and gold, still a third viceroy took up once more the idea of ports of refuge in California, though nothing of any great importance was done about it.

In that same year, however, a sea captain from Macao, Pedro de Unamuno, sent out to look for some wholly imaginary islands, sailed along the very real coast of California from 32° to 39° and found a bay, probably Monterey, with "an infinite number of fish of various kinds," also "trees suitable for a ship's masts, and water and firewood, and many shellfish." A river near by, was "well shaded by willows and osiers of considerable size, with other and lofty trees which look like the asp" and there were "many fragrant plants, such as samomile, pennyroyal and thyme." Inland there were many well-trodden trails. It was all just about the kind of thing which the Portolá expedition would find in about the same area, two hundred years later. The alleged voyage of Juan de Fuca, if it ever took place, adds nothing to what we know of those ancient days on the coast.

A few years later, however, there was more news from California. Sebastian Rodriguez Cermenho, another Portuguese in Spanish service, commanding the Manila galleon *San Augustin,* ran far enough north to sight the California coast near Cape Mendocino at about 41°, ran along the coast—missing the Golden Gate and San Francisco Bay, like everybody else—but did round Point Reyes and find Drake's Bay once more. Here, like Drake, he went inland and was there impressed by the number of deer. Deciding to explore in more detail, he built a vessel small enough to do so, when his big galleon, driven ashore, was completely wrecked. This ended exploration. Getting his crew to Mexico in the tiny new ship that was now his only hope was hard enough. He bore away for the Farallones on a course which took him out of sight of the Golden Gate, just as Drake had done, rediscovered Monterey Bay, and in the Santa Barbara Channel met Indians who hailed his crew as "Cristianos!" Though they were now nearly home, Cermenho paused to explore a little more, visited Point Loma and San Diego Bay, and after nearly starving in Lower California, got safely home.

On board the *Santa Ana* when Cavendish seized it, had been Sebastian Vizcaino, an adventurous business man from Mexico, who watched ruefully as commodities representing a good part of his fortune vanished from the galleon's hold into that of the English pirates. Some years after this, in 1594, he went "on a discovery" to California or Lower California—a venture of which nothing further is recorded; but as he was now "of all persons in New Spain best acquainted with that coast," he tried again in 1596, this time in the Gulf of Lower California. This expedition failed, though Vizcaino came back sure that there were many pearls, "for the number of shells is very great," and the Indians "all were eaters of the oyster." Next, he tried a coastal voyage. That failed, too.

In 1602, he set out once more to find a harbor for the Manila galleons and also to find the mythical Strait of Anian, through which the Spaniards suspected the French and English were already sailing. Running up the west coast, Vizcaino examined a forest on the northwest shore of San Diego Bay, tall oaks and other trees, mingled with "some shrubs resembling rosemary, and a great variety of fragrant and wholesome plants." The California climate made an instant hit. Vizcaino's crew "were highly delighted with the mildness of the climate and the goodness of the soil." Better yet, there were "a great variety of fish, as oysters, muscles, lobsters, soles, &C. and in some of the rocks up the country were found geese, ducks, quails; rabbits and hare were also here in great numbers."

Through fog and headwinds, with many men suffering from scurvy, he fought his way as far north as Monterey Bay—"the best harbor that could be desired." Around it was "a great extent of pine forest," mingled with live oaks, white oaks, firs, willows, poplars, chestnuts, vines, roses. Game filled the country, deer "larger than cows," bear, rabbits, "flying birds," partridges. The pines were straight and smooth, "fit for masts and yards," the oaks "of a prodigious size proper for building ships." And here for the first time the Spanish noted "a large shell fish with conques equal to the finest mother of pearl." This was the abalone. It was to be some centuries before anyone discovered the merits of that uniquely Californian delicacy, abalone "steaks."

Vizcaino went on north to Cape Mendocino—missing San Francisco Bay—and then, with his ship badly battered, decided to return. It was his last adventure on the California coast.

Not till the second half of the eighteenth century did the Spaniards begin serious land exploration in California with a view to permanent occupation. The missionary priest, Father Kino, had, it is true, crossed the southeastern corner of the state on his way to Arizona and New Mexico in 1701, but he had not paused to establish missions. In the meantime, the Spaniards had found plenty to do in the provinces they already held; but now there were rumors that the Russians were commencing to push dangerously far south from Alaska. Then too, the English heretics still claimed New Albion as a result of Drake's exploration and—whether the Spaniards knew it or not—would soon be exploring again where Drake had sailed almost two hundred years before.

In 1769, a newly appointed governor of California, Gaspar de Portolá, took command of three separate parties which were sent out, one by sea and two by land, to meet at San Diego. The advance guard went overland under command of Captain Fernando Rivera, an officer of the royal forces in Mexico, with the devoted missionary, Father Juan Crespi, a Franciscan who had been born in the Mediterranean island of Mallorca. They were soon followed by the main body led by Portolá himself, with the famous California missionary, Father Junipero Serra. Portolá's soldiers were to set up garrisons at San Diego and Monterey, while the priests established missions under the general direction of

Father Serra. The ships were to carry part of the colony and the heavier equipment.

The first overland party started March 24, 1769, reaching San Diego May 13, to find the two ships at anchor and waiting for them. Portolá and Serra set out from Mexico on May 14, just one day after Rivera and Crespi arrived at San Diego.

Thanks to several indefatigable diarists, we know a good deal about what these first land adventurers saw in primitive California. The country around San Diego harbor was "a large level place in the midst of great meadows and plains," with so few trees that the firewood for the explorers had to come mostly from the mountains. The San Diego River, however, had banks covered with willows, alders, poplars, and cottonwoods, and overgrown, like all the rest of the country, with "very fragrant roses," while the eternal wild grapevines covered the plains. Like other wild California meadows, these were "thickly dotted with shrubs"; and the explorers were pleased to find the soil wholly without stones.

The San Diego, like most of the California rivers, was a dream of beauty, perhaps not quite so lovely as some others. The Sacramento, says a later explorer, was "like a park, because of the verdure and luxuriance of its groves of trees," though the San Joaquin was miry, with "nothing but tule, without a tree." The whole country through which they had now passed was wooded, except the coast meadows and marshy places where the tule reed dominated. The meadows offered good pasture, an important matter for horsemen, and the stream banks were covered with water cress. Few Indians were to be seen, but well-trodden paths showed their presence, as earlier sea explorers had already noted in hasty trips ashore.

California meadows such as the first explorers saw have now been much changed by the introduction of cattle, which wiped out many of the native bunch grasses, and by overgrazing produced a good deal of erosion. After Spanish settlement began such European weeds as black mustard, wild oat, and filaree, began to take over the landscape of the coastal hills. Later still the '49-ers and the introduction of hydraulic mining turned streams from their beds, piled up mounds of stone wherever they needed them, and created terrific scars on the landscape; but in the intervening century Nature has smoothed over most of the damage that they did. Sheep-grazing later damaged the flowered and beautiful mountain meadows, but even here Nature has repaired the ravages of man. Lumbering destroyed many of the groves of redwoods, but many of them still rise into the sky, proudly as of old; and even at their worst, California lumbermen never created such wreckage and deforestation as the worst of their eastern brethren.

As soon as the whole force had been assembled at San Diego, Portolá himself led a small group to find Monterey. Following the coast as far as modern Los Angeles, they went up the San Fernando Valley, back to the sea again, down the Santa Clara Valley, north along the coast, then a little way inland to San Luis Obispo, once more to the sea, along the coast, over the Sierra Santa Lucia down the Salines Valley, and again along the coast to the vicinity of San Francisco, a journey through rich country. There were herds of antelope, many rabbits, flocks of migrant wild geese and ducks, settling down for the winter in the mild climate. "It was impossible to estimate the number of flocks of these birds," says one diarist. Captain Juan Bautista Anza, who opened the permanent land route to California, found San Jacinto Lake "as full of white geese as of water." There were so many that "it looked like a large, white grove." Today both the lake and the geese have vanished from the San Jacinto Valley. Wild geese were easy to kill—one Spaniard brought down nine with three shots. "Pleasant and affable heathen," bobbing around in the streams on rafts of bundled reeds, hunted wild ducks and geese, sometimes using stuffed geese as decoys.

Occasionally, along their route, a strange black liquid trickled out of the earth. From time to time, there were "large swamps of a certain material like pitch which was bubbling up." They could see that the stuff was oily and they called it "bitumen," interested to see that it flowed "amid the water of the streams without commingling with it or giving it a bad flavor." The Indians, they found, used the queer substance for calking boats and water vessels, but it seemed of little importance or value otherwise.

It was an arduous rather than a dangerous adventure. The going was hard. Though trails ran in every direction, they were at best mere footpaths which no horse had ever trodden. An advance party of Spaniards and Indians had to ply spades, picks, axes, and crowbars mightily to get a way open for the pack train. The horses were nervous at every strange sight and smell. A coyote, fox, bird, even a whirl of dust was enough to set them stampeding through the woods, falling over precipices, laming or otherwise injuring themselves, "defying human effort to restrain them." The travelers killed some antelope and bears, heard mountain lions, were disturbed by earthquakes (on one alarming occasion, nine in five days), and were shocked to find some of the Indians, though friendly, *totalmente desnudos*. But roses were with them all the way—sometimes "an infinity of rosebushes in full bloom"; and there were fine woods, springs, rivers, "fragrant wild rosemary" and "other shrubs not known to us," various grass seeds which the Indians used as grain and which, when roasted, "tasted like almonds," not to mention "an abundance of wild fruit of the cocoba" all along the way. Indians, adept in the use of their bone-pointed reed spears, brought in fish and piled them up—sometimes dried, sometimes "both fresh and roasted, so large that we had to tell them not to bring us any more, because they would be spoiled." The coastal Indians practiced little or no agriculture. Why trouble? Nature gave them all they needed.

Various Spanish explorers a few years later sometimes found themselves surrounded by perfume as they rode along. One priest mentions the fragrance of ambergris, which came and went several times, especially between San Louis Obispo and Monterey, sometimes very strong, then barely perceptible, then vanishing altogether, with no air stirring. Repeatedly he dismounted to sniff the wild flowers. They were fragrant enough but never did he find "a scent like that or so sweet." It must, he thought, be ambergris washed up along the coast or "some sweet vapor which the land gives forth." Nor were others able to explain what produced "so marvellous and so fragrant an effect."

From the moment of their arrival at San Diego, the Spanish had been delighted by sturgeon and sole "of delicate taste," and weighing fifteen to twenty pounds—all very well for flounders, though eastern explorers would have thought the sturgeon very small. You could catch all the bonito you wanted. Sardines ran as thickly as in the Mediterranean and there were shell fish for anyone who wished to gather them, though the Pacific oyster was very small and not all Spaniards liked its flavor. There were doves, quail, larks, thrushes, cardinal birds, hummingbirds, daws, crows, and hawks, besides the omnipresent waterfowl.

Indians brought trays of seeds, acorns, pine-nuts. Other Indians gave them "sweet preserve like little raisins" and a strange sweet "made of the dew which sticks to the reed grass"—apparently the exudation of aphids, known to modern schoolboys as "honeydew." One officer describes this as "a kind of sweet paste and sugar, which is not unworthy of the name." He also admired the Indians' skill in utilizing "vegetables which in themselves do not look very promising." They made, for instance, a good *atole,* or gruel, from cattail reeds and palatable bread from cattail roots. Roast *mescale,* or century plant, was another local delicacy.

The Spaniards saw "troops of bears," or their traces all the way along the route from San Diego northward. Sometimes the creatures had torn the earth, leaving it "plowed up and full of the holes which they make in searching for the roots they live on." Like the eastern Indians, those in California sometimes caught young bear cubs and fattened them for slaughter.

San Francisco Bay, which everyone had missed for more than two hundred years, was discovered at last—quite by accident. A party of soldiers, chasing a deer, reached the crest over which the animal had disappeared and came suddenly upon a great inland sea at their feet, blue waters stretching away into hills which sheltered distant bays, the extent of which they could only guess at. The simple soldiers left no description of San Francisco at the moment when the white man came, but their superiors did:

"The land surrounding this immense base offers, when seen from the sea, a very pleasing view. For, looking south, one sees the Sierra de Santa Lucia, sending out its foothills which grow lower as they approach the shore and whose ridges, crowned with pines and covered with pasturage, form a magnificent amphitheatre. Its beauty is enhanced by the verdure of the different canyons which intersect the country, presenting an admirable variety and harmony to the eye."

More thorough exploration a few years later tells what they saw. Much of the country around the Golden Gate was forested with laurel, ash, oaks, live oaks, and redwoods—full of bears, deer and elk—with some stretches of sand, marsh or green flats near the shore. Whales were spouting. Sea otter, with priceless pelts, and sea lions played among the rocks. Far down San Francisco Bay stood the tall redwood from which modern Palo Alto takes its name. As redwoods go, it was not a very tall tree—a mere 140 or 150 feet; but it stood out so clearly, "rising like a great tower," that two Spanish parties paused to measure it. The tree still stands, having in the intervening 175 years added at most a few feet.

The beach of San Francisco Bay was "not clean, but muddy, miry and full of sloughs," while San Pablo Bay, to the north seemed to have cleaner beaches. The tableland where today the Presidio stands was "very green and flower-covered, with an abundance of violets." Looking out from this, a missionary priest reflected: "If it could be well settled like Europe there would not be any thing more beautiful in all the world, for it has the best advantages for founding in it a most beautiful city." Indians fished or gathered mussels—piling their empty shells about their villages—or collected grasses, herbs, and roots. There was a curse of "long-billed mosquitoes."

The Oakland side of the bay was a mingling of open country, forest and small pools with small Indian villages and a thick growth of iris and other plants with edible roots, and just as full of bears as the western shore, with occasional large herds of elk. Suisim and Honker Bays, into which the Sacramento River pours a flood of fresh water, puzzled the first Spaniards, who at first mistook them for one huge river. Beyond modern Antioch was the tule marsh which still blocks the way and one could look off northeast across "a level plain of immeasurable extent" to the mountains, "white from the summit to the skirts." To the west lay another "immense plain," which was actually the lower Sacramento Valley.

Pushing north around San Francisco Bay, the earliest Spanish explorers came, on October 10, 1769, to their first sight of one of the great wonders of the western world—"some tall trees of reddish-colored wood of a species unknown to us, having leaves very unlike those of the Cedar, and without a cedar odor; and as we knew not the names of the trees, we gave them that of the color of the wood, *palo colorado"* —and so in the twentieth century they are "redwoods."

They were an astonishing spectacle. Sailors looking landward had often noticed tall timber; but from a mile or two offshore, an extra hundred feet or so of height makes very little difference, so that no one had any real idea how very big the big trees were. For the first time, white men realized their hugeness. Miguel Costanso, the engineer of the expedition, with the usual engineer's passion for figures, describes them as four to five yards in diameter, with wood "of a dull, dark, reddish color, very softly brittle, and full of knots."

"Eight men all holding hands could not span one of them," wrote another officer. A late Spanish explorer, passing a heavy grove of redwoods below San Francisco, near Watsonville (where there are none today), amused his comrades by riding his horse into a cavity in one of them, exclaiming: "Now I have a house in case it rains."

Presumably these were specimens of *Sequoia sempervirens,* which ranged naturally from the coastal canyons below Monterey as far north as Oregon. Costanso's measurements do not indicate particularly big specimens, for the sequoias were often five to seven, occasionally eight, yards in diameter, many being two hundred feet high and some running well over three hundred. The Spaniards may have been observing another species of the same genus, *Sequoia gigantea,* which does not grow in continuous belts but stands in isolated groves between the American River and the Tule. It would have stirred the good Father Crespi's sincerely pious heart, had he guessed that the great and ancient trees beneath which he stood had been standing in the time of Christ.

The trouble was that, as Portolá and his men pushed some miles north of San Francisco, they began to find landmarks which, though they had never seen them, they could recognize from mariners' descriptions. There was no doubt about Point Reyes and Drake's Bay. Their white cliffs and sands had long been familiar to Spanish sailors. Now, for the first time, they realized that they had missed Monterey Bay entirely and were far north of the place they had set out to find. Having passed Monterey Bay without recognizing it on their northward journey, they managed to do the same thing on the way back to San Diego—though they paused to erect a cross on its very shores!

They were safely back in San Diego January 24, 1770, after a blunder not quite so great as it appears. Finding the bay from the sea was one thing. Finding it from the shore side in the luxuriant primitive wilderness that then was California, was quite another. Besides, they had been led to expect a protected harbor, not an open bay. They consoled themselves by doubting whether there was such a bay at all. "The illusion that Monterey exists has been dispelled," wrote Portolá.

But he tried again, more successfully, a few months later; and by May was safely camped there, again admiring the Sierra Santa Lucia, full of deer and antelope, "whose ridges, crowned with pine and covered with pastures, form a magnificent amphitheatre," the beauty of the mountains enhanced by the verdure of canyons intersecting here and there, the brilliant green oak, pine, juniper, cypress, tall reeds, and grass which in some places "would entirely cover a man on horseback, proof of the fertility of the soil." He built a fort and prepared to defend California "from the atrocities of the Russians, who were about to invade us."

Once the Portolá expedition had opened the way overland and garrisons and missions had been established, it was time for further exploration. The very next year (1770), Pedro Fages—a Catalan soldier who had shared Portolá's adventures and who was later also to become governor of the Californias—led a party from Monterey to the Santa Clara Valley, which seems to have been a beautiful, if dampish, blend of forest and reedy marsh, with occasional Indian villages, herds of fifty antelope at a time, and the inevitable waterfowl everywhere. Fages went downstream to San Francisco Bay and thence along its eastern shore nearly to Alameda. Before turning back they climbed a hill and so caught a glimpse of the north arm of the bay.

In March of 1772, Fages took out another exploring party, to make a more thorough exploration of San Francisco Bay. Not until 1775, however, did the first ship pass through the Golden Gate. Fages and his party were the first white men in the Sacramento and San Joaquin valleys.

Other Spanish exploration swiftly followed and missions began to develop in California; but since the missionaries who built them were more intent on saving souls than on describing the country that they found, their letters and diaries add little to the picture of the country given by the first arrivals.

Though the Spaniards had sailed along the coasts of Oregon, Washington, and Canada, they had done little more. In the meantime, Russian explorers, working separately, Vitus Bering and Alexei Cherikov, had reached the northern coast of North America by 1741, and Bering may have come as far south as 46°. Characteristic Russian secrecy kept news of their discoveries from reaching Europe promptly. But the return of Bering's crew, after his death on his second voyage, with one thousand otter skins and news of the breeding grounds, started a wild craze for the fur trade. By 1750, the Muscovites were pouring so many furs into China that other nations woke to the opportunity.

Though the forests of the Pacific coast provided furs of almost every kind, the great prize was the sea otter, found nowhere else in the world. Herds of several hundreds at a time splashed about from Kamchatka to Alaska and all the way down the American coast to Lower California. The animals were about four and a half feet long, with a loosely folded skin that could be stretched to a full six feet. They haunted the thick beds of kelp near reefs and rocky islands. The Pacific kelp formed a kind of submarine jungle in which the animals were safe from their only enemies—sea lions, sharks, and killer whales. Said to be able to swim under water for a mile at a time, they lived almost entirely in the water, almost fearless of man. The Indians had always killed a few; but as late as 1803 the otters were still tame enough to allow boats to come very close before they dived. After the white man had begun his ruthless killing, they grew so alert that they were believed to flee from smoke or human scent several miles down wind. Like all otters, they were playful, juggling bits of seaweed as they lay on their backs in the water, or playing with their pups, which paddled about in the water with their mothers, "when no larger than rats."

John R. Jewett, a sailor captured and enslaved by the Indians about 1803, wrote after he had been rescued: "Nothing can be more beautiful than one of these animals when seen swimming, especially when on the lookout for any object. At such times it raises its head quite above the surface, and the contrast between the shining black and the white, together with the sharp ears and a long tuft of hair rising from the middle of its forehead, which look like three small horns, render it quite a novel and attractive object."

The pelt was jet black—"shining silky black," says Jewett—except for white markings on the head, an exquisite, thick, soft fur, making a perfect accompaniment to the silk garments of the luxury-loving Chinese upper classes. The fine close fur of the stubby tail was an especially valuable bit, often sold separately.

Relentless hunting soon practically exterminated the animals, though in the 1920's an occasional pelt, was sold, with dubious legality, for $2,400. Protected by international treaty after 1911, however, the almost extinct species began to increase so rapidly that by 1936 it was estimated there were one or two thousand in American waters. In 1938 a small herd, the first in a century, appeared at Carmel, California, where they have been ever since; and it is believed that there are now (1950) about 12,500. Like the buffalo, the sea otter is now probably safe from extinction.

But at the end of the eighteenth century, the possible extinction of a beautiful and interesting species troubled the Pacific traders not a whit. They simply rushed in where there was a chance for profits, and the profits were enormous. A single cargo might be worth a million dollars. One guileless Indian tribe traded $8,000 worth of furs for an old chisel. Discovering the eagerness of the Indians for one-inch chisels, and blue beads (in preference to beads of all other colors), the traders made them standard mediums of exchange, at great advantage to themselves.

Governments began to take an interest in country like this. England had a vague claim to New Albion, based on Drake's original discovery. While the American Revolution was still being fought out, Captain James Cook, with two ships, put out for a journey round the world, which was to include the west coast of the United States.

Since both the Russians and the Spaniards kept what they knew to themselves, this region was still a good deal of a mystery to the rest of the world. In this purely British exploration, the rebellious colonies had a very small share. In view of the exclusively scientific object of Cook's voyage, American men-of-war were ordered not to molest him; and among Cook's marines was the Connecticut Yankee, John Ledyard, whom Thomas Jefferson was later to encourage in an unsuccessful effort to explore the unknown lands between the Mississippi and the coast.

Cook raised the coast of North America at 44° 30′, on March 6, 1778, and moved southward as far as 43° 30′ (Cape Gregory), standing on and off the coast in the hope of finding a harbor. He was nervous about rocks, and what he could see of the land, as when he approached it in tacking, did not seem particularly inviting. It was "of a moderate height, though, in some places, it rises higher within. It was diversified with a great many rising grounds and small hills; many of which were entirely covered with tall, straight trees, and others, which were lower, and grew in spots like coppices; but the interspaces, and sides of many of the rising grounds, were clear." Captain Cook thought that though it "might make an agreeable summer prospect," it had at the moment too much snow and "an uncomfortable appearance." There was also some sleet. The captain was a little acid about "a large entrance or strait," which geographers had placed here, but which turned out to be entirely imaginary.

He stood north along the coast of Oregon and Washington—of a moderate and pretty constant height, well covered with wood—and again found occasion to be caustic about another strait that wasn't there. By the end of the month he was along the Canadian coast, which "differed much" from that of the United States, mainly because the mountains came down close to the coast when he could see them. Indians came off in big dugout canoes, one ornamented with "a singular head, which had a bird's eye and bill, of an enormous size," and traded sea otter and otter skins for iron. They were so eager for brass that "whole suits of clothes were stripped of every button; bureaus of their furniture; and copper kettles, tin cannisters, candlesticks, and the like, all went to wreck."

The sea otter was already known from Russian descriptions, but Cook for a time suspected that the skins he saw came from a different species, later realizing that he was merely seeing differences due to the age of the animals. The fur was "certainly softer and finer than that of any others we know of." Even then the Chinese were paying eighty to one hundred rubles apiece for them. When Cook's ships later reached Macao, one sailor sold his sea otter skins for eight hundred dollars and a few prime skins brought $120 apiece. Cook thought his crew's whole stock was worth about £2,000, in China, though they had already disposed of two-thirds of their stock in Kamchatka and had used some of them for bedclothes. Ledyard says that "skins which did not cost the purchaser sixpence sterling sold in China for 100 dollars."

It was Cook's last venture in exploration. From Nootka he ran north, met the Russians in Alaska, sailed on to Hawaii, and was killed there by natives.

News of the small fortunes that Cook's men had made in the Chinese fur trade spread quickly; and in 1792 another British expedition under Captain George Vancouver, a naval officer whose family had originally been Dutch, set out for a voyage around the world, which was to include further exploration on the coast. At about the same time, a group of Boston merchants, scenting profits, sent out two vessels. One of these was the *Columbia* which eventually, under the Rhode Island-born Captain Robert Gray, discovered the Columbia River. The Spaniards, too, were by this time sending ships as far north as Nootka Sound, on the Canadian coast.

Like Cook, as he approached the coast, Vancouver noted much driftwood, grass and seaweed in the water, and "many shags, ducks, puffins, and other aquatic birds" and knew that land could not be far off. Presently he found himself at about 39° 20′ within two miles of a shore that seemed "perfectly compact, formed, generally speaking, by cliffs of moderate height and nearly perpendicular." A member of the *Chatham*'s crew thought, at his first glimpse, California "had a very pleasing appearance, high and covered to the top with tall pines with here and there some rich verdant lawns." Close to the sea the land was open, "beautifully green, with a luxuriant herbage, interrupted by streaks of red earth." Vancouver thought he recognized Cape

Mendocino. In the morning he was in a thick haze and numerous whales were playing all around him.

Running north he noted the mountains rising inland; "a high steep mass, which does not break into perpendicular cliffs, but is composed of various hills that rise abruptly, and are divided by many deep chasms." There were only "a few dwarf trees," the general surface being a dull green with some stretches of red earth. Farther north at Cape Orford (42° 52′) the woods came down to the surf line, after which they came to white sand—probably what Captain Cook had mistaken for snow.

Presently they were passing Cape Foulweather (44° 49′) and were soon along the coast which Mears had already described—high country inland, mountains reaching toward the sea, tall timber, sometimes barren hummocks along the sea. Probably they were near what Mears called Cape Disappointment (46° 19′), opening into Deception Bay. The sea had now "river coloured water, the probable consequence of some streams falling into the bay." In fact, he was now looking at the coastal area lying west of the future site of Portland—"a most luxuriant landscape." High country inland was "agreeably diversified with hills, from which it gradually descended to the shore, and terminated in a sandy beach. The whole had the appearance of a continued forest extending as far north as the eye could reach"—but there was no harbor, the sandy beach sloping under shallow water three or four miles to sea.

On April 29, 1792, he met the ship *Columbia,* nineteen months out of Boston, commanded by Captain Robert Gray, from whom Vancouver learned to his disgust that the "river coloured water" came from the mighty Columbia, which he had himself just missed and which Gray had discovered and explored, shortly after Vancouver's own departure.

Gray's discovery of the Columbia was due to his grim persistence. Where others had suspected the presence of a great river, looked for it a little while, and then sailed on, Gray stubbornly stayed. For nine days a powerful current, whose source he could not see, held his ship off the coast. It was clear that the current must come from a river somewhere, out of sight. Then a favorable wind came at last, strong enough to enable him to force the *Columbia* into the great estuary, and up the river itself on May 12, 1792. When Vancouver learned of the Yankee achievement, eight days later during a chance meeting at sea, he sent Lieutenant William Broughton, commanding the little H.M.S. *Chatham,* 119 miles upstream, using a rough chart which Gray had supplied. Broughton stopped at about modern Washougal, or Cottonwood Point.

It was such a landscape as none of the discoverers had ever seen. Outside the estuary, the Clatsop Plains were deep with grass and bright with flowers most of the year. In May, when the newcomers saw them, they were at their best. Off the shore were spermaceti and right whales, seals, herds of sea otter by the hundreds. On the shore were clams— so many that the shell mounds left by hungry Indians still occupy many acres. Within the river's mouth the banks were "covered with forests of the very finest pine timber, fir, and spruce, interspersed with Indian settlements. Unlike Atlantic coastal forests, these were crowded with underbrush and the ground was often swampy, so that hunters sometimes found it impossible to penetrate at all. Lewis and Clark mention "bogs which the wate of a man would Shake for ½ an Acre." Some travelers found the forests terrifying—"their deep and impervious gloom resembles the silence and solitude of death." Though birds of every kind were numerous on the coast and in the open parts of the forest, they shunned the deeper woods, just as most songbirds shunned the sombre eastern woods.

If the Oregon and Washington trees did not quite equal the gigantic California redwoods, they were still enormous. One fir near Astoria, Oregon, was ten feet through and rose 150 feet before its branches began. It had been blasted by lightning before white men measured it; but its original height was estimated at three hundred feet. "Le Roi des Pins," Canadian traders named it. Another had a circumference of fifty-seven feet and rose 216 feet before its limbs began. The Lewis and Clark expedition found dead trunks two hundred feet long floating in the stream. Mingled with the big conifers were oak, ash, beech, poplar, crabapple, alder, cottonwood. At one strange place a whole forest had been submerged by the river, so that Lewis and

View of the Dalles of the Columbia River. From *March of the Mounted Riflemen.*

Mount Hood from the Columbia River. From *Picturesque America*, 1872.

Clark in their canoes floated above it, looking curiously down at the trunks still standing on the riverbed.

The banks of the Columbia had none of the monotony of so many wooded rivers, for, as one of the *Columbia's* officers noted, "the land was beautyfully divercified with forists and green verdant launs." Often these were low meadows reaching back to higher land "of easy ascent," and "agreeably variegated with clumps and copses of pine, maple, alder, birch, poplar, and several other trees." In autumn this gave a brilliant variety of color.

Up the river in the spring came the salmon, ascending into Rocky Mountain streams to spawn. There were sturgeon, a "sweet little anchovy," and other fish. Bears stood by the riverside, flipping the great salmon out with their paws. There were so many bears that the Indians found it profitable to set deadfalls, baited with fish, along the river banks. Seals and sea otter came far inland up the stream. Wild ducks, geese, and cranes haunted the river as well as the coast. At times flocks of geese were so big that their passage overhead cut off the light like the drawing of a curtain. Bark nets, flung from canoes by torchlight might sometimes take fifty or sixty geese at a throw; but at other times waterfowl were hard to take. The Lewis and Clark expedition were once reduced to eating hawks.

Indian settlements were dotted here and there along the river, busy in season catching and drying salmon, which were a staple the year round. Early white visitors wearied of the hard dried fish, which had to be pounded before it could be eaten, though often it was all there was to eat. The Lewis and Clark expedition thought pounded salmon only a little better than starvation, and a Jesuit who politely told his Indians hosts he thought it good, confided later that he really meant "a good mortification."

Since seamen never went much more than a hundred miles up the Columbia, they missed much of its finest scenery, which was first described by the Lewis and Clark *Journals.* Broughton's men simply heard that there were rapids upstream. They never saw the splendid pictures of the violent torrents of the Long and Short Narrows, the Cascades and the Dalles pouring between the wild shores. Lewis and Clark were the first to describe the towering rock precipices, the delicate lace of waterfalls tumbling a sheer hundred feet or more, towers, castles, and pinnacles in the colored rock.

From the mouth of the Clearwater, near Lewiston, Idaho, Lewis and Clark traveled down the Columbia in 1805, being the first white men to see the river between this point and the point to which Lieutenant Broughton had ascended. It was a wild canoe journey with many wrecks, though none of them was fatal. The great snow-crowned peaks of Mount Adams, Mount St. Helens, Mount Hood, and the rest, loomed up at huge distances when the weather was fair, vanished into the mists for days at a time when Oregon winter rains set in. At the Short Narrows, the whole tremendous stream was compressed between rock walls only forty-five yards apart, but the expedition shot the swift water with their canoes, "notwithstanding the horrid appearance of this agitated gut swelling, boiling & whorling in every direction." Beyond this the river boiled between walls of black rock "in a most tremendious manner," and at the Cascades, where the river dropped 60 feet in two miles, not even these daring canoemen risked the passage. They portaged and were soon discoverers no longer, floating down the lower river where white men had already journeyed.

Epilogue

AFTER A LITTLE less than four hundred years, there was little left for the Eyes of Discovery to seek in North America. Through most of the early nineteenth century there had still remained a few strange, untamed, half-known areas to lure the adventurous. Even that land of tourist wonders, the Yellowstone Park, was not really known to white men till the second half of the century was well advanced—though John Colter had left the Lewis and Clark expedition when it was only part way home, to risk his scalp and visit "Colter's hell." But when the latter years of the nineteenth century came, there was no part whatever of North America that the white man had not seen, except perhaps a few obscure areas of Canada, hidden here and there in regions like the barren grounds.

Today, as the twentieth century moves into its second half, the continent has changed so much that the Eyes of the Discoverers would not recognize it for the land they found. The great forests that swept across the United States, unbroken from the Atlantic coast to the Great Plains, are gone, leaving only here and there a few tracts of virgin timber, preserved by some fortunate accident. Most of Canada, too, has been lumbered over, once at least. In the wilder parts of the the continent, second growth timber has come back, re-creating mighty woodlands, which, though smaller than the great woods of ancient days, give some faint likeness of the forested glory of primitive America. Sometimes, for an instant, grazing cattle—black, distant dots on the prairie—suggest the wandering herds of buffalo; but the hard-riding, war-bonneted Sioux will never again, except in moving pictures, sweep up over the prairie hillocks and ride hell-for-leather upon the casual traveler.

There are some things that not even the destructive white man can change. The Rockies and Sierras tower to the sky, now as always, and will tower forever, changeless, with icy rocky summits that nothing can alter. Staunch conservationists have saved a few magnificent remnants of the redwood forests. A few of the great trees still grow, as they have been growing through the whole of the Christian era. Rolling Dakota grasslands are often much the same as the prairies where the Sioux roamed in ancient days. The Painted Desert, except for a few automobile roads and transitory buildings here and there, is what it always was.

The Grand Canyon is another of the magnificent spectacles that nothing will ever change. Only twice have white men traversed the whole length of its roaring, foaming river and lived to tell the tale. Coronado's explorers would find the Canyon had been cut, by the Colorado River's violent waters, a little deeper than the rocky gash down into which they gazed in wonder four hundred years ago. That is all. Otherwise Coronado's men, or Father Garcés, or the American trapper, Pattie, would find the colored strata exactly what, blind to their beauty, they found long since, though they might be surprised to find casual tourists, intent upon amusement only, visiting easily, mounted on sure-footed burros, the deep-sunk, distant river, at which they looked down, thirstily but in vain, from the upper edges of unscalable cliffs.

In the changeless Canyon, the Havasupai still live a life almost unchanged from primitive days. The Indian has not gone from his ancient hunting grounds by any means. It is said that there are in 1950 as many individuals with the blood of the tribes in their veins as there were when Columbus landed—though it is true that much of the red blood is mixed with white by this time.

Here and there—in pueblos, in the mountains, in some Canadian forests, even in New York State, not very far from Manhattan, the ancient red man's faiths still live, the voices of the spirits still speak, the rites of immemorial ages still are practiced, for there is a stubborn conservatism about the red man. There still live a few white men who can remember the terror of an Indian raid—today something faint and far-off, a tale from story-books, in the minds of most Americans. There are red hunters and red trappers still, roving North American woods, living almost the life of primitive times. But, for the most part, the Indian is on his reservations or is embracing the citizenship of a country that belongs to him at least as much as it can ever belong to any white man. He enters the white man's life. The wife of one recent President boasted the blood of Pocahontas. A recent vice-president had the blood of the Kaws. Navajo speech proved to be one of the U.S. Army's best and most secret codes in World War II. The modern Mohawk Indians, though some of them keep the old religion, reveal a strange gift for the most characteristic of the twentieth century American crafts. They are better structural steelworkers than most white men, because, for some strange reason, the dizzy height of a skyscraper's rising skeleton does not disturb them.

Even the animals the red men hunted are still about. The red fox lurks almost in the outskirts of New York City. An occasional hawk builds in the skyscrapers. Eagles soar near New England factories. The possum breeds in sight of the United Nations, undisturbed by international squabbles. Lordly moose still come down to many a northern stream to splash among the lily-pads at dusk. In parts of North America there are more deer today than when the white man came. They even raid suburban gardens; and their old enemies, the wolf and cougar, are not by any means extinct, though constantly hunted.

Only a few creatures, the great auk, the heath hen, the passenger pigeon, perhaps the Carolina parroquet and the ivory-billed woodpecker, are really gone for good. The buffalo and sea-otter, once on the verge of extinction, have been saved. The buffalo has even become a domestic animal on one or two specialized ranches. Bison and sea-otter are now alike increasing.

Changed though it is, the land that the Eyes of the Discoverers found slowly through the arduous years, still remains implicit with adventure, facing new perils where peril always was, but always also finding new achievement where achievement never ceased. One wonders what those first travelers—in ships, longboats, keelboats, pirogues, canoes, on foot and horseback and in the prairie schooners, wandering the forests, piercing the canebrakes, riding the prairies, scrambling dangerously in desolate mountain passes, wet, cold, sun-scorched and hungry, hunted, ever in danger of their lives—might think if they could see today the land they found, now that the first four hundred years have passed.

NOTES

Notes are given by page and paragraph numbers. The first figure in each pair below is a page reference, the second a paragraph reference. Thus, "49.3" means "paragraph three, page 49." Part of a paragraph running over to the top of a new page is counted as paragraph one of that page.

The usual abbreviations for the various states are used. Other abbreviations are:

DAB, for *Dictionary of American Biography*.
EWT, for R. G. Thwaites: *Early Western Travelers*.
Hbk, for Frederick Webb Hodge: *Handbook of American Indians North of Mexico*.
N. Am., for "North America."
MVHR, for *Mississippi Valley Historical Review*.

Chapter I. Based on S. E. Morison: *Admiral of the Ocean Sea*.

21.2 For a long list of writers who have held this singular delusion, *see* James Adair: *Hist. of the Am. Indians* (S. C. Williams, ed.), p. xxix.
21.5. John Bartram: *Observations* (1751, repr. 1895), pp. 76-77.
26.3. David Bushnell: "Tribal migrations east of the Mississippi," *Smithsonian Misc. Colls.*, 89: 1-9 (1934).
28.2. Adair, *op. cit.*, pp. 457, 437-438.
29.1. Bartram, *op. cit.*, pp. 169-170.
29.2. E. G. Bourne (ed.): *Narratives of . . . De Soto*, II, 98-99; W. Lowery: *Spanish settlements*, I, 228.
30.4. Adair, *op. cit.*, p. 433; *Am. Pioneer*, I, 143.
31.2. Pierre Margry: *Découvertes et établissements des Français*, IV, 174, 176, 183.
31.4. Henri Tonty: Memoir, 1682. In L. P. Kellogg: *Early Narr.*, pp. 302-303.

33.2. Lowery, *op. cit.*, I, 128.

34.1. F. W. Hodge suggests St. Clement's Point, near the entrance. *See* his *Sp. expl. in the Southern US*, p. 4; Lowery, *op. cit.*, p. 177 and App. J; Wm. Roberts: *Acct. of the first disc. and nat. hist. of Florida* (1763), p. 3.

34.3. Hodge, *op. cit.*, p. 21; G. F. de Oviedo y Valdés: *Historical general* (1853), III, 583, 615.

35.3. Stefan Lorant: *New world*, pp. 49, 96; Christian Schultz: *Travels* (1810), II, 124.

36.3 ff. Wm. Bartram: "Travels in Georgia and Florida," *Trans. Am. Philos. Soc.* (NS), 33: 151-152 (1943).

37.2. Hugh L. Willoughby: *Across the Everglades*, p. 72.

37.4. Lorant, *op. cit.*, pp. 39-40.

38.4. Ignaz Pfefferkorn: *Sonora: a description of the province* (Coronado Cuarto Centennial Publs., XII), p. 126.

41.1. Roberts, *op. cit.*, p. 96.

41.2. *Ibid.*, p. 98.

44.3. Buckingham Smith (tr.): *Letter of . . . De Soto and memoir of Hernando de Escalante Fontaneda*, pp. 49-50; I. A. Leonard: *Spanish approach to Pensacola*, p. 270; Margry, *op. cit.*, V, 480; *Ala. Hist. Qy.*, 5: 270 (1943).

46.1. Hodge, *op. cit.*, p. 175.

48.1. *Ibid.*, p. 175.

49.1. Bourne, *op. cit.*, II, 68, 71; Edward Johnson: *Wonder-working providence, Mass. Hist. Soc. Colls.*, 2nd ser., 4: 42 (1826, repr. 1846).

49.5. Bourne, *op. cit.*, II, 77; Hodge, *op. cit.*, p. 169.

50.1. Hodge, *op. cit.*, p. 173; Bourne, *op. cit.*, II, 88; Roberts, *op. cit.*, p. 95.

51.2. Wm. Bartram: *Travels* (1940), pp. 39, 89-90; *Ala. Hist. Qy.*, 5: 300-301 (1943).

51.4. Adair, *op. cit.*, pp. 449, 551.

52.3. Henry Timberlake: Memoirs (S. C. Williams, ed., 1927), p. 35; Adair, *op. cit.*, p. 443; Charles C. Jones: *Antiquities of Southern Indians* (1873), p. 16.

52.4. Adair, *op. cit.*, p. 452.

52.5. *Ibid.*, p. 8.

54.3. Bourne, *op. cit.*, II, 102, 103.

54.5. Adair, *op. cit.*, pp. 432-433; Wm. Bartram: *Travels*, p. 144; Jones, *op. cit.*, pp. 327 ff.; J. Bartram: *Observations*, p. 44; Hbk., I, 273.

54.6. Adair, *op. cit.*, p. 343.

55.1. Wm. Bartram: *Travels*, p. 144.

55.2. Bourne, *op. cit.*, II, 96, 106.

55.4. Adair, *op. cit.*, pp. 440, 449.

56.3. Cyrus Thomas: *Cherokees in pre-Columbian times*, p. 28; Wm. Bartram: *Travels*, p. 380; John Smith: *Generall Historie* (1907), II, 26.

57.1. S. W. Geiser: *Naturalists of the frontier*, p. 257; "Autobiography of Gideon Lincecum," *Miss. Hist. Soc. Publs.*, 8: 469 (1904); Bourne, *op. cit.*, II, 107.

57.4. Bourne, *op. cit.*, II, 100; Hodge, *op. cit.*, p. 175.

58.3. Hodge, *op. cit.*, p. 175.

58.4. *Ibid.*, p. 177; Lowery, *op. cit.*, p. 365.

59.3. ff. Bourne, *op. cit.*, II, 144, 117, 113.

60.4. Hodge, *op. cit.*, p. 183.

60.5. Hbk., II, 791.

61.1. Bourne, *op. cit.*, II, 112.

61.2. Wm. Bartram: *Travels*, p. 38; D. G. Brinton: *Notes on the Floridian peninsula* (1859), p. 94 and note.

62.1. Bourne, *op. cit.*, II, 127. Ranjel gives a different set of figures.

62.2. ff. Hodge, *op. cit.*, pp. 193-204; and Hbk., II, 347.

64.5. Bourne, *op. cit.*, II, 137.

65.3. Bourne, *op. cit.*, II, 138.

65.4. "A Dragoon" (J. Hildreth): *Dragoon campaign to the Rocky Mountains* (1836), pp. 76-77.

66.1. Hodge, *op. cit.*, p. 206; Bourne, *op. cit.*, II, 146.

66.3. Hodge, *op. cit.*, p. 210.

67.1. Hodge, *Ibid.*, pp. 215, 220.

67.4. J. F. McDermott (ed.): *Tixier's travels*, p. 73.

68.4. Lorant, *op. cit.*, p. 38.

69.1. *Ibid.*, pp. 42, 48, 64, 90, 117.

71.3. G. P. Hammond and A. Rey: *Narrs. of the Coronado expedition*, pp. 66-68.

73.2. Hodge, *op. cit.*, p. 289.

73.5. Hammond and Rey, *op. cit.*, pp. 75, 78, 79, 145; Hodge, *op. cit.*, pp. 289-290.

75.6. Hammond and Rey, *op. cit.*, pp. 6, 109.

76.4. *Ibid.*, p. 7.

77.4. Hammond and Rey, *op. cit.*, pp. 206-207, 351-352; Hodge, *op. cit.*, 348-350. The translations do not wholly agree.

78.2. H. E. Bolton (ed.): *Kino's hist. mem. of Pimeria*, I, 127-129, 172; Bolton (ed.): *Font's complete diary*, p. 35; Bolton (ed.): *Anza's California expedition*, III, 215.

79.4. Hammond and Rey, *op. cit.*, pp. 98, 99, 165, 167, 170, 173, 208.

81.2. Hodge, *op. cit.*, p. 360; Hammond and Rey, *op. cit.*, translate this "inland," rather than "up."

81.4. *Journal of Diego Pérez de Luxán* (Los Angeles: Quivira Soc., 1929), p. 106; Hammond and Rey, *op. cit.*, pp. 215-216.

83.3 ff. Elliott Coues: *On the trail of a Spanish pioneer*, I, xxvi; II, 336, 341-n; EWT, XXVII, 131-132, 138.

85.3. Frank Waters: *The Colorado*, p. 376; EWT, XVIII, 104; Pfefferkorn, *op. cit.*, pp. 112-113.

86.2. Hodge, *op. cit.*, p. 325. *See* Hammond and Rey, *op. cit.*, p. 231, for a somewhat different translation.

86.3. Bolton: *Kino's hist. mem.*, I, 252, 317; Bolton: *Anza's California exp.*, III, 42, 323, 325; Coues, *op. cit.*, I, pp. 179, 184, 189.

87.2. F. W. Hodge: *Hist. of Hawikuh*, p. 42; Hbk., *s.v.* "Hawikuh"; Hammond and Rey, *op. cit.*, p. 182.

87.4. Hodge: *Sp. expl.*, pp. 311-312.

88.2. Hammond and Rey, *op. cit.*, p. 223; *Journal of Diego Pérez de Luxán*, pp. 87. 92; Espejo's *Narr.*, p. 183; Hbk., I, 26; F. W. Hodge: "Prehistoric irrigation in Ariz.," *Am. Anthropologist*, 6:323-330 (1893).

88.5. *Journal of Diego Pérez de Luxán*, pp. 60-62, 120-121.

90.1. *Ibid.*, pp. 65-69; Coues, *op. cit.*, I, 31, 33; Bolton: *Anza's Calif. exp.*, II, 323.

91.1 ff. Hammond and Rey, *op. cit.*, pp. 219, 327-328.

92.3. J. V. Brower: *Harahey*, p. 63.

92.5. Hammond and Rey, *op. cit.*, pp. 235-236, 262, 310, 311.

93.4. Hammond and Rey: *New Mexico in 1602*, pp. 53-54.

94.2 ff. Hammond and Rey: *Narr. of the Coronado exp.*, pp. 236, 261, 279, 311; EWT, XVIII, 50.

95.1. Hammond and Rey: *Narr. of the Coronado exp.*, pp. 236, 238, 186, 279.

95.3. EWT, XVIII, 56.

96.1. Hammond and Rey: *Narr. of Coronado exp.*, p. 238.

97.4 ff. *Ibid.*, p. 243.

97.6. *Ibid.*, p. 145.

98.3. Bolton: *Kino's hist. mem.*, I, 247; *Journal of Diego Pérez de Luxán*, pp. 105, 67.

99.1. Hammond and Rey: *Narr. of Coronado exp.*, p. 303.

100.1. R. M. Peck: "Recollections of early times in Kansas," *Kansas Hist. Colls.*, 8: 489 (1904).

100.2. J. R. Mead: "Wichita Indians in Kansas," *Kansas Hist. Colls.*, 8: 174 (1904).

100.3. Hodge's version in Hbk. The text in Hammond and Rey's version of Jaramillo (*Narr. of Coronado exp.*, p. 304) differs slightly.

101.4. *Ibid.*, p. 27; Hbk., II, 346-347; Hodge: *Sp. expl.*, 302-n, 337-n.; *Mail and Breeze* (Topeka), 26 July, 1902; *Kansas Hist. Colls.*, 8: 158-161 (1904).

102.5. H. P. Biggar (ed.): *Voyages of Jacques Cartier*, pp. 6-7; Edna Kenton (ed.): *Indians of N. Am.*, I, 61.

105.5. Biggar, *op. cit.*, p. 31.

106.1-2. M. R. Audubon: *Audubon and his journals*, I, 361; Kenton, *op. cit.*, I, 5.

107.1. Biggar, *op. cit.*, p. 32; H. S. Burrage: *Early English and French voyages* (Original Narr. Am. Hist.), pp. 107-108.

107.3. Biggar, *op. cit.*, p. 34; *Bull. Soc. Géog. de Quebec*, 16: 142, note 13 (1922).

108.4. *Ibid.*, note 13.

110.1 ff. Biggar, *op. cit.*, pp. 103, 110, 124, 155-156.

112.2. *Account of two voyages* (1674), p. 100; Biggar, *op. cit.*, p. 147.

116.3. Biggar, *op. cit.*, p. 213; L. H. Morgan: *League of the Ho-dé-no-sau-nee* (1901), I, 321, II, 252, note 90.

118.3. Original MS. is in the John Carter Brown Library, Providence, R. I.

119.3. E. G. Bourne (ed.): *Voyages of Champlain*, II, 157-159.

120.2. *Ibid.*, II, 184, 189.

120.4. J. B. Brebner: *Explorers of N. Am.*, p. 188.

123.1. Charles Le Beaux: *Avantures*, II, 157-158. [Rare Book Room, Yale.]

128.2. Francis Parkman: *Pioneers* (1904), p. 364; Kenton, *opp. cit.*, II, 278; Father Gabriel Sagard-Théodat: *Long journey*, p. 64; Quaife's ed. of *Alexander Henry's travels*, p. 238; R. G. Lillard: *Great Forest*, pp. 90, 98; *Wyoming Hist. and Geol. Soc. Proc. and Colls.*, 8: 54 (1904); Bartram's Diary, in *Trans. Am. Philos. Soc.*, XXXIII, Pt. II, p. 50 (1942).

128.4. R. G. Thwaites: *Jesuit relations*, LXVII, 289, 295, 311; R. G. Thwaites: *Lewis and Clark journals*, II, 197-n; F. M. Perrin du Lac: *Travels* (1807), p. 44.

129.1. Rudolph Friedrich Kurz: *Journal*, Aug. 4, 1851. In Smithsonian Inst. (Bur. Am. Ethn.), *Bulletin* 115 (1937), p. 89.

130.4. Hbk., I, 206, 184.

130.5. C. P. Medsger: *Edible wild plants*, p. 16; Gray's *Manual* (7th ed.), pp. 411-412.

131.2. Margry, *op. cit.*, I, 203.

132.2. John Josselyn: *New Englands rarities* (1675), p. 71.

135.2-3. Kenton, *op. cit.*, II, 44, I, 5, 86, 122-123, 347.

141.3. An obvious scribal repetition has been omitted.

142.1-3. *Voyages of Pierre Esprit Radisson* (1943), pp. 55-56.

143.3. Kenton, *op. cit.*, II, 62, 81-83; Stanley Vestal: *King of the fur traders*, p. 98.

145.2. Radisson, *op. cit.*, pp. 99-100.

145.4-5. E. Coues: *New Light*, I, 89, 101, 106; Josselyn: *New Englands rarities*, p. 13.

146.5. Kenton, *op. cit.*, II, 531; J. S. Clark: *Cayuga history*, p. 33.

147.1. Kenton, *op. cit.*, II, 84-85.

148.1. Margry, *op. cit.*, I, 132.

150.1-2. J. G. Kohl: *Kitchi-gami* (1860), p. 365; Radisson, *op. cit.*, pp. 142-143; Margry, *op. cit.*, I, 61; Quaife's *Henry*, p. 212; *Wis. Hist. Colls.*, XVI, 24; Kenton, *op. cit.*, II, 370.

152.2. G. W. Featherstonhaugh: *Canoe voyage up the Minnay Sotor*, I, 144-146;

Charles Lanman: *Summer in the wilderness*, pp. 158-159; Margry, *op. cit.*, I, 164; Coues: *New Light*, I, 91.

152.5. Vestal, *op. cit.*, p. 107; Kenton, *op. cit.*, II, 145-146; *Jesuit relations*, 1659-1660; Margry, *op. cit.*, I, 53-55.

156.2. Radisson, *op. cit.*, p. 190; *Vestal, op. cit.*, p. 156; Paul Foundatin: *Great Northwest* (1904), p. 325.

156.3. Margry, *op. cit.*, I, 159-160.

157.1. Radisson, *op. cit.*, p. 191; Vestal, *op. cit.*, p. 307.

159.3. L. J. Burpee, in the introduction to his edition of *Journals and letters of La Vérendrye*, says everything beyond Lake Nipigon was "little else but conjecture."

160.3. This follows Burpee, *op. cit.*, p. 49-n. But see *Trans. Royal Geog. Soc. Canada*, I, 23 (1905); Eduard Richard: *Report on Canad. arch.* (1899), p. 138.

160.4. Burpee, *op. cit.*, pp. 50-51.

161.1. *Ibid.*, pp. 55-59, 92.

162.2. Lanman, *op. cit.*, pp. 113-114, 158, 182; Kohl, *op. cit.*, p. 329; Burpee, *op. cit.*, pp. 141, 96-97, 104, 116, 192, 221.

164.1. *Ibid.*, pp. 270, 275, 303, 312-n.

165.5. Warren Upham: "Explorations of Vérendrye and his sons," MVHR, 1: 49 (1907-1908).

166.4 ff. Burpee, *op. cit.*, pp. 318-319, 328-387.

171.4. *Ibid.*, pp. 407-408; *Wis. Hist. Colls.*, 18: 188 ff. (1904); *S.D. Hist. Colls.*, 7: 200-201 (1914).

173.1. *S.D. Hist. Colls.*, 7: 217 (1914); Burpee, *op. cit.*, p. 420.

173.3. *Wis. Hist. Colls.*, 16: 413-414 (1902); Burpee, *op. cit.*, p. 416-n; F. Parkman: *Half century of conflict* (1904), II, 14; John Brown Dunbar: "Massacre of the Villazur expedition," *Kansas Hist. Colls.*, 11: 397-423 (1910).

174.2. *S.D. Hist. Colls.*, 7: 264-270 (1914).

175.2. Burpee, *op. cit.*, p. 427.

181.2. The original is British Museum, Sloane MS. 1447, fols. 1-18. It has been reprinted in P. J. C. Weston: *Docs. connected with the history of S.C.* (1856). See also Hakluyt (1810 folio), III, 622; Jared Sparks: *American Biography*, XVII, 79-n.

182.1. Robert Beverley: *Hist. and pres. state of Va.* (Wright, ed., 1947), pp. 153-154.

182.3. Wm. Strachey: *Hist. of travaille into Virginia Britannia* (Hakluyt Soc. ed.), p. 130.

183.2. Oscar Handlin: *This was America*, p. 27.

183.3 ff. George Percy: *Discourse of Virginia* (1606), pp. 11-12. (Am. Hist. Beverley, *op. cit.*, p. 140; Strachey, *op. cit.*, p. 130.

183.6. MS. Harl. 7009, fol. 68; Strachey, *op. cit.*, p. xxxii.

185.2. Lorant, *op. cit.*, p. 114.

186.2. Haywood J. Pearce: "New light on the Roanoke colony," *Journ. Southern Hist.*, 4: 148-163 (1938).

186.4. Strachey, *op. cit.*, p. 34 and note. See also *Discovery of New Brittain (1651)*, passim.

187.2. Beverley, *op. cit.*, pp. 153-154; Percy, *op. cit.*, p. 10; Raphe Hamor: *True discourse*, pp. 20-21. Percy's book is also in Purchas (1625), Pt. IV, pp. 1685-1690.

187.3. Strachey, *op. cit.*, pp. 26-27.

187.4. Beverley, *op. cit.*, pp. 30-31.

188.1. Strachey, *op. cit.*, p. 124; Josselyn: *New Englands rarities*, p. 13.

188.2. Strachey, *op. cit.*, pp. 31-32, 122.

188.3. *Ibid.*, pp. 31-32.

188.4. Beverley, *op. cit.*, pp. 144-145.

189.2. Percy, *op. cit.*, p. 7; Strachey, *op. cit.*, p. 127; C. Burrage (ed.): *John Pory's descr. of Plymouth* (1918), p. 40; John Josselyn: *Account of two voyages* (1674), p. 110.

190.1. Lorant, *op. cit.*, p. 234. White's paintings are reproduced in this book.

190.2. Strachey, *op. cit.*, pp. 60, 117: Smith: *Generall Historie, passim.*

191.1. Josselyn: *Acct. of two voyages*, p. 122.

191.2. Hamor, *op. cit.*, p. 23; Percy, *op. cit.*, pp. 7, 11, 12; Beverley, *op. cit.*, p. 131.

191.4. Strachey, *op. cit.*, p. 120.

191.5. Hamor, *op. cit.*, p. 23.

192.1. Eleanour Sinclair Rohde: *Herbs and herb gardeners*, p. 185; Medsger, *op. cit.*, pp. 75-76; Josselyn: *New Englands rarities*, p. 66.

192.2. Strachey, *op. cit.*, p. 122.

192.3. Smith, *op. cit.*, I, 53; Henry Spelman: *Relation of Va.* (1872 ed.), p. 29; Hamor, *op. cit.*, p. 23.

192.4. Elias Pym Fordham: *Personal Narr.*, p. 143; Beverley, *op. cit.*, p. 130.

193.2. Gray's *Manual* (7th ed.), p. 717; Luigi Castiglioni: *Viaggi negli Stati Uniti* (1790), II, 231.

193.3. Josselyn: *New Englands rarities*, pp. 28-29; 40; Edward Valentine Mitchell: *It's an old State of Maine custom*, pp. 156-157.

194.2. Jeremy Belknap's *Journal* (1882), June 28, 1796.

194.3. Percy, *op. cit.*, p. 10; *Mass. Hist. Colls.*, ser. 3, 8:97 (1843).

195.1. Strachey, *op. cit.*, p. 126; Hamor, *op. cit.*, p. 21.

195.2. Strachey, *op. cit.*, pp. 75, 127; Andrew Burnaby: *Travels* (Wilson, ed., 1904), p. 41; Percy, *op. cit.*, *passim*; Beverley, *op. cit.*, pp. 146-151; Hamor, *op. cit.*, p. 21.

196.2. Josselyn: *Acct. of two voyages*, p. 105; Josselyn: *New Englands rarities* (1675), p. 32.

198.1. Brebner, *op. cit.*, p. 115; Henry F. Howe: *Prologue to New England*, pp. 85-86.

199.1. Wm. Bradford: *Hist. Plymouth Plantation.* In Wm. T. Davis (ed.): *Original Narr. Am. Hist.*, I, 96-99; Frank Strong: "Forgotten danger to the New England colonies," *Ann. Rept. Am. Hist. Assn.*, 1898, p. 91.

200.4. Smith, *op. cit.*, I, 3; Arthur Barlow: *First voyage* (Prince Soc. ed., 1884), p. 110; Am. Scenic and Hist. Pres. Soc., *15th Ann. Report* (1910), p. 183.

201.1. Gabriel Archer: *Relation* (Old South Leaflet, No. 120), p. 2; *Winthrop Papers, Mass. Hist. Soc.*, 6: 269 (1931); John Winthrop: *Hist. New England* (1853), I, 27, 28.

201.2. *Whole and true discoverye of Terre Florida* (1563), *passim*; G. M. Asher: *Henry Hudson the navigator*, p. 80; S. Lorant: *New world*, pp. 11, 90; D. Denton: *Brief descr. of N.Y.* (Gowans, ed., 1845), p. 55.

201.5. Francis Higginson's *Journal.* In *Founding of Mass.* (Mass. Hist. Soc. Tercentenary ed., 1930), p. 72.

203.2. Janette Mary Lucas: *Where did your garden grow?* p. 48.

204.4. Winthrop, *op. cit.*, I, 231.

205.2. Josselyn: *Acct. of two voyages*, p. 124.

205.4. W. D. Miller: "Narragansett planters," *Proc. Am. Antiquarian Soc.*, April, 1933; "America dissected," App. to *Hist. Narragansett Church*, p. 525; Winthrop, *op. cit.*, I, 175.

206.4. James Rosier: *True relation.* In *Gorges Soc. Publs.*, III, 95; *Mass. Hist. Soc. Colls.*, 2nd ser., 4: 53-54, 231, 250, 267; 8: 112-116 (Repr. 1846).

207.2. *Ibid.*, p. 143.

208.2. J. Palairet: *Concise description* (1755), p. 51.

209.1. Archer, *loc. cit.*; John Brereton: *Briefe and true relation.* In *Mass. Hist. Soc. Colls.*, 3rd ser. (1843), *passim*.

209.3. *The Relation* (Popham and Gilbert, 1607). In *Gorges Soc. Publs.*, IV, 43, 75.

209.4. *Joyfull newes out of the new founde worlde, passim;* D. C. Peattie: "Sassafras and witch hazel," *Atlantic Monthly*, 182: 69-71 (1949).

210.3. Rosier, *op. cit.*, III, 95; *Mourt's relation* (Dexter, ed.), p. 20; Higginson, *op. cit.*, p. 72; Brereton, *op. cit.*, 8: 89 (1843).

211.3. Francis Higginson: *New Englands plantation* (1630). In *Founding of Mass.* (Mass. Hist. Soc. Tercentenary ed., 1930), p. 87; Peter Force: *Tracts*, I, 8.

211.4-5. Rosier, *op. cit.*, *Gorges Soc. Publs.*, III, 93; IV, 42, 65.

212.1. *New English Canaan*. In P. Force: *Tracts*, II, 61.

212.2. *New England's plantations*. In P. Force: *Tracts*, I, 9; Josselyn: *Acct. of two voyages*, p. 109; Pory, *op. cit.*, p. 40.

214.2. Bradford, *op. cit.*, p. 121.

214.4. G. B. Dorr: "Our seacoast national park," *Appalachia*, 15: 177-178 (1921).

215.3. Josselyn: *New Englands rarities*, p. 57; Thomas Campanius Holm: "Short descr. of New Sweden," *Mem. Hist. Soc. Pa.*, 3: 42 (1834); Pfefferkorn: *Sonora: a descr. of the province*, p. 57; *Journal of Jasper Dankers and Peter Sluyter*. In *Mem. Long Island Hist. Soc.*, I, 219 (1867).

216.1. Josselyn: *Acct. of two voyages*, pp. 99-100.

216.3. Josselyn: *New Englands rarities*, p. 7; Sagard-Théodat, *op. cit.*, pp. 218-219; Kenton, *op. cit.*, I, 157; Holm, *op. cit.*, 3: 161.

218.3. Bradford, *op. cit.*, pp. 110-111; Caroline Thomas Foreman: *Indians abroad*, pp. 16-17.

219.1. Bourne: *Champlain*, I, 126.

219.2. Bradford, *op. cit.* (1898 ed.), p. 99.

220.2-3. Smith, *op. cit.*, II, 2; DAB, XVII, 295.

221.3 ff. Smith, *op. cit.*, II, 3, 13, 24, 34, 48.

222.5. *Winthrop's Journal* (Orig. Narr. Early Am. Hist.), p. 90; Pory, *op. cit.*, pp. 37-39.

223.4-5. Johnson, *op. cit.* 7: 28; Pory, *op. cit.*, p. 40.

224.1-6. "Juet's Journal," *Am. Scenic. and Hist. Pres. Soc.*, 15: 270, 320-321 (1910); Smith, *op. cit.*, II, 57, 28.

225.1-4. Benjamin G. Willey: *Hist. White Mts.* (1870), pp. 13-18; *Appalachia*, 15: 125-126 (1921): Josselyn: *New Englands rarities*, p. 3.

226.1. Asher, *op. cit.*, pp. xcii, xciii, cxlv.

228.2-3. J. Franklin Jameson: *Narr. of New Netherland*, pp. 38, 103-105; *Journal of Jasper Danckaerts* (James and Jameson, eds.), p. 64; Denton, *op. cit.*, pp. 26-27.

231.2-3. *Ibid.*, p. 15; Burnaby, *op. cit.*, p. 106; *Mem. Long Island Hist. Soc.*, I, 270-271 (1867); Perrin du Lac: *Travels*, pp. 12-13.

232.4. Josselyn: *New Englands rarities*, p. 17; Josselyn: *Acct. of two voyages*, p. 93.

233.1. Jameson, *op. cit.*, pp. 222-223; Belknap, *op. cit.*, p. 12.

233.3. Thomas Anburey: *Travels*, II, 471; William Eddis: *Letters from America* (1792), p. 426; Denton, *op. cit.*, pp. 53-54.

233.4. Joel Munsell: *Annals of Albany* (1869), I, 34-36.

233.5. Jameson, *op. cit.*, p. 71.

235.1. Asher, *op. cit.*, p. 173; N.Y. Hist. Colls. (NS), I, *passim*.

238.1. Jameson, *op. cit.*, pp. 38, 49.

240.2. A. C. Myers: *Early Narr. of Pa., West N. J., and Del.*, pp. 19-20.

240.3. *Ibid.*, p. 8; Amandus Johnson: *Swedish settlements on the Delaware*, pp. 170-171.

241.2-3. Myers, *op. cit.*, p. 15; Thomas Pownall: *Topographical Descr.* (L. Mulkearn, ed.), p. 41.

241.5-6. Myers, *op. cit.*, pp. 74, 265.

242.4-6. L. H. Gipson's ed. of Lewis Evans: *Brief account of Pennsylvania*, p. 96; Josselyn: *New Englands rarities*, p. 9.

243.2. Holm, *op. cit.*, 3:41, 49-50.

243.3. Myers, *op. cit.*, pp. 48-49; Evans, *op. cit.*, p. 96.

243.4. *Mem. Long Island Hist. Soc.*, 1: 172 (1867).

244.1. *Brief relation.* In P. J. C. Weston: *Docs. connected with the history of S. C.* (1856), p. 60; Joshua Gilpin: "Journal of a tour," *Pa. Mag.* 51: 158 (1927).

244.5. Lloyd L. Smith, Jr., and John B. Moylan: *Biological survey and fishery management plan* (Tech. Bull. No. 1, Minn. Dept. Conservation, 1944), p. 144; George Shiras: "Wild life of Lake Superior," *Nat. Geog. Mag.*, 40:155-159 (1921); *Geol. and Nat. Hist. Survey Minn.*, (1879), p. 133.

245.1. Myers, *op. cit.*, pp. 272, 265; *Brief relation.* In P. J. C. Weston: *Docs. . . S. C.*, p. 59.

245.3. Stewart Pearce: *Annals of Luzerne Co.*, p. 499; *Atlas of Am. Hist.*, Map. No. 78.

246.3. W. M. Darlington: *Christopher Gist's Journals*, pp. 72-73.

246.4-5. H. W. Shoemaker: *Juniata memories*, pp. 203-204: 318-319, and correspondence with Colonel Shoemaker.

247.2-4. Margry, *op. cit.*, IV, 170; Myers, *op. cit.*, p. 321; *New York Times*, 30 April, 1949.

247.5. Myers, *op. cit.*, p. 322.

248.2-6. Strachey, *op. cit.*, pp. 122-123; Josselyn: *Acct. of two voyages*, p. 85; EWT, V, 53-54; Sagard-Théodat, *op. cit.*, p. 224; Kenton, *op. cit.*, I, 157; Evans, *op. cit.*, p. 119; Henry Wansey: *Excursion to the U. S.* (2nd ed., 1798), p. 206.

249.2. Weston, *op. cit.*, p. 59.

249.3. J. D. Schoepf: *Travels* (tr. 1911), *passim.*

249.5. *Mem. Hist. Soc. Pa.*, 3:42 (1834).

250.2-4. Josselyn: *Acct. of two voyages*, p. 116; *Mem. Long Island Hist. Soc.*, I: 219 (1867); *Ra. Gaz.*, 1 June, 1749; Evans, *op. cit.*, p. 121.

251.2-3. *Mem. Hist. Soc. Pa.*, 3:162 (1834); Wansey, *op. cit.*, p. 89.

255.4. J. F. Meginness: *Otzinachson* (1852), pp. 30-31.

256.2. *Moravian journals* (Onondaga Hist. Assn., 1916), p. 10.

256.3. Evans, *op. cit.*, pp. 10-11.

257.3. *Moravian journals*, p. 158.

257.4. W. C. Reichel: *Memorials*, Vol. I, p. 102.

257.5. *Moravian journals*, p. 158.

259.4. *Ibid.*, p. 159.

259.5-6. Bartram: *Observations*, pp. 38-39.

260.2. Reichel, *op. cit.*, I, 89-90 and note; *Docs. rel. col. hist. N. Y.* (1853), IV, 82.

260.4. Philip Tome: *Pioneer life* (1928), pp. 68-72; Josselyn: *Acct. of two voyages*, p. 72.

260.5. Evans, *op. cit.*, p. 114.

261.3. Information from Dr. Kimber Kuster, State Teachers College, Bloomsburg, Pa.

261.4-5. *Moravian journals*, pp. 158-166, 221.

262.4. Frederick C. Johnson: "Count Zinzendorf," *Wyoming Hist. and Geol. Soc. Proc. and Colls.*, 8: 30 (1904); Charles A. Miner: *Hist. Wyoming* (1845), p. xiv and note; Stewart Pearce, *op. cit.*, pp. 500-502; Zenas T. Gray: *Prose and poetry of the Susquehanna and Juniata* (1893), p. 31.

263.5. DeWattville's *Journal, Wyoming Hist. and Geol. Soc. Proc. and Colls.*, 8:43-44 (1904).

263.6-7. Reichel, *op. cit.*, I, 93-94.

264.2. Thomas Ashe: *Travels.* In *Coll. modern and contemp. voyages and travels,* V, 17; Pownall, *op. cit.,* p. 6.

264.4. *Travels in N. Am.* (1828), p. 348-n.

265.1. Schoepf, *op. cit.,* pp. 159-170.

265.2. Thaddeus Mason Harris: *Travels* (1905), p. 29.

267.2. Solon J. Buck: *Planting of civilization in W. Pa.,* pp. 11-12; Gilpin, *op. cit.,* 51: 178.

268.1. "New Yorker": *Winter in the west* (1836), I, 7.

268.3. H. W. Shoemaker: *Legends of the Juniata,* 315-317, 242, 86-87.

269.1. Francis Parkman: *Pioneers* (1904), p. 234-n, quoting Thevet MS. 1586.

269.3. Pownall, *op. cit.,* p. 8.

269.4. Ashe, *op. cit.,* pp. 48-49; also in *Coll. modern and contemp. voyages and travels,* V, 39-41.

270.2. John T. Faris: *Seeing Pennsylvania,* pp. 169-170.

270.4. Perrin du Lac, *op. cit.,* p. 34; Tome, *op. cit.,* pp. 87-88; J. S. Illick: *Pennsylvania Trees,* p. 159.

271.4. Schoepf, *op. cit.,* p. 342.

271.5. Fordham, *op. cit.,* p. 151.

272.3. *Coll. modern and contemp. voyages and travels,* V, 14; Pownall, *op. cit.,* p. 6.

272.6. Schoepf, *op. cit.,* pp. 213-214.

273.4. Ashe, *op. cit.* (1811), pp. 16-17, 80; EWT, III, 247.

274.1. Tome, *op. cit.,* p. 102.

274.3. Francis Higginson: *New Englands plantation.* In *Founding of Mass.,* p. 91; *Mem. Hist. Soc. Pa.,* 3:53 (1834).

275.3. Charles Beatty: *Journal* (1768), pp. 18-19.

275.4. Tome, *op. cit.,* pp. 31-35.

276.2. MVHR, 14: 195 (1928).

276.4. Kenton, *op. cit.,* II, 471-479; Adair, *op. cit.,* p. 250.

277.1-2. C. Hale Sipes: *Indian chiefs of Pa.,* pp. 160-161; F. Parkman: *Old regime* (1904), p. 80; Kellogg, *op. cit.,* pp. 189-190; Kenton, *op. cit.,* pp. 84-86; Burnaby, *op. cit.,* p. 71; Timberlake, *op. cit.,* p. 72.

277.3. Beatty, *op. cit.,* p. 16.

277.5. Schoepf, *op. cit.,* pp. 226-227; Beatty, *op. cit.,* p. 20-n; Shoemaker, *Legends,* p. 315.

278.1. Pownall, *op. cit.,* p. 33.

278.2. EWT, III, 329; Gilpin, *op. cit.,* p. 351.

278.3. Morris Birkbeck: *Notes on a journey in America* (1818), pp. 43-45.

279.2. Pownall, *op. cit.,* pp. 9, 33.

279.3. Schoepf, *op. cit.,* p. 235.

280.2. *Coll. modern and contemp. voyages and travels,* V, 18.

281.2. Francis Parkman: *LaSalle* (1904), p. 18.

283.1. Margry, *op. cit.,* II, 81, 273.

283.3. EWT, IV, 178, V, 38, I, 127-130; Schultz, *op. cit.,* II, 24-n; Robert Baird: *Valley of the Mississippi* (1832), p. 117.

284.4. Harris, *op. cit.,* p. 65; Fordham, *op. cit.,* p. 119.

285.3. Baird, *op. cit.,* p. 114.

285.4. Ashe, *op. cit.* (1811), p. 71; *Publs. State Hist. Soc. Wis.,* vol. 22 (1916), *passim.*

286.2. MVHR, 14: 145 (1927); Schultz, *op. cit.,* I, 140-141.

286.3. F. H. Herrick (ed.): *Delineations of Am. scene,* pp. 60-61; A. D. Jones: *Illinois and the west* (1838), p. 218.

287.1. *Relations . . . du Père Gravier* (1700; Cramoisy ed., 1859, p. 9; *Moravian journals,* p. 201; Perrin du Lac, *op. cit.,* pp. 57-61.

287.3. *Hennepin's New Disc.* (Thwaites, ed., 1903), I, 53-56, 317-323.

288.1. Margry, *op. cit.*, I, 441-442.

288.2. Charles Lyell: *Travels* (1845), p. 28; Palairet, *op. cit.*, pp. 39-40.

288.4. Map by Capt. John Montresor, Chief Engineer in America, now in British Museum, No. CXXI, 73.

290.1. Margry, *op. cit.*, II, 81, 95, 97.

290.2. Harris, *op. cit.*, p. 61. There is no doubt about the size of the grape vines. Some reached ten inches, and the great vine at Windsor Park is credited with a diameter of two feet nine inches. See G. C. Swallow: *Geol. Report of the country along the line of the South-Western Branch* (1859), p. 12-n.

293.4. Excerpts from original surveys in *Indiana Hist. Soc. Publs.*, 6: 442-446 (1916-1919).

294.1. J. S. Buckingham: *Eastern and western states of America* (1842), III, 216.

294.2. Milo M. Quaife: *Glimpses of Illinois* (Lakeside Classics), p. 77.

295.2. Calvin Cotton: *Tour of the American lakes* (1833), I, 173-175; Margry, *op. cit.*, II, 170.

295.3. Margry, *op. cit.*, II, 247.

297.1. Parkman: *LaSalle* (1904), pp. 186-187.

300.1. Ashe, *op. cit.* (1811), p. 66; Harris, *op. cit.*, p. 39; Schultz, *op. cit.*, I, 117.

301.1. *Journals of Robert Rogers* (1883), pp. 190, 199, 201; Timothy Flint: *Recollections* (1826), p. 43.

302.1. EWT, III, 346.

303.3. *Docs. rel. col. hist. N.Y.*, IV, 98-99; Margry, *op. cit.*, IV, 341-342.

304.3. Harlan Hatcher: *Western Reserve*, p. 209.

305.1. Harris, *op. cit.*, p. 146; A. D. Jones, *op. cit.*, p. 35.

305.2. Pownall, *op. cit.*, p. 7; EWT, IV, 262.

306.1. Draper MS. 6 S 85-86; Darlington, *op. cit.*, pp. 42-43.

306.2. Harris, *op. cit.*, p. 178; EWT, XVIII, 354.

307.1-2. A. D. Jones, *op. cit.*, pp. 211-213, 217, 222; Quaife: *Glimpses of Ill.*, pp. 60-62.

307.3. *Ibid.*, p. 71; Harris, *op. cit.*, pp. 179-180.

307.4. EWT, I, 124-125.

308.2 "New Yorker," *op. cit.*, I, 175-176.

308.3. *Ibid.*, II, 63-64; Quaife, *Glimpses of Ill.*, pp. 74-77.

308.4. Fordham, *op. cit.*, p. 235.

309.2. Schultz, *op. cit.*, II, 69-70.

309.3. Pownall, *op. cit.*, p. 41; EWT, V, 247-248; Brebner, *op. cit.*, p. 447.

309.4. Darlington, *op. cit.*, p. 35; Ashe, *op. cit.* (1811), p. 49.

309.5. Birkbeck, *op. cit.*, pp. 70-72; EWT, I, 133.

310.1. Birkbeck, *op. cit.*, p. 71; Harris, *op. cit.*, p. 113; "New Yorker," *op. cit.*, I, 100.

310.2-3. Schultz, *op. cit.*, II, 24; Rogers, *op. cit.*, p. 20; "Notes" to Thomas Hutchins's map of 1762 (Beverly W. Bond, Jr., ed., 1942); Meginness, *op. cit.*, p. 28; D. C. Peattie: *American Heartwood*, p. 117.

311.1. Birkbeck, *op. cit.*, p. 79.

311.2. A. D. Jones, *op. cit.*, p. 199; "Reminiscences of Frederick Chouteau," *Kansas Hist. Colls.*, 4: 428 (1904); Margry, *op. cit.*, I, 264; Draper MS. 6 S 215; Josselyn: *Acct. of two voyages*, p. 22; J. Bakeless: *Daniel Boone*, p. 358; Birkbeck, *op. cit.*, passim.

312.2. J. Filson: *Kentucke*, p. 7.

314.2. Felix Walker: "First settlement of Kentucky," *DeBow's Review*, 16:152 (1854);

Draper MS. 48 J 10; W. R. Jillson: *Tales of the dark and bloody ground*, pp. 70-71.

314.4. Filson, *op. cit.*, p. 16.

314.5. Brent Altsheler: "Long hunters," *Filson Club Hist. Qy.*, 5: 169-185 (1931).

315.2. *DeBow's Review*, 15: 152 (1854).

315.3. Flint, *op. cit.*, p. 43; J. F. Buisson de St. Cosme in J. G. Shea: *Early voyages up and down the Mississippi* (1861), p. 5.

315.4. Baird, *op. cit.*, p. 204.

315.5. Harris, *op. cit.*, p. 178; Fordham, *op. cit.*, pp. 136, 112.

316.1-2. "New Yorker," *op. cit.*, II, 58; A. D. Jones, *op. cit.*, pp. 170-171, 236.

316.3. Harris, *op. cit.*, pp. 116-117; Perrin du Lac: *op. cit.*, p. 37.

317.1. Tome, *op. cit.*, p. 95.

317.2. *Hist. and Phil. Soc. Ohio Publs.*, (NS) 1:69 (1873).

317.3. "Journal of Colonel John May, 1789," *Pa. Mag.* 45:45:32 (1921).

320.2. Shea, *op. cit.*, p. xi.

321.1. *Ibid.*, pp. xxi-xxvii.

324.2. *Ibid.*, pp. 10-14.

325.3. Margry, *op. cit.*, VI, 72.

325.5. "New Yorker," *op. cit.*, I, 168, 184, 201, 267.

327.2. Henry Ker: *Travels* (1816), p. 33.

327.3. "New Yorker," *op. cit.*, I, 184.

327.4. Shea, *op. cit.*, p. 79.

328.2. Margry, *op. cit.*, V, 281.

329.1. Schultz, *op. cit.*, II, 144-145; *Mo. Hist. Rev.*, 15: 676 (1921); Perrin du Lac, *op. cit.*, p. 61.

329.4. Margry, *op. cit.*, I, 261, 269.

329.5. Margry, *op. cit.*, II, 244.

330.3. Kurz: *Journal*. In Smithsonian Inst. (Bur. Am. Ethn.), *Bull.* 115: 14-15 (1937).

332.1. There is a particularly fine example in the Missouri Pacific Lines Museum, St. Louis.

332.3. [Henri] *Joutel's journal* (Chicago: Caxton Club, 1896), p. 165.

333.1-3. Shea, *op. cit.*, pp. 65-66; Wm. McAdams: *Records of ancient races* (1887), pp. 40-41; John Russell: "The Piasa—an Indian tradition," *Evangelical Mag. and Gospel Advance*, 19: 224 (1848) [file in Tufts College Library]; Amos Stoddard: *Sketches of Louisiana* (1812), p. 17; A. D. Jones, *op. cit.*, pp. 53-60.

334.1. L. F. Thomas and J. C. Wild: *Valley of the Mississippi* (1841), pp. 71-72.

334.3. Bureau of American Ethnology: *Annual Report*, 1888-1889, p. 78; Kurz, *op. cit.*, pp. 15-16.

335.2. A. D. Jones, *op. cit.*, p. 219; Stoddard, *op. cit.*, pp. 208-209; Schultz, *op. cit.*, II, 38.

335.3. Baird, *op. cit.*, p. 31; Ker, *op. cit.*, p. 34.

335.4-6. McAdams, *op. cit.*, p. 104; J. G. McDermott (ed.) *Tixier's travels*, pp. 67, 72.

336.3. Schultz, *op. cit.*, II, 144-145.

336.4. McAdams, *op. cit.*, p. 104.

337.3-5. Margry, *op. cit.*, II, 180; Schultz, *op. cit.*, II, 42.

338.1. A. D. Jones, *op. cit.*, p. 42; Shea, *op. cit.*, p. 65; Perrin du Lac, *op. cit.*, p. 49; *Mo. Hist. Soc. Colls.*, 6: 218, 219, 243 (1928-31).

339.2. Samuel S. Forman: *Narr. of a journey down the Ohio and Mississippi in 1789-90*, p. 45.

339.3. A. D. Jones, *op. cit.*, p. 43.

339.4. Schultz, *op. cit.*, pp. 18-19.

340.3. Margry, *op. cit.*, I, 265.

341.2. Otto Jespersen: *Language,* pp. 181-182.

344.1. Margry, *op. cit.,* II, 168.

344.2. Bénard La Harpe: *Journal historique* (1831), pp. 394-395.

345.4. Margry, *op. cit.,* I, 258; VI, 182.

346.2. Ray Allan Billington: *Westward expansion,* pp. 434-435; Stoddard, *op. cit.,* pp. 30-34.

346.4. Margry, *op. cit.,* VI, 193-194, 200-202.

347.3. Grant Foreman: *Adventure on the Red River,* pp. 138-139; EWT, XX, 254 ff.; U. S. House Report No. 474, 23rd Congress, 1st Sess.

348.2. Margry, *op. cit.,* VI, 253, 257.

348.3. The distance is given as ten leagues in Margry, *op. cit.,* VI, 230. See also Mrs. Dunbar Rowland: *Life, letters, and papers of William Dunbar,* pp. 164, 170.

348.4. Grant Foreman, *op. cit.,* p. 137; MVHR, 15: 34 ff. (1928-29).

349.1. Norman W. Caldwell: "Red River raft," *Chronicles of Oklahoma,* 19: 253-268 (1941).

349.4. *DeBow's Review,* 19: 438-439 (1858); EWT, XXVIII, 114-115; *Arkansas Gazette,* 9 Sept., 16 Sept., 1828; *Niles' Weekly Register,* 12: 320 (1817); Stoddard, *op. cit.,* pp. 158, 166.

350.1. Stoddard, *op. cit.,* pp. 167, 178; Margry, *op. cit.,* IV, 122.

350.2. Margry, *op. cit.,* V, 161, 174, 185, 313; McDermott, *op. cit.,* p. 33; Schultz, *op. cit.,* II, 32.

351.3. William E. Dunn: "Spanish reaction against the French advance toward New Mexico," MVHR, 2: 354-362 (1915).

351.5. Margry, *op. cit.,* 392-397; Henri Folmer: "De Bourgmont's exp. to the Padoucahs," *Colorado Mag.,* 14: 121-128 (1937).

352.5. Margry, *op. cit.,* VI, 415, 428-431.

353.3. See map in *Colorado Mag.,* 16: 164 (1939).

353.4. Louis Pelzer: *Marches of the dragoons,* p. 71; "Diary of William Marshall Anderson" (TS. copy of original MS.), fol. 9 [in possession of Mr. J. S. Holliday, Yale Library]; EWT, XVIII, 140-141.

354.4 ff. Pelzer, *op. cit.,* pp. 38, 54, 71, 348, 353, 343-346, 338; Pelzer: "Journal of marches of dragoons," *Iowa Journ. Hist. and Politics,* 7: 38, 54, 71, 338, 343-346, 348, 353, 338; George Catlin: *N. Am. Indians,* II, 505.

357.2. A. H. Abel: *Tabeau Narr.,* pp. 11-12; A. P. Nasatir: "John Evans, explorer and surveyor," *Mo. Hist. Rev.* 25: 440-441 (1930); Knox to Harmer, 20 Dec. 1789, MS. in Clements Library, University of Michigan.

359.5. Abel, *op. cit.,* p. 27.

361.3. "Journals of Capt. Thomas Becknell," *Mo. Hist. Rev.,* 4:84 (1909).

361.4-5. EWT, VI, 84, V. 72, 90.

362.2. EWT, VI, 67; W. A. Maxwell: *Crossing the plains* (1915), pp. 23.

362.6. Hugh L. Scott: *Some memories of a soldier,* p. 114.

363.1. Kurz, *op. cit.,* p. 27; EWT, XXI, 47.

363.2. EWT, VI, 81; *Original Journals of Lewis and Clark* (Thwaites, ed.), I, 159.

363.3. Abel, *op. cit.,* p. 59; Thwaites: *Lewis & Clark.,* I, 297.

363.4. EWT, VI, 37, 87.

364.1. Abel, *op. cit.,* pp. 60-61; EWT, V, 57.

364.3. Abel, *op. cit.,* pp. 58-60; EWT, V, 57, VI, 38.

364.4. *Mo. Hist. Rev.,* 31: 57-60 (1936); Samuel Parker: *Journal of an exploratory tour* (1835-37), *passim.*

365.1. "Captain Flack": *Hunter's experiences* (1866), pp. 349-351; W. Irving: *Adventures of Captain Bonneville* (Lovell ed., n.d.), pp. 89-90; *Mo. Hist. Rev.,* 31:57-60 (1936).

365.3. EWT, XXI, 125, 134, 157.

365.4-5. *Mo. Hist. Rev.*, 31: 181-184 (1936); McDermott, *op. cit.*, p. 106; EWT, XXI, 47, 134, 139, VI, 49.

366.3. McDermott, *op. cit.*, pp. 112, 277; Thwaites: *Lewis & Clark*, I, 59, 370; EWT, VI, 69; Coues: *New Light*, I, 90.

367.1. Scott, *op. cit.*, p. 39; *Mo. Hist. Rev.*, 31:60 (1936).

367.3. Thwaites: *Lewis & Clark*, I, 67; EWT, VI, 39, 49, 81.

367.6. EWT, XXI, 133, VI, 90.

368.3. EWT, V, 124; Scott, *op. cit.*, p. 52.

368.4. EWT, V, 188-189.

369.2. Thwaites: *Lewis & Clark*, V, 199.

369.3. EWT, XXI, 161, 170.

370.1. W. C. Kennerly: *Persimmon Hill*, p. 149.

370.2. *Chronicles of Oklahoma*, V, 386 (1927).

370.5-6. Thwaites: *Lewis & Clark*, I, 153-154; EWT, XXI, 174.

371.4. Thwaites: *Lewis & Clark*, I, 293; EWT, XXI, 157, VI, 88.

372.2 ff. Brebner, *op. cit.*, pp. 291-292, 296; J. F. Kenney: "Career of Henry Kelsey," *Roy. Soc. Canada Trans.*, 3rd ser., vol. 23, section II, pp. 37-71 (1929); A. G. Doughty and C. Martin (eds.): *Kelsey papers* (Ottawa, 1929), pp. xxiii, 12; G. N. Bell: *Journal of Henry Kelsey, passim;* EWT, XXI, 52, 101, 204-205, 218; Grant Foreman (ed.): *Traveler in Indian Terr.*, pp. 163-164; Coues: *New Light*, I, 99; Dunbar: *Life, letters . . . ,* p. 244; Thwaites: *Lewis & Clark*, II, 49.

374.2 ff. Kennerly, *op. cit.*, p. 148; Coues: *New Light*, I, 121; EWT, XVIII, 62-64, 158.

375.1. Tome, *op. cit.*, p. 102.

375.2. E. Coues (ed.): *Journal of Jacob Fowler*, pp. 41-45.

382.1. Alfred Powers: *Redwood country*, pp. 12-19; Charles G. Leland: *Fusang, passim.*

383.1. H. R. Wagner: *Voyage of Francisco de Ulloa* (1925), p. 22.

383.3. H. R. Wagner: *Juan Rodrigo de Cabrillo* (Calif. Hist. Soc., 1941), pp. 10-12; *Herrera's account* (Wagner, ed.), p. 70.

383.4-5. "Summary journal." In Wagner: *Cabrillo*, pp. 18, 45-47, 49, 83; Wagner: *Herrera's account*, p. 67.

385.2. Billington, *op. cit.*, p. 426.

385.3. *English hero, or Sir Francis Drake reviv'd* (1692), p. 105.

386.1. J. M. Dixon: "Drake on the Pacific coast," *Overland Monthly*, 2nd ser. 53: 537-545 (1914).

386.2. Dixon, *op. cit.*, pp. 544-545.

386.3. H. R. Wagner: *Drake's voyage around the world*, pp. 132-137.

387.2. *Drake's plate of Grass* (San Francisco: Calif. Hist. Soc., 1937).

388.4. Vincent T. Harlow: *Voyages of great pioneers*, p. 223; J. A. Williamson: *Sir John Hawkins*, p. 393.

388.5. G. B. Ramusio: *Delle navigationi e viaggi* (1565), III, 343.

389.1. *Hist. Soc. Southern Calif. Publs.*, 2:17 (1891); H. R. Wagner: "Unamuno's voyage to Calif.," *Calif. Hist. Soc. Qy.*, 2: 140-160 (1923); Justin Winsor: *Narr. and crit. hist.*, II, 456-457; H. H. Bancroft: *North Mex. states*, I, 146; H. H. Bancroft: *Northwest coast*, I, 71-80.

389.3. I. B. Richman: *Calif. under Spain and Mexico*, pp. 25-26; H. R. Wagner: "Unamuno's voyage to Calif.," *Calif. Hist. Soc. Qy.*, 2: 140-160 (1923).

390.2. *Voyage of Sebastian Viscaino* (Calif. Book Club, 1933), p. 4; *Hist. Soc. Southern Calif. Publs.*, 2:25, 29-32, 35 (1891).

390.3. *Ibid.*, pp. 10, 13.

391.1. *Hist. Soc. Southern Calif. Publs.*, 2:47, 67, 71 (1891); *Voyage of Sebastian Vizcaino*, p. 31; Richman, *op. cit.*, *passim.*

392.3. Miguel Costanso: "Narr.," *Acad. Pac. Coast Hist. Publs.*, 1:29 (1909); Bolton: *Fray Juan Crespi*, p. 4; Pedro Fages: *Hist., pol., and nat. descr. of Calif.*, p. 35.

392.4. "Diary of Fray Narciso Duran," *Acad. Pac. Coast Hist. Publs.*, 2:9, 19 (1911).

393.2. Costanso, *op. cit.*, p. 117; Bolton: *Anza's Calif. exp.*, II, 93, 202, 345; Brebner, *op. cit.*, p. 420; Pedro Fages: "Diary," *Acad. Pac. Coast Hist. Publs.*, 2:13 (1911); Bolton: *Font's complete diary*, p. 358.

393.3. Fages: *Hist . . . . of Calif., and nat. descr.* p. 52.

394.1. Costanso, *op. cit.*, p. 43; Bolton: *Fray Juan Crespi*, p. 117.

394.2. Bolton: *Font's complete diary*, pp. 318-319.

395.2. Costanso, *op. cit.*, p. 31; Fages: *Hist . . . . of Calif.*, pp. 22, 50.

402.4. E. S. Meaney: *New Vancouver journal*, p. 2; G. Vancouver: *Voyage of disc.* (1798), I, 197.

403.2. Vancouver, *op. cit.*, I, 198, 207, 214-215, II, 268.

404.1. *Dict. Am. Hist.*, I, 430.

404.2-3. Ross Cox: *Adventures on the Columbia River*, I, 116, 113, 119.

405.2. Vancouver, *op. cit.*, II, 55, 58.

405.3. J. R. Jewett: *Narr.* (1815), pp. 164-165.

405.4. Father Cataldo's MS. "Sketch of Spokane Mission," 1865-1866. Jesuit Archives, Oregon Province, Mt. St. Michael's, Spokane, Washington.

INDEX

A CATALOGUE OF SELECTED DOVER BOOKS
IN ALL FIELDS OF INTEREST

A CATALOGUE OF SELECTED DOVER BOOKS
IN ALL FIELDS OF INTEREST

THE NOTEBOOKS OF LEONARDO DA VINCI, edited by J.P. Richter. Extracts from manuscripts reveal great genius; on painting, sculpture, anatomy, sciences, geography, etc. Both Italian and English. 186 ms. pages reproduced, plus 500 additional drawings, including studies for Last Supper, Sforza monument, etc. 860pp. 7⅞ x 10¾.   USO 22572-0, 22573-9 Pa., Two vol. set $15.90

ART NOUVEAU DESIGNS IN COLOR, Alphonse Mucha, Maurice Verneuil, Georges Auriol. Full-color reproduction of Combinaisons ornamentales (c. 1900) by Art Nouveau masters. Floral, animal, geometric, interlacings, swashes — borders, frames, spots — all incredibly beautiful. 60 plates, hundreds of designs. 9⅜ x 8¹/₁₆ .   22885-1 Pa. $4.00

GRAPHIC WORKS OF ODILON REDON. All great fantastic lithographs, etchings, engravings, drawings, 209 in all. Monsters, Huysmans, still life work, etc. Introduction by Alfred Werner. 209pp. 9⅛ x 12¼.   21996-8 Pa. $6.00

EXOTIC FLORAL PATTERNS IN COLOR, E.-A. Seguy. Incredibly beautiful full-color pochoir work by great French designer of 20's. Complete Bouquets et frondaisons, Suggestions pour étoffes. Richness must be seen to be believed. 40 plates containing 120 patterns. 80pp. 9⅜ x 12¼.   23041-4 Pa. $6.00

SELECTED ETCHINGS OF JAMES A. McN. WHISTLER, James A. McN. Whistler. 149 outstanding etchings by the great American artist, including selections from the Thames set and two Venice sets, the complete French set, and many individual prints. Introduction and explanatory note on each print by Maria Naylor. 157pp. 9⅜ x 12¼.   23194-1 Pa. $5.00

VISUAL ILLUSIONS: THEIR CAUSES, CHARACTERISTICS, AND APPLICATIONS, Matthew Luckiesh. Thorough description, discussion; shape and size, color, motion; natural illusion. Uses in art and industry. 100 illustrations. 252pp.
                                                      21530-X Pa. $3.00

TEN BOOKS ON ARCHITECTURE, Vitruvius. The most important book ever written on architecture. Early Roman aesthetics, technology, classical orders, site selection, all other aspects. Stands behind everything since. Morgan translation. 331pp.
                                                      20645-9 Pa. $3.75

THE CODEX NUTTALL. A PICTURE MANUSCRIPT FROM ANCIENT MEXICO, as first edited by Zelia Nuttall. Only inexpensive edition, in full color, of a pre-Columbian Mexican (Mixtec) book. 88 color plates show kings, gods, heroes, temples, sacrifices. New explanatory, historical introduction by Arthur G. Miller. 96pp. 11⅜ x 8½.   23168-2 Pa. $7.50

CREATIVE LITHOGRAPHY AND HOW TO DO IT, Grant Arnold. Lithography as art form: working directly on stone, transfer of drawings, lithotint, mezzotint, color printing; also metal plates. Detailed, thorough. 27 illustrations. 214pp.
21208-4 Pa. $3.50

DESIGN MOTIFS OF ANCIENT MEXICO, Jorge Enciso. Vigorous, powerful ceramic stamp impressions — Maya, Aztec, Toltec, Olmec. Serpents, gods, priests, dancers, etc. 153pp. 6⅛ x 9¼. 20084-1 Pa. $2.50

AMERICAN INDIAN DESIGN AND DECORATION, Leroy Appleton. Full text, plus more than 700 precise drawings of Inca, Maya, Aztec, Pueblo, Plains, NW Coast basketry, sculpture, painting, pottery, sand paintings, metal, etc. 4 plates in color. 279pp. 8⅜ x 11¼. 22704-9 Pa. $5.00

CHINESE LATTICE DESIGNS, Daniel S. Dye. Incredibly beautiful geometric designs: circles, voluted, simple dissections, etc. Inexhaustible source of ideas, motifs. 1239 illustrations. 469pp. 6⅛ x 9¼. 23096-1 Pa. $5.00

JAPANESE DESIGN MOTIFS, Matsuya Co. Mon, or heraldic designs. Over 4000 typical, beautiful designs: birds, animals, flowers, swords, fans, geometric; all beautifully stylized. 213pp. 11⅜ x 8¼. 22874-6 Pa. $5.00

PERSPECTIVE, Jan Vredeman de Vries. 73 perspective plates from 1604 edition; buildings, townscapes, stairways, fantastic scenes. Remarkable for beauty, surrealistic atmosphere; real eye-catchers. Introduction by Adolf Placzek. 74pp. 11⅜ x 8¼. 20186-4 Pa. $3.00

EARLY AMERICAN DESIGN MOTIFS, Suzanne E. Chapman. 497 motifs, designs, from painting on wood, ceramics, appliqué, glassware, samplers, metal work, etc. Florals, landscapes, birds and animals, geometrics, letters, etc. Inexhaustible. Enlarged edition. 138pp. 8⅜ x 11¼. 22985-8 Pa. $3.50
23084-8 Clothbd. $7.95

VICTORIAN STENCILS FOR DESIGN AND DECORATION, edited by E.V. Gillon, Jr. 113 wonderful ornate Victorian pieces from German sources; florals, geometrics; borders, corner pieces; bird motifs, etc. 64pp. 9⅜ x 12¼. 21995-X Pa. $3.00

ART NOUVEAU: AN ANTHOLOGY OF DESIGN AND ILLUSTRATION FROM THE STUDIO, edited by E.V. Gillon, Jr. Graphic arts: book jackets, posters, engravings, illustrations, decorations; Crane, Beardsley, Bradley and many others. Inexhaustible. 92pp. 8⅛ x 11. 22388-4 Pa. $2.50

ORIGINAL ART DECO DESIGNS, William Rowe. First-rate, highly imaginative modern Art Deco frames, borders, compositions, alphabets, florals, insectals, Wurlitzer-types, etc. Much finest modern Art Deco. 80 plates, 8 in color. 8⅜ x 11¼. 22567-4 Pa. $3.50

HANDBOOK OF DESIGNS AND DEVICES, Clarence P. Hornung. Over 1800 basic geometric designs based on circle, triangle, square, scroll, cross, etc. Largest such collection in existence. 261pp. 20125-2 Pa. $2.75

150 MASTERPIECES OF DRAWING, edited by Anthony Toney. 150 plates, early 15th century to end of 18th century; Rembrandt, Michelangelo, Dürer, Fragonard, Watteau, Wouwerman, many others. 150pp. 8⅜ x 11¼. 21032-4 Pa. $4.00

THE GOLDEN AGE OF THE POSTER, Hayward and Blanche Cirker. 70 extraordinary posters in full colors, from Maîtres de l'Affiche, Mucha, Lautrec, Bradley, Cheret, Beardsley, many others. 9⅜ x 12¼. 22753-7 Pa. $5.95

SIMPLICISSIMUS, selection, translations and text by Stanley Appelbaum. 180 satirical drawings, 16 in full color, from the famous German weekly magazine in the years 1896 to 1926. 24 artists included: Grosz, Kley, Pascin, Kubin, Kollwitz, plus Heine, Thöny, Bruno Paul, others. 172pp. 8½ x 12¼. 23098-8 Pa. $5.00
23099-6 Clothbd. $10.00

THE EARLY WORK OF AUBREY BEARDSLEY, Aubrey Beardsley. 157 plates, 2 in color: Manon Lescaut, Madame Bovary, Morte d'Arthur, Salome, other. Introduction by H. Marillier. 175pp. 8½ x 11. 21816-3 Pa. $4.00

THE LATER WORK OF AUBREY BEARDSLEY, Aubrey Beardsley. Exotic masterpieces of full maturity: Venus and Tannhäuser, Lysistrata, Rape of the Lock, Volpone, Savoy material, etc. 174 plates, 2 in color. 176pp. 8½ x 11. 21817-1 Pa. $4.50

DRAWINGS OF WILLIAM BLAKE, William Blake. 92 plates from Book of Job, Divine Comedy, Paradise Lost, visionary heads, mythological figures, Laocoön, etc. Selection, introduction, commentary by Sir Geoffrey Keynes. 178pp. 8½ x 11.
22303-5 Pa. $4.00

LONDON: A PILGRIMAGE, Gustave Doré, Blanchard Jerrold. Squalor, riches, misery, beauty of mid-Victorian metropolis; 55 wonderful plates, 125 other illustrations, full social, cultural text by Jerrold. 191pp. of text. 8⅛ x 11.
22306-X Pa. $6.00

THE COMPLETE WOODCUTS OF ALBRECHT DÜRER, edited by Dr. W. Kurth. 346 in all: Old Testament, St. Jerome, Passion, Life of Virgin, Apocalypse, many others. Introduction by Campbell Dodgson. 285pp. 8½ x 12¼. 21097-9 Pa. $6.00

THE DISASTERS OF WAR, Francisco Goya. 83 etchings record horrors of Napoleonic wars in Spain and war in general. Reprint of 1st edition, plus 3 additional plates. Introduction by Philip Hofer. 97pp. 9⅜ x 8¼. 21872-4 Pa. $3.50

ENGRAVINGS OF HOGARTH, William Hogarth. 101 of Hogarth's greatest works: Rake's Progress, Harlot's Progress, Illustrations for Hudibras, Midnight Modern Conversation, Before and After, Beer Street and Gin Lane, many more. Full commentary. 256pp. 11 x 14. 22479-1 Pa. $7.95

PRIMITIVE ART, Franz Boas. Great anthropologist on ceramics, textiles, wood, stone, metal, etc.; patterns, technology, symbols, styles. All areas, but fullest on Northwest Coast Indians. 350 illustrations. 378pp. 20025-6 Pa. $3.75

MOTHER GOOSE'S MELODIES. Facsimile of fabulously rare Munroe and Francis "copyright 1833" Boston edition. Familiar and unusual rhymes, wonderful old woodcut illustrations. Edited by E.F. Bleiler. 128pp. 4½ x 6⅜. 22577-1 Pa. $1.50

MOTHER GOOSE IN HIEROGLYPHICS. Favorite nursery rhymes presented in rebus form for children. Fascinating 1849 edition reproduced in toto, with key. Introduction by E.F. Bleiler. About 400 woodcuts. 64pp. 6⅞ x 5¼. 20745-5 Pa. $1.50

PETER PIPER'S PRACTICAL PRINCIPLES OF PLAIN & PERFECT PRONUNCIATION. Alliterative jingles and tongue-twisters. Reproduction in full of 1830 first American edition. 25 spirited woodcuts. 32pp. 4½ x 6⅜. 22560-7 Pa. **$1.25**

MARMADUKE MULTIPLY'S MERRY METHOD OF MAKING MINOR MATHEMATICIANS. Fellow to Peter Piper, it teaches multiplication table by catchy rhymes and woodcuts. 1841 Munroe & Francis edition. Edited by E.F. Bleiler. 103pp. 4⅝ x 6. 22773-1 Pa. $1.25

THE NIGHT BEFORE CHRISTMAS, Clement Moore. Full text, and woodcuts from original 1848 book. Also critical, historical material. 19 illustrations. 40pp. 4⅝ x 6. 22797-9 Pa. **$1.35**

THE KING OF THE GOLDEN RIVER, John Ruskin. Victorian children's classic of three brothers, their attempts to reach the Golden River, what becomes of them. Facsimile of original 1889 edition. 22 illustrations. 56pp. 4⅝ x 6⅜.
20066-3 Pa. **$1.50**

DREAMS OF THE RAREBIT FIEND, Winsor McCay. Pioneer cartoon strip, unexcelled for beauty, imagination, in 60 full sequences. Incredible technical virtuosity, wonderful visual wit. Historical introduction. 62pp. 8⅜ x 11¼. 21347-1 Pa. $2.50

THE KATZENJAMMER KIDS, Rudolf Dirks. In full color, 14 strips from 1906-7; full of imagination, characteristic humor. Classic of great historical importance. Introduction by August Derleth. 32pp. 9¼ x 12¼. 23005-8 Pa. $2.00

LITTLE ORPHAN ANNIE AND LITTLE ORPHAN ANNIE IN COSMIC CITY, Harold Gray. Two great sequences from the early strips: our curly-haired heroine defends the Warbucks' financial empire and, then, takes on meanie Phineas P. Pinchpenny. Leapin' lizards! 178pp. 6⅛ x 8⅜. 23107-0 Pa. $2.00

ABSOLUTELY MAD INVENTIONS, A.E. Brown, H.A. Jeffcott. Hilarious, useless, or merely absurd inventions all granted patents by the U.S. Patent Office. Edible tie pin, mechanical hat tipper, etc. 57 illustrations. 125pp. 22596-8 Pa. $1.50

THE DEVIL'S DICTIONARY, Ambrose Bierce. Barbed, bitter, brilliant witticisms in the form of a dictionary. Best, most ferocious satire America has produced. 145pp. 20487-1 Pa. $1.75

THE BEST DR. THORNDYKE DETECTIVE STORIES, R. Austin Freeman. The Case of Oscar Brodski, The Moabite Cipher, and 5 other favorites featuring the great scientific detective, plus his long-believed-lost first adventure — 31 New Inn — reprinted here for the first time. Edited by E.F. Bleiler. USO 20388-3 Pa. $3.00

BEST "THINKING MACHINE" DETECTIVE STORIES, Jacques Futrelle. The Problem of Cell 13 and 11 other stories about Prof. Augustus S.F.X. Van Dusen, including two "lost" stories. First reprinting of several. Edited by E.F. Bleiler. 241pp.
20537-1 Pa. $3.00

UNCLE SILAS, J. Sheridan LeFanu. Victorian Gothic mystery novel, considered by many best of period, even better than Collins or Dickens. Wonderful psychological terror. Introduction by Frederick Shroyer. 436pp. 21715-9 Pa. $4.50

BEST DR. POGGIOLI DETECTIVE STORIES, T.S. Stribling. 15 best stories from EQMM and The Saint offer new adventures in Mexico, Florida, Tennessee hills as Poggioli unravels mysteries and combats Count Jalacki. 217pp. 23227-1 Pa. $3.00

EIGHT DIME NOVELS, selected with an introduction by E.F. Bleiler. Adventures of Old King Brady, Frank James, Nick Carter, Deadwood Dick, Buffalo Bill, The Steam Man, Frank Merriwell, and Horatio Alger — 1877 to 1905. Important, entertaining popular literature in facsimile reprint, with original covers. 190pp. 9 x 12. 22975-0 Pa. $3.50

ALICE'S ADVENTURES UNDER GROUND, Lewis Carroll. Facsimile of ms. Carroll gave Alice Liddell in 1864. Different in many ways from final Alice. Handlettered, illustrated by Carroll. Introduction by Martin Gardner. 128pp. 21482-6 Pa. $2.00

ALICE IN WONDERLAND COLORING BOOK, Lewis Carroll. Pictures by John Tenniel. Large-size versions of the famous illustrations of Alice, Cheshire Cat, Mad Hatter and all the others, waiting for your crayons. Abridged text. 36 illustrations. 64pp. 8¼ x 11. 22853-3 Pa. $1.50

AVENTURES D'ALICE AU PAYS DES MERVEILLES, Lewis Carroll. Bué's translation of "Alice" into French, supervised by Carroll himself. Novel way to learn language. (No English text.) 42 Tenniel illustrations. 196pp. 22836-3 Pa. $3.00

MYTHS AND FOLK TALES OF IRELAND, Jeremiah Curtin. 11 stories that are Irish versions of European fairy tales and 9 stories from the Fenian cycle — 20 tales of legend and magic that comprise an essential work in the history of folklore. 256pp. 22430-9 Pa. $3.00

EAST O' THE SUN AND WEST O' THE MOON, George W. Dasent. Only full edition of favorite, wonderful Norwegian fairytales — Why the Sea is Salt, Boots and the Troll, etc. — with 77 illustrations by Kittelsen & Werenskiöld. 418pp.
22521-6 Pa. $4.50

PERRAULT'S FAIRY TALES, Charles Perrault and Gustave Doré. Original versions of Cinderella, Sleeping Beauty, Little Red Riding Hood, etc. in best translation, with 34 wonderful illustrations by Gustave Doré. 117pp. 8⅛ x 11. 22311-6 Pa. $2.50

EARLY NEW ENGLAND GRAVESTONE RUBBINGS, Edmund V. Gillon, Jr. 43 photographs, 226 rubbings show heavily symbolic, macabre, sometimes humorous primitive American art. Up to early 19th century. 207pp. 8⅜ x 11¼.
21380-3 Pa. $4.00

L.J.M. DAGUERRE: THE HISTORY OF THE DIORAMA AND THE DAGUERREOTYPE, Helmut and Alison Gernsheim. Definitive account. Early history, life and work of Daguerre; discovery of daguerreotype process; diffusion abroad; other early photography. 124 illustrations. 226pp. 6⅙ x 9¼.
22290-X Pa. $4.00

PHOTOGRAPHY AND THE AMERICAN SCENE, Robert Taft. The basic book on American photography as art, recording form, 1839-1889. Development, influence on society, great photographers, types (portraits, war, frontier, etc.), whatever else needed. Inexhaustible. Illustrated with 322 early photos, daguerreotypes, tintypes, stereo slides, etc. 546pp. 6⅛ x 9¼.
21201-7 Pa. **$6.00**

PHOTOGRAPHIC SKETCHBOOK OF THE CIVIL WAR, Alexander Gardner. Reproduction of 1866 volume with 100 on-the-field photographs: Manassas, Lincoln on battlefield, slave pens, etc. Introduction by E.F. Bleiler. 224pp. 10¾ x 9.
22731-6 Pa. **$6.00**

THE MOVIES: A PICTURE QUIZ BOOK, Stanley Appelbaum & Hayward Cirker. Match stars with their movies, name actors and actresses, test your movie skill with 241 stills from 236 great movies, 1902-1959. Indexes of performers and films. 128pp. 8⅜ x 9¼.
20222-4 Pa. $3.00

THE TALKIES, Richard Griffith. Anthology of features, articles from Photoplay, 1928-1940, reproduced complete. Stars, famous movies, technical features, fabulous ads, etc.; Garbo, Chaplin, King Kong, Lubitsch, etc. 4 color plates, scores of illustrations. 327pp. 8⅜ x 11¼.
22762-6 Pa. $6.95

THE MOVIE MUSICAL FROM VITAPHONE TO "42ND STREET," edited by Miles Kreuger. Relive the rise of the movie musical as reported in the pages of Photoplay magazine (1926-1933): every movie review, cast list, ad, and record review; every significant feature article, production still, biography, forecast, and gossip story. Profusely illustrated. 367pp. 8⅜ x 11¼.
23154-2 Pa. $7.95

JOHANN SEBASTIAN BACH, Philipp Spitta. Great classic of biography, musical commentary, with hundreds of pieces analyzed. Also good for Bach's contemporaries. 450 musical examples. Total of 1799pp.
EUK 22278-0, 22279-9 Clothbd., Two vol. set $25.00

BEETHOVEN AND HIS NINE SYMPHONIES, Sir George Grove. Thorough history, analysis, commentary on symphonies and some related pieces. For either beginner or advanced student. 436 musical passages. 407pp.
20334-4 Pa. $4.00

MOZART AND HIS PIANO CONCERTOS, Cuthbert Girdlestone. The only full-length study. Detailed analyses of all 21 concertos, sources; 417 musical examples. 509pp.
21271-8 Pa. **$6.00**

THE FITZWILLIAM VIRGINAL BOOK, edited by J. Fuller Maitland, W.B. Squire. Famous early 17th century collection of keyboard music, 300 works by Morley, Byrd, Bull, Gibbons, etc. Modern notation. Total of 938pp. 8³/₈ x 11.
ECE 21068-5, 21069-3 Pa., Two vol. set $15.00

COMPLETE STRING QUARTETS, Wolfgang A. Mozart. Breitkopf and Härtel edition. All 23 string quartets plus alternate slow movement to K156. Study score. 277pp. 9³/₈ x 12¼.
22372-8 Pa. $6.00

COMPLETE SONG CYCLES, Franz Schubert. Complete piano, vocal music of Die Schöne Müllerin, Die Winterreise, Schwanengesang. Also Drinker English singing translations. Breitkopf and Härtel edition. 217pp. 9³/₈ x 12¼.
22649-2 Pa. $5.00

THE COMPLETE PRELUDES AND ETUDES FOR PIANOFORTE SOLO, Alexander Scriabin. All the preludes and etudes including many perfectly spun miniatures. Edited by K.N. Igumnov and Y.I. Mil'shteyn. 250pp. 9 x 12.
22919-X Pa. $6.00

TRISTAN UND ISOLDE, Richard Wagner. Full orchestral score with complete instrumentation. Do not confuse with piano reduction. Commentary by Felix Mottl, great Wagnerian conductor and scholar. Study score. 655pp. 8¹/₈ x 11.
22915-7 Pa. $11.95

FAVORITE SONGS OF THE NINETIES, ed. Robert Fremont. Full reproduction, including covers, of 88 favorites: Ta-Ra-Ra-Boom-De-Aye, The Band Played On, Bird in a Gilded Cage, Under the Bamboo Tree, After the Ball, etc. 401pp. 9 x 12.
EBE 21536-9 Pa. $6.95

SOUSA'S GREAT MARCHES IN PIANO TRANSCRIPTION: ORIGINAL SHEET MUSIC OF 23 WORKS, John Philip Sousa. Selected by Lester S. Levy. Playing edition includes: The Stars and Stripes Forever, The Thunderer, The Gladiator, King Cotton, Washington Post, much more. 24 illustrations. 111pp. 9 x 12.
USO 23132-1 Pa. $3.50

CLASSIC PIANO RAGS, selected with an introduction by Rudi Blesh. Best ragtime music (1897-1922) by Scott Joplin, James Scott, Joseph F. Lamb, Tom Turpin, 9 others. Printed from best original sheet music, plus covers. 364pp. 9 x 12.
EBE 20469-3 Pa. $7.50

ANALYSIS OF CHINESE CHARACTERS, C.D. Wilder, J.H. Ingram. 1000 most important characters analyzed according to primitives, phonetics, historical development. Traditional method offers mnemonic aid to beginner, intermediate student of Chinese, Japanese. 365pp.
23045-7 Pa. $4.00

MODERN CHINESE: A BASIC COURSE, Faculty of Peking University. Self study, classroom course in modern Mandarin. Records contain phonetics, vocabulary, sentences, lessons. 249 page book contains all recorded text, translations, grammar, vocabulary, exercises. Best course on market. 3 12" 33¹/₃ monaural records, book, album.
98832-5 Set $12.50

MANUAL OF THE TREES OF NORTH AMERICA, Charles S. Sargent. The basic survey of every native tree and tree-like shrub, 717 species in all. Extremely full descriptions, information on habitat, growth, locales, economics, etc. Necessary to every serious tree lover. Over 100 finding keys. 783 illustrations. Total of 986pp.
20277-1, 20278-X Pa., Two vol. set $9.00

BIRDS OF THE NEW YORK AREA, John Bull. Indispensable guide to more than 400 species within a hundred-mile radius of Manhattan. Information on range, status, breeding, migration, distribution trends, etc. Foreword by Roger Tory Peterson. 17 drawings; maps. 540pp.
23222-0 Pa. $6.00

THE SEA-BEACH AT EBB-TIDE, Augusta Foote Arnold. Identify hundreds of marine plants and animals: algae, seaweeds, squids, crabs, corals, etc. Descriptions cover food, life cycle, size, shape, habitat. Over 600 drawings. 490pp.
21949-6 Pa. $5.00

THE MOTH BOOK, William J. Holland. Identify more than 2,000 moths of North America. General information, precise species descriptions. 623 illustrations plus 48 color plates show almost all species, full size. 1968 edition. Still the basic book. Total of 551pp. 6½ x 9¼.
21948-8 Pa. $6.00

HOW INDIANS USE WILD PLANTS FOR FOOD, MEDICINE & CRAFTS, Frances Densmore. Smithsonian, Bureau of American Ethnology report presents wealth of material on nearly 200 plants used by Chippewas of Minnesota and Wisconsin. 33 plates plus 122pp. of text. 6⅛ x 9¼.
23019-8 Pa. $2.50

OLD NEW YORK IN EARLY PHOTOGRAPHS, edited by Mary Black. Your only chance to see New York City as it was 1853-1906, through 196 wonderful photographs from N.Y. Historical Society. Great Blizzard, Lincoln's funeral procession, great buildings. 228pp. 9 x 12.
22907-6 Pa. $6.95

THE AMERICAN REVOLUTION, A PICTURE SOURCEBOOK, John Grafton. Wonderful Bicentennial picture source, with 411 illustrations (contemporary and 19th century) showing battles, personalities, maps, events, flags, posters, soldier's life, ships, etc. all captioned and explained. A wonderful browsing book, supplement to other historical reading. 160pp. 9 x 12.
23226-3 Pa. $4.00

PERSONAL NARRATIVE OF A PILGRIMAGE TO AL-MADINAH AND MECCAH, Richard Burton. Great travel classic by remarkably colorful personality. Burton, disguised as a Moroccan, visited sacred shrines of Islam, narrowly escaping death. Wonderful observations of Islamic life, customs, personalities. 47 illustrations. Total of 959pp.
21217-3, 21218-1 Pa., Two vol. set $10.00

INCIDENTS OF TRAVEL IN CENTRAL AMERICA, CHIAPAS, AND YUCATAN, John L. Stephens. Almost single-handed discovery of Maya culture; exploration of ruined cities, monuments, temples; customs of Indians. 115 drawings. 892pp.
22404-X, 22405-8 Pa., Two vol. set $9.00

CONSTRUCTION OF AMERICAN FURNITURE TREASURES, Lester Margon. 344 detail drawings, complete text on constructing exact reproductions of 38 early American masterpieces: Hepplewhite sideboard, Duncan Phyfe drop-leaf table, mantel clock, gate-leg dining table, Pa. German cupboard, more. 38 plates. 54 photographs. 168pp. 8⅜ x 11¼. 23056-2 Pa. $4.00

JEWELRY MAKING AND DESIGN, Augustus F. Rose, Antonio Cirino. Professional secrets revealed in thorough, practical guide: tools, materials, processes; rings, brooches, chains, cast pieces, enamelling, setting stones, etc. Do not confuse with skimpy introductions: beginner can use, professional can learn from it. Over 200 illustrations. 306pp. 21750-7 Pa. $3.00

METALWORK AND ENAMELLING, Herbert Maryon. Generally conceded best all-around book. Countless trade secrets: materials, tools, soldering, filigree, setting, inlay, niello, repoussé, casting, polishing, etc. For beginner or expert. Author was foremost British expert. 330 illustrations. 335pp. 22702-2 Pa. $4.00

WEAVING WITH FOOT-POWER LOOMS, Edward F. Worst. Setting up a loom, beginning to weave, constructing equipment, using dyes, more, plus over 285 drafts of traditional patterns including Colonial and Swedish weaves. More than 200 other figures. For beginning and advanced. 275pp. 8¾ x 6⅜. 23064-3 Pa. $4.50

WEAVING A NAVAJO BLANKET, Gladys A. Reichard. Foremost anthropologist studied under Navajo women, reveals every step in process from wool, dyeing, spinning, setting up loom, designing, weaving. Much history, symbolism. With this book you could make one yourself. 97 illustrations. 222pp. 22992-0 Pa. $3.00

NATURAL DYES AND HOME DYEING, Rita J. Adrosko. Use natural ingredients: bark, flowers, leaves, lichens, insects etc. Over 135 specific recipes from historical sources for cotton, wool, other fabrics. Genuine premodern handicrafts. 12 illustrations. 160pp. 22688-3 Pa. $2.00

DRIED FLOWERS, Sarah Whitlock and Martha Rankin. Concise, clear, practical guide to dehydration, glycerinizing, pressing plant material, and more. Covers use of silica gel. 12 drawings. Originally titled "New Techniques with Dried Flowers." 32pp. 21802-3 Pa. $1.00

THOMAS NAST: CARTOONS AND ILLUSTRATIONS, with text by Thomas Nast St. Hill. Father of American political cartooning. Cartoons that destroyed Tweed Ring; inflation, free love, church and state; original Republican elephant and Democratic donkey; Santa Claus; more. 117 illustrations. 146pp. 9 x 12.
22983-1 Pa. $4.00
23067-8 Clothbd. $8.50

FREDERIC REMINGTON: 173 DRAWINGS AND ILLUSTRATIONS. Most famous of the Western artists, most responsible for our myths about the American West in its untamed days. Complete reprinting of Drawings of Frederic Remington (1897), plus other selections. 4 additional drawings in color on covers. 140pp. 9 x 12.
20714-5 Pa. $5.00'

How to Solve Chess Problems, Kenneth S. Howard. Practical suggestions on problem solving for very beginners. 58 two-move problems, 46 3-movers, 8 4-movers for practice, plus hints. 171pp. 20748-X Pa. **$3.00**

A Guide to Fairy Chess, Anthony Dickins. 3-D chess, 4-D chess, chess on a cylindrical board, reflecting pieces that bounce off edges, cooperative chess, retrograde chess, maximummers, much more. Most based on work of great Dawson. Full handbook, 100 problems. 66pp. 7⅞ x 10¾. 22687-5 Pa. $2.00

Win at Backgammon, Millard Hopper. Best opening moves, running game, blocking game, back game, tables of odds, etc. Hopper makes the game clear enough for anyone to play, and win. 43 diagrams. 111pp. 22894-0 Pa. $1.50

Bidding a Bridge Hand, Terence Reese. Master player "thinks out loud" the binding of 75 hands that defy point count systems. Organized by bidding problem—no-fit situations, overbidding, underbidding, cueing your defense, etc. 254pp. EBE 22830-4 Pa. **$3.00**

The Precision Bidding System in Bridge, C.C. Wei, edited by Alan Truscott. Inventor of precision bidding presents average hands and hands from actual play, including games from 1969 Bermuda Bowl where system emerged. 114 exercises. 116pp. 21171-1 Pa. **$2.25**

Learn Magic, Henry Hay. 20 simple, easy-to-follow lessons on magic for the new magician: illusions, card tricks, silks, sleights of hand, coin manipulations, escapes, and more —all with a minimum amount of equipment. Final chapter explains the great stage illusions. 92 illustrations. 285pp. 21238-6 Pa. $2.95

The New Magician's Manual, Walter B. Gibson. Step-by-step instructions and clear illustrations guide the novice in mastering 36 tricks; much equipment supplied on 16 pages of cut-out materials. 36 additional tricks. 64 illustrations. 159pp. 6⅝ x 10. 23113-5 Pa. $3.00

Professional Magic for Amateurs, Walter B. Gibson. 50 easy, effective tricks used by professionals —cards, string, tumblers, handkerchiefs, mental magic, etc. 63 illustrations. 223pp. 23012-0 Pa. $2.50

Card Manipulations, Jean Hugard. Very rich collection of manipulations; has taught thousands of fine magicians tricks that are really workable, eye-catching. Easily followed, serious work. Over 200 illustrations. 163pp. 20539-8 Pa. $2.00

Abbott's Encyclopedia of Rope Tricks for Magicians, Stewart James. Complete reference book for amateur and professional magicians containing more than 150 tricks involving knots, penetrations, cut and restored rope, etc. 510 illustrations. Reprint of 3rd edition. 400pp. 23206-9 Pa. $3.50

The Secrets of Houdini, J.C. Cannell. Classic study of Houdini's incredible magic, exposing closely-kept professional secrets and revealing, in general terms, the whole art of stage magic. 67 illustrations. 279pp. 22913-0 Pa. $3.00

THE MAGIC MOVING PICTURE BOOK, Bliss, Sands & Co. The pictures in this book move! Volcanoes erupt, a house burns, a serpentine dancer wiggles her way through a number. By using a specially ruled acetate screen provided, you can obtain these and 15 other startling effects. Originally "The Motograph Moving Picture Book." 32pp. 8¼ x 11. 23224-7 Pa. $1.75

STRING FIGURES AND HOW TO MAKE THEM, Caroline F. Jayne. Fullest, clearest instructions on string figures from around world: Eskimo, Navajo, Lapp, Europe, more. Cats cradle, moving spear, lightning, stars. Introduction by A.C. Haddon. 950 illustrations. 407pp. 20152-X Pa. $3.50

PAPER FOLDING FOR BEGINNERS, William D. Murray and Francis J. Rigney. Clearest book on market for making origami sail boats, roosters, frogs that move legs, cups, bonbon boxes. 40 projects. More than 275 illustrations. Photographs. 94pp. 20713-7 Pa $1.50

INDIAN SIGN LANGUAGE, William Tomkins. Over 525 signs developed by Sioux, Blackfoot, Cheyenne, Arapahoe and other tribes. Written instructions and diagrams: how to make words, construct sentences. Also 290 pictographs of Sioux and Ojibway tribes. 111pp. 6⅛ x 9¼. 22029-X Pa. $1.75

BOOMERANGS: HOW TO MAKE AND THROW THEM, Bernard S. Mason. Easy to make and throw, dozens of designs: cross-stick, pinwheel, boomabird, tumblestick, Australian curved stick boomerang. Complete throwing instructions. All safe. 99pp. 23028-7 Pa. $1.75

25 KITES THAT FLY, Leslie Hunt. Full, easy to follow instructions for kites made from inexpensive materials. Many novelties. Reeling, raising, designing your own. 70 illustrations. 110pp. 22550-X Pa. $1.50

TRICKS AND GAMES ON THE POOL TABLE, Fred Herrmann. 79 tricks and games, some solitaires, some for 2 or more players, some competitive; mystifying shots and throws, unusual carom, tricks involving cork, coins, a hat, more. 77 figures. 95pp. 21814-7 Pa. $1.50

WOODCRAFT AND CAMPING, Bernard S. Mason. How to make a quick emergency shelter, select woods that will burn immediately, make do with limited supplies, etc. Also making many things out of wood, rawhide, bark, at camp. Formerly titled Woodcraft. 295 illustrations. 580pp. 21951-8 Pa. $4.00

AN INTRODUCTION TO CHESS MOVES AND TACTICS SIMPLY EXPLAINED, Leonard Barden. Informal intermediate introduction: reasons for moves, tactics, openings, traps, positional play, endgame. Isolates patterns. 102pp. USO 21210-6 Pa. $1.35

LASKER'S MANUAL OF CHESS, Dr. Emanuel Lasker. Great world champion offers very thorough coverage of all aspects of chess. Combinations, position play, openings, endgame, aesthetics of chess, philosophy of struggle, much more. Filled with analyzed games. 390pp. 20640-8 Pa. $4.00

SLEEPING BEAUTY, illustrated by Arthur Rackham. Perhaps the fullest, most delightful version ever, told by C.S. Evans. Rackham's best work. 49 illustrations. 110pp. 7⁷/₈ x 10¾.   22756-1 Pa. $2.00

THE WONDERFUL WIZARD OF OZ, L. Frank Baum. Facsimile in full color of America's finest children's classic. Introduction by Martin Gardner. 143 illustrations by W.W. Denslow. 267pp.   20691-2 Pa. $3.50

GOOPS AND HOW TO BE THEM, Gelett Burgess. Classic tongue-in-cheek masquerading as etiquette book. 87 verses, 170 cartoons as Goops demonstrate virtues of table manners, neatness, courtesy, more. 88pp. 6½ x 9¼.
                                                                        22233-0 Pa. $2.00

THE BROWNIES, THEIR BOOK, Palmer Cox. Small as mice, cunning as foxes, exuberant, mischievous, Brownies go to zoo, toy shop, seashore, circus, more. 24 verse adventures. 266 illustrations. 144pp. 6⁵/₈ x 9¼.   21265-3 Pa. $2.50

BILLY WHISKERS: THE AUTOBIOGRAPHY OF A GOAT, Frances Trego Montgomery. Escapades of that rambunctious goat. Favorite from turn of the century America. 24 illustrations. 259pp.   22345-0 Pa. $2.75

THE ROCKET BOOK, Peter Newell. Fritz, janitor's kid, sets off rocket in basement of apartment house; an ingenious hole punched through every page traces course of rocket. 22 duotone drawings, verses. 48pp. 6⁷/₈ x 8³/₈.   22044-3 Pa. $1.50

CUT AND COLOR PAPER MASKS, Michael Grater. Clowns, animals, funny faces . . . simply color them in, cut them out, and put them together, and you have 9 paper masks to play with and enjoy. Complete instructions. Assembled masks shown in full color on the covers. 32pp. 8¼ x 11.   23171-2 Pa. $1.50

THE TALE OF PETER RABBIT, Beatrix Potter. The inimitable Peter's terrifying adventure in Mr. McGregor's garden, with all 27 wonderful, full-color Potter illustrations. 55pp. 4¼ x 5½.   USO 22827-4 Pa. $1.00

THE TALE OF MRS. TIGGY-WINKLE, Beatrix Potter. Your child will love this story about a very special hedgehog and all 27 wonderful, full-color Potter illustrations. 57pp. 4¼ x 5½.   USO 20546-0 Pa. $1.00

THE TALE OF BENJAMIN BUNNY, Beatrix Potter. Peter Rabbit's cousin coaxes him back into Mr. McGregor's garden for a whole new set of adventures. A favorite with children. All 27 full-color illustrations. 59pp. 4¼ x 5½.
                                                                    USO 21102-9 Pa. $1.00

THE MERRY ADVENTURES OF ROBIN HOOD, Howard Pyle. Facsimile of original (1883) edition, finest modern version of English outlaw's adventures. 23 illustrations by Pyle. 296pp. 6½ x 9¼.   22043-5 Pa. $4.00

TWO LITTLE SAVAGES, Ernest Thompson Seton. Adventures of two boys who lived as Indians; explaining Indian ways, woodlore, pioneer methods. 293 illustrations. 286pp.   20985-7 Pa. $3.50

HOUDINI ON MAGIC, Harold Houdini. Edited by Walter Gibson, Morris N. Young. How he escaped; exposés of fake spiritualists; instructions for eye-catching tricks; other fascinating material by and about greatest magician. 155 illustrations. 280pp. 20384-0 Pa. $2.75

HANDBOOK OF THE NUTRITIONAL CONTENTS OF FOOD, U.S. Dept. of Agriculture. Largest, most detailed source of food nutrition information ever prepared. Two mammoth tables: one measuring nutrients in 100 grams of edible portion; the other, in edible portion of 1 pound as purchased. Originally titled Composition of Foods. 190pp. 9 x 12. 21342-0 Pa. $4.00

COMPLETE GUIDE TO HOME CANNING, PRESERVING AND FREEZING, U.S. Dept. of Agriculture. Seven basic manuals with full instructions for jams and jellies; pickles and relishes; canning fruits, vegetables, meat; freezing anything. Really good recipes, exact instructions for optimal results. Save a fortune in food. 156 illustrations. 214pp. 6⅛ x 9¼. 22911-4 Pa. $2.50

THE BREAD TRAY, Louis P. De Gouy. Nearly every bread the cook could buy or make: bread sticks of Italy, fruit breads of Greece, glazed rolls of Vienna, everything from corn pone to croissants. Over 500 recipes altogether. including buns, rolls, muffins, scones, and more. 463pp. 23000-7 Pa. $4.00

CREATIVE HAMBURGER COOKERY, Louis P. De Gouy. 182 unusual recipes for casseroles, meat loaves and hamburgers that turn inexpensive ground meat into memorable main dishes: Arizona chili burgers, burger tamale pie, burger stew, burger corn loaf, burger wine loaf, and more. 120pp. 23001-5 Pa. $1.75

LONG ISLAND SEAFOOD COOKBOOK, J. George Frederick and Jean Joyce. Probably the best American seafood cookbook. Hundreds of recipes. 40 gourmet sauces, 123 recipes using oysters alone! All varieties of fish and seafood amply represented. 324pp. 22677-8 Pa. $3.50

THE EPICUREAN: A COMPLETE TREATISE OF ANALYTICAL AND PRACTICAL STUDIES IN THE CULINARY ART, Charles Ranhofer. Great modern classic. 3,500 recipes from master chef of Delmonico's, turn-of-the-century America's best restaurant. Also explained, many techniques known only to professional chefs. 775 illustrations. 1183pp. 6⅝ x 10. 22680-8 Clothbd. $22.50

THE AMERICAN WINE COOK BOOK, Ted Hatch. Over 700 recipes: old favorites livened up with wine plus many more: Czech fish soup, quince soup, sauce Perigueux, shrimp shortcake, filets Stroganoff, cordon bleu goulash, jambonneau, wine fruit cake, more. 314pp. 22796-0 Pa. $2.50

DELICIOUS VEGETARIAN COOKING, Ivan Baker. Close to 500 delicious and varied recipes: soups, main course dishes (pea, bean, lentil, cheese, vegetable, pasta, and egg dishes), savories, stews, whole-wheat breads and cakes, more. 168pp. USO 22834-7 Pa. $2.00

COOKIES FROM MANY LANDS, Josephine Perry. Crullers, oatmeal cookies, chaux au chocolate, English tea cakes, mandel kuchen, Sacher torte, Danish puff pastry, Swedish cookies — a mouth-watering collection of 223 recipes. 157pp.
22832-0 Pa. $2.25

ROSE RECIPES, Eleanour S. Rohde. How to make sauces, jellies, tarts, salads, potpourris, sweet bags, pomanders, perfumes from garden roses; all exact recipes. Century old favorites. 95pp.
22957-2 Pa. $1.75

"OSCAR" OF THE WALDORF'S COOKBOOK, Oscar Tschirky. Famous American chef reveals 3455 recipes that made Waldorf great; cream of French, German, American cooking, in all categories. Full instructions, easy home use. 1896 edition. 907pp. 6⅝ x 9⅜.
20790-0 Clothbd. $15.00

JAMS AND JELLIES, May Byron. Over 500 old-time recipes for delicious jams, jellies, marmalades, preserves, and many other items. Probably the largest jam and jelly book in print. Originally titled May Byron's Jam Book. 276pp.
USO 23130-5 Pa. $3.50

MUSHROOM RECIPES, André L. Simon. 110 recipes for everyday and special cooking. Champignons à la grecque, sole bonne femme, chicken liver croustades, more; 9 basic sauces, 13 ways of cooking mushrooms. 54pp.
USO 20913-X Pa. $1.25

THE BUCKEYE COOKBOOK, Buckeye Publishing Company. Over 1,000 easy-to-follow, traditional recipes from the American Midwest: bread (100 recipes alone), meat, game, jam, candy, cake, ice cream, and many other categories of cooking. 64 illustrations. From 1883 enlarged edition. 416pp.
23218-2 Pa. $4.00

TWENTY-TWO AUTHENTIC BANQUETS FROM INDIA, Robert H. Christie. Complete, easy-to-do recipes for almost 200 authentic Indian dishes assembled in 22 banquets. Arranged by region. Selected from Banquets of the Nations. 192pp.
23200-X Pa. $2.50

Prices subject to change without notice.
Available at your book dealer or write for free catalogue to Dept. GI, Dover Publications, Inc., 180 Varick St., N.Y., N.Y. 10014. Dover publishes more than 150 books each year on science, elementary and advanced mathematics, biology, music, art, literary history, social sciences and other areas.